The Economic Analysis of Public Policy

A critical analysis of public policy decisions requires a far greater depth of knowledge than one receives from news reports and political speeches. Issues such as how best to reduce traffic congestion, reduce acid rain, improve airline safety, or develop a parcel of land are better understood by organizing, measuring, and weighing the effects of alternative policies. William K. Bellinger's new text book is an ideal introduction to benefit–cost analysis, the economics of efficiency, risk analysis, and present value discounting for those with only a modest background in mathematics and economics.

Dr Bellinger presents the key concepts for analyzing public policy with frequent problems, discussion questions, and case studies throughout the book. Placing a great emphasis on teaching as well as sharing knowledge, this book encourages its readers to both understand and apply each concept and learn to appreciate policy analysis as part of an interdisciplinary, analytical, and political process that can lead to better government policy decisions.

This book is an ideal teaching tool for undergraduate and Master's students engaged in Public Administration, Public Economics, and Public Policy.

William K. Bellinger is Associate Professor of Economics at Dickinson College, Pennsylvania.

The Economic Analysis of Public Policy

William K. Bellinger

Routledge
Taylor & Francis Group

LONDON AND NEW YORK

First published 2007
by Routledge
2 Park Square, Milton Park,
Abingdon, Oxon 0X14 4RN

Simultaneously published in the USA and Canada
by Routledge
270 Madison Ave, New York, NY 10016

Routledge is an imprint of the Taylor & Francis Group, an informa business

© 2007 William K. Bellinger

Typeset in Times New Roman by Keyword Group Ltd
Printed and bound in Great Britain by Antony Rowe Ltd, Chippenham, Wiltshire

British Library Cataloguing in Publication Data
A Catalogue record for this book is available
from the British Library

Library of Congress Cataloguing in Publication Data
Bellinger, William Kenneth, 1950-
   The economic analysis of public policy / William K. Bellinger.
   p. cm.
   Includes bibliographical references and index.
   1. Policy sciences–Economic aspects. 2. Political planning–Economic aspects.
   3. Economic policy. I. Title.
   H97.B4655 2007
   320.6–dc22
   2006102504

ISBN10: 0-415-77277-X (hbk)
ISBN10: 0-415-77278-8 (pbk)
ISBN10: 0-203-94648-0 (ebk)

ISBN13: 978-0-415-77277-8 (hbk)
ISBN13: 978-0-415-77278-5 (pbk)
ISBN13: 978-0-203-94648-0 (ebk)

Contents

PART II

Economics for policy analysts   49

Acknowledgments

While hundreds of former and current students and dozens of local and regional private and public sector officials provided indirect and often unintended inspiration for this book, a smaller number of individuals provided more direct and substantial aid in its completion. I particularly wish to thank Jonathan Rogers, a former student, who contributed many of the review questions found in this book as well as an undergraduate's point of view on the clarity and substance of the text. I also owe a debt of thanks to Drs. Stacy Dickert-Conlin, Nicola Tynan, and Kristin Skrabis for detailed comments on selected chapters, and to Robert Langham for encouraging my association with the publishers, Routledge, and greasing the wheels of the editorial and review process. Also, I wish to express my appreciation to former instructors and colleagues for introducing me to the disciplinary, interdisciplinary, and applied contexts of policy economics. W. Kip Viscusi, Gerald Goldstein, Cyril Dwiggins, Mara Donaldson, Chris Gulatta, James Hoefler, and Eugene Hickok were particularly memorable in this regard. Finally, I wish to express my thanks and love to Jane, Brian, and Lynne. Even the tiniest fleet needs a home port.

Part I
Policy analysis, politics, and ethics

The first chapter of the book introduces the reader to the basic meaning of policy analysis and its various uses in the political process. The chapter also discusses the process of critical thinking about the arguments and evidence presented in policy research and political discussion. The second chapter introduces the reader to a set of basic ethical goals for public policy, as well as three theories of distributional justice that can be productively applied to some applications of policy analysis. Those who wish to get right to the economics might be tempted to skip this section. In my view the costs of that choice will ultimately outweigh its benefits.

1 The meaning of policy analysis

Do not believe in anything simply because you have heard it. Do not believe in anything simply because it is spoken and rumored by many. Do not believe in anything simply because it is found written in your religious books. Do not believe in anything merely on the authority of your teachers and elders. Do not believe in traditions because they have been handed down for many generations. But after observation and analysis, when you find that anything agrees with reason and is conducive to the good and benefit of one and all, then accept it and live up to it.[1]

(Gautama Siddharta, the founder of Buddhism)

... my way is to divide half a sheet of paper by a line into two columns; writing over the one Pro and over the other Con. ... If ... thus proceeding I find ... where the balance lies ... I come to a determination accordingly. ... I have found great advantage from this kind of equation, in what may be called moral or prudential algebra.[2]

(Benjamin Franklin)

At the most general level, efforts to weigh the benefits and costs of a public or private decision involve some version of the type of rational analysis presented in this book. At one extreme this decision process can take the form of a list of pluses and minuses, as in the quote by Benjamin Franklin. At the other extreme the decision process can include efforts to measure all relevant benefits and costs using a common scale such as dollars in order to determine the wisdom of a decision. In either case, the goal is to organize and compare the various effects of a decision in order to choose the action that most effectively improves individual or societal well-being.

Your Turn 1.1: Create a list of the benefits and costs of attending college. Include benefits that will occur in the future as well as the present, effects on others and on society as a whole as well as yourselves, and non-monetary as well as financial benefits and costs. After making some judgment about which benefits and costs are most important, do your benefits outweigh your costs?

If policy analysis involved only lists of positive and negative effects of decisions such as attending college it would not warrant an entire semester of your time or your purchase of this book. Moreover, a simple list of positives and negatives would not answer the following crucial questions: (1) Are the total benefits of this policy greater than the total costs? (2) Does this product or policy offer greater net benefits than another alternative? (3) How large a budget is required for this policy? A detailed analysis of policy alternatives can help one to answer such questions.

The degree of accuracy and detail of professional policy analysis depends on the amount of information available to the analyst and the setting in which the analysis takes place. The most thorough form of policy analysis is **benefit–cost analysis,** which attempts to estimate dollar values for all benefits and costs, even when the good in question is never actually bought or sold and has no explicit market value. For example, the benefits of a new section of highway include time savings for travelers as well as possible reductions in energy use and air pollution due to the lessening of congestion. Costs include construction spending, the loss of the benefits of alternative projects, added noise, increased danger from higher speeds, and an increase in road kill. Most of these benefits and costs are not determined in the marketplace. However, some common denominator is needed in order to compare the project's benefits and costs. Policy analysis usually relies on estimated dollar values for judging benefits and costs even when market prices are not available. This dollar valuation of non-traded goods is among the most difficult and controversial aspects of the economic approach to policy analysis.

A brief history of U.S. policy analysis

Princeton University professor, and later U.S. president, Woodrow Wilson led a movement for the scientific administration of government in the late 1800s, and the explicit goal of achieving positive net benefits from a United States governmental program dates back at least to the 1930s. However, the main proliferation of policy analysis in the U.S. federal government began in the 1960s. The foundation for the U.S. federal government's regular use of policy analysis was provided by the Planning Programming and Budgeting System (PPBS) established in the Department of Defense by then Secretary of Defense Robert McNamara. Policy analysis became an established part of other agencies' operations during the mid-1960s' War on Poverty. Policy analysis offices were established in the Office of Economic Opportunity and the Department of Health, Education, and Welfare during that time (see Radin 2000: 13-27). At the same time a large number of studies of the Johnson administration's War on Poverty's job training programs were undertaken by university professors. Academic analysis remains one of the most common sources of information about public policy. Also, independent research institutes, or think tanks, sprang up or increased in number and research emphasis during this period, and over 100 such organizations currently exist around the Washington DC area (Radin 2000: 39).

Research institutes vary in their degree of specialization and their ideological framework. Some specialize in a limited range of policy areas, such as the environment, transportation, or defense policy, while others offer analysis and opinion on a wide range of topics. Some of the most prominent of these organizations have evolved into ideological combatants on a wide range of policy issues. A few examples of organizations with identifiable ideologies and a wide range of policy concerns are the Cato Institute (http://www.cato.org/) and the American Enterprise Institute (http://www.aei.org/), which tend to produce conservative analyses of a wide range of issues, the Brookings Institution (http://www.brookings.edu/), which is considered more centrist in ideology, and the Economic Policy Institute (http://www.epinet.org/), which has a liberal or progressive viewpoint. Because the ideology of such organizations is often aligned with that of a subset of one of the major U.S. political parties, the political independence of these organizations is sometimes unclear. However, comparing the work of various think tanks can be an illuminating experience for any student, since their work tends to be far more substantive than that of general-interest publications, television and radio news, or political debates.

The goals of public policy

While this book will occasionally consider the role of institutions and interest groups in policy debate and implementation, its primary role is to present and apply a set of basic economic concepts that can be used to judge and compare alternative public policies. Policy analysis analyzes alternative policies according to at least three criteria: efficiency, equity, and political practicality. Each of these concepts involves some degree of controversy regarding meaning, measurement, and relative importance. In the case of economic analysis, efficiency is usually the dominant policy goal.

Efficiency

According to economic theory, a society achieves allocative efficiency if it provides the greatest possible level of well-being for society given a limited set of resources. At the level of an individual policy, efficiency is generally translated into maximizing the difference between the total benefits and total costs of that policy. These benefits and costs include non-monetary as well as monetary factors, and both direct and indirect effects. While the economic theory of efficiency is well established, the analysis of efficiency often involves significant challenges when defining and measuring specific benefits and costs. Also, the goal of efficiency may conflict with other policy goals such as equity or fairness, producing legitimate debate among those on different sides of the issue. Efficiency will be discussed in much greater detail in Chapter 4.

Equity

As a goal of public policy, equity generally involves the pursuit of one or more broad goals such as income equality, minimum standards of treatment, or freedom.

As with efficiency, determining a policy's ability to meet equity goals can be difficult, and conflict between ethical and other policy goals presents a frequent challenge for policy makers. For example, equality can be divided into multiple subtopics including equal income, equal rights, equal opportunity, and equal access to public services. Many of these dimensions of equality are difficult to define or measure, and in some cases these alternative dimensions of equality may be contradictory.

Furthermore, there are many ethical theories with conflicting conclusions and policy prescriptions. Three examples of ethical theories will be presented in Chapter 2. The lack of an accepted ethical paradigm for policy analysis tends to lessen the practical importance of ethical theory, yet the view of this book is that ethical goals provide an important basis for weighing the legitimacy of competing political positions. Since many policy debates involve claims of injustice or immorality, the failure to include ethical considerations in this text would leave the student without the means of judging these frequent, and frequently misused, claims of right and wrong. The challenge for those who wish to seriously consider the moral dimension of public policy is to learn enough about ethical theories to be able to logically and dispassionately judge the claims of right and wrong in political debates. That process will not be completed in this book.

Political practicality

A third goal of public policy is political practicality. A policy will be politically practical if it has sufficient support to be passed into law and practice by the legislative and administrative branches of government. Political practicality also involves meeting the broader rules and norms of government, such as the United States Constitution or British Common Law, in order to survive a possible judicial review. In addition to passing constitutional review by the courts, a successful policy must achieve popular and legislative support in order to pass into the legal code, and must then be effectively administered in order to have a significant effect on the public. There are many possible barriers to the establishment of a fully effective law or public program. A brief review of the economic analysis of the political process and its challenges is included in Chapter 5.

The steps in policy analysis

A useful guide to the policy analysis process is provided by the U.S. government's Office of Management and Budget (OMB).[3] The five steps for policy analysis suggested by the OMB are: (1) **state the policy rationale,** or the goal of the policy, (2) **explicitly state the assumptions** used in the analysis, (3) **evaluate alternatives,** including different program sizes, program methods, and public sector involvement, (4) **identify and measure benefits and costs,** and (5) **verify results** through follow-up studies. A more complete and readable list of steps comes from Eugene Bardach (2000: 1-47), who suggests an eight-step policy analysis process. These steps are: (1) **define the problem,** (2) **assemble evidence,**

(3) **select criteria for making the decision,** (4) **construct alternatives,** (5) **predict the outcome of each alternative,** (6) **confront the tradeoffs,** (7) **make recommendations,** and (8) **tell your story.** I reversed Bardach's steps 3 and 4 in order to separate the general analysis of the problem more completely from the analysis of a specific policy.

These two lists of steps overlap in several ways. For example, stating a policy rationale generally requires one to identify the problem being addressed and how the policy will reduce or eliminate that problem. Explicitly stating one's assumptions is part of defining the problem and the criteria for judging alternative solutions. Given imperfect information about a problem and the effects of alternative policies, assumptions are usually an important part of one's measurement of benefits and costs, particularly when predicting the future effects of a proposed policy.

The primary difference in the two lists is that the OMB procedures do not include policy recommendations. This difference is a matter of debate within the field of policy analysis, and reflects different views of the role of the analyst. Within government agencies, decisions regarding policy are usually made by high-ranking officials with political as well as administrative responsibilities. In this context it is often not the place of a staff economist or policy analyst to make recommendations regarding policy. On the other hand, there are situations within government where analysts' conclusions and recommendations can be part of the process of advising decision makers. Also, analysts working outside of government have fewer constraints on their role, and often include policy recommendations in their analysis.

Views of government and the roles of the policy analyst

Like policy professionals from any field, economists have several potential roles to play in the policy process. Three such roles are discussed in an article by Robert Nelson (1987). These roles are based on differing theories of government that have been popular at some point during the past century. Nelson's first role for the policy analyst is the "**progressive neutral expert**" (1987: 52). This role is based on the progressive era's[4] view that the administration of government should be above corrupting interests and based on sound management principles (see Wilson 1941, reprint). In this vision of government, the rational analysis of policy has a powerful role in determining government's course of action. While the growing importance of benefit–cost analysis over the past few decades suggests a continuing role for this view, reality suggests that political power remains a more important force in the success of a policy initiative.

Robert Nelson's second role for the policy economist is labeled the "**entrepreneur for efficiency**" (1987: 54). The entrepreneur for efficiency conducts policy analysis and also actively promotes economics or efficiency-based policy designs. This more active role for the analyst is based on a newer theory of government behavior that was developed in the 1950s and remains influential today. This view sees government, and particularly the legislative process, as a struggle among competing groups promoting their own self-interest (Truman 1941, reprint).

Within this view of government policy analysis serves at least two purposes. First, the evidence provided by policy analysts serves as support for arguments in favor of particular policy positions. Studies and research findings are regularly used as evidence by advocates of a particular political party or private interest group, and such groups often fund research that is likely to support their point of view. On the other hand, independent policy research may serve to mediate or resolve debates among interest groups. At some point decision makers may be persuaded by evidence that one or both sides are offering inaccurate or misleading facts or argument in a policy debate.

Nelson's third role for the government economist is the "**ideological combatant**". This role is based on the idea that ideology as well as self-interest guide policy makers, and that the battle of ideas may be as important as the battle of interests in determining public policy. In the intellectual arena, the primary ideological debates between economists and others often occur over the role of markets and incentives in policy design, the role of private business in a just society, and the economists' efforts to place dollar values on non-marketed goods such as environmental resources and human life.

Nelson's primary example of an ongoing ideological battle occurs between economists and non-economists in the area of environmental policy. Many environmental policy arguments combine scientific evidence of environmental harm with relatively absolute views of right and wrong. Environmental advocates often frame their discussion in terms of greedy corporations and the infinite value of nature and human life. This approach leads to support for stringent environmental standards and the rejection of any consideration of the costs of such standards. On the other hand, environmental economists usually advocate the impartial weighing of all benefits and costs of environmental policies, including non-environmental factors such as jobs and income. These different values and methods tend to produce differing conclusions regarding the appropriate amount of pollution reduction. Non-economists often support the greatest technically feasible level of clean-up, while economists tend to support the greatest level of clean-up for which the benefits outweigh the costs. Another dimension of the debate over environmental policy is the method by which pollution is to be controlled. Economists tend to favor incentive-based approaches such as taxes or pollution permits, while non-economists with less faith in self-interest or market forces tend to advocate explicit regulatory standards. Elements of this debate are presented in Chapter 13.

Advocacy and analysis

Nelson's entrepreneurs for efficiency and ideological combatants operate within a world of partisan politics and political influence. In the context of competing interests and ideals, conflict often exists between relatively objective analysis and political advocacy. An **advocate** is one who "pleads the cause of another" or "supports any cause by argument" (*Webster's* 1939). Most modern legal systems are based on opposing advocates for the prosecution and the defense, a system that has its roots in Roman law. The duty of a legal advocate is to build a case supporting one side in a trial. The duty of the judge or jury is to weigh the evidence and argument from the two sides in order to render a balanced decision. In the case of public policy, advocacy involves the support of a specific policy goal or point of view, and also tends to act by building a case for one side of even the most debatable policy proposals. Advocates for a particular viewpoint are likely to be biased in a number of ways, and being able to identify these sources of bias is crucial if a student is going to be able to think critically and objectively about policy.[5]

Most policy debates among advocates are likely to involve disagreements over values, definitions of the problem, evidence, and policy conclusions. Advocates for a particular interest group or ideology will provide a set of value arguments, definitions, evidence, and policy recommendations designed to support their point of view. Of course, the use of policy analysis as part of a persuasive argument requires that the findings in the policy study are consistent with the goals of the advocate. Hence, selective use of policy analysis and other evidence is a near certainty in political debates.

In addition to the selective use of evidence, it is possible that policy analysts might be pressured to modify their results or the way they are expressed. In order to reduce the probability of such political influence at the federal level, U.S. staff analysts have protection from political interference other than in the choice of their research assignments. The federal government's Office of Personnel Management acts under the following policy statement:

> Federal employees are hired, promoted, paid, and discharged solely on the basis of merit and conduct ... their ability to do their job. They provide special protections for veterans, victims of discrimination, and those who expose Government waste or fraud. They also guarantee our public employees due process in any action that threatens their employment, as well as the right to join unions and bargain collectively. With these enabling principles, our civil service system ensures that politics and political party, as well as other non-merit factors, have no bearing on the tenure of our civil servants, from the entry level clerk to the career members of our Senior Executive Service who lead them.[6]

This system of protection from political pressure is supported by a system of due process for handling complaints. However, efforts to influence results may still take place. The Union of Concerned Scientists' survey of fisheries scientists reported that nearly one-quarter of respondents had been pressured to alter or cut technical information from a report (Smith 2005). The director of Public Employees for Environmental Responsibility stated that its Washington office received three complaints per day from government scientists during the Clinton administration and about five complaints per day during the George W. Bush administration (Smith 2005). Academic researchers are more likely to be independent of direct political influence, but all research supported by private or public funding sources could be subject to some degree of financial influence.

Another interesting dimension of policy analysis is that results can be stored and reconsidered when a crisis emerges or the issue becomes newsworthy for some other reason. For example, in the aftermath of Hurricane Katrina in 2005 some looked at images of the largely submerged city of New Orleans, saw a predominantly African-American population, and responded with arguments about race, class, and the lack of access to transportation for the poor. Others saw visions of looting and violence among some of the same population and drew conclusions regarding the moral decay of at least some parts of American society. Environmentalists pulled out old papers on the costs of losing wetlands and barrier islands. Macroeconomists pulled out their models and forecast macroeconomic slowdowns and higher energy prices. Engineering studies of south Louisiana's system of levies were reconsidered and widely quoted. Very little of this analysis was actually completed after the hurricane, but the new evidence provided by the aftermath of the storm created important applications for older analysis, as well as a catalyst for the re-emergence of old political debates.

Interdisciplinary analysis

Another important part of the policy analyst's job is the need to consider ideas from multiple academic disciplines. An effective policy analyst must be able to trade ideas with engineers, other social scientists, lawyers, government officials, and the general public. For example, the analysis of infrastructure investments such as highways or mass transit systems requires input from transportation engineers, while the analysis of crime policy may require input from criminologists with backgrounds in sociology or other social sciences, as well as experts in law enforcement. Informed discussions of environmental policy require information from biological, chemical, geological, or environmental scientists. In addition, communication with public administrators, elected officials, and other interested parties is essential to the effectiveness of policy analysis, in part because one or more of these groups is probably sponsoring the analysis, and also because they have an active role in implementing legislation or regulations related to the policy in question. When communicating with administrators, an economic analyst may have to defend, or at least explain, the method and results of benefit–cost analysis. In that sense analysts also take the role of teachers. The same communication ability applies to one's interaction with clients in the private sector.

Critical thinking as a policy tool

The rest of the chapter will critically review some of the elements of argumentation and critical thinking, and then briefly critique benefit–cost analysis in light of these elements. Sound policy analysis depends on one's ability to organize analysis using established principles of logic and evidence. A brief review of a few important critical thinking concepts may improve the quality of your own analysis, as well as improve your ability to critically analyze the analysis of others. These concepts are useful when analyzing several levels of policy analysis from the "sound byte" in a political advertisement to professional journal articles.

Models and assumptions

Analytical models provide the underlying definitions and logic that are part of any well-constructed argument. These models may be based on social science, physical or biological science, legal scholarship, moral philosophy, or other academic fields. Any analytical model will contain the following components: (1) underlying assumptions and value judgments, (2) definitions of terms, (3) causal relationships, and (4) logical conclusions.[7] Models usually are judged on their ability to explain, predict, or productively guide human actions. In the social sciences the conclusions of theoretical models take the form of predictions about human behavior or the effects of policy alternatives.

Assumptions, definitions, and causal relationships are worthy of additional discussion. Assumptions are probably the most controversial components of economic models. **Assumptions** are stated or unstated value judgments, definitions, and interpretations of fact that are usually made without supporting evidence. Their primary role in an analytical model is to simplify and focus the analysis. For example, economists often assume that markets are competitive and efficient unless otherwise noted. Similarly, Marxists assume a set of social relations between classes that include elements of oppression and exploitation of the working class. Finally, analysis based on race, class, gender, or other categories of the population implicitly assumes that members of a given group are similar enough to be analyzed without explicit reference to individual differences. As with the economic assumptions of pure competition, these are simplifying assumptions that are essential to creating a relatively clear analysis. Assumptions, whether or not they are explicitly stated, are absolutely essential as the foundation of any subsequent argument. However, because assumptions are not supported with logic or evidence, they should always be used with care and humility.

Interpreting evidence

A strong argument must be supported by evidence. This section will present a brief review of types of evidence and their limitations. There are at least three general categories of evidence used to support policy analysis and policy recommendations. They are case studies, expert opinion and research, and general statistics. Each will be discussed briefly.

Case studies

A case study involves a detailed evaluation of an individual person, firm, industry, or geographic area. Case studies are deliberately limited in scope in order to emphasize detailed information. Case studies can be useful for identifying the process through which a problem develops. For example, case studies of sexual harassment in the workplace can identify ways in which harassment occurs as well as the psychological and physical effects of the harassment on its victims. Because of the individual detail possible in case studies, they are uniquely capable of displaying the human effects of a particular problem, and thereby can bring forth an emotional response from the public and the decision maker.

The primary weakness of the case study is its inability to answer a few fundamental questions about a policy problem. Most obviously, case studies are inherently incapable of identifying how frequently a problem occurs. It is usually necessary to know the frequency of a problem in order to determine the resources needed to deal with it. Similarly, the broader causes and effects of a policy problem, such as total costs or global impacts, cannot be addressed effectively through case studies. Also, the subjects of case studies might be chosen in a biased manner and therefore may be misleading or unrepresentative. Whether or not the case chosen for analysis is actually biased, the limits of the case study make such a charge difficult to refute without further evidence. Overall, case studies can play a positive role through their ability to add detail and a human touch to one's argument, but because they cannot determine the frequency or seriousness of a social problem, they are most effective when used in combination with more broadly-based forms of evidence such as scientific studies or broadly-based statistics.

Expert opinion and research findings

Expertise is usually measured by one's academic degrees, publication record, and experience. However, an expert's opinions can be subject to the same ideological bias as those of a layman or politician, and can be analyzed using the same type of questions. For example, is an expert's conclusion typical of research in that area? Is her argument fully supported by logic and evidence, or is it weak in one or both respects? Such questions help guide one's critical thinking about any issue. Advocates sometimes have a range of experts or studies to choose from, and their choice is likely to be highly influenced by their policy goals and points of view.

Another dimension of interpreting policy studies involves the range of estimated effects of a given policy or problem. When one considers a literature review of a policy topic, he or she should pay attention to the range of results in addition to the typical median estimate. For example, at this time there is a relatively wide range of estimates of the expected rise in global temperatures over the next century. A wide range of estimates implies a significant degree of uncertainty about the facts and models related to an issue. Environmental advocates are likely to tell stories based on relatively high estimates of temperature change, while a common position of environmental conservatives is to argue that the wide range of evidence suggests that further study is needed before any action should be taken. Sometimes a closer look can lead to a narrowing of the range. For example, a review of the employment effects of the minimum wage (Brown *et al.* 1982) found that while a relatively wide range of predictions exists, more sophisticated studies tended to cluster near the bottom of the range, indicating that the employment effects of the minimum wage tend to be relatively minor, at least in the short run.

Occasionally you will hear that a particular study has disproven an entire set of previous studies about a particular topic. In some cases this type of statement may be true, but often this is a slanted conclusion based on ideology. For example, political supporters of a higher minimum wage sometimes argue that a study by Card and Krueger (1994) disproved the idea that a higher minimum wage causes a decrease in employment. After many decades of research about the minimum wage, it is a rather large leap of faith to suggest such a conclusion based on one or a few contradictory studies. The minimum wage is discussed in greater detail in Chapter 15.

Official statistics

Statistics from the government and other public and private organizations provide another prime source of evidence for public policy analysis and debate. In some ways, official statistics are at the opposite extreme from case studies. Their primary strength is their ability to identify the frequency or breadth of a problem based on large samples of the population.[8] Anyone who has taken a basic statistics course should understand that even official statistics are estimates rather than facts. However, given the large samples used for most national statistics, measurement error is likely to be small. The controversies surrounding government statistics are usually based on their definitions or their use by advocates rather than their measurement accuracy. Understanding the limits of commonly used statistics is important for critical thinking about problems relating to those measures. Other issues arise regarding how statistics are presented, and in some cases which statistics are used. Each of these sources of controversy will be discussed in turn.

The definitions of common official statistics are sometimes arbitrary and controversial. In other cases the specific statistic has been found to offer a biased or incomplete interpretation of the problem it is meant to assess. Sources of bias in commonly used measures such as the inflation rate, the unemployment rate, and the poverty rate have been studied in detail. The inflation rate is discussed in more detail in Chapter 9, while the poverty rate is discussed in Chapter 14. Another example of potentially biased statistics based on a limited definition is the unemployment rate, which will be discussed below.

The unemployment rate is based on a very specific and somewhat arbitrary set of definitions and assumptions. In the U.S. the unemployment rate is defined as the number of persons "unemployed" divided by the number of persons "in the labor force", multiplied by 100 percent. A person is considered **unemployed** if she is not currently working for pay, but is actively seeking employment. Similarly, a person is counted as **in the labor force** if he is either working or actively looking for work. In other words, the labor force is made up of two groups: the employed and the unemployed. However, not everybody who doesn't work is part of the labor force. Retirees, full-time students, homemakers, and others who are neither working nor actively looking for work are considered to be out of the labor force.

Your Turn 1.2: Based on the previous paragraph, answer the following questions: (1) If a lawyer is currently working as a cashier at K-Mart, is she counted as unemployed? (2) Is someone who wants to work full time but only works one hour per week unemployed? (3) Is a full-time student who is not currently working for pay unemployed? (4) Are you currently unemployed?

Despite its widespread use as an indicator of economic health, the unemployment rate is actually a relatively narrow statistic that measures only one aspect of labor market conditions. One problem that the unemployment rate does not measure is under-utilized skills, as with the lawyer above. The under-utilization of skills is sometimes labeled **under-employment**. Similarly, people who are involuntarily working part time are still employed, as are those working for very low wages. Finally, those who are not currently looking for work are not included in the labor force and are therefore not unemployed. Individuals who are not actively looking for work but would take a job if offered are called either **marginally attached workers** or **discouraged workers,** depending on their reason for not actively searching for work, and are now measured separately by the U.S. Bureau of Labor Statistics.

Critics of the unemployment rate are often displeased with its inability to measure broader labor market problems. The significance of this example is that a single benchmark number such as the unemployment rate may provide an indication of trends in the labor market or in the national economy, but it cannot define the entirety of the issue it is meant to represent.

The presentation of statistics

Another aspect of critical thinking about statistics lies in observing how they are presented. One might discuss unemployment, poverty, profits, or virtually any statistic as a total number or as a percentage of some larger sum.

Your Turn 1.3: Consider these statements: (A) Raising the minimum wage by one dollar will decrease employment by 270,000 jobs. (B) Raising the minimum wage by one dollar will decrease employment by only one-fifth of 1 percent. Which piece of evidence sounds more reasonable to you? Why?

Statistics presented as large totals often sound more impressive than percentages. One important suggestion regarding the interpretation of statistics is to **beware the big number**. In a large economy, billions of euros or thousands of people do not always represent socially significant sums. For example, corporate profits are often presented as large annual totals, but a large annual total profit does not necessarily mean the company is exploiting the consuming public or its workers. A large company might have an annual profit level in the billions but still have a low percentage of profits to total sales or to stockholders' equity. For example, Wal-Mart profits totaled $10.27 billion for 2004. These profits amounted to 3.56 percent of total revenue, which is not an unusually high level (*Pacific Business News* 2005).

Advocacy and statistics

A much more difficult issue in interpreting statistics involves determining whether the statistics are accurate. First, both the advocate and the actual source of the statistics may be biased. Ideology and self-interest may affect who is chosen to do the research, and possibly how the actual research is undertaken. So another question to ask when considering policy research is what group sponsored the research, and how do the conclusions of the research relate to the sponsor's ideology or self-interest? Ideology or self-interest also may affect which results are actually quoted by an advocate, and how they are presented.

Another difficulty in interpreting statistics is that different statistics with contradictory trends are sometimes used to identify the same problem. For example, there is a common perception that the U.S. manufacturing sector is being replaced by foreign production. However, until recently evidence for this trend was mixed. The trends in employment and output provided below suggest two very different patterns.

Your Turn 1.4: The following table (source: *Economic Report of the President*, 2000) presents data on the relation between durable goods manufacturing and the total economy. Durable goods are things that last a long time, such as cars or major appliances.

(A) Try to explain the difference between the trends in the percentage of production and the percentage of jobs. Also discuss the differences between the total number and the percentage of durable goods manufacturing jobs. Which sets of data suggest that the U.S. is "de-industrializing"?

Table 1.1 U.S. output and employment trends

Year	U.S. durable goods output ($billions)	U.S. gross domestic product	*Durable goods production (% of GDP)*	Total U.S. jobs (thousands)	Durable goods jobs	*Durable goods jobs (% of total payroll jobs)*
1959	95.3	507.4	**18.8%**	53,270	9,342	**17.5%**
1960	96.9	527.4	**18.4%**	54,189	9,429	**17.4%**
1998	1,567.8	8,759.9	**17.9%**	125,826	11,170	**8.9%**
1999	1,643.6	9,248.4	**17.8%**	128,610	10,986	**8.5%**

Output is from Table B-8 and equals final sales plus change in inventories. Employment is from Table B-44 in the 2000 Economic Report of the President.

Continued

(B) Look up more recent data for total output by sector and total employment by industry group at the *Economic Report of the President's* website (http://a257.g.akamaitech.net/7/257/2422/17feb20051700/ www.gpoaccess.gov/eop/tables05.html). Based on more recent figures, is the erosion of the U.S. manufacturing sector worsening in the new century? Finally, does the use of total goods production instead of durable goods production change these conclusions?

Another common fallacy in the use of evidence is to assume that when two events are correlated, one event caused the other. This is referred to as ***post hoc, propter hoc analysis,*** or **false cause reasoning.** Proving a cause-and-effect relationship requires a combination of theory and evidence, and cannot be accomplished through a statistical correlation alone. For example, opponents of free trade in the U.S. sometimes claim that free trade is counterproductive because the U.S. experienced its primary industrial revolution in the 1800s while under a system of high tariffs. This historical correlation is true. However, proving a causal relationship between tariffs and growth requires that (1) growing U.S. industries would have been subject to debilitating competition from foreign producers in the absence of tariffs; (2) that our industries couldn't successfully compete with those of other countries without the tariffs; and, most importantly, (3) that the resources invested in those industries couldn't have been used more productively elsewhere. Less plausible examples of false cause reasoning can be found in any number of subjects. For example, the hemline theory of stock prices hypothesized that average stock prices could be predicted based on that season's skirt length (rising hemlines meant rising stock prices). Another less than scientific model of stock prices is the Super Bowl theory, which predicts that a victory by the U.S. football's National Football Conference leads to rising stock prices.

Political interpretations of even the most valid statistics should give anyone reason for caution. The supporting evidence used in the arguments of public officials or interest groups is particularly prone to being chosen selectively, represented and interpreted in a biased way, and presented with too much certainty. The evidence found in the policy papers of advocacy organizations should be interpreted with extreme caution whether or not you are inclined to agree with the advocate's position.

Critical thinking about policy analysis

While policy analysis has become a relatively common part of the implementation and administration of public programs, it also remains controversial and subject to fundamental criticisms. The previous section on critical thinking in policy analysis can and should be turned back on the subject itself. Among the many critiques of benefit–cost analysis, three seem to be particularly common. These critiques relate to the utilitarian philosophy that underlies the benefit–cost model, the appropriateness and accuracy of assigning dollar values to non-marketed goods, and objections to the microeconomic foundations of benefit–cost analysis. The critique of utilitarianism is presented in Chapter 2, while a critique of assigning dollar values to non-marketed goods is presented in Chapter 10. Other critiques will be discussed in this chapter.

Two related sources of complaint about benefit–cost analysis can be categorized as primarily ideological. One is the common view of institutional and radical economists that market forces are dominated more by power and oppression than supply and demand (Dorman 1996). If this is true, then measuring benefits and costs on the basis of market concepts is likely to be both misdirected and inaccurate. Another ideological objection to benefit–cost analysis arises from populists, who consider the desires of the people to be the primary basis for policy, and any expert analysis to be at least somewhat anti-democratic. In a populist vision, there may be some justification for policy analysis if the primary client for the research is the public itself rather than bureaucrats or interest groups, but for the most part the will and thinking of the people are seen as trumping any type of professional analysis.

Conclusion

This book is arranged in four parts. Following the introductory chapter, the principles of ethics and efficiency that underlie benefit–cost analysis are considered in Chapters 2 through 5. The tools of policy analysis are covered in Chapters 6 through 11. These chapters discuss the basics of benefit–cost analysis, methods for comparing present and future net benefits, benefit–cost analysis in the presence of risk and uncertainty, dollar estimates of the value of human life and other non-marketed goods, and economic impact analysis. The final chapters present more detailed overviews of a set of policy issues, and are meant to add two elements to the text. The first goal of these applied chapters is to expose the student to the range of possible policies related to a specific policy problem. The second goal is to expose the reader to breadth and differing sources of knowledge required for specific policy areas. For example, in Chapter 13 we consider the role of the physical and biological sciences in analyzing environmental policy, while input from other social scientific fields is considered in the analysis of poverty and anti-poverty policy in Chapters 14 and 15.

While the main topic of this book is the analysis of public policy, the opening quote of this chapter promotes critical thinking, while the second is about careful and rational decision making. These are totally appropriate quotes for a policy analysis text, for regardless of how many of this book's analytical tools or policy topics are remembered, any significant improvement in one's ability to see beneath the sound bites and shallow reasoning of many of our public policy debates will provide an important benefit. I hope that this benefit is worth its cost.

Review questions

Conceptual questions

1. Review each part of Bardach's eight-step process of policy analysis as well as the five-step procedure of the Office of Management and Budget (OMB).

   (A) Why might an analyst operating within a bureaucracy such as the federal government feel less free to include policy recommendations as part of his or her report? Discuss the pluses and minuses of excluding this step or leaving it to others.

   (B) The OMB requires that the goals and assumptions of one's policy analysis be stated explicitly. Where might this requirement fit into Bardach's list? How is a study that fails to explicitly and thoroughly state its assumptions less reliable or more difficult to interpret?

2. Discuss how the three goals of efficiency, equity, and political practicality might apply to the following public policy issues. For each goal, construct a list of relevant questions that might be applied to the case in question.

   (A) Rebuilding the poorer neighborhoods of New Orleans or leaving some of them as green space after Hurricane Katrina.

   (B) Establishing a universal health insurance program in the U.S. with no fees for any resident.

   (C) Invading Iraq and establishing a democratic government as a means of fighting Islamic terrorism.

3. Nelson's three roles for the policy analyst (the progressive neutral expert, the entrepreneur for efficiency, and the ideological combatant) are based on three different views of the operation of government and formation of public policy.

   (A) Review these three roles and the views of government related to each. Which role strikes you as most favorable? Most realistic?

   (B) Discuss how a policy analyst might react to a proposal to raise the minimum wage. In your discussion, does the analyst favor or oppose such a policy?

4. Find a discussion of a common economic policy issue such as the merchandise trade deficit or the minimum wage on the website of a conservative organization such as the Cato Institute (http://www.cato.org/) or the American Enterprise Institute (http://www.aei.org/), and also on the site of the Economic Policy Institute (http://www.epinet.org/). Note in detail the arguments raised and the evidence used to support their conclusions.

Computational questions

This book relies on your knowledge of introductory economics and the basic mathematics often seen in the analysis of markets and individual decisions.

The following questions can be thought of as a test of the basic concepts and skills that will be utilized later in the text.

5. A market equilibrium can be summarized in the following three equations:

>   **(1) Demand curve:** $P_d = 100 - 2Q_d$, where P_d and Q_d equal the demand curve's price and quantity, respectively.
>
>   **(2) Supply curve:** $P_s = 10 + Q_s$, where P_s and Q_s equal the supply curve's price and quantity, respectively.
>
>   **(3) Equilibrium condition:** At equilibrium, Demand = Supply, which means that $P_d = P_s$ and $Q_d = Q_s$.

(A) Graph the demand and supply curves in Figure 1.1. Label the endpoints and slopes of each curve.

(B) Find the equilibrium values for quantity and price using algebra.

(C) Draw lines from the equilibrium point to the quantity and price axes. Total spending equals price•quantity. Identify this rectangle on the graph. What is the value of total spending in this market?

(D) Consumer surplus is defined as the area beneath the demand curve and above the price. This area usually forms a right triangle. Identify this triangle in the graph. What is the formula for the area of a right triangle? What is the area of the consumer surplus triangle in Figure 1.1?

6. Identify the tangency point in Figure 1.2. $\frac{100 - 0}{0 - 100} = -1$

(A) At that point what is the slope of the straight line? _____ the curved line? _____

(B) About how many cans of each beverage is this person consuming?

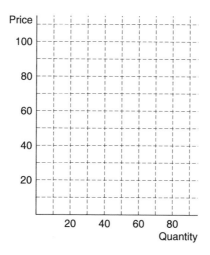

Figure 1.1 Demand-and-supply curves

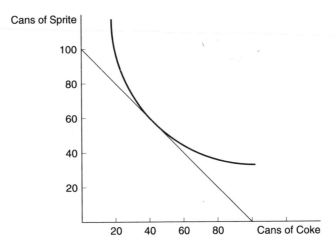

Figure 1.2 A tangency example

7. Solve the following compound fractions.

(A) $\dfrac{3/8}{3/32}$ = _____   (B) $\dfrac{2/3}{16/21}$ = _____

2 Ethics for policy analysts

If liberty and equality ... are chiefly to be found in democracy, they will be best attained when all persons alike share in the government to the utmost.[1]

(Aristotle)

Our task as humans is to find the few principles that will calm the infinite anguish of free souls.[2]

(Albert Camus)

All animals are equal but some animals are more equal than others.[3]

(George Orwell)

While economics is often thought of as the study of market value, ethics can be thought of as the study of moral value. Ethics is the study of the meaning of right versus wrong or moral versus immoral actions, and the application of these concepts to everyday life. In Western thought, ethics dates back at least to the ancient Greeks, particularly Plato and Aristotle. General ethical principles operate at the personal and institutional levels and are, or should be, an important part of our lives as well as our policies.

One important challenge in studying ethics arises from its many conflicting ethical theories. In modern ethics these theories range in time of origin from Plato and Aristotle through the present day and in ideology from highly conservative to revolutionary. Ethics may arise from religious or secular sources, and all major religions have one or more related codes of ethics. Because there are so many views of right and wrong, informed ethical choice is often very difficult.

Another challenge for the student of ethics arises from the need to think about the meaning of right and wrong with an open mind. This is difficult because as children many of us are taught about right and wrong in a rather authoritarian or paternalistic manner that doesn't allow much room for thought. A final challenge is that, like statistics, values and value judgments can be misused or misinterpreted, and must be considered cautiously.

Your Turn 2.1: What are your views on each of the following questions? Think about how you would explain or support your views. Are you satisfied with the quality of your arguments? If possible, discuss them with friends or classmates.

(A) Does an individual have a right to engage in self-destructive behavior, and does government have the right to prevent him or her from doing so?

(B) Does an affluent society have the responsibility to provide an adequate minimum level of income for those who cannot support themselves? For those who choose not to support themselves?

(C) Is it ethically necessary to provide the highest technically possible level of safety in transportation, factories, and homes, regardless of the cost to consumers, taxpayers, or workers?

(D) Should income equality be an important goal of tax-and-spending policies? Should the rich pay a higher percentage of their income in taxes than the poor?

Ethical goals

While the field of ethics includes a wide range of ideologies, arguments, and ways of writing, there are a few common goals for society which guide the writings of most of the great moral philosophers. Three of these ethical goals, in no particular order, are basic human rights, freedom, and equality.

Basic human rights

Philosophers sometimes establish ethical principles based on a set of minimum human rights. Essential questions about human rights include these three:

1   What are rights?
2   Which rights are basic?
3   What is the basis in argument for these rights?

Each will be discussed briefly.

In this context a **right** is a power or privilege to which one is entitled. If one has rights, then others have a corresponding duty to act in accordance with that person's rights. For example, if a person has a right to own possessions (property rights), we have a duty not to steal those possessions. If a person has a right to life, we have a duty not to kill her. In policy terms, rights tend to represent a set of minimum standards for an acceptable human existence, and the concept of equal rights means that we have a responsibility not to violate the basic rights of anyone.

But what items should we include in our list of human rights? Different answers to this question arise from different sources. One set of rights is found in John Locke's theory of the state of nature from which society arises:

> The state of nature has a law of nature to govern it, which ... teaches that, being all equal and independent, no one ought to harm another in his life, health, liberty, or possessions.
>
> (Locke 1955: 5-6)

There is a corresponding set of responsibilities based on these rights. According to Locke, these are to not "harm another" in his rights. In other words, one should not take another's life, deliberately injure or sicken another, restrict their liberty or take their possessions.

The policy role of basic rights and liberties is to establish what Henry Shue (1980) calls a "moral minimum – the lower limits on tolerable human conduct, individual and institutional" (p. ix). At a minimum, these basic human rights require us to not actively deprive another of his life, health, liberty or property or, more generally, to not harm other humans. An argument for why we choose to honor the rights of others comes from Plato:

> ... to do wrong is, in itself, a desirable thing; on the other hand, it is not at all desirable to suffer wrong, and the harm to the sufferer outweighs the advantage to the doer. Consequently, when men have had a taste of both, those who have not the power to seize the advantage and escape the harm decide that they would be better off if they made a compact neither to do wrong nor to suffer it.
>
> (Jones *et al.* 1969: 26)

Doing wrong in this context means stealing from or otherwise exploiting another person for one's own gain. As advantageous as such actions may seem to the perpetrator, they clearly harm the victim. Since in an amoral society any of us might be victims, it is in our best interest to accept social norms which reject victimizing others. Within the Judeo-Christian tradition an even more familiar statement of the responsibilities consistent with these rights is found in some of the Ten Commandments, most notably "thou shall not kill" and "thou shall not steal."

In a modern and more affluent context, however, some argue that the rights to life and health require society to provide sufficient resources to maintain the life and health of those who might not be capable of doing so on their own (Shue 1980: 22-4). Shue's argument that we are morally required to support the destitute expands Locke's view of our responsibilities to the poor and is widely accepted in modern policy, in part because the greater affluence of modern developed countries makes such aid less of a burden on others. In conclusion, adherence to the principle of basic human rights requires us not to harm other person's rights, and perhaps to provide sufficient aid to those whose basic human rights are being inadequately preserved.

Freedom

Freedom is an important component of basic human rights, yet is subject to many different interpretations. In the most common ethical definition, freedom means the absence of limits or constraints on an individual's actions. As Locke states:

> To understand political power aright, and derive it from its original, we must consider what state all men are naturally in, and that is a state of perfect freedom to order their actions … as they think fit, within the bounds of the law of nature, without asking leave, or depending upon the will of any other man.
>
> (Locke 1955: 4)

In a policy context, freedom can also be usefully thought of as freedom of choice, as in the freedom to choose any job, political party, religion, intoxicating substance, or point of view.

Of particular importance in a policy context is the distinction that is sometimes drawn between the phrases **freedom to** … and **freedom from** …, as in the freedom to do something and the freedom from a harmful or unjust situation. The most notable example of "freedom from" as a separate concept comes from Marxists who often emphasize freedom from oppression, exploitation, or alienation (Lukes 1985: Ch. 5). Often, however, these phrases do not conflict. One may be free to vote or free from barriers to voting.

Freedom as a basic human right is not the same thing as political freedom or democracy. The freedom to choose between two or more oppressive political parties would not impress most defenders of individual liberty. However, freedom to act as we wish has always been understood to be limited in a civilized society. Perhaps the most common policy question relating to liberty involves the degree to which government should limit our freedom in order to protect others from harm. Ethical theories that emphasize the evils of inequality, exploitation, or sin tend to see an intrusive government as a necessary means of controlling these evils. Theories which emphasize freedom and individual choice tend to see government control as harmful, and individual vice as the lesser of two evils.

Another long-standing issue involving the limits of liberty is whether an individual should have the freedom to act in a self-destructive way. Most modern libertarians argue that no limits should be placed on individual behavior unless it involves direct and significant harm to others, but even among the greatest philosophers of freedom there is disagreement over this issue. John Locke, for instance, states that "though man in that state [of nature] has an uncontrollable liberty to dispose of his person or possessions, yet he has not the liberty to destroy himself" (1955: 5). On the other side of the issue, Robert Nozick states that, "My non-paternalistic position holds that someone may choose (or permit another) to do to himself anything, unless he has acquired an obligation to some third party not to do or allow it" (Nozick 1974: 58). The question of whether society is morally required to place controls on deviant or self-destructive individual behavior is one of many legitimately debatable ethical issues.

Equality

Ethics also involves determining how to distribute the rights, incomes, legal status, and other aspects of society which we deem to be important. This dimension of ethics is often referred to as distributional justice. Equality is the most common norm in ethics for determining how various rights and resources in society should be distributed. The dominance of equality in ethics is suggested by Amartya Sen:

> … a common characteristic of virtually all the approaches to the ethics of social arrangements that have stood the test of time is to want equality of something – something that has an important place in the particular theory. Not only do income-egalitarians … demand equal incomes, and welfare-egalitarians ask for equal welfare levels, but also classical utilitarians insist on equal weights on the utilities of all, and pure libertarians demand equality with respect to an entire class of rights and liberties. They are all "egalitarians" in some essential way.
>
> (Sen 1992: ix)

The fundamental issue raised by Sen's quote involves the multitude of goals to which equality may be applied. The implications of Sen's observation are profound indeed, for it calls into question the common debate over the roles of equality and liberty and its implications for the size and role of government. Those who favor equality of freedoms and individual rights tend to favor minimal government since those in positions of authority or power are likely to have greater individual and legal rights than others. Those who are most concerned with equal incomes and living standards tend to favor stronger government as the most efficient means of redistributing income and protecting minimum standards of living. For example, a crucial element in the ongoing debate over affirmative action policies in U.S. higher education is the ethical debate over equal opportunity versus equal outcomes. Notice that equality is the stated goal of both sides of this debate, but the interpretation of the goal is very different.

While equality is among the most general theoretical standards for judging the ethics of public policy, other distributional goals exist. Maximizing a goodness is also consistent with many ethical theories, and meeting minimum standards of behavior is also important for some policy issues. This list of basic philosophical principles is limited to a selection of goals related to public policy, specifically basic human rights, liberty, and equality, but others exist, particularly those relating to individual behavior. Honesty, courage, purity, and generosity are examples of important ethical goals that are more personal in nature.

The next section of this chapter will provide an overview of three ethical theories representing a wide range of ethical goals and policy implications. The primary purposes of this discussion are to illustrate the diversity and sophistication of ethical theory and to establish a minimal theoretical base for considering the ethical challenges that arise in public policy. The theories chosen are secular in nature, though religious ethics are equally broad in their implications for public policy and individual behavior. For example, Christian views on policy may range from highly conservative (Falwell *et al.* 1981) to radical (Miranda 1974; Wallis 1984). The three theories discussed below are either recent or have significant recent support, and range from strongly supportive of equality, including the equality of incomes, to libertarian and opposed to the involuntary redistribution of income. The three theories are utilitarianism and the theories of John Rawls and Robert Nozick.

Utilitarianism

Utilitarianism is the branch of ethics most closely associated with economics and benefit–cost analysis. Utilitarianism began with the writing of Jeremy Bentham in the early nineteenth century. Other utilitarians writing in the 1800s include John Stuart Mill and Henry Sidgwick. Modern writers associated with utilitarianism include J.J.C. Smart, Amartya Sen, and Partha Dasgupta. Brief discussions of utilitarian ethics usually begin with the famous utilitarian goal, **the greatest good for the greatest number**. The most basic questions that come to mind when analyzing this phrase are: **(1) What do we mean by good**, and **(2) What is the greatest number?**

Utilitarianism defines the good in a very general and relative sense. As Bentham defines the term:

> By utility is meant that property in any object, whereby it tends to produce benefit, advantage, pleasure, good, or happiness …, or to prevent the happening of mischief, pain, evil, or unhappiness to the party whose interest is considered.
>
> (Jones *et al.* 1969: 308)

Two aspects of this quote are particularly significant. First, utility involves an unusually broad definition of the good, including items such as pleasure which in some contexts might be considered immoral or sinful. According to this definition, something that is useful to a person is good because it adds utility, and something which is pleasantly intoxicating to the same person is also good for the same reason.

Secondly, each person's utility is determined by his or her own tastes. Laws and social norms may influence a person's utility by imposing feelings of guilt, social pressure, or actual punishment on those actions which violate social rules, but the basic judgment about personal utility still rests with the individual. In this sense utilitarianism is relatively weak in its ability to provide moral judgments about individual behavior. On the other hand, it is unusually capable of avoiding paternalistic or authoritarian judgments about what is good and bad in a given situation. This tension between individual pleasure and social norms has led to varying interpretations of utilitarianism, which will be discussed later.

Now let us consider the meaning of the term "greatest number." According to Jeremy Bentham, the greatest number represents the total number of individuals in a given community:

> The community is a fictitious body, composed of the individual persons who are constituting … its members. The interest of the community then is … the sum of the interests of the several members who compose it.
>
> (Jones *et al*. 1969: 308)

Interestingly, there is little support in utilitarianism for the usual limits placed on the size or inclusiveness of a community. Sidgwick, among others, defines the ultimate goal of utilitarianism as "*universal* happiness" (1962: 413). There is little basis in utilitarianism for limiting our analysis to citizens of a particular nation, ethnic group or religion, or even of a particular species.

> Are we to extend our concern to all the beings capable of pleasure and pain whose feelings are affected by our conduct? Or are we to confine our view to human happiness? The former view is the one adopted by Bentham and Mill, and (I believe) by the Utilitarian school generally.
>
> (Sidgwick 1962: 414)

Clearly, utilitarianism requires us to consider the well-being of the citizens of all nations as equally important. Nationalism is inconsistent with utilitarianism. Also, utilitarian thinking may require that the well-being of non-human species be considered when setting policy. When considering environmental or international policy, the greatest number is a very large number indeed!

Perhaps we should consider a more structured interpretation of the meaning of utilitarian ethics. Sen and Williams (1982) offer three basic principles for utilitarian theory. These principles are listed and defined below:

1. **Welfarism** implies that individual utility, or welfare, is the basis for assigning an ethical value for the utilitarian. Therefore the value of an action is based on the net benefits to those affected by the action, as opposed to its consistency with some overarching principle. Furthermore, the benefits and costs of income redistribution are based on the utility gained or lost, rather than on the actual dollar amount transferred.

2. **Sum-ranking** means that society should determine the overall net benefits of a policy to society by adding the utilities of all affected individuals. It further means that all individual utilities should be weighted equally.

3. **Consequentialism** means that policy choices should be made with regard to the consequences (ends) of the policy, rather than the means by which the ends are achieved.

(Sen and Williams 1982: 3-4)

The first two principles, welfarism and sum-ranking, are unique to utilitarianism, while consequentialism is true of some important alternative ethical theories.

Extreme versus restricted utilitarianism

Scholars largely agree that under some interpretations, utilitarianism can be inconsistent with the observance of human rights and even with the basic meaning of ethics itself. If one allows the net gains in society's total utility to determine policy, no matter how badly one individual is hurt in the process, individual rights are clearly at risk. Because of these tensions between utilitarianism and basic human rights, as well as discomfort with the role of hedonism in Bentham's analysis, utilitarianism has been interpreted in a more limited way by most of the utilitarians who followed him. John Stuart Mill, Henry Sidgwick, and Amartya Sen, among others, might be best characterized as **restricted utilitarians**, after the terminology of J.J.C. Smart (1956), while Bentham's theory would be categorized as **extreme utilitarianism**.

Restricted utilitarianism uses the logic of utilitarianism at a general level in order to establish a set of guiding principles for society. Each of these principles is judged according to its ability to achieve the greatest good for the greatest number, or equivalently the greatest net good for society as a whole, according to the principles of welfarism, the rank-sum rule, and consequentialism. If a rule provides the greatest level of pleasure minus pain for society, it should be adopted. Once a rule is adopted, however, each individual should act according to the rule whether or not it is in his or her best interest. On the other hand, in **extreme utilitarianism** an individual may judge each action according to its utility independent of any general rules. If rules exist under extreme utilitarianism, they are not absolutely binding on the individual. Smart describes the difference between extreme and restricted utilitarianism as follows:

> A more modest form of utilitarianism ... [holds] that moral rules are more than rules of thumb. In general the rightness of an action is *not* to be tested by evaluating its consequences but only by considering whether or not it falls under a certain rule. Whether the **rule** is to be considered an acceptable moral rule is, however, to be decided by considering the consequences of adopting the rule. Broadly, then, actions are to be tested by rules and rules by consequences.
>
> (Smart 1969: 625-6)

The actual rules which are likely to pass such a test vary with the author, but usually bear a close relationship to basic human and legal rights. For example, John Stuart Mill suggests six rules of justice which promote the greater good. These are (1) not depriving people of their legal rights, (2) of their basic human rights, or (3) of things they deserve. Also, one must (4) not break promises and agreements, (5) show unjust favoritism toward some over others, or (6) treat people unequally (Mill 1957: 54-7). Writing from a libertarian perspective,

Hayek uses utilitarian logic to argue that liberty should be the primary goal of government:

> Our faith in freedom does not rest on the foreseeable results in particular circumstances but on the belief that it will, on balance, release more forces for the good than for the bad.
>
> (Hayek 1960: 31)

Restricted utilitarianism therefore can be used to establish rules which defend basic human rights by weighing the societal benefits and costs of those rules.

An example of how extreme and restricted utilitarianism might differ regarding a policy issue is the death penalty. An extreme utilitarian would be willing to support the death penalty if the benefits of execution to society in terms of satisfaction, future safety, or cost outweigh the disutility to the individual who is executed. A follower of Mill or Locke might question the death penalty due to its violation of the condemned person's right to life.

Weaknesses of utilitarianism

Because of utilitarianism's role as the philosophical cornerstone of benefit–cost analysis, some mention should be made of the many criticisms of the theory. In spite of its widespread use and wide range of policy applications, utilitarianism is not an ideal means of analyzing many moral issues. A selection of critical arguments will be arranged as they relate to consequentialism, the rank-sum rule, and welfarism.

As stated earlier, consequentialism says that a policy is just if its results are just, or that the ends justify the means. Because of its consequentialism, extreme utilitarianism offers a relatively poor defense of human rights. If a policy results in net gains to society, it is of relatively little importance to extreme utilitarians whether some people's rights are violated in the process. Similarly, it matters little whether a redistribution of income is accomplished through voluntary charity, or by government policy, or by theft. A consequentialist theory will see little difference between aiding the poor through the Salvation Army, Robin Hood's merry men, or government, though their methods differ considerably.

When one adds the rank-sum rule to consequentialism, the logic of extreme utilitarianism permits even tragic consequences for the few to be outweighed by modest improvements in well-being for the many. The basic logic of the rank-sum rule suggests that a policy is acceptable whenever the added utility to the winners outweighs lost utility for the losers, even if the losers suffer a loss of basic human rights. For example, extreme utilitarian thought might say that a group of starving persons would be morally right to sacrifice and consume one member in order for others to survive. Many other theories would disagree.

Furthermore, some argue that utilitarianism is inconsistent with the goal of income equality or with the transfer of income to the poor. Because the utility of the rich and poor are equally weighted through the rank-sum rule, gains to the poor through income transfers would be offset by losses to the rich. This argument isn't necessarily true, however, as long as the utility the poor gain from the income transfer is greater than the utility lost by the rich. If the economic principle of diminishing marginal utility applies to income, the utility benefits of an income transfer to the poor are likely to outweigh the utility losses by the rich, unless there is significant waste caused by the transfer program. The tendency of non-economists to confuse income and utility is the likely source of this critique of utilitarianism. However, benefit–cost analysis generally weighs individual monetary gains and losses equally, and is therefore more subject to this critique than the utilitarian principles on which it is based.

Welfarism is also the basis for much criticism. Bentham's emphasis on pleasure as the basis for well-being is rejected by many moral philosophers, including restricted utilitarians. Most religions consider the pursuit of some pleasures to be immoral. For example, extreme utilitarianism suggests that if a person's pleasure from heavy drinking outweighs the pain caused to him and others, then drinking is morally justified. The same logic applies to any intoxicating substance. Similarly, because utility is based on each individual's preferences, utilitarian thought includes a large degree of moral relativism. One is reminded of such 1960s expressions as "if it feels good, do it." Individual morality is generally considered a reasonable goal for society, and extreme utilitarianism offers a relatively weak basis for such moral judgments.

Furthermore, despite Bentham's effort to measure utility through a detailed categorization of types and degrees of pleasure and pain, utility is usually not measurable. If one cannot measure the utility gains and losses of an action, one also cannot add or subtract them. Unless indirect means of measuring utility are used, this problem has the potential to destroy the usefulness of the rank-sum rule. Fortunately for utilitarianism and for policy analysis, economists have developed indirect measures of utility that allow the theory to be applied in a more explicit way than many alternative theories. However, these methods are inexact and controversial, and present a challenge for utilitarian theory.

In conclusion, utilitarianism is the closest thing to a paradigm for analyzing the ethics of public policy, but it is subject to relatively serious flaws and limitations. Compared to most ethical theories, utilitarianism tends to be more concerned with efficiency and its potential to increase the overall wealth of a society. It also emphasizes individual tastes and choice more than most ethical theories. Ironically, utilitarianism might be the strongest ethical theory in situations where ethics is least important. In other words, utilitarianism may be most useful for analyzing policies if lives are not threatened and the least well-off in society are not seriously harmed.

John Rawls and the difference principle

The next two theories arise from single individuals, John Rawls and Robert Nozick, both of whom published their most influential works in the 1970s. The first of these works is *A Theory of Justice* by John Rawls (1971). The major characteristic of Rawls' theory is its strong emphasis on equality of incomes, wealth, political rights, and other outcomes, along with its dominant concern for the least well-off in society.

Rawls' strong defense of equality makes his theory relatively consistent with a liberal political ideology and a highly egalitarian approach to social policy.

The original position

Rawls develops his theoretical approach through an abstract model that is somewhat related to Locke's theory of the social contract. The primary difference between the assumptions of Rawls and Locke is that Rawls' analysis of the formation of the social contract begins with a set of abstract assumptions, rather than as a set of (debatable) fundamental truths about the state of nature. Rawls' goal is to create a situation where thought can be applied to the question of distributional justice without the corrupting combination of self-interest and social differences. Rawls calls this abstract situation the **original position**. As Rawls describes it,

> The original position … is a state of affairs in which the parties are equally represented as moral persons and the outcome is not conditioned by arbitrary contingencies or the relative balance of social forces.
>
> (p. 120)

This original position assumes that all parties have equal rights and equal access to the decision-making process, so that any decision made by the group while in the original position is fair (pp. 128-9).

The most important assumption regarding the original position is the information each person lacks. All persons in the original position are assumed to be ignorant about their own status in society, income level, natural ability, and any groups or coalitions to which they belong. Any individual may be powerful or dependent, rich or poor, part of an influential group or alone, but in the original position nobody will be aware of these indicators of privilege or power. This lack of awareness of one's social, political, or economic standing is called the "**veil of ignorance**."

This veil of ignorance serves a very important purpose in determining how the group will decide its principles of justice. As Rawls states, "No one knows his situation in society nor his natural assets, and therefore no one is in a position to tailor principles to his advantage" (1971: 139). In other words, people behind the veil of ignorance are not in a position to bargain for political, social, or economic advantages for themselves or others in a similar situation because they don't know their situation. Therefore, those in the original position will have no alternative except to choose society's laws and norms in a truly impartial manner.

The difference principle

Rawls suggests that those in an original position will choose total equality as a starting point for their society:

> Since it is not reasonable for him to expect more than an equal share in the division of social goods, and since it is not rational for him to agree to less, the sensible thing for him to do is to acknowledge as the first principle of

justice one requiring an equal distribution. ...Thus, the parties start with a principle establishing equal liberty for all, including equality of opportunity, as well as an equal distribution of income and wealth.

(pp. 150-1)

However, equality of income need not persist if individuals display different skills and levels of effort in their work. In such a case, allowing the most productive to earn and keep extra income may help to increase the overall productivity of society. A wealthier society then has the potential to increase the well-being of those who are least well off. This brings us to Rawls' primary contribution to the concept of distributive justice, the difference principle:

> **[The difference principle:]** All social primary goods – liberty and opportunity, income and wealth, and the bases of self-respect – are to be distributed equally unless an unequal distribution of any or all of these goods is to the advantage of the least favored.
>
> (1971: 303)

The most fundamental and controversial part of the difference principle is its complete focus on the least well-off person. Only when the least well-off person benefits from inequality is that inequality justifiable, according to Rawls. The difference principle is also expressed in more mathematical terms as a **maxi-min** solution to the problem of social justice, where maxi-min is an abbreviation for **maximizing the minimum**, or maximizing the well-being of the least well-off person. This aspect of Rawls' theory is discussed in the final section of this chapter.

Your Turn 2.2: Assume that you are one of three people in a very small society, and that your group is under the veil of ignorance. You may choose any of the following three distributions of income. Which income distribution do you choose? Which distribution is consistent with the difference principle? If your preferred choice differs from that of the difference principle, discuss why. If not, defend the difference principle against any challenges.

	Distribution 1	*Distribution 2*	*Distribution 3*
Person 1	$15,000	$14,000	$13,000
Person 2	$15,000	$20,000	$1,000,000,000
Person 3	$15,000	$20,000	$1,000,000,000

Distribution 1 gives everyone $15,000, distribution 2 gives each person a 2/3 chance of earning $20,000 and a 1/3 chance of earning $14,000, and distribution 3 gives each person a 2/3 chance of becoming a billionaire and a 1/3 chance of earning $13,000.

Rawls is not concerned with income distribution alone. Liberty, equality, and productivity are all goals in Rawls' theory of justice. Within this brief list of primary goods, Rawls establishes definite priorities regarding their relative importance. The first priority within the difference principle is assigned to liberty, which means that liberty cannot be restricted in pursuit of any other goal except liberty itself. Furthermore, any restriction on liberty must meet two conditions: "(a) a less extensive liberty must strengthen the total system of liberty shared by all; and (b) a less than equal liberty must be acceptable to those with the lesser liberty." (Rawls 1971: 302) Once these conditions for liberty are established and maintained, then society can consider the goals of equality and efficiency. Here also, Rawls argues that equality should have a clear priority over efficiency, and that equality should be compromised only if the least well-off benefits.

The difference principle implies that once liberty is fairly distributed, the financial well-being of the least well-off person is of primary importance to society. Clearly this view imposes a greater pressure for equality than utilitarianism, which weighs the utility of the poorest persons equally with that of others. Indeed, Rawls is among the most egalitarian of all well-known philosophers.

Robert Nozick and the ethics of the minimalist state

Both utilitarians and John Rawls can be classified as consequentialists, meaning that the justice of an outcome is more fundamental to their theories than the process by which that outcome is achieved. Many libertarian conservatives find this apparent lack of concern with the method of redistribution to be unjust. For those individuals, the ethical theory of Robert Nozick stands as a beacon. Nozick's ethical theory emphasizes the process by which society evolves from the state of nature into a civil and affluent society and how this evolution affects the status of individuals. Nozick's approach begins with a state of nature similar to John Locke's in which perfect liberty and equality exist. Two issues that arise as society evolves from this natural state are the evolution of government and of social inequality.

Mutual protection and the minimal state

In Nozick's theory government evolves as a solution to the dangers that exist in a pure state of nature. Conflict between individuals may arise in a state of nature, and without the rule of law the resolution of disagreements is likely to involve violence. If agreements are made between individuals, in the absence of law enforcement of those agreements may also involve violence. In order to reduce this threat of force individuals form organizations for mutual protection. Extended families, clans, or tribes are early forms of these organizations. These organizations offer a means of resolving disputes among members as well as protection against violence from non-members. However, if several such organizations exist conflict is not eliminated and battles are likely. Therefore, merger of these organizations is the most peaceful alternative. When a single mutual protection society has been formed within a region, it can be called a government.

In this story the most unique feature of government is its monopoly on the use of force, since all members agree to give up the use of force against other members when they join the mutual aid societies. Also, the most basic tasks of government are the enforcement of law and the protection of order. This is Nozick's view of the minimal state, one that provides a system of law and order through its monopoly on the use of force.

Just acquisition and just transfer

Other policy implications of Nozick's theory arise from his description of the process by which inequality develops, and the degree to which government should control this inequality. First, Nozick rejects the usual meaning of the term distribution in a society with a minimal government:

> There is no *central* distribution, no person or group entitled to control all the resources, jointly deciding how they are to be doled out. What each person gets, he gets from others who give to him in exchange for something, or as a gift. In a free society ... new holdings arise out of the voluntary exchanges and actions of persons.
>
> (Nozick 1974: 149-50)

Rather than worry about the degree of inequality of wealth or income, Nozick proposes that we should concern ourselves with how wealth or income is acquired: "A distribution is just if it arises from another just distribution by legitimate means" (p. 150). As this sentence suggests, the most fundamental dimension of Nozick's theory of distribution involves determining which **means** of acquiring income or wealth are ethical and which are not.

Starting from Locke's state of nature, where no individual or group owns any land or resources, wealth may be acquired in two steps. The first step is the initial acquisition of wealth or property. The second is the transfer of wealth or property from one person to another. Either of these steps may be accomplished by just or unjust means. Property may be claimed initially by individuals or groups for ownership through **just acquisition** if certain criteria are met. Locke argued that an individual can justly claim unowned property if she mixes her labor with the resources of the land (Locke 1955: 22). For example, picking an apple from a common tree allows an individual to claim ownership of the apple. However, the right to claim ownership of land and resources also has ethical limits. First, one person's labor may not be owned by another. Slavery is unjust in Nozick's theory. More generally, Nozick suggests that if the property is not spoiled, if adequate property remains for others, and if the property is used productively, the acquisition of unowned property is just.

The second method for acquisition is the transfer of income or wealth from one person to another. Transfers are considered just by Nozick if they are made through voluntary and informed exchange between the two parties. If a person offers a service which many people are freely willing to pay for, then there is no ethical limit on that person's earned income. His best-known example of this principle, which I will update a bit, involves a basketball star. Michael Jordan, formerly of the Chicago Bulls, is widely considered to be the best basketball player who ever lived. Let's assume that Mr. Jordan signed a contract that required $5 of each ticket purchased to go to him. Customers know this, and with the purchase of each ticket drop their $5 for Mr. Jordan in a separate slot. If 4 million fans each pay $5 of the ticket price to Michael, he would earn a hefty salary of $20,000,000. If firms hired him to represent their products or star in their cartoons, he would gain additional income. Since this endorsement process involves voluntary and informed exchange, it is fair within the Nozick framework.

The fairness of government redistribution can also be considered through Nozick's argument. According to Nozick, appropriating a large part of Jordan's income through the tax system in order to bring it into line with some preconceived pattern of income distribution would be quite unfair. To Nozick, the compulsory payment of taxes is a form of forced labor because it claims the fruits of one's labor without her agreement. The same logic suggests that no individual should be forced to contribute to the payment of a minimum level of income for the poor, although voluntary contributions to charity are encouraged. The claiming of money by government through the threat of force is not consistent with Nozick's principle of a just transfer.

Moral side constraints

A third concept which is often ignored in brief summaries of Nozick's work is the principle of moral side constraints. **Moral side constraints** refer to limits on what individuals, groups, or institutions may do in pursuing their ethical or other goals. These constraints need not be the same as the goals themselves. As an example, Nozick states that basic rights could be viewed as side constraints. In Nozick's theory, side constraints are crucial to understanding the difference between just and unjust acquisitions of property or transfers of income.

Side constraints differ from moral goals in potentially important ways. A constraint creates an absolute limit on certain unjust actions. For example, the goal of protecting human rights might allow the state to violate the rights of a few violent criminals in order to eliminate their ability to violate the rights of others. However, a constraint which precludes any violation of human rights would not permit the state to violate the rights of criminals. Society's means for dealing with criminals would be limited to those which did not violate their fundamental rights. On the other hand, once the basic rights constraint is met, there is no further obligation for individuals or government to pursue the issue. If an affluent society adopts a social policy which says that society should maximize its total welfare subject to the constraint that it provide basic nutrition to all individuals, the provision of food for the least well off is all that would be required. One interesting application of side constraints is the strong case Nozick makes for extending these side constraints to non-humans. Nozick makes a convincing case for the non-exploitation of animals, including vegetarianism, based on his side constraints involving basic rights (1974: 35-42).

In conclusion, moral side constraints play an important role in Nozick's theory. However, constraints may also be utilized to prevent unjust results that might be permitted under any other ethical theory. Side constraints represent a useful supplement for any theory whose goals offer inadequate moral guidance in a particular policy area.

A graphical representation of income redistribution and ethical theory

Graphical analysis of the tradeoff between income equality and efficiency can aid in our understanding of the degree to which various theories support income redistribution. This section begins by presenting a simple two-dimensional model within which income distribution can take place. The basic principles of utilitarianism, John Rawls, and Robert Nozick will then be presented in graphical terms, and the degree of income redistribution prescribed by each theory will be analyzed.

The utility possibilities frontier

Generally the first graph one sees in introductory economics is the production possibilities frontier, which displays the combinations of two goods a society can produce given limited resources and technology. The utility possibilities frontier (UPF) is very similar in appearance to the production possibilities frontier. The UPF connects all possible combinations of total utility that may be achieved by two individuals given fixed resources and technology. Let's begin with a simple model of society with several simplifying assumptions. The model assumes that there are two people, Ritchie Rich and Paul Poorly, who have identical preferences. The model also assumes that only Ritchie is productive while Paul produces nothing. We also assume that Ritchie and Paul do not care about each other, meaning that neither receives utility from the other's well-being. Given these assumptions, without a government-mandated transfer of income Ritchie will receive a utility level U_1 on the horizontal axis in Figures 2.1 and 2.2, and Paul will receive no utility and presumably starve.

The slope of a UPF curve equals the change in Paul's utility divided by the change in Ritchie's utility $(-U_P/U_R)$. Figures 2.1 and 2.2 are based on different assumptions about the productivity effects of an income transfer. Figure 2.1 assumes that the transfer of income from Ritchie to Paul does not affect anyone's behavior, including Ritchie's. Therefore, even if the government took all of Ritchie's income he would continue to produce the original amount of goods. Therefore, it would be possible to achieve a utility level for Paul of U_1 on the vertical axis, which is identical to Ritchie's original utility level, by giving all of Ritchie's income to Paul. More generally, the UPF will be symmetric on either

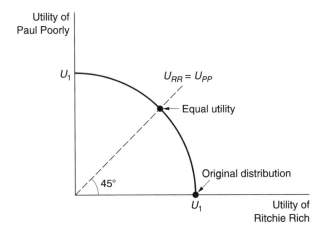

Figure 2.1 Utility possibilities frontier with neutral transfers

side of the 45-degree line representing equal utility. Transfers of income that don't affect behavior are called neutral transfers.

> **Definition: A neutral transfer** is a transfer of income which does not alter either party's behavior.

Figure 2.2 is based on the assumption that an income transfer from Ritchie to Paul will reduce Ritchie's productivity due to a reduction in his motivation and ability

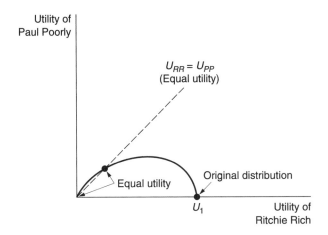

Figure 2.2 Utility possibilities frontier with non-neutral transfers

to work. Also, in Figure 2.2 the utility possibilities frontier touches the dashed line indicating equal utilities twice, once at zero utility for both, and once at a somewhat higher point. This higher point occurs if one assumes that in a situation of total equality Paul will still produce enough to provide a positive level of income for himself and for Paul, because the alternative (zero utility for both) would not be pleasant for Ritchie. A transfer that affects behavior is called a non-neutral transfer.

Definition: A non-neutral transfer alters at least one party's behavior. In this example a non-neutral transfer reduces Ritchie's productivity.

Utility frontier models with neutral and non-neutral transfers provide a two-fold test of various ethical theories as they relate to income distribution. The neutral transfer model tests whether a theory favors total equality if there is no corresponding loss of productivity. The non-neutral transfer model allows us to compare the degree of redistribution favored by various theories when redistribution causes a loss of output and income. The utilitarian approach, the Rawlsian difference principle, and two interpretations of Nozick's libertarian theory will be compared through this two-fold test.

It might be worth reviewing briefly why the utility possibilities curve bows outward in the neutral transfer case. First, the role of income in this story should be made explicit. In Figure 2.3, the solid line displays all possible distributions of income (not utility) assuming that all transfers are neutral and the total income available to the two individuals is fixed. This income possibilities curve with neutral transfers shows that one dollar more for Paul means one dollar less

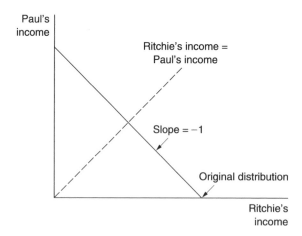

Figure 2.3 Income possibilities with neutral transfers

for Ritchie. This linear **income** possibilities curve is consistent with the bowed UPF in Figure 2.1 because of a crucial economics concept, **the law of diminishing marginal utility**. The law of diminishing marginal utility states that as more units of a good are consumed, less additional (marginal) utility will be gained from consuming another unit. In our example, at the original income distribution Paul has no income. Therefore, the first few dollars Paul receives from Ritchie will provide a great deal of added utility because of Paul's high marginal utility for the food or other goods he can buy with those dollars. On the other hand, Ritchie starts out with a great deal of money, so the utility he loses when the first few dollars are taken away will be small since the marginal utility of the last few goods he could purchase with that money will be low. Therefore, if the two men have equal tastes, transferring a dollar from Ritchie to Paul will add more to Paul's total utility than it takes away from Ritchie's. Therefore, redistributing some income from the rich to the poor is likely to add to society's utility if tastes are approximately equal.

In order to compare the ideal degree of redistribution under these different philosophical principles, we need a tool that identifies an explicit redistribution goal for each ethical theory. This principle is easily incorporated in a mathematical model called the social welfare function. Generally defined, the social welfare function defines the well-being of society as some function of the utilities of its members. However, the weight given to the well-being of different individuals varies across different ethical theories. Each will be identified in the analysis to follow.

Utilitarian redistribution

The most fundamental utilitarian principle is summarized in the phrase "the greatest good for the greatest number." This phrase means that society is best off when it maximizes the sum of the utilities of all individuals when each individual's utility is equally weighted. If U_R and U_P represent the utilities of Ritchie and Paul, respectively, then the utilitarian social welfare function will appear as follows:

$$SWF_{Utilitarian} = U_R + U_P \qquad (2.1)$$

or, equivalently, that

$$U_P = SWF_{Utilitarian} - U_R \qquad (2.2)$$

The first equation defines the utilitarian social welfare function, while the second identifies the same function in a form that can be interpreted graphically as social indifference curves. **Social indifference curves** identify all possible combinations of utilities that provide an equal level of social welfare for society. The slope for a utilitarian social indifference curve is equal to a negative one, as seen by the minus sign in the second equation.

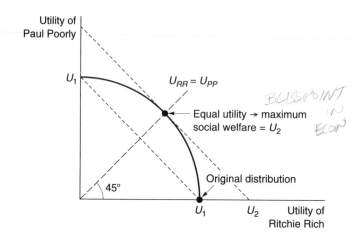

Figure 2.4 Utilitarian optimal transfer with neutral transfers

The first graphical test of our ethical theories involves the just distribution given neutral transfers. Figure 2.4 shows that if transfers are neutral and people have equal tastes, the highest level of utilitarian social welfare is achieved where utility levels and incomes are totally equal.

> **A proposed definition:** An ethical theory may be categorized as **income-egalitarian** if it favors total equality of incomes in the presence of neutral and cost-less transfers.

Under this definition, utilitarianism would be categorized as an income-egalitarian ethical theory.

A graph with non-neutral transfers such as Figure 2.5 allows us to judge the optimal amount of income redistribution when there is a tradeoff between equality and efficiency. In the case of utilitarianism, the ideal amount of redistribution would leave Ritchie with utility level U_{R2} on the horizontal axis and Paul with level U_{P2} on the vertical axis. Compared to the Rawlsian case to follow, this graphical analysis of a non-neutral transfer suggests that utilitarian theory prescribes some redistribution but leaves a relatively large degree of inequality.

Utilitarianism offers the following general rule for income redistribution in the neutral and non-neutral transfer cases.

> **The utilitarian redistribution rule:** Redistribute income as long as the marginal utility of the income gained is greater than the marginal utility of the income lost.

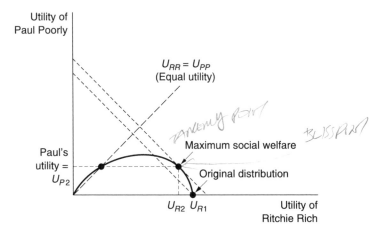

Figure 2.5 Utilitarian optimal transfer with non-neutral transfers

The greatest challenge in applying this principle is the generally impossible task of measuring and comparing the utilities of two different persons. Therefore, in practice, the utilitarian approach is not likely to provide exact guidance for redistribution policy. However, it is important to know that utilitarian principles favor some redistribution under non-neutral circumstances, and favor total equality under ideal circumstances.

Rawlsian redistribution

The essential principle for a formal Rawlsian model of redistribution is the **difference principle**. To repeat, Rawls (1971: 62) states the difference principle as follows:

> All social values … are to be distributed equally unless an unequal distribution of any, or all, of these values is to everyone's advantage.

The difference principle is also labeled the **maxi-min** principle, which states that the goal of society is to maximize the well-being of the least well-off person. In our example, if a state of total equality results in a large decrease in Ritchie's productivity, then both Ritchie and Paul may be better off if a degree of inequality is allowed to exist. However, if productivity is unaffected by redistribution, as in the case of neutral transfers, Rawls' difference principle would prescribe total income equality.

Mathematically, the difference principle implies that social welfare depends only on the well-being of the least well-off person. In terms of a formula, **the Rawlsian social welfare function** is defined as follows:

$$SWF_{Rawls} = \min[U_{Ritchie}, U_{Paul}], \tag{2.3}$$

where **min** is short for minimum, and society's goal is to maximize this function given its limited resources. In terms of numbers, if Ritchie's utility is 10 and Paul's is 5, society's social welfare equals 5. If Ritchie's utility is 1,000,000 and Paul's is 5, then society's welfare still equals 5. Only the well-being of the poorest person matters under Rawls' theory when measuring social welfare.

Graphically, this function produces social indifference curves which are L-shaped. In Figure 2.6 the dashed 45-degree line defines all points of equal utility for Ritchie and Paul. Everywhere to the right of the 45-degree line Ritchie has a higher level of utility than Paul, and therefore only Paul's utility (the lower of the two) will count in the Rawlsian social welfare function. For example, at point C in Figure 2.6 Paul has the lowest utility, so the Rawlsian social welfare function at that point equals $\min[U_{Ritchie}, U_{Paul}] = U_{Paul}$. From point C, any increase Paul receives will increase the well-being of the least well-off person and therefore society's social utility. However, from point C added income for Ritchie leaves social welfare unchanged. Another important implication of the difference principle can be seen in the level of social welfare achieved at the original income distribution (point A). According to Rawls, this point represents a social welfare of zero, because the least well-off person (Paul) has zero utility.

We can consider the redistributional implications of the Rawlsian difference principle by viewing Figure 2.7. In this graph both the neutral and non-neutral transfer UPFs are included. In the case of neutral transfers complete equality is the preferred result and welfare level 4 is the highest of any possible distribution. However, the non-neutral case does not necessarily lead to total equality. Consider points A and B on the non-neutral utility possibilities curve. Point A represents total equality, but point B provides greater utility for both Paul and Ritchie. Therefore, since the least well-off party benefits from the inequality at point B, it is the preferred point according to the difference principle.

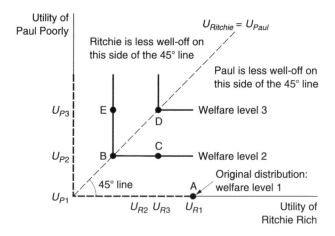

Figure 2.6 Rawlsian social indifference curves

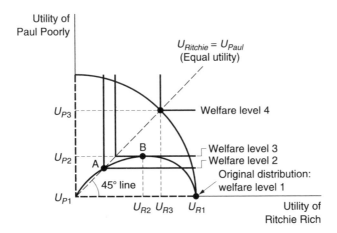

Figure 2.7 Rawlsian optimal transfers

Nozick: zero transfers versus a minimum income

As noted earlier, Nozick argues that minimal government should not require individuals to pay taxes in order to transfer income to the least well-off in society. According to a strict application of Nozick's theory, the original distribution in our model is moral if Ritchie's income was achieved by just means. On the other hand, if we allow a minimum income level for all as a basic right or moral side constraint, then society would accept as moral any distribution that provided at least that minimum income level for each person. In Figure 2.8 both neutral and

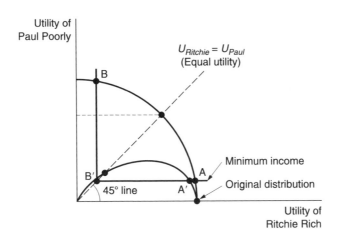

Figure 2.8 Zero Transfers and A minimum income level

non-neutral UPFs are presented, and a hypothetical minimum income level for both individuals is represented by the social indifference curve labeled "Minimum income." If neutral transfers exist, a required minimum income implies that Paul should receive at least enough income to get to point A and Ritchie must achieve at least point B. Any point between A and B meets the minimum income constraint for both people and is therefore just. Similarly, with non-neutral transfers Paul must receive income consistent with point A′ and Ritchie is guaranteed at least B′. One major challenge in this policy is to determine the minimum income level. The minimum moral requirement under a basic rights theory is that it must be at least enough to ensure survival, although affluent societies may adopt a somewhat higher standard. However, Nozick's basic principle of just distribution does not require a governmentally imposed minimum level of redistribution.

According to this graphical analysis, different ethical theories suggest very different answers to the issue of how much equality or income redistribution is consistent with a just society. The utilitarian approach prescribes a totally equal income distribution in the case of neutral transfers and equal tastes, but a relatively unequal distribution in the non-neutral case. Rawls' difference principle also prescribes total equality in the neutral transfer case, but its primary concern with the least well-off person allows for far less inequality, and far more efficiency loss, than the utilitarian approach if transfers are non-neutral. Nozick's basic theory does not require any income transfer to Paul unless it is voluntary. If the basic human right to survival is added as a moral side constraint, redistribution must be sufficient to allow Paul to survive. Since Paul's survival does not depend on the degree of lost productivity from Ritchie, the minimum amount of income Paul receives is the same in the neutral and non-neutral cases. The rather extreme graphical difference between the Rawls and Nozick models mirrors the substantial differences in their theories.

Conclusion

These few examples from ethical theory may help to illustrate the importance of ethics in formulating and administering public policy. They also serve to point out the difficulty in applying different ethical theories to specific situations. The greatest possible total happiness, the greatest possible equality, the greatest possible achievement of basic human rights, and the greatest possible adherence to a fair process are very different goals for society, and inevitably lead to conflicting policy judgments.

Your Turn 2.3: If you had to choose, would you identify yourself as most in agreement with utilitarians, Rawls, or Nozick? In groups, discuss the reasons for your preferences. If people have different choices, discuss how the group might resolve these differences through reasoning. Don't be disappointed if you cannot resolve your differences.

Because of the diversity of ethical theory, we face a challenge in applying ethics to policy decisions. One way to apply ethics to policy is to choose a particular ethical perspective which most generally satisfies your ideology or sense of justice and apply it in every possible situation to which it relates. However, if our brief tour through ethical thought results only in a new language for defending your previous beliefs or self-interest, then our tour hasn't been as productive as it should have been. Ethics is most effective when it leads to the universal application of norms which, for many, involve a degree of personal sacrifice for the social good.

However, even if your choice is primarily based on ideology, understanding more about ethics may deepen your understanding of the logic and limitations of your particular ethical and ideological preferences, and also introduce a healthy degree of open-mindedness to your policy positions. It is also necessary to understand that adopting a particular moral theory does not make one morally superior to someone with a different moral compass. The dedicated critical thinker can find logical weaknesses and fundamental questions in any theory, including one's particular favorite. Therefore, a degree of tolerance is required when discussing ethical issues with people who hold different viewpoints.

Finally, and most importantly, moral claims may be counterproductive in policy debates if they are used as an excuse for not thinking seriously about an issue or listening carefully to other viewpoints. Intolerance and ignorance of detail are often justified through moral claims, and this common misuse of ethics can lead to poor societal outcomes. Finally, the passion with which one defends a particular view shouldn't be allowed to mask weaknesses in her position or lead to an exaggerated view of her ethical standing. People who speak with great passion and certainty about what is right and wrong are at least as likely to be incorrect or unclear as those who speak cautiously. All of these cautions are useful in guiding your defense or critique of any ethical viewpoint, but should not prevent you from adopting a world view with which you are comfortable.

Rather than defining oneself in terms of a dominant ethical viewpoint, one might apply different ethical approaches in different situations through a careful weighing of the moral questions raised by a particular policy issue. For example, Rawls' difference principle seems relatively inconsistent with the moral dimension of decisions involving present and future generations,[4] extreme utilitarianism seems inconsistent with questions of basic human rights, and Nozick's theory seems disconnected from issues involving the very poor. On the other hand, each theory also has its strengths, as we have seen.

A third method of utilizing ethics in formulating policy is to adopt a set of moral standards as side constraints on policy, and then leave policy makers free to pursue other ethical, economic, or political goals. For example, one might choose policies which best combine political and economic goals subject to the constraint that basic human and legal rights not be violated. Retaining only enough ethical thought to maintain minimum moral standards seems to place ethics in a secondary position compared to political and economic factors, and some readers will prefer to adopt a view that sets the goal of justice as their highest priority.

However, those rights which are accepted as constraints would be fundamental to the design of policy in either case.

Review questions

1. Near the beginning of this chapter, four policy questions were suggested for discussion. This time, consider the same four considerations not in terms of your own opinions, but in terms of what Rawls, Nozick, and utilitarians might say about each issue. In some cases one or more of the theories may not seem to apply to the question.

    (A) Does an individual have a right to engage in self-destructive behavior, and does government have the right to prevent him or her from doing so?
    (B) Does an affluent society have the responsibility to provide an adequate minimum level of income for those who cannot support themselves? For those who choose not to support themselves?
    (C) Is it ethically necessary to provide the highest technically possible level of safety in transportation, factories, and homes, regardless of the cost to consumers, taxpayers, or workers?
    (D) Should income equality be an important goal of tax-and-spending policies? Should the rich pay a higher percentage of their income in taxes than the poor?

2. Consider the following policies regarding the distribution of grades in a typical class. Discuss the ethics of each policy alternative and the effect that each would have on one's effort in the class. In terms of ethics, is the explicit redistribution of grades different from the redistribution of income? Why or why not?

    (A) Everybody gets an A regardless of individual performance.
    (B) Everybody receives the class average regardless of individual performance.
    (C) Everyone above the class average places half of the difference between their score and the class average into a pool. The pool is distributed in such a way as to bring the neediest students to a minimum acceptable passing grade (perhaps a C-). Any extra points are wasted. How do you interpret the word "neediest"?
    (D) Those with low grades are eligible for special remedial class sessions and extra credit.
    (E) Everybody earns the grade they receive based on their performance. No redistribution takes place.

3. In the 1990s a new cancer drug called Taxol was discovered. At the time it could only be produced from the bark of an endangered species of yew tree. Discuss the ethics of destroying the last of the trees versus letting current

cancer sufferers die. Consider both the ethical standing of other living things and the ethical standing of future generations.

4. The Association of Community Organizations for Reform Now (or ACORN), spearheads a movement to adopt "living wage" ordinances in U.S. cities. The basic goal of this movement is to establish minimum wages for government workers and contractors, or sometimes the entire working population of an area, at a level sufficient for one full-time worker to raise a family of four above the poverty line or some similar standard. Visit their website (http://www.livingwagecampaign.org/) for definitions, measurement issues, and supporting studies. Also, review a Cato Institute study by Carl Horowitz (http://www.cato.org/pubs/pas/pa493.pdf) for a critique of the living wage, and then answer the following questions:

   (A) Discuss the wisdom of a poverty-proof minimum wage from the point of view of our main ethical theories.
   (B) From an ethical point of view does it matter whether the policy covers the entire low-wage population or only the employees of government or government contractors? Why might an organization propose covering only government-related employment? Who benefits from this approach in addition to the workers themselves?
   (C) What are some possible alternative assumptions for setting a living wage level? (See the living wage site.) Does the poverty level or cost-of-living basis for this policy seem more convincing from an ethical point of view?
   (D) According to economic theory, a price floor such as a minimum wage above equilibrium creates an excess supply or surplus. As an employer, how would you decide who to hire if faced with a large excess number of applicants (experience, race or gender, dress, speech, etc.)? Check Horowitz's evidence regarding the characteristics of persons who experience the least job loss from a higher minimum wage. Are those who are harmed least the same groups you would hire first?
   (E) Is the possibility of job loss sufficient reason to oppose this policy from an ethical point of view?

5. Tens of thousands of U.S. residents die in automobile accidents every year. Should automobiles be banned? Why or why not? Are there ethical as well as efficiency reasons for allowing the continued use of the automobile? Consider this issue in light of the three schools of thought presented in this chapter.

Part II

Economics for policy analysts

Starting at a very basic level, this section introduces microeconomic tools for analyzing the efficiency of markets and the behavior of economically rational individuals. Chapter 3 begins with a basic overview of the competitive market. It then introduces the components and meaning of the net benefits of market exchange to consumers and producers. The model of the utility maximizing consumer is then introduced and related to a set of policy examples. Chapter 4 introduces various concepts of market efficiency, including Pareto optimality, and then reviews the efficiency losses arising from a series of market imperfections using a single market model. Chapter 5 extends the analysis of market efficiency by considering efficiency effects of government in both competitive and imperfectly competitive markets. The primary conclusion of this chapter is that while government creates efficiency losses in competitive markets, market imperfections create a window of opportunity for government policy to improve efficiency. This conclusion establishes the economic basis for analyzing public policy in the following chapters.

3 A review of markets and rational behavior

... while the law [of competition] may be sometimes hard for the individual, it is best for the race, because it ensures the survival of the fittest in every department.[1]

(Andrew Carnegie)

Markets change, tastes change, so the companies and the individuals who choose to compete in those markets must change.[2]

(Attributed to An Wang, founder of Wang Laboratories, a defunct computer company)

A commodity appears at first sight an extremely obvious, trivial thing. But its analysis brings out that it is a very strange thing, abounding in metaphysical subtleties and theological niceties.[3]

(Karl Marx)

The analysis of markets and rational individual behavior dominates the typical introductory microeconomics course. For those who have a good recollection of introductory economics, early sections of this chapter will probably be unnecessary. For those who welcome a review of the subject, the entire chapter may be valuable. This chapter reviews two building blocks for the upcoming analysis of market inefficiency and public policy, the competitive market and the utility-maximizing individual.

What is "perfect" competition?

In the real world of business many decisions are required in order to compete effectively. These decisions include choosing the price, quality, and quantity of one's product as well as the method of production, the location of one's production facility, and many others. Like most abstract models in the social sciences, mainstream economics starts its analysis of competition by assuming away many important aspects of the real world in order to present an explicit and easy-to-understand overview of the essential components of competition. These simplifying assumptions are called the classical assumptions of a perfectly competitive market.

Classical assumptions for perfect competition:

1 **Many buyers and sellers:** This assumption implies that no single producer or consumer will be a large enough part of the market to influence prices through their individual actions. One case which violates this assumption is a monopoly, or a single seller of a product. Oligopoly, or a market with a few competing sellers, is another exception.

2 **Perfect information:** This means that every buyer and seller is aware of the price and quality of the products offered for sale and can make fully informed decisions about what to buy or sell.

3 **Homogeneous product:** This means that the output of each firm in the market is identical. Examples include shares of General Motors stock offered for sale by various stockholders, and raw agricultural or mineral products. Any product which has a brand name or unique qualities violates this assumption to some degree. Otherwise competitive markets with product differences or brand names are referred to as **monopolistically competitive** markets.

4 **Freedom of entry and exit, or perfect mobility:** According to this assumption individual buyers or sellers can enter or leave a market without restriction or significant transactions costs. For example, firms will tend to enter a market when demand and profits are unusually high, workers apply for jobs when and where wages are high, shoppers come to stores for sales, etc. For this assumption to hold, no legal or technical barriers to entry or exit may exist.

5 **No collusion:** Collusion means group decision making. Collusion among sellers may allow them to fix their prices above the competitive price for that market. This is particularly likely in oligopolistic markets or when government permits collusion. Examples of collusion include cartels such as the Organization of Petroleum Exporting Countries (OPEC), the business trusts of the nineteenth century, and labor unions.

If the competitive assumptions are approximately true for a given market, both buyers and sellers will be **price takers**, meaning that no buyer or seller will have the power to influence the market price of the product. For example, if General Motors stock is currently trading at $29 per share and I offer to sell some shares for $35, no informed buyer will purchase my shares since there are many shares available, everybody in the market knows the current price, and all shares are identical.

Your Turn 3.1: Can you think of any other goods besides some stocks and bonds for which markets are likely to be perfectly competitive? Which of the competitive conditions are violated in the labor market, and which are not?

In reality, effective competition does not require that all of these conditions be fully met, but it does require at a minimum that buyers and sellers have multiple alternatives and sufficient information to make wise decisions. Also, in order for competition to work well in the long run neither economic nor legal barriers can prevent the movement of buyers and sellers into and out of the market.

Demand

The model of the competitive market depends on the interaction of the behavior of buyers (demand) and the behavior of sellers (supply). Each side of the market will be discussed in turn. **Demand** is a concept that summarizes the decisions of buyers in a market. In addition to the price of a product, the quantity demanded is also affected by one's income, the prices of related goods, consumer tastes, the number of consumers in the market, and other factors. This list of factors affecting quantity demanded is summarized in a **demand function**, which in general form is merely a list of variables in the demand relationship. Equation (3.1) provides a general demand function for cola:

$$Q_{Dcola} = f (P_{cola}, \text{ income, other prices, tastes, the number of consumers}) \quad (3.1)$$

A demand function can be represented on a two-dimensional graph by graphing one relationship, usually the relationship between quantity and price, while holding all other variables constant. This graphical relation between price and quantity demanded, holding other factors fixed, is called the **demand curve**. It is generally true that the lower the price the more of a good people will buy. Therefore, the price of a good has an inverse or negative relationship to the quantity demanded.

Other demand concepts

The relationships between the quantity demanded and other components of the demand function involve some additional concepts. The prices of other goods may affect the demand curve for Coke if the other goods are **substitutes** for or **complements** to Coke. For example, Pepsi and Coke are similar products serving the same basic functions (thirst quenching, caffeine). Therefore, a lower price for Pepsi will tend to lead some people to buy more Pepsi and less Coke. These goods are called **substitutes**. On the other hand, pizza and Coke (or pizza and beer) are goods which tend to be consumed together. Cheaper pizza will lead consumers to buy more pizza and also more Coke. Goods such as pizza and Coke are referred to as **complements**.

Another set of concepts describe the relation between the demand curve and the consumer's level of income. Goods that have a positive relationship between income and demand are called **normal goods**. Goods for which demand falls when income rises are called **inferior goods**. Inferior goods may include generic or off-brand products at the grocery store, older used cars, or less savory examples such as discarded food from restaurants or grocery stores. As people's incomes grow, they are less likely to consume inferior goods. Because total consumer spending grows with income, we know that the average good is normal.

Shifts in the demand curve

If there are changes in any of the demand factors besides price, the demand curve will shift either leftward or rightward. Similarly, a change in price (or a shift in supply) will *not* lead to a shift in the demand curve. The rule for how the change in a variable affects demand can be summarized in the following rule:

> **If you see the variable on the axis (i.e. price) its relationship to quantity is seen in the slope. If you don't see the variable on an axis its effect is seen as a shift in the curve.**

Your Turn 3.2: In Figure 3.1, the initial demand curve for cola is D_1. Label the location of the demand curve after each of the following events. Is each event below consistent with a new demand at D_1, D_2, or D_3?
(A) Researchers find that Coke cures warts. _____
(B) Papa Joe's pizza goes on sale. _____
(C) The population of caffeine addicts declines. _____
(D) Pepsi goes on sale. _____
(E) Coke goes on sale. _____

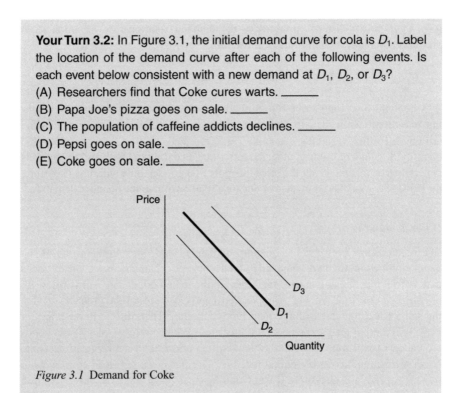

Figure 3.1 Demand for Coke

A mathematical example may help to explain why a change in one of the invisible-demand variables such as income shifts the demand curve. Assume that Spuds' daily demand for Coke is determined by the price of Coke, the price of Pepsi, and income, as in equation (3.2):

$$Q_{coke} = 2 + 0.05 \; Income + 0.5 P_{pepsi} - 1 P_{coke} \tag{3.2}$$

If his daily spendable income is $40 and the price of Pepsi is $1, substituting the $40 for income produces

$$Q_{coke} = 2 + 0.05(40) + 0.5(1) - 1P_{coke} \text{ or } Q_{coke} = 2 + 2 + \frac{1}{2} - 1P_{coke} \quad (3.3)$$
$$\text{or } Q_{coke} = 4.5 - 1P_{coke}$$

Solving this equation for price gives us the usual graphical form of the demand curve.

$$P_{coke} = 4.5 - Q_{coke}. \text{ This is } D_1 \text{ in Figure 3.2.} \quad (3.4)$$

Now, if his daily income falls to $20, the demand function in equation (3.2) becomes:

$$Q_{coke} = 2 + 0.05(20) + 0.5(1) - 1P_{coke}, \text{ or } P_{coke} = 3.5 - Q_{coke} \quad (3.5)$$

This is D_2 in Figure 3.2. Notice by comparing equations (3.2) and (3.5) that the slope of the demand curves are the same but the endpoint is lower after income falls. Also, the positive relationship between the demand for Coke and income means that Coke is a normal good, while the positive relationship between the price of Pepsi and the quantity demanded of Coke means that the goods are substitutes.

Your Turn 3.3: If income rises to $60 per day, find the new demand curve equation and compare it to the original curve in Figure 3.2.

Supply

Supply is a concept that summarizes the decisions of producers in a market. The rational decision to produce a product involves weighing the benefits and costs of producing each additional unit of a good and choosing the quantity for which the marginal benefit or revenue equals the marginal cost. As with demand, the

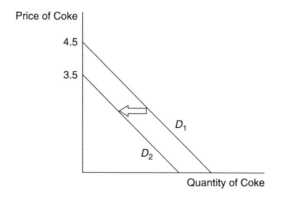

Figure 3.2 Demand shift

quantity of goods supplied to the market depends on many different factors, which can be summarized in a supply function. A simple supply function will include one or more groups of input prices, technology, and the product's price. As with consumers, the number of producers in a market also affects supply. Equation 3.6 presents a simple supply function:

$$Q_{supplied} = f(\text{price, labor cost, other input costs, technology, the number} \quad (3.6)$$
$$\text{of firms})$$

The supply curve is a graph of the relation between the price of the product and the quantity produced holding all other factors fixed. It is generally true that a rise in the price will lead to higher levels of production. Therefore, the price of a good has a positive or direct relationship to the quantity supplied. If any other factor affecting supply changes, this change will appear as a leftward or rightward shift in the supply. Note that a rightward shift is correctly labeled as an increase in supply due to the higher quantity offered at each price, even though the curve is moving downward vertically.

Your Turn 3.4: Possible supply shifts. See Figure 3.3. Starting from S_1, will each event below lead to a new curve like S_2, S_3, or S_1?
(A) Bean beetles decimate the cola crop. ____
(B) Cola workers demand higher wages. ____
(C) Sugar prices tumble. ____
(D) New technology allows firms to transport beans directly to the factory ("Beam them up, Scotty"). ____
(E) The demand for cola rises. ____

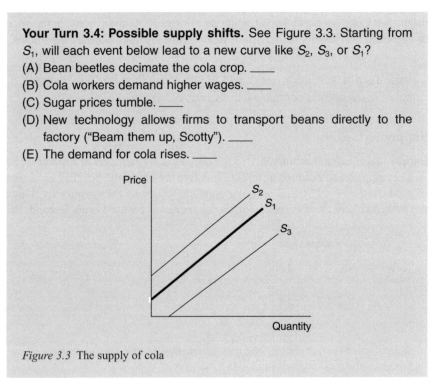

Figure 3.3 The supply of cola

Equilibrium

Equilibrium exists in a market when the quantity supplied equals the quantity demanded at a single price, or where the supply and demand curves cross.

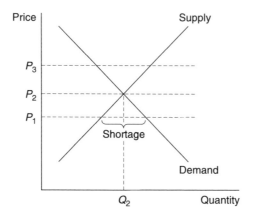

Figure 3.4 The cola market

Markets will tend to move toward an equilibrium price and quantity from any other point. For instance, if the price is below equilibrium (as with P_1 in Figure 3.4), more cola is demanded than is being produced. Since some who are willing to buy Coke at price P_1 cannot do so because of the shortage, they may offer to pay a higher price. Similarly, dealers may notice the lines of people waiting for Coke or the low inventory of Coke on their shelves, and raise the price on their own. Either way, the rising price will discourage some consumers, and also lead to a larger quantity of Coke supplied, until the shortage disappears at price P_2 and quantity Q_2.

Equilibrium using equations

As Figure 3.4 shows, equilibrium involves a single price at which the quantity demanded equals the quantity supplied. In algebraic form, an equilibrium will involve three simple equations: a demand equation, a supply equation, and an equilibrium equation, which simply states that $P_s = P_d$ or $Q_s = Q_d$, since at equilibrium both price and quantity are the same. Here are two examples.

Your Turn 3.5: Find the equilibrium price and quantity for the following sets of equations:

Example A: Cola

Demand: $P_d = 100 - \frac{1}{2}Q_d$

Supply: $P_s = 20 + \frac{1}{2}Q_s$

Equilibrium: $P_d = P_s$

Example B: Cola

$Q_d = 200 - 2P_d$

$Q_s = -40 + 2P_s$

$Q_d = Q_s$

The price elasticity of demand

Another concept from introductory microeconomics that has important implications for some public policies is elasticity, particularly the price elasticity of demand. To review briefly, the elasticity of demand provides a numerical value of the responsiveness of the quantity demanded to a change in the price. In general terms, the price elasticity of demand is defined as the percentage change in quantity divided by the percentage change in price (%ΔQ/%ΔP). More specifically, demand elasticity at the introductory level is usually defined by the mid-point formula, where the percentage changes in price and quantity are measured using the average of the old and new prices and quantities. If one moves from point A to point B on the demand curve, the elasticity of demand along that range is represented by the mid-point formula, which is presented below:

$$Elasticity = \frac{\dfrac{\Delta Q}{(Q_a + Q_b)} \Big/ 2}{\dfrac{\Delta P}{(P_a + P_b)} \Big/ 2} = \Delta Q \,/\, average\ Q \div \Delta P \,/\, average\ P \tag{3.7}$$

Because price and quantity move in opposite directions along a downward-sloping demand curve, price elasticity will always be negative. Because it is more difficult to refer to negative numbers verbally, economists and policy analysts generally discuss price elasticity in terms of its absolute value.

In reviewing the meaning of this elasticity measure, let's assume that the price of oil is rising. If the absolute value of elasticity is greater than one, the demand for oil is referred to as **elastic**. This means that the proportional decrease in quantity purchased is larger than the proportional rise in price. On the other hand, if the percentage decrease in the quantity demanded for oil is less than the percentage rise in price, the absolute value of elasticity will be less than one, and demand will be referred to as **inelastic**. It is also possible, though far less common, that the percentage decrease in quantity (measured by the mid-point formula) will equal one, meaning that the percentage decrease in quantity will equal the percentage increase in price. This unusual result is labeled **unit elastic**.

Your Turn 3.6: Assume that the government of Amnesia recently increased the minimum wage from $4.75 to $5.25. The Amnesian government knows that an economist predicted that employment of Amnesian teens would drop from 101 to 99 as a result of the higher wage, but they don't remember why this is important.

(A) Using the mid-point formula, find the price elasticity of demand for Amnesian teens. Is demand elastic, inelastic, or unit elastic over this price range?

(B) Another economist claims that teen employment would fall from 120 to 80 as a result of the same wage increase. Find her predicted elasticity of demand. Is this elasticity elastic, inelastic, or unit elastic?

The primary implication of price elasticity is its ability to directly predict the effect of a change in price on total spending in a market. Total spending equals price times quantity. If demand is elastic, a price increase leads to a proportionally larger decrease in quantity, and total spending falls. If demand is inelastic, a price increase causes customers to reduce their quantity demanded by a smaller proportion and total spending will rise.

Your Turn 3.7: The total earnings of minimum wage teenage labor (per hour) in Amnesia will equal the wage times the number of employees. Find the total earnings for these teens before and after the wage increase for both sets of predictions. Are the results consistent with the elasticity of demand for Amnesian teens?

The net benefits of consumption

One of the most profound contributions of early classical economists such as Adam Smith is the principle of **mutually beneficial trade**, which in simple terms states that free and informed trade in a market benefits both consumers and producers. Defining these net benefits for consumers and producers involves two crucial concepts in policy analysis: consumer and producer surplus. Each will be explained carefully below.

In theory the consumer will weigh the benefits and costs of each unit purchased and buy only those units for which the marginal benefits are greater than or equal to the marginal costs. The benefits of consumption are not directly measured in terms of money, and for good reason. The pleasure we receive from consumption is generally experienced in terms of an emotional or perceptual response, such as increased happiness or decreased discomfort. Economists summarize these non-monetary benefits in the rather dull word, **utility**, which was discussed at some length in Chapter 2.

Definitions:
- **Marginal utility** is the utility gained by consuming one more unit of the product.
- **Total utility** is the satisfaction gained from all units consumed. It also equals the sum of the marginal utilities of all units consumed.

For most consumers and most products, the marginal utility of the second unit is less than that of the first unit, the marginal utility of the third is less than that of the second, and so on. This behavioral principle is called **the law of diminishing marginal utility**. For example, a hiker emerging from a desert trail may be in extreme discomfort due to thirst. His first glass of water will provide a high level of marginal utility because it eliminates the most urgent discomfort caused by his thirst. A second glass probably will also offer considerable marginal utility, but less than the first. This pattern of positive but decreasing marginal utility will continue for additional glasses of water, until eventually the marginal utility reaches zero and then becomes negative.

As noted in Chapter 2, under most circumstances utility cannot be directly measured. However, in order to assess the benefits of public policy we must have some way of measuring these benefits. Fortunately, the demand curve offers a simple way of approximating the marginal utility of consumption in dollar terms. The height of the demand curve at a given quantity represents the maximum consumers are willing to pay for that particular unit of the good. In Figure 3.5 we assume that Carrie has a relatively high marginal utility for coffee. Therefore, she is willing to pay a maximum of $8 for her first mug of the day. As a rational consumer she will pay as little as possible for coffee, but if she was forced to, she would buy the first mug for any amount up to $8.

Since $8 is the **maximum** amount she would be willing to pay, the utility of the first mug of coffee is about equal to the utility she could get by spending the $8 on her next best alternative choice. This thought experiment suggests that the maximum a person is willing to pay for a particular unit of a good provides a useful way of estimating the benefits of consuming that unit in terms of dollars.

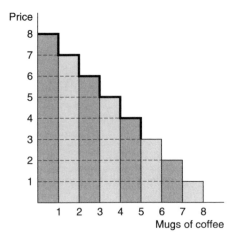

Figure 3.5 Carrie's demand for coffee

> **Definitions:**
> - The **marginal value** of consumption is the maximum a person is willing to pay for a particular unit of a good.
> - The **total value** of consumption is the sum of the marginal values for all units actually consumed.

Figure 3.5 represents Carrie's demand for coffee. If we assume that Carrie can buy only whole mugs, we can draw her demand as a series of steps ending at each whole number. This type of graph is called a **step function**, for obvious reasons.

Your Turn 3.8: See Figure 3.5. If Carrie consumes five mugs of coffee, what is the marginal value of the last mug? ____ What is the total value of all five mugs combined? ____

If the demand curve is represented by a straight line rather than a step function, the marginal value and total value concepts are the same, but the method one uses to find numerical values for these concepts changes. In Figure 3.6 consumers are buying 10 mugs of coffee at a price of $4 each. The height of the demand curve determines the marginal value, as before. With a linear demand curve, however, total value will equal the area under the demand curve between the vertical axis and the quantity bought in the market. For those with a calculus background, a definite integral will suffice. For others, dividing the total value into two areas, the rectangle below the price and the triangle above the price, allows one to find the total value by calculating the areas of the rectangle and triangle (areas A and B in Figure 3.6) and adding them.

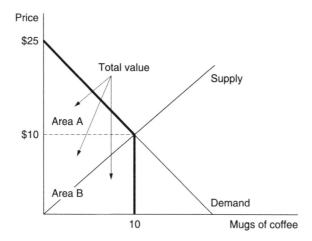

Figure 3.6 Total value

Your Turn 3.9: Find the total value for coffee purchased given the demand curve in Figure 3.6.

The marginal and total value concepts are sufficient to provide a measurable dollar-based estimate of the satisfaction one receives from consuming a good such as coffee.

The cost and net benefits of consumption

As noted in the elasticity section, a consumer's total spending on a good equals the price of the good times the number of units purchased. Total spending appears in a market graph as a rectangle bounded by the equilibrium price and quantity.

Your Turn 3.10: Total spending in Figure 3.6 equals _____.

If we define total value as our measure of the benefits of consumption and total spending as the cost of consumption, then the net benefits will equal the total benefits minus the total cost, or total value minus total spending.

> **Definition:** The net benefit of consumption, or the difference between total value and total spending, is called **consumer surplus.**

In Figure 3.7, Carrie's demand for coffee is reconsidered using this new concept. For example, $8 is Carrie's marginal value for the first mug of coffee.

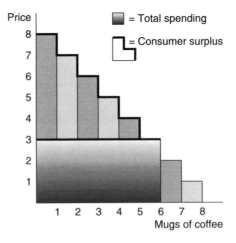

Figure 3.7 Carrie's consumer surplus for coffee

If the price of coffee is $3 per mug, Carrie receives a net benefit or consumer surplus of $5 for the first mug. The consumer surplus for each additional unit can be calculated in the same way. The total consumer surplus is then found by adding the consumer surpluses of each unit actually purchased. As long as the price is less than or equal to the maximum willingness to pay, Carrie will buy that mug. In Carrie's case, she will buy six mugs, rather than five.

Your Turn 3.11: Carrie's consumer surplus. See Figure 3.7. Find the number of mugs Carrie will purchase at a price of $3, and then find her total spending, consumer surplus, and total value in dollars.

If demand curves are linear, the consumer surplus equals the area of the triangle above the price but below the demand curve (area A) in Figure 3.6, while the rectangle below the price (area B) equals total spending for that good.

Your Turn 3.12: Calculate the consumer surplus, total spending, and total value for Figure 3.6.

The primary lesson of this analysis is that if rational consumers are able to make free and informed decisions, they will only buy those units which provide a positive or zero marginal consumer surplus. By doing this they will maximize their total consumer surplus.

Your Turn 3.13: Combining the equilibrium and consumer surplus concepts is an important starting point for considering the efficiency of markets and the effects of policy, analysis that begins in the next chapter. Assume that the following demand and supply equations define a market for public transportation. Assume Q measures thousands of bus rides.
   Demand: *Price* $= 12 - 2Q$ **Supply:** *Price* $= 3 + Q$
(A) Find the equilibrium price and quantity, and sketch the demand and supply curves including endpoints and equilibrium values.
(B) Find the consumer surplus, total spending, and total value to the consumer of this market.
(C) Assume the government passes a $3 per ride subsidy which shifts the supply curve down to *Price* $= 0 + Q$. Find the new equilibrium price and quantity, and the new consumer surplus. How much better off are consumers with the subsidy? (Hint: find the difference between the new and old consumer surplus values.)

The net benefits of production

In a competitive market model, producers are also assumed to be rational, informed, and powerless with regard to the price they charge for their product. Like the consumer, they may produce and sell as much or as little as they wish given the market prices for the product, the cost of the inputs they buy, and the limits of their technology. Like the consumer, the seller wishes to maximize her well-being, and will produce and sell any unit of a good which offers marginal benefits greater than or equal to its marginal costs. Because the basic model of the rational producer bears many similarities to that of the consumer, we can explain the basic net gains to producers relatively briefly. We will assume that the only measurable gross benefit to producers is the revenue they make through sales of their product. Sellers' total revenue is equal to the total spending of consumers which equals the price per unit (P) times the number of units sold (Q), and appears as a rectangle on a supply–demand graph.

In order to consider suppliers' costs and net benefits, we must reconsider the meaning of the supply curve by asking the following question: **What is the minimum price at which the firm is willing to produce and sell a given unit?** The height of the supply curve for any unit defines the minimum price at which that unit would be produced and sold. The height of the competitive firm's supply curve at a particular quantity also equals the marginal cost of producing that unit. Therefore, the supply curve tells us that the minimum price at which a particular unit will be produced must be high enough to equal the marginal opportunity cost of producing that unit.

If the price is greater than the marginal cost of producing a given unit, then producing that unit will provide a net benefit to the producer. The net benefits to the suppliers of goods in a market are known as **producer surplus**.

Definitions:
- **Marginal producer surplus** is the difference between the market price and the height of the supply curve for a given unit of a good.
- **Total producer surplus** is the sum of the marginal producer surplus for all units sold.

For example, the first unit in Figure 3.8 costs 50 cents to produce but brings in $3 in revenue. Therefore the producer will receive a marginal producer surplus of $2.50 for that unit. Similarly, the third unit costs $1.50 to produce and has a marginal producer surplus of $1.50.

Your Turn 3.14: Calculate the total spending, opportunity cost, and producer surplus for Figure 3.8. Why won't firms produce the seventh unit?

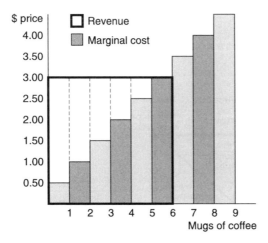

Figure 3.8 Costs and benefits of production

Given a linear supply curve, producer surplus is represented as the area above the supply curve and below the market price, while opportunity cost is the area below the supply curve up to the quantity produced. Total revenue is the sum of producer surplus and opportunity cost. All general definitions involved (total revenue, marginal opportunity cost, and producer surplus) remain the same.

Your Turn 3.15: Calculate the producer surplus and opportunity cost for Figure 3.9.

The components of producer surplus: economic profit and economic rent

Producer surplus is composed of two related components: economic profit and economic rent. They cannot be distinguished in a market graph such as Figure 3.10, but they are significantly different for the economist. Let's compare their definitions and then consider their meaning in a bit more detail.

Definitions:
- **Economic rent:** Total revenue minus opportunity cost for owners of inputs such as land or resources.
- **Economic profit:** Total revenue minus the opportunity cost of production for owners of capital goods such as factories, stores, or machines.

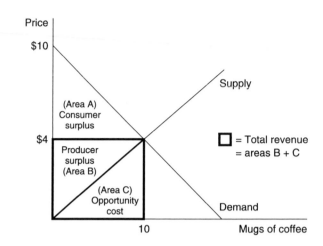

Figure 3.9 Producer surplus, opportunity cost, and revenue

Economic profit is usually less than a firm's net income (or accounting profit). This difference arises because the owner's opportunity cost includes more than her spending on labor, materials, and other inputs. Opportunity cost is defined as the cost of foregone alternatives, or the value one could have received from choosing the next best action.

For the owner of a store, opportunity cost includes **two components**. The first component is the **total spending on inputs** used in the production process. These inputs include labor, building space (factory, store, office, etc.), energy, raw materials, machinery, and others. The second component of opportunity cost is the total market value of the inputs an owner contributes to the business. The owner's contributions of time and money to the business are called **implicit costs**. For example, if an owner works 50 hours per week in the business he's giving up the chance to work 50 hours for a wage. If his labor is worth $10 per hour, his **implicit wage** would equal $10 per hour, or $500 per week, or $26,000 ($500 × 52) per year. Similarly, if an owner invests $50,000 of her own money into the business, she gives up the chance to earn interest by saving that money. For example, if the interest rate is 6 percent, she could be earning 0.06 × $50,000, or $3,000 per year, in interest. This lost interest is called **implicit interest**. While there are other components of implicit cost, the essential concept is consistent with these two examples. Now we can review the difference between economic profit and accounting profit in more detail.

Economic profit equals total revenue minus opportunity cost, or total revenue minus spending on inputs minus implicit costs.

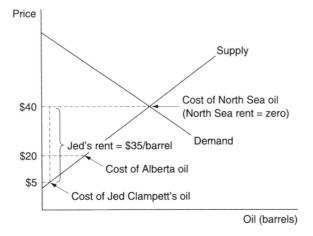

Figure 3.10 Economic rent

If **economic** profits are zero, the owner is doing just as well as he could if he allocated his time and money to their best alternative use, and there is no financial reason for firms to either enter or leave this market. On the other hand, if economic profits are positive, firms are earning higher than average profits and new firms will tend to enter the industry in the long run. As firms enter the short-run supply will shift outward, decreasing the market price and eventually reducing economic profits to zero. The concept of long-run equilibrium arises at this point.

Concept: Long-run equilibrium. A market is in long-run equilibrium if (1) supply equals demand and (2) economic profits are zero. If both conditions exist, there is no incentive for firms to enter or exit the market.

If economic profits equal zero, as in a long-run competitive equilibrium, all of the producer surplus must be made up of economic rent.

As the previous sentence makes clear, economic rent is often the more important than economic profit for the policy analyst. Let's consider the conditions that lead to economic rent before discussing the differences between economic rent and economic profit. The owners of a particular resource will earn economic rent when that resource is more productive, cheaper to extract, or in a more accessible location.

Consider the example of crude oil in Figure 3.10. While there are differences in the quality of crude oil, the primary difference between oil extracted from different places is the cost of drilling, pumping, and transporting the oil. Many of you are probably familiar with either the television or film versions of the Beverly Hillbillies. As the famous theme song by Lester Flatt and Earl Scruggs goes, "Then one day he was shootin' at some food, when up through the ground come a-bubblin' crude." This strikes most people as a very inexpensive way of discovering oil. Figure 3.10 assumes that Jed's oil can be pumped and shipped for an opportunity cost of $5 per barrel. Therefore $5 is the minimum price needed to keep Jed in the oil business.

However, oil discovered by gunshot is far less than what is needed to meet demand. People must actually test and drill for oil. This is more expensive, but at a high enough market price the resulting revenue will still more than cover the costs. As a second example, Alberta oil is deeper in the ground, and therefore more costly to extract. It is also farther from major refineries and therefore more expensive to ship. If the price is high enough, however, producing oil in Alberta is still rational. Finally, if demand rises still higher, seemingly impossible locations may be explored and exploited. During the oil crises of the 1970s, prices rose high enough to justify exploring and drilling in very expensive locations such as northern Alaska and the North Sea. In Figure 3.10, North Sea oil is assumed to cost $40 per barrel to produce, which in the example just happens to equal the market price of crude in the graph. At a price of $40 per barrel, oil is just valuable enough to justify the extraordinary cost of drilling in the North Sea. North Sea producers will be making a normal return in this situation, but no economic rent.

But what about Jed? If the market price is $40 per barrel, the difference between the price and opportunity cost of Jed's oil is $40 − $5, or $35 for each barrel. This $35 is Jed's economic rent. Another line from the song goes, "The first thing you know ol' Jed's a millionaire." The source of his wealth is economic rent.

To conclude this section on producers' net benefits, recall that for a particular unit of output the marginal producer surplus equals the difference between the price and the marginal opportunity cost of that unit. Total producer surplus equals the sum of the marginal producer surplus for all units sold in the market, or the area of the triangle formed by the price of the product and the supply curve. Finally, the two sources of producer surplus are economic profit, which will tend toward zero in a competitive market, and economic rent, which will persist as long as production depends on resources of differing cost or productivity.

The net benefits of markets

As Figure 3.11 shows, the total net gains from a private competitive market equal the sum of the consumer and producer surplus. The total net gains from trade also equal the total value of consumption minus the opportunity cost of production. In this figure consumer surplus equals $\frac{1}{2} \cdot 10 \cdot (10-4)$, or $30, and producer surplus equals $\frac{1}{2} \cdot 10 \cdot 4$, or $20. Total net gains from trade therefore equal $50. In the next chapter these basic concepts will be applied to situations where markets are not perfectly

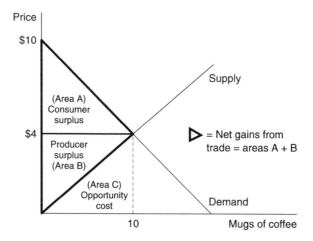

Figure 3.11 Net gains from trade

competitive, and in Chapter 5 they will be applied to various forms of government policy.

Rational consumer choice and the role of incentives

While the market model provides a basis for analyzing the efficiency effects of market imperfections and public policy, the microeconomic model of the rational consumer plays a useful role in analyzing the effects of policy on individual behavior and well-being. The model of consumer choice includes a utility function to measure the benefits of consumption and a budget line to measure the effects of prices and income on one's choices.

The budget line

The more active part of the consumer model in most graphical problems is the budget line. For this simple concept we assume two goods (X and Y until further notice), prices given by the market (P_X and P_Y, respectively), and a fixed amount of spendable income (I). The budget equation is as follows:

$$I = P_X \cdot X + P_Y \cdot Y = spending\ on\ X\ plus\ spending\ on\ Y \qquad (3.8)$$

Solving this equation for the quantity Y gives us the typical endpoint-slope equation

$$Y = \frac{I}{Py} - \frac{Px}{Py} \cdot X \qquad (3.9)$$

for a straight line. The *Y* endpoint represents the amount of the good *Y* that a person can afford if he buys no *X*. For example, if a person has $20 and each unit of *Y* (yogurt) costs $2, then she can afford at most 10 yogurts.

Formulas :

$$Y \ endpoint = \frac{Income}{Py} \qquad Slope \ of \ budget \ line = \frac{\Delta X}{\Delta Y} = -\frac{Px}{Py} \qquad (3.10)$$

The meaning of the budget line's slope is a bit less obvious. If the price of *X* is $1 and the price of *Y* is $3, then a person who gives up one unit of *Y*, thereby saving $3, can buy three more units of *X*. This tradeoff is determined by the price ratio $-P_X/P_Y$, or $-\frac{1}{3}$. Similarly if P_X is 3 and P_Y is 1, the person has to give up three units of *Y* in order to afford one more unit of *X*. In this case the slope of the budget line will equal $-\frac{3}{1}$ or -3.

> **Your Turn 3.16:** Assume that you have $20, that a bottled water machine charges $1.25 per bottle, and that a soda machine charges $0.50 per can. Find the endpoints and the slope for your budget line. If you buy 10 sodas, how many waters can you afford?

The utility function and indifference curves

The graphical analysis of consumer choice relies on the utility function to identify the benefits of consumption. A utility function depends on three assumptions regarding the preferences of the consumer:

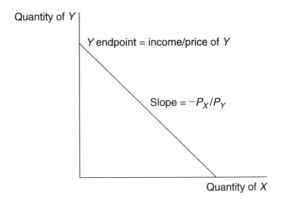

Figure 3.12 Budget line

Assumption 1: Preferences are complete. For any two combinations (1 and 2) of goods X and Y a person will know whether she prefers combination 1, prefers combination 2, or is indifferent between the two. In practice this means that every point on a graph will correspond to some level of utility and a corresponding indifference curve.

Assumption 2: Preferences are transitive. If a person prefers combination 1 to combination 2, and combination 2 to combination 3, then the person must prefer combination 1 to combination 3. For our graphs this means that indifference curves, which represent different levels of total utility, cannot cross.

Assumption 3: *Usually*, **marginal utility is positive,** meaning that a person prefers more to less of a good. Exceptions to this rule will be noted later.

With these assumptions in place, a utility function relates a person's total utility to the quantities of the two goods X and Y, as in the following general equation:

$$\text{Utility} = f(X,Y) \tag{3.11}$$

This utility function has three dimensions: the level of total utility, the quantity of good X, and the quantity of good Y. This function is displayed in Figure 3.13. Since the level of utility is generally unobservable, and because a three-dimensional graph is very difficult for your professor or my publisher to work with, we can remove the utility dimension from the graph and display the utility function as a series of curves on a plane defined by the quantities of X and Y. Each of these curves, labeled U_1, U_2, and U_3, connect all combinations of X and Y with equal total utilities. All points on U_3 are preferred to any point on U_2 because U_3 provides a greater level of total utility. These curves are referred to as **indifference curves** because each point on a given indifference curve offers equal total utility.

The slope of the indifference curve has two basic definitions which can be useful in interpreting its meaning. The most basic definition of the slope is the simple rise over run formula $\Delta Y/\Delta X$, holding total utility constant. The second relates the slope to the marginal utilities of the two goods.

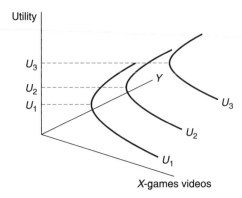

Figure 3.13 Utility function

Concept:
Indifference curve slope = $\Delta Y/\Delta X$, holding total utility constant
$$= -(MU_X/MU_Y)$$
where MU_X and MU_Y = the marginal utilities of X and Y.[4]

Your Turn 3.17: If an indifference curve is totally flat and Y is a typical good with finite marginal utility, what is the marginal utility of X?

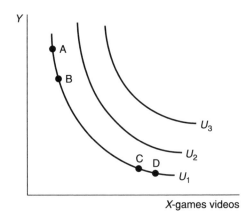

Figure 3.14 Indifference curves

Because any two points on an indifference curve provide the same total utility, the movement from one point to another involves an equal tradeoff between the utility lost from giving up one good and the utility gained by adding the other. Where the slope of an indifference curve is steeper than 1 in absolute value the marginal utility of Y is lower than the marginal utility of X, meaning that one needs relatively few additional units of X to make up for the loss of a larger number of units of Y. Furthermore, the gradual flattening associated with the typical indifference curve relates directly to the diminishing marginal utility for additional units of both goods.

Your Turn 3.18: Explain how the diminishing marginal utility of *X* leads to a flatter slope for the indifference curve. Use the slope formula in your answer.

The marginal utility definition of the slope of the indifference curve also applies to situations where a consumer has a choice between a typical good and an item which she actively dislikes, such as unemployment, the risk of death, or lima beans. If the marginal utility of X is less than zero, the negative sign in the formula $-(MU_X/MU_Y)$ creates a double negative or positive value. In more common-sense terms, in order to remain equally happy when facing more risk the hero of Figure 3.15 will require more beer. This graph offers our first view of the concept of compensating differentials, which proposes that workers facing poor working conditions will require higher wages in order to accept or keep that job, all else equal.

Utility maximization

The goal of the rational consumer is to allocate her limited budget so as to achieve the highest possible total utility. This involves combining the budget line and set

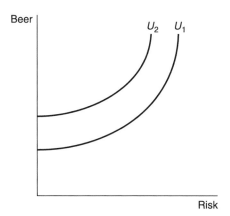

Figure 3.15 Negative marginal utility of X

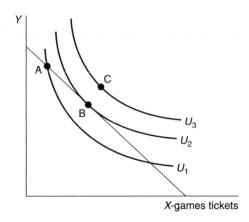

Figure 3.16 Utility maximization

of indifference curves as shown in Figure 3.16. In that figure, point B on the indifference curve U_2 represents the highest utility level possible given the budget line. Point A is equally affordable (also on the budget line) but offers less total utility, while point C is not affordable. Point B represents a tangency point between indifference curve U_2 and the budget line. At this point the slopes are equal. Using the formulas for each slope, this equality of slopes implies that

$$-MU_X/MU_Y = -P_X/P_Y \text{ or that } MU_X/P_X = MU_Y/P_Y \tag{3.12}$$

The second formula is the common model for consumer equilibrium or utility maximization found in introductory economics texts.

Changing incomes and prices

The primary uses for this consumer model relate to the effects of changes in income and prices on the individual's choice of goods and total utility. All else equal, income changes produce parallel shifts in the budget line because neither price changes, so that the slope of the budget line will be the same. Income changes are presented in Figure 3.17. In this graph, higher levels of income lead to higher quantities of both goods. Therefore, both goods are **normal**.

Price changes produce two effects. First, a change in the price of one good will change the slope of the budget line. Holding total utility constant, this change in relative prices creates a movement along the initial indifference curve away from the more expensive good. This movement, called the **substitution effect**, takes place between points A and B in Figure 3.18.

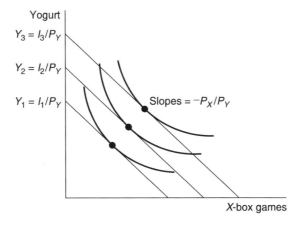

Figure 3.17 Income changes

Secondly, because higher prices mean less purchasing power, the person's total utility will also be affected. Holding relative prices fixed at their new level, this change in total purchasing power and utility appears in Figure 3.18 as a parallel shift from point B to point C. This parallel shift appears identical to an income change (Figure 3.17) because it shows a change in purchasing power and utility holding relative prices constant. This parallel movement from point B to C is referred to as an **income effect**. Together, the substitution and income effects explain the impact of a price change on an individual's consumption choices and utility. These effects can be very useful in exploring the incentive effects of policy choices related to assistance to the poor or subsidies for particular goods.

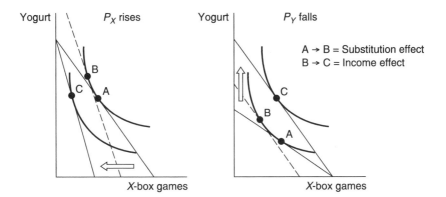

Figure 3.18 Price changes

Your Turn 3.19: Referring to Figure 3.18, sketch the income and substitution effects of a rise in the price of yogurt (Y). In your graph do the quantities of yogurt and X-box games rise or fall after this price change? Referring to the change in the quantity of X, are yogurt and X-box games substitutes or complements in your graph?

Incentives and policy problems

The importance of the indifference curve model can now be made clearer through some policy examples. We already know that lower prices and/or higher incomes raise the well-being of consumers. More challenging problems involve comparing the effects of alternative policies for helping the poor or encouraging socially positive behavior through price incentives.

The gas tax-rebate problem

During the oil crises of the 1970s it became popular to discuss policies designed to reduce the consumption of gasoline and other petroleum products. John Anderson, an independent candidate for U.S. President in 1980, proposed a conservation policy that included a 50 cent tax on gasoline along with an income tax cut equal to the expected revenue from the gasoline tax. The proposal was not well-received. A graphical analysis will help to explain why. Figure 3.19 shows that the

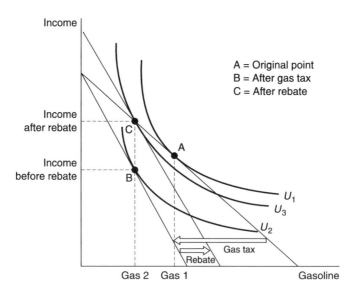

Figure 3.19 Gas tax and rebate

gasoline tax has the same effect as a price increase. It raises the relative price of gasoline and lowers the purchasing power and utility of the consumer. The income tax rebate acts as a pure income increase, preserving the higher relative price of gasoline while increasing the consumer's purchasing power. The amount of revenue received from the gasoline tax can be seen by comparing the height of the post-gasoline tax budget line with the original line at the new quantity of gas (Gas 2). In this example the rebate does not affect the quantity of gasoline. This is somewhat of an oversimplification, but does not significantly affect the overall results.

The primary issue arising from the case is that a revenue-neutral rebate, where the income tax cut equals the gas tax revenue, will not return the consumer to her original indifference curve. This is true because the gas tax presumably reduces the amount of gas consumed and thereby the amount of tax collected. In other words, if the gas tax works, a revenue-neutral rebate will leave the consumer worse off. However, if the income tax cut was large enough to return the consumer to the original indifference curve (U_1) the net effect on the consumer's well-being would be zero.

Free goods and co-payments

According to marginal utility theory, goods that are entirely free are consumed until the marginal utility of the last unit falls to zero. This can lead to relatively high consumption even when the need of or pleasure from the last unit of consumption is negligible. A private sector example of this phenomenon occurred in the mid-1990s when America On-Line (AOL) announced that it would begin offering an unlimited internet service for about $20 per month as well as a separate option of paying an hourly charge of about $3.

The public responded very enthusiastically to the monthly fee, signing up and logging on in much larger numbers than anticipated. Shortages developed and busy signals became common for the dial-up internet service. The result was a temporary public relations nightmare that was eventually solved through a significant expansion of capacity and automated log-off capability. This example is seen in Figure 3.20. In this case the consumer's total monthly income equals $120 before the $20 charge and yogurt ($Y$) costs $1. The consumer can either pay $3 per hour of on-line service or pay a flat fee of $20 per month and pay nothing per hour. As the graph shows, with unlimited service the quantity of on-line time per month is likely to increase significantly, and most people will be better off in terms of utility. Since those early days, all internet service providers have adopted a flat monthly fee as their primary pricing option.

The overuse of free goods has policy implications in several areas, including highways, healthcare, and several aspects of resource and environmental policy. Some of these examples are considered in the applied topics chapters later in the book. One example of the overuse of free goods concerns the demand for prescriptions and visits by doctors under public or private health insurance policies. Many European countries provide fully insured healthcare to their citizens.

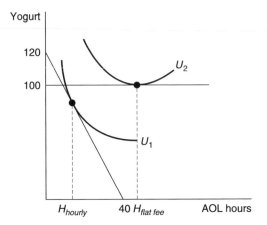

Figure 3.20 Free AOL

However, there has been a trend toward increasing use of co-payments (partial payment by customers) as a method of controlling unnecessary use of healthcare services.

One well-documented example occurred in Germany, whose near-universal healthcare system was significantly modified in 1997. In supporting the 1997 reform, insurance companies argued that 25 percent of all prescriptions were unnecessary and drugs worth 4 billion Deutschmarks were thrown away each year (Winkelmann 2004: 1081). The healthcare reform raised prescription co-payments by varying percentages with smaller quantities of drugs seeing up to 200 percent increases. After controlling for several related factors Winkelmann estimated that the new policy lowered the quantity of prescriptions by 17 percent and caused a drop of about 10 percent in visits to doctors' offices (p. 1086). While additional examples of the value of pricing as a means of reducing the overuse of free goods will be provided in later chapters, particularly Chapters 12 and 13, the case of healthcare co-payments provides a useful first view of the issue.

The limits of consumer surplus

The earlier discussion of consumer surplus in this chapter overlooked an area of controversy regarding the consumer surplus concept. Consumer surplus is based on the observation that the height of the demand curve represents a consumer's maximum willingness to pay for that particular unit, a measure of what that unit is worth to her. Indifference curve analysis is necessary in order to see the possible inaccuracy of this concept. There are two concepts related to the concept of willingness to pay: compensating variation (CV) and equivalent variation (EV).

> **Concepts:**
> - **Compensating variation** in income is the maximum amount a person is willing to pay for a marketed or non-marketed good.
> - **Equivalent variation** in income is the minimum amount a person will **accept** in order to face a marketed or non-marketed cost such as a price increase or an increased non-monetary harm.

Compensating and equivalent variations differ because they involve moving the budget line in different directions. In Figure 3.21, the graph to the left shows a decrease in the price of X. The compensating variation for this price cut is the decrease in income (from point B to C) that leaves the person just as well off as before the price cut occurred. Similarly, the graph to the right shows the effect of a price increase in X (from A′ to B′) and the minimum increase in income (B′ to C′) that would return him to his original level of utility.

The problem for policy analysts is that the typical demand curve, which is based on the relation between price and quantity without a corresponding change in income, is not necessarily consistent with the maximum willingness to pay for a good (CV), or the minimum willingness to accept income in response to a cost (EV). In order to capture these effects accurately one would have to calculate the change in X demanded associated with a price change *and* the corresponding income change that would leave the person equally well off. For example, in Figure 3.21 the maximum willingness to pay for a price cut would be measured by the movement from X_A to X_C, while the change in X associated with the minimum income one would accept for a price increase is from Xa' to Xc'. Neither point C nor C′ is directly observable from consumer behavior. The bias between the normal, or Marshall, demand curve and the actual willingness to pay for a price increase requires one more concept, the Hicks demand curve.

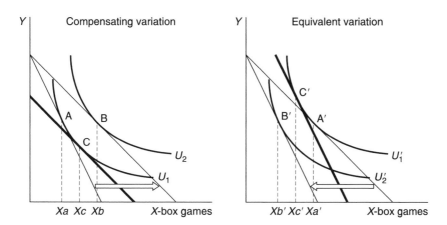

Figure 3.21 Compensating and equivalent variations

Concept: The Hicks demand curve measures the change in the quantity of X associated with the substitution effect of a price change after any change in utility is eliminated through a change in income. This is also called the **income-compensated demand curve**.

Figure 3.22 provides a good example of this bias in the case of a price increase. The biased Marshall demand curve shows the effects of a price increase without any corresponding change in income, while the Hicks demand curve shows the effect of the price rise on X with the corresponding increase in income (from B to C).

The true loss of consumer surplus from the price increase would be the area under the Hicks demand from point a to c and to the left, while the normal Marshall demand curve understates this lost surplus. When a price decrease occurs, the Marshall demand curve tends to exaggerate the increase in consumer surplus for the same reason. In Figure 3.22 the graphs on the right show one circumstance where the two demand curves are identical. In the indifference curve

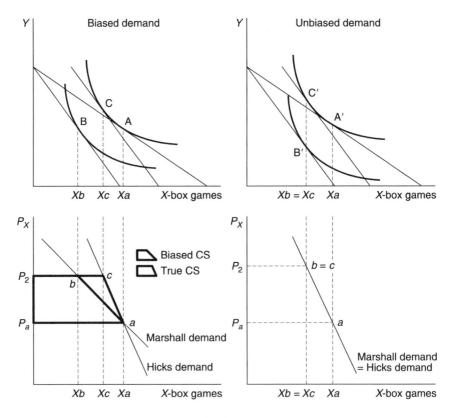

Figure 3.22 Equivalent variation of a price increase

graph the increase in income needed to return the person to her original indifference curve does not change the quantity of X. In this case X is neither a normal nor an inferior good, and therefore the income increase has no effect on X.

Your Turn 3.20: See Figure 3.23. Follow the instructions in the graph. If you prefer, graph your results on a separate piece of paper.

More generally, the finding that normal demand curves understate the harm done by a price increase and overstate the harm done by a price decrease suggest that humility is appropriate when using consumer surplus in policy analysis. However, a crucial but highly technical article by Willig (1976) demonstrated that under normal conditions these biases in the normal Marshall demand curve are small, and probably less than the normal bias in the estimate of the demand curve itself. After Willig's paper was published, the use of single market welfare analysis using surplus measures became less controversial. As with other texts, we will continue to utilize surplus-related concepts when considering market imperfections, government policy, and the valuation of benefits and costs.

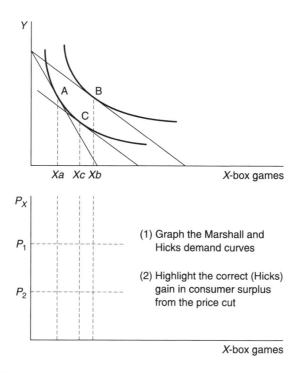

Figure 3.23 Bias in compensating variation, Your Turn 3.20

Conclusion

This chapter provides a review of microeconomic models of the competitive market and the rational consumer. These models will be the cornerstone of much of the remainder of the book, beginning with the next chapter. In Chapter 4 we will consider the efficiency implications of consumer surplus and producer surplus. The reader will also learn what happens when markets are not perfectly competitive. In Chapter 5 the role of government in promoting market efficiency will be discussed by considering the negative efficiency effects of government involvement in markets when perfect competition exists, and the potentially positive effects of government when markets are imperfect. This will allow us to see when government intervention in markets might be beneficial and what types of policies might be effective in various situations. Chapters 6 through 10 will integrate these models into various dimensions of benefit–cost analysis and provide additional policy examples. The final four applied chapters will utilize both the market and consumer models to analyze issues such as the work incentive effects of alternate public assistance programs, the effects of alternate approaches to controlling pollution and traffic congestion, and the effects of alternative policies for the working poor. Readers with relatively little background in applied microeconomics are likely to be surprised and impressed with the rich potential of these basic tools.

Review questions

Conceptual questions

Use your knowledge of supply and demand in the competitive market to answer questions 1 to 4 about the market for pizza on your college or university campus.

1. Based on the competitive assumptions listed in the chapter, is pizza a perfectly competitive good in your town? Which competitive assumptions are true and which are not?

2. Consider the following events. Assume that the initial supply and demand curves are denoted by S_1 and D_1. In each case, determine the final demand-and-supply curves after the event, and note any movement up or down in price and quantity. (Note: it is usually not necessary for both curves to shift.)

   (A) A poor growing season causes a shortage of tomato sauce.   D _____ S _____

   (B) Pizza workers suffer indigestion and reduced productivity.   D _____ S _____

   (C) A new chicken wings restaurant opens on campus.   D _____ S _____

   (D) A winter storm makes traveling and delivery impossible.   D _____ S _____

   (E) OPPC (the Organization of Pizza Producing Companies) cuts the overall pizza supply.   D _____ S _____

   (F) Pizza goes on sale.   D _____ S _____

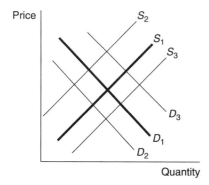

The competitive pizza market

3. The First Year Class Officers are hosting a pizza-eating marathon. They observe that although the participants were initially willing to pay $2 per slice, after three hours pizza consumption has virtually stopped. Explain in terms of marginal utility why this might be true.

4. Explain, in your own words, why raising the price of pizza might not increase total revenue for pizza producers.

5. Neoclassical economics assumes that people are rational maximizers of utility. However, many people donate their time and money to charitable causes. Are these individuals irrational in the economic sense? Explain this behavior economically and elaborate on how volunteerism might be an important component of a policy decision.

6. Differentiate between the following terms:

   (A) Income effect and substitution effect.
   (B) Economic profit and economic rent.

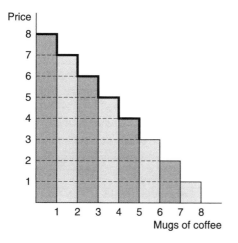

Quantity	Marginal value	Total value
1	8	8
2	7	15
3		21
4		
5		
6		
7		
8		

Computational problems

7. Given the step function above, complete the adjoining table in pencil or on a sheet of paper.

8. A town in the mid-Atlantic region of the U.S. is trying to determine demand for a municipal snow-plowing service. Complete the table below, assuming that the demand curve is linear, and then create an equation to describe the demand curve. How many plows should the town buy? At that quantity, what is its consumer surplus? Explain your reasoning. As you can verify in the table, total consumer surplus can be found in either of two ways: (1) finding the marginal consumer surplus for each mug, and then adding the individual surpluses to find the total, or (2) calculating the total value for all mugs purchased and the total spending, then subtracting total spending from the total value. Check to see that both methods work.

Quantity	Marginal value	Total value	Price	Total spending	Marginal consumer surplus	Total consumer surplus
0						
1	210		40			
2	180					
3						
4						
5						

9. A school district is trying to determine exactly how many school buses to hire for the academic year and how much it will cost. The supply of school buses is represented by $P_s = 4,000 + 8Q_s$ and the district's demand for school buses is represented by $P_d = 10,000 - 2Q_d$.

    (A) Find the equilibrium price and quantity.
    (B) How much will it cost to hire as many buses as the school needs to meet demand?
    (C) Find the consumer and producer surpluses associated with this equilibrium.
    (D) Now suppose that only half of the buses needed by the school district are actually available for hire. At that quantity, how much would the school district be willing to pay for each bus?
    (E) Identify the new consumer surplus at this price and quantity.
    (F) Using the prices and quantities demanded you found in parts a and d, calculate the price elasticity of demand for buses using the mid-point formula.

10. Let's consider two alternative policies for providing aid to the poor: cash assistance and housing vouchers. Housing vouchers act like a coupon that

can only be spent on housing, but leaves the recipient with considerable additional money for other expenditures. Let's compare the two policies using indifference curves and budget lines. Assume that John Smith earns $1,200 per month. Housing (on the horizontal axis) costs $150 per unit, and a week's worth of food (on the Y axis) costs $100. A housing unit can be thought of as some combination of square feet of space and utilities such as plumbing.

(A) Graph the budget line for John, and choose any utility-maximizing point you wish using an indifference curve. Label the endpoints and determine the slope of the budget line.

(B) Assume that the government now contributes $300 in cash to John, all else equal. Graph his new budget line, and choose a new utility-maximizing point. Explain how the graph demonstrates that John is better off.

(C) Now assume that the government cancels the cash assistance program and instead offers a coupon or voucher worth $300 that can only be spent on housing. This means he can buy two units of housing using only the voucher, but must pay the original market price for any additional housing. (1) How will this added funding that can only be used for housing change his endpoint for food? (2) With this voucher, how many units of food must he give up in order to afford the first two units of housing? (Careful.) (3) Graph his new budget line given the voucher. (Hint: It will have a different slope for the first two units than for any additional units.)

(D) How is the budget line with the cash assistance different from the budget line with the housing voucher? Is John better off with the voucher, the cash assistance, or is he equally well off under either program? If John prefers to live with a friend and has a very low marginal utility for his own housing, will he be better off with the cash grant or with the housing voucher? Why? Show this situation on a graph.

11. Harry Truckdriver pays $2 per gallon for diesel fuel (X) and $1 per unit for "little white pills" (Y). He has $150 per week to spend on these two goods. Let's assume that he originally consumes 50 gallons of diesel fuel and 50 little white pills per week. Graph the budget line and indifference curve for this result carefully. Two additional bits of information will help. First, the vertical distance between the pre-gasoline tax and post-gasoline tax budget line will be equal to the total revenue from the tax for that quantity of gasoline. Secondly, note how much tax revenue the government would receive at Butch's original quantity of gasoline, and use the first hint to measure the size of the income tax cut on your graph.

(A) Senator Ghost proposes a 50 cents per gallon tax on diesel fuel, which we will assume raises the price of diesel by 50 cents (it won't in reality), along with an income tax cut that will increase Butch's disposable income by $25 per week. Graph the effects of the diesel tax, then on the same graph show the effects of the income tax cut.

(B)   With both programs in effect, will Harry buy less fuel, more fuel, or the same amount as before the tax changes? Will he be better off, equally well off, or worse off. Why? With both programs in effect, will the government deficit be slightly larger, slightly smaller, or exactly the same? Why? (Hints: If you graph the tax changes correctly, the final budget line will go through the original utility-maximizing point but with a different slope.)

Computational problems

12. The graphs below begin to illustrate compensating variation and equivalent variation. On each graph, draw two indifference curves and a new budget line illustrating what change in income would be needed to return to the original level of utility. Which income change seems larger in your graph, if any?

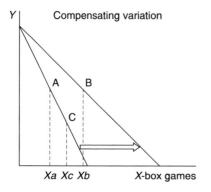

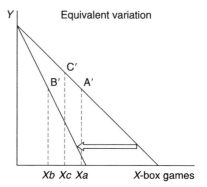

4 Efficiency and imperfect markets

Obviously, the highest type of efficiency is that which can utilize existing material to the best advantage.[1]

(Jawaharlal Nehru, former Prime Minister of India)

We want the spirit of America to be efficient; we want American character to be efficient; we want American character to display itself in what I may, perhaps, be allowed to call spiritual efficiency – clear disinterested thinking and fearless action along the right lines of thought.[2]

(Woodrow Wilson, former President of the U.S.)

I don't like a man to be too efficient. He's likely to be not human enough.[3]

(Felix Frankfurter, former Supreme Court Justice)

Of the three basic dimensions of policy analysis emphasized in the introductory chapters of this book (efficiency, equity, and political context), the analysis of efficiency involves the most widely accepted set of concepts among policy analysts. Debates about efficiency occur frequently, but they often involve specific questions about its measurement or its importance relative to other policy goals. There is little debate about its general meaning.

What is efficiency?

The reader will be glad to know that the common-sense definition of efficiency does resemble its formal meaning in policy analysis. In common-sense terms, an individual is working efficiently if she is working to her capacity with a minimum of wasted effort. Alternatively, a person is playing efficiently if he is having the greatest possible time with minimum costs or other negative effects on himself or others.

In a general sense, this concept of efficiency is also applicable to the operation of business, government, and other institutions. A business is operating efficiently if it produces the greatest value of product at the lowest possible cost. A government is operating efficiently if it is providing the greatest possible well-being for its citizens at the least possible cost. And society as a whole is operating efficiently if its citizens are as well off as possible given the society's resources.

As you can see, the intellectual challenge associated with efficiency does not arise because of problems with its basic meaning, but in how that meaning can be applied to real-world situations.

Because individual utility is not measurable under most circumstances, individual and societal well-being are both subject to measurement problems. The first set of problems occurs at the individual level. In Chapter 3 the benefits of consumption are defined in terms of marginal value, or the maximum willingness to pay for a particular unit of a good. As noted at the end of Chapter 3, there is a potentially important difference between the maximum a person is willing to pay in order to receive a benefit (compensating variation) and the amount the person is willing to accept in order to forego a benefit (equivalent variation). This measurement issue has not become a serious barrier to policy analysis, but does introduce a degree of uncertainty into the meaning and accuracy of consumer surplus.

More broadly, an efficient society is presumed to maximize the welfare (or utility) of society as a whole. At the societal level two basic measurement problems exist with this concept. First, individual utilities are only observable in terms of the ranking of different combinations of goods. This limitation means that one cannot easily or accurately compare the intensity of two persons' preferences, or how strongly a given policy will affect each person's utility. Secondly, the total well-being of society depends on how much weight each person's utility receives. The different social welfare functions defined in our discussion of ethics (Chapter 2) produce very different weights for the utility of different individuals. To review, utilitarianism weighs each individual's utility equally, while John Rawls' difference principle assigns all weight to the least well-off person. These two problems, among others, make the task of measuring society's overall well-being more or less impossible in any direct sense.

These measurement problems are real, but they do not and should not preclude the economic analysis of efficiency. Approximate answers to policy questions are all that any discipline can offer, including economics, and a certain degree of humility and care is needed in the process of analyzing public policy from any point of view. With this caution in mind, we can now plow ahead.

Pareto optimality

The most fundamental economic concept in the analysis of societal efficiency is **Pareto optimality**, named after Vilfredo Pareto (1848-1923). This concept has a wonderful simplicity because it manages to avoid the impossible task of adding the well-being of individuals from the ground up. Instead, Pareto optimality offers a marginal test of allocative efficiency.

Definition: Pareto optimality. A situation is Pareto optimal if it is impossible to make any person better off without making at least one person worse off.

In other words, Pareto optimality requires that all possible opportunities for efficient production and mutually beneficial trade have been fulfilled. A related concept is Pareto improvement.

Definition: Pareto improvement. An action leads to a Pareto improvement if it makes at least one person better off without making at least one person worse off. A Pareto improvement can also be achieved if anybody who would otherwise lose due to a policy is fully compensated for his or her losses.

Pareto optimality relates to Pareto improvement in the following way. If society, or a relevant portion of society, has achieved Pareto optimality, no Pareto improvements are possible.

Your Turn 4.1: Before proceeding any further, the reader might take a few moments to consider the meaning of these concepts. Consider whether or not the following actions produce Pareto improvements.
(A) Robin Hood robs Prince John to feed his merry men.
(B) The Sheriff of Nottingham arrests Robin Hood, thereby preventing further theft.
(C) The U.S. government increases aid to the homeless, paying for the program with a slight increase in the corporate income tax.
(D) The Salvation Army feeds the hungry with voluntary donations from the well-to-do.

The lesson from these examples is that the redistribution of income, by itself, will not be a Pareto improvement unless it is wholly voluntary. While some people are proud to pay their taxes in order to support public anti-poverty programs, the non-voluntary nature of taxes makes it unlikely that everyone will feel better off when their taxes are due.

Another simple example may aid in understanding the policy implications of the Pareto improvement concept. If a policy costs Jack $10 and provides $20 in benefits to Jill, it is not a Pareto improvement. However, if Jill compensates Jack for his loss by paying him $10 of her benefits, then Jill would still be $10 better off, Jack would be equally well off, and a Pareto improvement is achieved. Therefore if the winner (Jill) fully compensates the loser (Jack) and has some benefits left over, the policy produces a Pareto improvement. On the other hand, if the policy costs Jack $10 and provides Jill with $10 in benefits, then in order to compensate Jack for his loss, Jill would have to pay him all of her benefits. After Jack is compensated nobody is worse off, but nobody is better off either.

This second policy would *not* be a Pareto improvement. This example indicates that there are two conditions which must be met in order for a policy to be a Pareto improvement.

Conditions for a Pareto improvement:
1 Total benefits must be greater than total costs.
2 Losers (if any) must be fully compensated for their net losses.

Together these conditions imply that nobody is made worse off (by condition 2), and that some net gains will remain after the losers are compensated (by condition 1).

More advanced: the Edgeworth box and the meaning of Pareto optimality

One theoretical tool for explaining the meaning of Pareto optimality is labeled the **Edgeworth box**. This model represents an abstract world with two individuals and no production. Instead of production, predetermined quantities of two goods can be traded in order to improve the well-being of the individuals. Therefore, the Edgeworth box also can be labeled as a pure exchange model. While this model has little or no direct use in the analysis of policy, it is useful in the identification of two important concepts that help to explain the meaning of Pareto optimality. These principles are mutually beneficial exchange and the endowment point. **Mutually beneficial exchange** states that informed individuals will not undertake a trade, purchase, or task unless the action makes them better off. The **endowment point** refers to the initial distribution of income or wealth from which exchange takes place.

The Edgeworth box model assumes that there are two individuals, Dottie and Schwartz, and two goods. Each individual starts with fixed quantities of the two goods. These initial quantities represent the endowment point. In order to identify trade between the two parties, the quantities and utilities of one of two persons are inverted. In the Edgeworth box figure, Schwartz's quantities of fruit and eggs start at zero on the upper right-hand corner, while Dottie's quantities start at zero from the bottom left. The dashed indifference curves represent Dottie's utility function, while the solid curves represent Schwartz's utility. Turning the book upside down for a moment will demonstrate that Schwartz's indifference curves are normally shaped.

The endowment point in Figure 4.1 represents the initial distribution of fruit and eggs between Dottie and Schwartz. In this particular case Dottie starts with the majority of the eggs and Schwartz with the majority of fruit. The utility each party receives from this endowment is shown by the indifference curve that passes through the endowment point. The area between these two curves is called the core. The **core** represents the space within which a Pareto improvement can take place. In other words, any point in the core will make at least one party better off without making the other worse off.

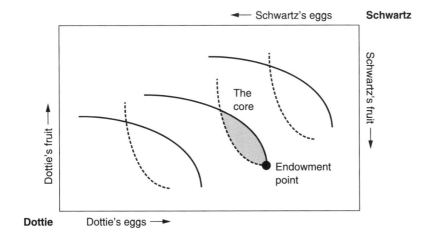

Figure 4.1 Edgeworth box

Within the Edgeworth box model the only way for the two parties to achieve a Pareto improvement is to trade with each other starting from the endowment point. Ideally, this trade will result in a Pareto optimal point. Such a result is displayed in Figure 4.2. In this graph Schwartz gave up some fruit and received eggs in trade, while Dottie gave up some eggs and received fruit. Notice that in this case both have moved to higher indifference curves after the exchange, and that the new allocation of goods at the point represented by the square is a triple

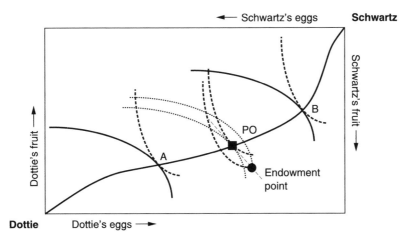

Figure 4.2 Edgeworth box with a Pareto-optimal point

tangency between the dashed line along which they could trade and each person's indifference curve. From this new allocation of goods it will be impossible to make one person better off without making the other person worse off. Therefore, the square represents a Pareto optimal outcome. Similarly, at tangency points like A or B it would also be impossible to increase one person's utility without reducing the utility of the other. Therefore, any tangency point between the two persons' indifference curves is Pareto optimal. In Figure 4.2 the thick line, commonly called a **contract curve**, represents all possible Pareto optimal points in this Edgeworth box. Notice that the contract curve extends through points A, B, and the square, but also includes the two corner points where one or the other person has no goods at all.

The Edgeworth box is useful in representing two important points regarding the meaning of Pareto optimality. First Pareto optimality can be achieved through the free and informed exchange of goods if the rate at which one good is exchanged for the other equals the slopes of the two persons' indifference curves at their point of intersection. This means that the slope of both party's indifference curves ($-MU_X/MU_Y$ in Chapter 3) will equal the rate of exchange, which in a monetary economy equals the slope of the budget line, or $-P_X/P_Y$. Therefore, individual utility maximization is a necessary condition for a Pareto optimal outcome. Secondly, and more importantly in a policy context, Pareto optimality and Pareto improvement are relative concepts that vary with the initial allocation of goods. An allocation of goods that leaves one person with everything and another with nothing will be Pareto optimal since transferring goods from the person with everything will cause him or her to be worse off. Therefore, it is often important to include ethical considerations as well as efficiency when analyzing the social impact of a public policy.

Other efficiency concepts

The Pareto improvement principle is an impractical efficiency standard for many public policy decisions. Public programs are often funded by taxation. Since taxes by definition lower the spendable incomes and well-being of taxpayers, programs that allocate tax revenues from the general public to specific groups violate the Pareto improvement principle. Similarly, regulations that restrict the actions of some in order to benefit society as a whole are also likely to make some individuals worse off. Unlike the earlier example of Jack and Jill, identifying and compensating all individuals who suffer losses from a government program is likely to be impractical. However, those with strong libertarian tendencies tend to approve of Pareto improvement as a standard, since it generally limits transfers of wealth or restrictions on freedom to those which are voluntary, and therefore mutually beneficial.

The Kaldor–Hicks principle

There are two common standards for judging efficiency that are less restrictive than Pareto optimality. The first is labeled the **Kaldor–Hicks principle**, or the

fundamental rule of policy analysis. The second and even less restrictive criterion is labeled the **leaky bucket principle**. Each will be introduced in this section.

The Kaldor–Hicks principle modifies the wording and meaning of the Pareto improvement criterion in the following way.

Definition: The Kaldor–Hicks principle states that a policy should be adopted if the winners could *in principle* compensate the losers. This principle requires that the total benefits outweigh the total costs but does not require that the losers actually be compensated.[4]

Adding the words "in principle" creates a substantial difference between the Pareto improvement concept and the Kaldor–Hicks principle. As stated above, a Pareto improvement requires that total benefits must be greater than total costs *and* that any losers must be fully compensated for their net losses. However, the Kaldor–Hicks principle does not require that the losers actually be compensated. The rule for analyzing public policy based on the Kaldor–Hicks principle is often labeled the fundamental rule of policy analysis.

The fundamental rule of policy analysis: Adopt a policy if total benefits are greater than total costs.

This rule, based on the Kaldor–Hicks principle, provides the basis for benefit–cost analysis, which is discussed in more detail in Chapter 6.

The Kaldor–Hicks principle also has a direct relationship to the utilitarian philosophy discussed in Chapter 2. As you may recall, utilitarianism argues that the well-being of all individuals should be equally weighted when considering the effects of a policy, and that the primary goal of any policy is to maximize the total benefits minus costs, or pleasure minus pain, for all members of society. Therefore, the Kaldor–Hicks principle is an application of utilitarianism. Because utility is not measurable, however, cost–benefit analysis based on the Kaldor–Hicks principle is usually measured in terms of dollars, or some other monetary measure. Monetary value makes a very useful measurement tool, but it does create one significant difference between utilitarianism and Kaldor–Hicks. As noted in Chapter 2, the law of diminishing marginal utility implies that transferring income from the rich to the poor without any efficiency losses will tend to make society as a whole better off. This distributional effect is lost when well-being is measured in terms of dollars. This is another reason why ethics should be considered in policy analysis.

The leaky bucket principle

While the Kaldor–Hicks principle is widely accepted as a test of the efficiency of a policy, it tends to reject many policies designed to redistribute income to the poor. This is because income redistribution programs are likely to decrease total production in a society somewhat in addition to increasing equality. Because the Kaldor–Hicks principle requires that total net benefits to society be positive for any policy, such a tradeoff between efficiency and equality will be rejected. As part of a brief but wonderfully insightful book entitled *Equality and Efficiency: The Big Tradeoff*,[5] Arthur Okun developed a model for analyzing redistribution programs based on a version of the following story.

A leaky bucket tale

When one transfers income through government policy, some of the spending does not end up directly benefiting the poor. Okun refers to any other use of a program's funds as "leaks." Leaks exist when the amount of money taken in taxes for a redistribution program is more than the increased income of the poor. Let's consider an example. It is a cold day, and kerosene is in short supply. Jill has two buckets of kerosene, and Jane has none. The mayor comes to Jill's house to take a bucket of kerosene to Jane. Jill reluctantly agrees to give up a bucket of the precious kerosene, but on the way to Jane's house some of the kerosene leaks out, leaving less than one bucket of kerosene for Jane. Clearly this process is likely to violate both the Pareto and Kaldor–Hicks principles because Jill's loss is greater than Jane's gain.

Most ethical principles require that such a tradeoff at least be considered in order to keep Jane from freezing. However, if Jane is getting far less kerosene than Jill is giving up, society may judge the transfer of kerosene to be too wasteful to be worthwhile. For example, no reasonable ethical principle could require that the transfer take place if **all** of the kerosene leaked on the way to Jane's house, because the only effects are that a bucket of kerosene is lost, and someone has wasted the effort to carry the bucket to Jane's house. Okun makes no judgment regarding the maximum acceptable leak. Rather, Okun's emphasis is on identifying the sources of leaks, or inefficiencies, associated with a redistribution program, and designing public policies to minimize these leaks.

Sources of leaks

Okun identifies several sources of leaks that may occur in a program which transfers income. One source of leaks is **administrative costs**. The salaries of government workers, computer costs, paper, printing, and other expenditures divert some tax revenue from the poor. A second category of leaks involves the **disincentive to work** caused by taxes and transfer payments. If the rich expect to sacrifice a substantial portion of their income in taxes, their incentive to earn income is reduced. Similarly, if the poor expect to receive adequate income through government transfer payments without having to work, their work incentive is also reduced. Okun also mentions two other possible leaks which he finds less well supported by statistical evidence. The first is the **disincentive to save and invest** caused by the taxes used to fund the program. In the policy context this is an indirect leak, since any actual loss of income occurs wherever and whenever the benefits of investment may have occurred. Okun also mentions **"socio-economic leakages"** (Okun 1975: 100), which refer to the adverse effect of transfer payments on the work ethic or other behaviors of those who receive benefits. Another source of leaks that Okun does not mention is the payment of benefits to those who are eligible for the program but are not poor. These payments to the non-poor can be labeled **misdirected funds**.

These leaks can be categorized into two groups related to our more general discussion of efficiency. **The first group of leaks involves the diversion of funds to the non-poor**. This group of leaks includes administrative costs and misdirected funds. The second group of leaks is caused by lost income for society as a whole, or **societal inefficiency**. This group is comprised of the disincentives to work, save, and invest caused by taxes, transfer payments, and any economic effects of attitude changes.

How large a "leak" is acceptable?

There is nothing in the basic logic of the leaky bucket analogy which suggests an answer to this question about the maximum acceptable leakage. However, various ethical theories will have different views on this question. For utilitarians a redistribution of income from a rich to a poor person with equal tastes might provide a net gain to society even if some leakage exists. This is because of the principle of diminishing marginal utility. A poor person with a relatively high marginal utility of income will gain more utility from a dollar of income than a corresponding rich person will lose when giving up the same dollar. Returning to our example of Jill, Jane, and the oil, it is quite possible that Jane will receive more utility from 3/4 bucket of oil than Jill will lose by sacrificing one bucket. If this is true the sum of pleasure minus pain is increased, and even extreme utilitarians will approve of the transfer. However, there is generally no way to know this information, since utility is extremely difficult to measure and compare across individuals. Under Rawls' difference principle, however, any redistribution that improves the well-being of the poorest person is acceptable regardless of the losses to others. Okun criticizes Rawls' exclusive concern for the least well-off person as being too extreme. Finally, Robert Nozick's basic theory would reject any non-voluntary transfer unless, perhaps, a moral side constraint is involved.

The competitive market and Pareto optimality

The assumptions of perfect competition discussed in Chapter 3 imply that any decision to buy or sell will be fully informed and subject to free choice among many alternatives. To review, the perfectly competitive market requires

(1) many buyers and sellers, (2) perfect mobility, (3) perfect information, (4) a homogeneous product, and (5) no collusion among buyers or sellers. Another assumption that is required for a fully efficient competitive market is fully defined property rights. Without this added condition, markets may produce externalities, a concept that will be discussed below. In this idealized competitive world, no rational consumer will buy a good unless he or she is made better off by doing so, and no rational producer will sell a good unless he or she is made better off. If these conditions are met, competition will provide a fully effective constraint on the exploitation of buyers by sellers, or vice versa. Furthermore, if a competitive market produces no externalities the resultant competitive equilibrium will be Pareto optimal and will maximize the total net gains from trade.

In Figure 4.3, the net gains for consumers and producers are identified as two triangles labeled consumer and producer surplus. Verify for yourself that if the price is raised above the equilibrium consumer surplus will decrease, and that if the price is lowered producer surplus will decline. This exercise suggests, but does not prove, that a competitive equilibrium is Pareto optimal. The Pareto optimality of a competitive equilibrium has been formally proven in multiple ways and is considered the basis for welfare economics, the analysis of the type of efficiency we are considering in these chapters.

Market imperfections and inefficiency

Since perfect competition maximizes net gains from trade, any violation of perfect competition will tend to reduce the net gains from trade as well as producing winners and losers relative to the competitive result. The following violations of perfect competition will be considered in this section: (1) violation of the assumption of many buyers and sellers, (2) violation of the assumption of perfect

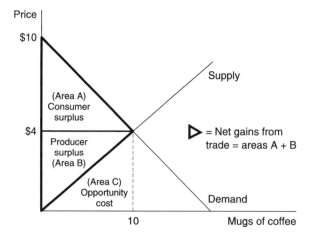

Figure 4.3 Net gains from trade

information, and (3) violation of the assumption of fully defined property rights, which allows externalities.

Monopoly versus many sellers

Monopoly is the economist's word for a single seller in a market. It is based on the Greek words *monos* (one) and *polein* (to sell). Clearly, if only one seller of a product exists in a market, the consumer's only choice is whether to buy the product from the monopolist or to not buy it at all. This lack of consumer choice gives the monopolist a degree of power over the price it charges, generally leading the profit-maximizing monopolist to charge a higher price than would exist in a competitive equilibrium.

A brief review of the introductory monopoly model will establish the reasoning behind the prediction that monopoly will tend to lead to a higher price and lower production than a competitive market. The basic monopoly model assumes that the monopolist, unlike the individual competitive firm, faces a downward-sloping demand curve for its product.

Figure 4.4 presents demand curves for the competitive firm and the monopoly. The competitive firm's demand curve is flat at the market price because it has no power over the price it charges. Since the monopoly is the only firm in the market, the demand curve it faces is the market demand curve. Therefore, the monopolist has the ability to choose any combination of price and quantity on the market demand curve.

The most basic monopoly model assumes that the monopoly may choose any single price for its product, but must sell each unit at that price. This model is called the **single price monopoly**. The primary implication of the downward-sloping demand curve for a single-price monopoly is that the price of the product (measured in dollars per unit) is no longer equal to the marginal revenue of selling another unit of output (marginal revenue equals the change in total revenue for a given change in output). Let's demonstrate the difference between the

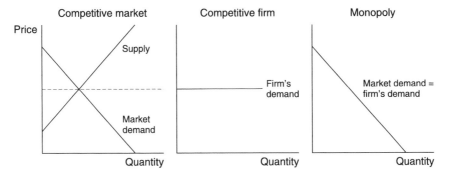

Figure 4.4 Individual and market demands

demand and marginal revenue curves for a monopoly, then explain briefly why the difference exists.

Example: Table 4.1 shows the total and marginal revenue for a monopoly at various combinations of price and quantity. Remember that total revenue (or total spending) equals price times quantity, and that marginal revenue equals the change in total revenue for each change in quantity.

Table 4.1 Monopoly demand and marginal revenue

Quantity (Q)	0	1	2	3	4	5	6	7	8
Price (P)	20	18	16	14	12	10	8	6	4
Total revenue (P × Q)	0	18	32	42	48	50	48	42	32
Marginal revenue	xx	18	14	10	6	2	−2	−6	−10

Notice that at each quantity beyond 1 the marginal revenue gained by selling another unit is less than the price of that unit. The marginal revenue is less than the price because each time the firm decides to sell another unit, it must move down the demand curve, thereby lowering the price for all of the units previously sold. For example, in Table 4.1 the monopolist can sell one unit for a total of $18. He can also sell two units at $16 each, producing $32 in total revenue. His marginal revenue for the second unit is 32 − 18, or $14. Why isn't the marginal revenue equal to the price of the second unit? His revenue increased by $16 through selling the second unit, but the first unit now brings in $16 instead of $18, for a loss of $2. Subtracting the lost $2 in revenue for the first unit from the added $16 from the second unit leads to the net marginal revenue of $14 for the second unit.

Your Turn 4.2: Using the same logic as in the previous paragraph, explain why the marginal revenue of the third unit in Table 4.1 is less than the price of $14.

Graphically, if the demand curve is linear the marginal revenue curve will be linear also, with the same vertical intercept and a slope twice as steep as the demand curve.[6]

Maximizing profits for any firm involves producing any unit for which the marginal revenue is greater than or equal to the marginal cost of production. It is also necessary to charge the highest possible price consistent with selling that quantity. One finds the maximum price the consumer is willing to pay from the height of the demand curve at the profit-maximizing quantity.

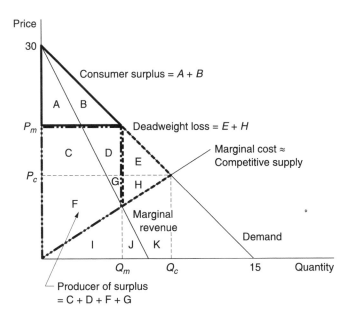

Figure 4.5 Monopoly

Figure 4.5 reviews the net gains from trade arising from a profit-maximizing monopoly. In Figure 4.5 the profit-maximizing quantity for a monopoly is Q_m and the profit-maximizing price is P_m. First, if this market was competitive, assuming equal costs of production, the equilibrium would occur at price P_c and quantity Q_c. The consumer surplus under competition would equal the area above the competitive price (P_c) and beneath the demand curve, which equals areas A + B + C + D + E, and the producer surplus would equal the triangle above the supply curve and below the competitive price, or F + G + H.

Because a monopoly produces fewer units and sells them at a higher price, consumer surplus is reduced to the triangle that includes areas A + B in Figure 4.5. The monopolistic producer surplus equals areas C + D + F + G. Producer surplus is no longer a triangle because the marginal opportunity cost of the last unit produced is now less than its price. However, this is still consistent with the basic definition of producer surplus, which equals the area beneath the price and above the marginal cost for all units sold.

Notice that producer surplus is both taller and narrower than under a competitive equilibrium. Area H represents the economic rent that has been lost because of the decrease in output. Areas C and D have been transferred from consumer surplus to producer surplus as monopoly profits due to the higher price. Finally, the lower quantity of goods bought and sold leads to a loss of total net gains from trade (CS + PS), also called a **deadweight loss**, of areas E + H (the dashed triangle in Figure 4.5). This deadweight loss triangle is typical of an equilibrium in which less than the optimal amount is being produced. It is bounded by the demand-and-supply curves and points to the right toward the competitive equilibrium point.

Concept: Deadweight loss equals the lost net gains due to a market inefficiency or government policy. It equals the total net gains under perfect competition *minus* the total net gains under another market situation.

Monopoly is an extreme form of imperfect competition among producers. Imperfect competition can exist whenever firms face a downward-sloping individual demand curve, giving them some choice regarding the price they charge to customers. Another form of imperfect competition exists when different firms produce products that are not identical. This type of imperfect competition is known as monopolistic competition. A **monopolistically competitive market** violates the competitive assumption of homogeneous products. For example, automobile companies produce differentiated models with identifiable brand names. A Toyota Camry is not identical to a Volkswagen Jetta or a Ford Focus. Some people are willing to pay extra for the Toyota based on looks, reputation for reliability, noise level, or many other characteristics. This willingness to pay more for a particular company's product is known as **brand loyalty**. Brand loyalty creates downward-sloping demand and marginal revenue curves like those of a monopoly. However, if there are no effective barriers to entry, positive economic profits will lead to the entry of new competing product lines, and will tend to reduce demand for Jettas or Camrys until profit reaches zero. As displayed in Figure 4.6, in the long run monopolistic competition produces an underproduction deadweight loss (area A) but zero economic profits.

Governments virtually never interfere with the pricing and production decisions of monopolistically competitive firms. However, because brand loyalty creates potential net benefits from advertising, the accuracy of the information imparted in advertising may be regulated. Biased information in advertising is considered as a form of imperfect information later in this chapter.

A third example of imperfect competition among producers exists when a few producers dominate a market. A market with a few producers is known as an **oligopoly**. The unique and interesting dimension of oligopoly markets is the strategic interaction between these few competing firms. A few competitors are more likely to have the opportunity to join in a price-fixing conspiracy than perfectly competitive firms. There are also strategic decisions among these competitors regarding engaging in price wars in order to eliminate competitors, the development of new product lines, and others. These strategic battles among competitors are analyzed in an interesting area of economics known as game theory. Most intermediate microeconomics texts include introductions to game theory. For a more thorough analysis of basic game theory see Luce and Raiffa (1957).

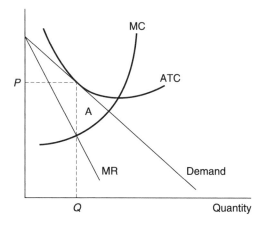

Figure 4.6 Monopolistic competition in long-run equilibrium

Game theory is not explicitly considered in this text, although some of its components are presented in Chapter 9.

The possibility of business strategies to harm competitors and increase market power leads to government policy controlling anti-competitive practices. More generally, these imperfectly competitive markets provide useful examples of equilibria where too little is produced. The next two examples of market imperfections, imperfect information and negative externalities, both lead to overproduction.

Imperfect information

Imperfect information is usually not included in introductory economics texts because it is somewhat difficult conceptually and of somewhat more recent interest to policy makers than monopoly or externalities. Imperfect information implies that buyers and/or sellers are not fully aware of the benefits and costs of their actions in the market, and will not be able to make fully informed choices when buying, selling, or producing a product. The implications of imperfect information depend on how that information is distributed between buyers and sellers, among other factors. In some cases, a product's effects on consumers may be genuinely unknown to both buyers and sellers. This equally distributed ignorance does have policy implications, best seen in our willingness to support basic research, the required testing of new products, and so forth. Questions of equally distributed but imperfect information will be considered in our chapter on risk and uncertainty.

In some common situations information is not equally distributed. A common example exists when a producer or advertiser attempts to exaggerate the benefits of her product or to hide the possible harms of the product from consumers. In this case the producer knows the true effects of the product, but chooses to provide biased information to the consumer in order to gain an advantage in the market. Job applicants who distort their employment experience or students who plagiarize a research paper provide other examples of unequally distributed information.

The effects of biased information can be seen in Figure 4.7. In this graph the lower demand curve D_1 is based on the true benefits of the product to consumers, while the higher demand curve D_2 represents the exaggerated benefits perceived by the consumer. In other words, in Figure 4.7 the consumer thinks he is receiving the value associated with D_2, but after buying the product will actually receive the benefits under demand curve D_1. Let's start by considering the net benefits that would occur in this market if the consumer knew the truth about the product. If the consumer knew the truth, they would be aware that demand curve D_1 is the accurate measure of the product's value. Therefore, they would demand Q_1 units at a price of P_1. At this equilibrium, consumer surplus equals areas B + C and producer surplus equals areas F + I. The total net gains from trade in this market therefore equal B + C + F + I.

Now let's consider the results if the consumer is fooled into acting as though D_2 is his demand curve. The new equilibrium would occur at price P_2 and quantity Q_2. Because of the higher price and higher quantity, producer surplus increases to area C + D + F + I. This increase in producer surplus demonstrates that the producer has an incentive to fool the consumer into thinking that the product is more desirable than is actually the case. The consumer surplus when

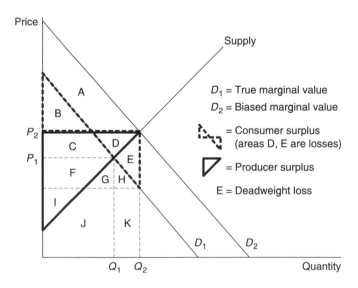

Figure 4.7 Unequal information

consumers are fooled is somewhat more difficult to see, however. Recall from Chapter 3 that consumer surplus equals the total value of the product (the area under the demand curve for all units purchased) minus the total expenditure on the product. In this case the consumers *think* they are receiving the marginal value of demand curve D_2, which leads to an equilibrium at price P_2 and quantity Q_2. Therefore, they make their purchasing decisions thinking that their consumer surplus will equal areas A + B. But this is **not** the surplus they actually receive. The true total value of Q_2 units equals the area under demand curve D_1 up to quantity Q_2, or areas B + C + F + G + H + I + J + K. Total spending at the higher price equals P_2 times Q_2, or areas C + D + E + F + G + H + I + J + K. Subtracting the total spending from the total value gives the consumer surplus. This surplus equals ($\mathbf{B}$ + C + F + G + H + I + J + K) − C − $\mathbf{D}$ − $\mathbf{E}$ − F − G − H − I − J − K. Canceling the areas in italics that appear twice (most areas appear twice in this case) leaves a consumer surplus of B − D − E. The negative signs in front of areas D and E are correct, since consumers are being fooled into buying some units of the product whose true marginal value is less than their cost. In other words, the consumer is literally not getting what he is paying for. To summarize, in a market where the consumer is being misled the producer surplus grows while the consumer surplus includes negative values and shrinks in total size. Such a result is likely to be unfair according to all of the ethical theories discussed in Chapter 2, including that of Robert Nozick.

Misleading the consumer is inefficient as well as unethical. Under perfect information, the consumer surplus equals areas B + C, the producer surplus equals areas F + I, and total net gains equal B + C + F + I. With imperfect information, total net gains equal the consumer surplus ($\mathbf{B} - D - \mathbf{E}$) plus producer surplus ($\mathbf{C} + D + \mathbf{F} + \mathbf{I}$), or (canceling the two D's) B + C + F + I − E. The difference between the net gains with perfect information and imperfect information equals the negative of area E, which is the deadweight loss caused by imperfect information. This triangle (area E) provides a good example of the typical deadweight loss from overproduction, a triangle that points leftward toward the competitive equilibrium point.

Externalities

Pollution flowing from an auto factory can harm people who have nothing to do with the production or consumption of cars. Similarly, the beauty of a well-designed building can provide pleasure to passers-by who neither work nor shop in the building. These negative or positive effects of markets on uninvolved parties are called externalities. An **externality** is a cost or benefit to a party not involved in the production or consumption of a good. In that sense, those experiencing external costs or benefits are outside of the market process, and generally will not be considered in the decisions of self-interested buyers or sellers. As noted earlier, a basic reason why some costs and benefits are external is the lack of defined property rights. For example, in most cases nobody owns the air or water into which pollutants are dumped. Therefore, nobody can charge for the use of the air or the water for waste, despite the real costs such use can bring.

Externalities can be harmful or helpful. For example, water pollution produced by farmers may negatively affect their neighbors or cities downstream. On the other hand, the air pollution from a chocolate factory could be positive externality by many people who experience it. Visitors to Hershey, Pennsylvania, are likely to enjoy the aroma rising from the chocolate factory near the amusement park and center of town. Another example of a positive externality is the more familiar case of the beekeeper and the apple orchard. A beekeeper's insects will provide great benefits to an orchard located next door through the pollination of its trees. This will happen whether or not the orchard owner pays for this benefit. Therefore, the pollination process is basically external, as are the benefits of pollination to the orchard owner.

Introductory texts often start the economic analysis of externalities by drawing a distinction between the private, external, and social costs of production. Let's assume that a factory on a river produces shoes and water pollution which harms fishermen downstream. The production of these shoes will produce two types of costs: private production costs for the shoe company and external costs to the fishermen. Since both groups belong to society, society's total costs include both the private and external costs.

Definitions:
- **Private cost** = the cost of production to the firm. This generally does not include external costs to outsiders from pollution or other effects. The usual market supply curve is based on the marginal costs of producers.
- **External cost** = the negative effect of production of a good on parties who are not involved with the production or consumption of the good. Positive externalities can be thought of as negative external costs.
- **Social cost** = private cost of production to the firm + external cost to others. For goods whose production or consumption leads to external harms, the good's social cost will be higher than its private cost. However, a good which offers external benefits, such as the beekeeper's honey bees or a beautiful building, will have a social cost which is lower than its private cost.
- **Marginal social cost** = the change in society's total cost for a given change in output. It also equals marginal private cost + marginal external cost. In this case the two costs are added vertically.

More explicitly, the firm's production will lead to two different cost curves, one representing marginal private costs, and the other curve representing marginal social costs. The difference in height between the two curves will equal the marginal **external** cost or benefit for that unit of production (see Figure 4.8). If no anti-pollution policy exists, the firm will have to pay only its private costs, while the external costs faced by the fishermen need not be paid by the firm.

When external costs or benefits exist, two distinct equilibria will exist in a market. The **private equilibrium** occurs where demand equals the supply curve

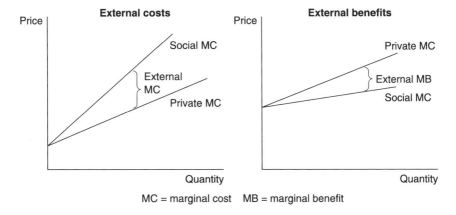

Figure 4.8 External costs and benefits

based on the private marginal costs of production. The **social equilibrium** exists where demand equals the social marginal cost of production. In a market with external costs, the private equilibrium will lead to overproduction and deadweight loss, while the social equilibrium will be Pareto optimal (see Figure 4.9).

> **Your Turn 4.3: Private and socially optimal equilibriums**
> Demand: $P = 120 - Q$
> Supply = Marginal private cost: $P = 30 + \frac{1}{2}Q$
> Marginal external cost: $MC_x = \frac{1}{2}Q$
> Marginal social cost: $MC_s = 30 + Q$
> Find the quantities and prices for the private and social equilibriums given these equations.

Introducing externalities adds a third group to our analysis of market efficiency. In addition to buyers and sellers, we must now consider outsiders who are affected by the market. The net benefits of a market to outsiders will be labeled **external surplus**.

> **Definition: External surplus** = external benefits − external costs, or the net benefits experienced by persons or firms not directly involved in production of a particular good. **A good whose production involves harmful pollution or other external costs will produce a negative external surplus,** while a good which offers positive externalities, such as the bees, will have a positive external surplus.

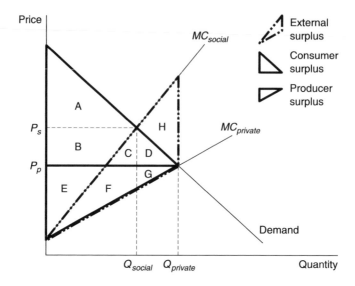

Figure 4.9 External costs

Figure 4.9 shows a market with external costs, or a negative external surplus, from production. The socially ideal level of production for such a market is where the marginal benefits of consumption equal the marginal social costs (which equal all of society's marginal costs). Therefore, the socially optimal equilibrium would be at quantity Q_s and price P_s. The total net gains in such a market include the net benefits to consumers, producers, and outsiders, or the consumer, producer, and external surpluses in that market.

Concept: The net benefits in a market with externalities equal Consumer Surplus (CS) + Producer Surplus (PS) + External Surplus (ES).

If the market in Figure 4.9 is at the socially ideal equilibrium with price P_s and quantity Q_s, consumer surplus equals area A, producer surplus equals area B + C + E + F, and external surplus (which is negative for external costs) equals − F − C. When one adds all three components together, the total net benefits are **A + B +** *C* + E + *F* − *C* − *F* or, after canceling the areas in italics, A + B + E. This seems likely to be the maximum possible net gains from trade, but one can't be sure until this result is compared with the private equilibrium.

At the private equilibrium at price P_p and quantity Q_p, consumer surplus grows to A + B + C + D, producer surplus is E + F + G, and the external surplus equals $-$ F$-$ G $-$ C $-$ D $-$ H. Adding these three surpluses together produces total net benefits of $(A + B + C + D) + (E + F + G) - F - G - C - D - H$. After canceling C, D, F, and G, we are left with A + B + E $-$ H. Comparing this answer to the social equilibrium is easy enough, since the only difference is the negative value of area H. Area H is the deadweight loss from a market with negative externalities. In addition to the overall efficiency loss from the private equilibrium, notice that there are also winners and losers from moving from a private to a social equilibrium. The consumers are worse off at the social equilibrium, while those suffering from the external costs are better off. This means that politically the correction of the overproduction caused by external cost is not a foregone conclusion.

Now review Figures 4.5, 4.7, and 4.9. In the case of monopoly (Figure 4.5), the imperfect market produces less output than the competitive result. This underproduction produces a deadweight loss triangle which points rightward toward the competitive equilibrium. On the other hand, both Figures 4.7 (unequal information) and 4.9 (external cost) involve higher levels of output than the ideal competitive case. In both of these overproduction examples the deadweight loss triangle points leftward toward the ideal equilibrium. In other words, these deadweight losses produced by an imperfect market not only identify the lost gains from trade, but also point to the ideal equilibrium solution. As we will see when considering more complicated cases in the next two chapters, this triangle pattern for deadweight losses is not always true, yet as a first view of the inefficiency created by market imperfections, it is instructive.

Numerical examples of net gains and deadweight loss

The analysis of the shapes and areas of the various components of a market's net gains is very useful for organizing one's thoughts about market inefficiency, but in order to make the connection to actual policy analysis we must be able to find the numerical values of the surplus and deadweight loss figures. Analyzing the numerical values for consumer and producer surplus, deadweight loss, and other components of our efficiency model requires three general steps. First, we must find the price and quantity values at various key points on the graph. We then find the areas of any rectangle or triangle representing part of the surplus values from a market. Finally the total net gains from the market equals the sum of all the surplus values. As long as linear demand and supply curves are used, all areas can be calculated by dividing any unusual shapes into smaller rectangles and triangles. I'll review the process as I go through our first numerical example. Your turn will follow.

A numerical example of monopoly
Figure 4.5 can now be reconsidered in numerical terms. Let's assume that the equations for the demand, marginal revenue, and supply curves can be summarized in the following equations.

Demand: $P = 30 - 2Q$
Marginal revenue: MR $= 30 - 4Q$
Supply or marginal cost: $P = 0 + Q$

Step 1: Find price and quantity values at points a, b, and c in Figure 4.5'

Point a is the competitive equilibrium where supply equals demand. Therefore, setting the demand-and-supply equations equal to each other allows us to find the equilibrium quantity and price:

$$Demand = supply$$
$$30 - 2Q = 0 + Q$$
$$30 = 3Q$$
$$10 = Q_a$$
$$10 = P_a \text{ (from either the demand or supply equation)}$$

So the values $P = 10$ and $Q = 10$ represent the competitive equilibrium price and quantity.

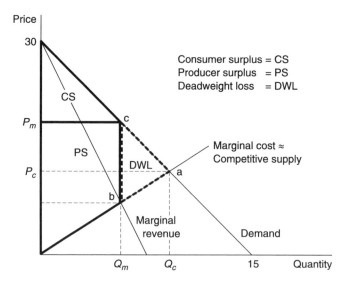

Figure 4.5' Monopoly again

Your Turn 4.4:
Point b is where the marginal revenue curve equals the marginal cost. Find its quantity and price values using the same steps as above. This point identifies the profit-maximizing quantity for the monopolist and the monopolist's marginal cost, but **not** its price.

Point c (the monopoly price and quantity) is somewhat different because it is not found at an intersection between two curves. Just plug the quantity of point b into the demand curve to find the price at point c.

Step 2: Finding numerical values for the areas

In this example all areas are either rectangles or triangles. The mathematical formulae needed for this step are those for the area of a rectangle (width times height) and a triangle ($1/2$ base times height). As long as the height of the triangle is measured perpendicularly to the base, this will work even if the triangle is not a right triangle.

Your Turn 4.5: Find the consumer surplus in dollars for this market at the competitive equilibrium point a, with price P_c and quantity Q_c in Figure 5.2′. Then find the consumer surplus for the monopoly (price = P_m and quantity = Q_m).

   Competitive CS: _____   **Monopoly CS:** _____

Now find the producer surplus for this market given a competitive equilibrium. The producer surplus for the monopoly is provided below.

   Competitive PS: _____   **Monopoly PS:** _____

In this case the PS is not a triangle. However, it is composed of the triangle below point b and the rectangle between points b and c. *Rectangle = 6 × $(18 − 6) = $72. Triangle = 1/2 × 6 × $6 = $18. Total = $100.*

Final step, find the deadweight loss

Find the total gains from trade (CS + PS) for the competitive and monopoly cases. Then find the difference between them. This difference will equal the deadweight loss. It also equals the area of the DWL triangle.

	(1) Competitive equilibrium	(2) Monopoly	(1) minus (2)
CS	_____	_____	_____
PS	_____	_____	_____
Total	_____	_____	_____

                           (This is the deadweight loss)

Check: Find the area of the deadweight loss triangle bounded by points a, b, and c to check your answer for the deadweight loss.

Example: Imperfect information with numbers

Firms have often been accused of and sometimes convicted for hiding the negative effects of a product from the consumer. Inaccurate information about a product creates a biased demand curve and a market result which is both inefficient and unfair. In Figure 4.7′, consumers think the total value of the product is consistent with demand D_2, but the true value of the product is seen in demand curve D_1.

True demand (D_1): $P = 90 - Q$

Perceived demand: $P = 110 - Q$

Supply: $P = 10 + Q$.

> **Your Turn 4.6:**
> (A) Find the price, quantity, and the dollar values of the consumer and producer surplus and total net gains (CS + PS) in a market with perfect information (use true demand only).
> (B) Now find the price, quantity, and the dollar values of the consumer and producer surplus and the deadweight loss when the consumers

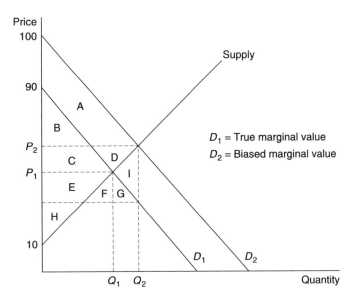

Figure 4.7′ Market for Viagra

are being fooled. Remember that this means they will choose the quantity and price based on demand curve D_2, but will receive actual total value based on demand curve D_1. Refer to the earlier graph of unequal information (Figure 4.7) to identify the consumer surplus. As before, find key points first, then areas. (Hint: As shown in the original Figure 4.7, consumer surplus will have both positive and negative areas.)

The primary conclusion from this example is that when given false information about the benefits or safety of a product, some consumers will literally not get the benefits they are paying for, and all will be disappointed with the product to some degree. Product labeling regulations undoubtedly help some people make more informed decisions, but in the U.S. the desire for consumer loyalty and the threat of lawsuits and negative public relations are probably more effective deterrents to false advertising and other forms of inaccurate information.

Example: External costs with numbers

Figure 4.9′ represents a market with external costs. Assume that the curves in Figure 4.9′ are based on the following equations:

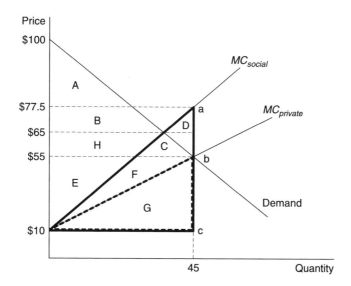

Figure 4.9′ External surplus

Marginal private cost $= 10 + Q$

Marginal external cost $= \frac{1}{2}Q$

Marginal social cost $= 10 + 1.5Q$

Demand: $P = 100 - Q$

We will find the net benefits in this market at the private equilibrium and then at the socially ideal equilibrium. Find the key points before finding the areas for Consumer, Producer, and External Surplus. Be careful, finding external surplus will be tricky and indirect.

Step 1: Private equilibrium

(A) Find the private equilibrium price and quantity:

(a) $100 - Q = 10 + Q$

$90 = 2Q$

$Q = 45$

(b) $P = 10 + Q = \$55$

(B) Then find the consumer and producer surplus for private equilibrium:

$CS = \frac{1}{2} \times 45 \times (\$100 - 55) = \$1{,}012.5$

$PS = \frac{1}{2} \times 45 \times (\$55 - 10) = \$1{,}012.5$

(C) The external surplus (negative) equals the area of solid triangle (areas D + C + F + G) minus the area of the dashed triangle (G only).

$Ex{\cdot}S = -[\frac{1}{2} \times 45 \times (\$77.5 - \$10) - \frac{1}{2} \times 45 \times (\$55 - 10)] = -[\frac{1}{2} \times 45 \times (\$67.5 - \$45)] = -\$506.25.$

(D) Total net gains then equal $\$1{,}012.5 + \$1{,}012.5 - \$506.25 = \$1{,}518.75$.

Step 2: Socially ideal equilibrium

In a market with pollution maximum net gains occur where the marginal social cost equals demand, and would equal the area between the demand and social marginal cost (MC_{social}) curves, or areas A + B + H + E in Figure 4.8.

(A) To find equilibrium quantity and price, set MC_{social} equal to demand.

$100 - Q = 10 + 1.5Q$

$$90 = 2.5Q$$

$$36 = Q$$

$$P = 10 + 1.5 \times 36 = \$64$$

(B) Total surplus = $^1/_2 \cdot 36 \cdot (100 - 64) + \frac{1}{2} \cdot 36 \cdot (64 - 10) = \$648 + \$972 = \$1,620$.

(C) To find the deadweight loss at a private equilibrium, compare the total net benefits from the socially ideal and private equilibria. In this case the **deadweight loss** due to the overproduction equals $1,620 − $1,518.75, or $101.25.

Public goods

Public goods are goods for which consumption is entirely external. Those purchasing a public good will consume no more of it than a neighbor who pays nothing for the same good. A public good has two characteristics which are different from a typical private consumer good. First, a public good has **no rivalry in consumption**. This means that a public good can be consumed or enjoyed by more than one person simultaneously. The second characteristic of public goods is non-excludability. **Non-excludability** means that one cannot prevent someone from consuming a public good if they have not paid. National defense is one example of this type of good. A missile defense system protects (or endangers) all those within its range equally. All consume the good simultaneously whether or not they are contributing taxpayers. With the exception of toll roads, most public roads are not excludable, and therefore meet the definition of public goods. On the other hand, rail travel is generally excludable, the occasional hobo notwithstanding, and is therefore not a public good.

The primary reason for government involvement in the production of public goods is the **free-rider problem**. If one can consume a public good or service without payment, he or she has a clear incentive not to pay. Voluntary payment for public goods is occasionally attempted, as in the case of U.S. public radio, but overall the lack of incentive to pay for the public good means that many consumers of the good will not do so, and the public good or service will not be adequately provided without public financing.

According to all but the most libertarian economists, public goods cannot be provided efficiently by a free private market. The lack of excludability and rivalry means that private consumers and producers have an inefficient set of incentives with regards to public goods. If people are not required to pay, the revenue potential of that product is obviously limited. Therefore, private demand for the good is insufficient to provide the good at the socially efficient level. Financing the provision of public goods generally includes some degree of government compulsion in order to avoid the free-rider problem.

Conclusion

A great deal of information has been presented in this chapter. However, the over-all outline is fairly short. We discussed general efficiency concepts such as Pareto optimality and the leaky bucket principle, the efficiency of a perfectly competitive market, and the effects of market imperfections on market efficiency. The major mathematical topics to be learned involve applying market equilibrium and the net benefits or surpluses to various parties in a number of contexts. Sometimes these were analyzed in terms of graphs only, and sometimes using equations and algebra.

Review questions

Conceptual questions

1. Determine whether or not the following actions are Pareto improvements. In each case, make an argument defending your claim and then also determine whether the action satisfies either the Kaldor–Hicks principle or the leaky bucket principle.

    (A) The government uses taxpayer dollars to increase government aid to the elderly.
    (B) The government buys back some commercial fishing licenses using a loan paid for by the owners of the remaining fleet.
    (C) A consumer purchases a car from a dealership.
    (D) The border between Pennsylvania and Ohio is closed to prevent smuggling.

2. Monetary assistance programs for the poor in virtually any nation could be criticized for their inefficiency. Name three possible sources of this inefficiency using the leaky bucket model. Also discuss the symptoms or effects of this inefficiency. Would a 10 percent leak in such a program would be acceptable to your class? Would a 50 percent leak be acceptable?

3. Discuss the Pareto optimality and Pareto improvement principles in light of Rawls' difference principle from Chapter 2. Would either Pareto principle be acceptable according to the difference principle? Why or why not?

4. Food From Above (FFA) has a monopoly in the production of Guano Burgers. FFA has the following demand, marginal revenue, and marginal cost functions:

    Demand: $P = 80 - \frac{1}{4}Q_d$

    Marginal Revenue: $MR = 80 - \frac{1}{2}Q$

    Marginal Cost $= 0.5Q$

In this problem you will calculate the effect of a monopoly on this market. Show each answer graphically as well as numerically.

(A) Find the level of output and the price which would exist if this market met the competitive result $P = MC$, or Demand = Supply. Find the consumer and producer surplus, and the total gains from trade $(CS + PS)$, for this result. Draw a graph first, and then find the numerical values.

(B) Now assume that Food From Above is a profit-maximizing single-price monopolist. What are its P and Q now? Find the consumer surplus, producer surplus, and deadweight loss graphically, then numerically.

5. Using the graph below, at private equilibrium $(P_p$ and $Q_p)$ identify the lettered sections that correspond to:

(A) Consumer surplus : _____
(B) Producer surplus : _____
(C) Deadweight loss : _____
(D) External costs : _____
(E) Total social costs : _____
(F) Total value : _____

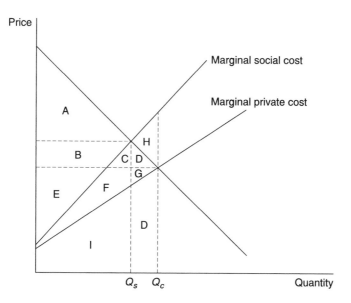

A market with external costs

6.   Now let's analyze a market with negative production externalities in numerical form. Assume that this graph can be summarized in the following equations:

Marginal private cost $= 10 + Q$

Marginal social cost $= 10 + 1.2Q$

Demand: $P = 120 - Q$

Find the price and quantity for a private equilibrium. Then find the consumer surplus, external surplus, and producer surplus for the private equilibrium in dollar values. Careful, external surplus will be tricky and indirect.

7.   Firms sometimes hide negative effects of a product from the consumer, thereby creating a biased demand curve and a market result which is both inefficient and unfair. In the sexy cigarette market, consumers think the total value of the product is consistent with demand D_2, but they have been fooled. The true value of the product is seen in demand curve D_1.

True demand is $P = 160 - 2Q$

Perceived demand is $P = 175 - 2Q$

Supply is $P = 10 + Q$

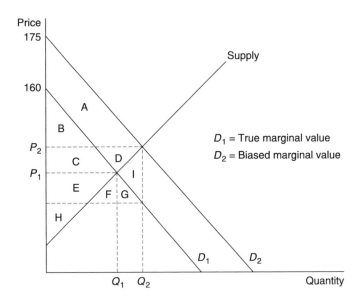

Market for sexy smokes

(A) Find the price, quantity, and the dollar values of the consumer and producer surplus in a market with perfect information (true demand).

(B) Now find the price, quantity, along with the **dollar values** of the consumer and producer surplus and the deadweight loss when the consumers are being fooled. See Figure 4.7 in the text for a view of the consumer and producer surplus for this type of problem.

5 Efficiency and the role of government

According to the system of natural liberty, the sovereign has only three duties to attend to ... first, the duty of protecting the society from the violence and invasion of other independent societies; secondly, the duty of protecting, so far as possible, every member of the society from the injustice or oppression of every other member of it, or the duty of establishing an exact administration of justice, and thirdly, the duty of erecting and maintaining certain public works and certain public institutions, which it can never be for the interest of any individual, or small number of individuals, to erect and maintain.[1]

(Adam Smith)

The primary goal of this chapter is to extend our analysis of market efficiency to include an analysis of the efficiency effects of government policy. For most economists, this issue starts with the minimum role for government most famously stated by Adam Smith in the quotation above. There is wide acceptance of Smith's principle that even in a world of very limited government there are a few essential societal functions that are best performed by the public sector. Government policies beyond these minimum functions may be justified by the efficiency losses from imperfect markets or the needs of the less fortunate based on equity concerns.

There are three steps to this analysis of government's role in promoting efficiency. The first step is to consider the effects of government intervention in **competitive markets** through taxes, subsidies, or regulation. These government policies in a competitive market tend to produce efficiency losses similar to those from private market imperfections. Secondly, government intervention in **imperfect markets** will be considered. If markets are imperfectly competitive, the government has the potential to counteract private efficiency losses and improve market efficiency. Thirdly, possible inefficiencies in the political and administrative processes of government will be discussed. These include the roles of interest groups, bureaucratic self-interest, and the enforcement of laws and regulations. Because of these procedural challenges, government may fail to provide the possible efficiency improvements predicted by economic theory.

The minimum role of government

Adam Smith's principle of **laissez-faire** states that government should allow private markets to operate with a free hand. However, Adam Smith allowed for three fundamental roles for government in a free-market economy. In simple terms, the fundamental roles of government include national defense, an impartial system of laws, and a set of public works and institutions.

While the concepts of *laissez-faire* and the three minimum roles of government offered by Adam Smith are extremely important, many current economists and policy analysts would argue that government involvement can be justified on other grounds as well. Some will support a degree of aid to the poor based on principles of distributive justice, as discussed in Chapter 2. Even if the discussion is limited to efficiency, however, properly designed government programs can improve the efficiency of a market if it violates one or more of the assumptions of perfect competition. If a market is monopolized by a single firm, then anti-trust laws or price regulations may improve that market's efficiency. If production leads to significant pollution, pollution control policies can improve the market's social net benefits. If information is imperfect, public-address announcements, product labeling requirements, truth in advertising laws, and subsidies for pure research may play a role in disseminating more complete and accurate information. These examples will be considered later in the chapter.

Taxes in competitive markets

Economic theory states that a perfectly competitive market maximizes net gains from exchange and as a result is Pareto optimal. Therefore, any divergence from the perfectly competitive outcome causes reduced gains from trade, or deadweight efficiency losses. In the previous chapter, examples were offered of the efficiency losses from private market imperfections such as monopoly, imperfect information, or externalities. Government involvement in perfectly competitive markets through taxes, subsidies, or regulations can create similar losses. Taxes tend to reduce production from its purely competitive level, thereby creating deadweight losses similar to those of monopoly. Subsidies tend to increase production beyond the private equilibrium, producing deadweight losses consistent with overproduction. Quotas, price floors, and price ceilings can all lead to underproduction when applied to a competitive market.

Before we begin this analysis we must add another group to our list of possible beneficiaries from a market. Like consumer surplus, producer surplus, and external surplus, government also may experience net benefits from intervening in a market. In the case of government, the benefits and costs are generally measured in a quite straightforward manner. Government benefits can be represented by tax revenue, while government costs arise from government spending. We will label the net benefits to government the **government surplus**.

> **Definition: Government Surplus (GS)** = government tax revenue − government spending.

> **Concept:** The net benefits in a market with externalities and government = Consumer Surplus (CS) + Producer Surplus (PS) + External Surplus (ES) + Government Surplus (GS)

In our simple examples government surplus (GS) will tend to be either entirely positive in the case of taxes or entirely negative in the case of government spending. For other types of government policies such as price regulation or quotas, we will ignore the costs of enforcement and assume that government surplus is zero.

Taxes on producers

Political debates over taxes sometimes include heated arguments over who should pay the tax. For example, the U.S. healthcare debate of 1992 included a dispute over whether employers or employees should pay for a required health insurance program. For economists, such debates are exaggerated because most of the costs of a tax to buyers and sellers do *not* depend on which party actually pays the government. An example will aid in understanding this assertion.

In Figure 5.1, the administration has proposed a tax on tobacco to be paid by the tobacco producers. In this case the tax can be interpreted in either of two ways. A tax of $1 on every pack of cigarettes would either lower the firm's revenue by $1 times the number of units or raise its costs by $1 times the number of units. There is no numerical difference between these interpretations. However, it is somewhat easier graphically to display tax payments as a reduction in revenue, so that the firm has a lower price after taxes but the same cost of production as before the tax. In this form the tax revenue appears as a rectangle rather than a parallelogram between two supply curves. The following example and its endnote will help explain this distinction.

Let's look more closely at Figure 5.1. Prior to imposing the tax, the equilibrium would be at price P_c and quantity Q_c. Consumer surplus equals areas A + B + C + D and producer surplus equals areas E + F + G + H + I. After the tax, the supply curve shifts vertically upward (a supply decrease) by the amount of the tax, forcing the quantity down to Q_2 and the price up to P_2. As a result the consumer surplus drops to area A only. After collecting total revenue of $P_2 \cdot Q_2$, the firm must pay the tax per unit times Q_2 to the government. As a result of this tax government surplus equals the rectangle B + C + E + F in Figure 5.1.[2] The producer surplus equals areas H+I, or the remaining revenue (after taxes) minus the cost of resources used in production. The total net benefits after the tax equal the sum of

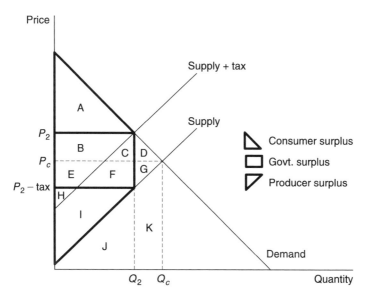

Figure 5.1 Tax on producers

the consumer, producer, and government surpluses, and the deadweight loss equals area D + G.

Taxes on consumers

Now assume that the National Tobacco Institute proposes that this tax be paid by consumers instead of producers in order to further decrease the harms of smoking. A tax on consumers will have the effect of shifting the *after-tax* demand curve downward by the amount of the tax. This example is seen in Figure 5.2. In this case the original demand curve represents the maximum willingness to pay for the good, as before. However, the price–quantity relationship shifts down because the consumer has to pay the tax in addition to the price. With this lower demand curve the equilibrium price and quantity move downward to P_2 and Q_2. Producers receive P_2 per pack, but the consumer pays P_2 **plus tax** for each pack.

Your Turn 5.1: Identify the consumer surplus, government surplus (tax revenue), and producer surplus for the consumption tax on Figure 5.2, along with the deadweight loss.

Given identical demand-and-supply curves, the net gains to all parties and the deadweight loss are identical whether the $1 tax is placed on producers or

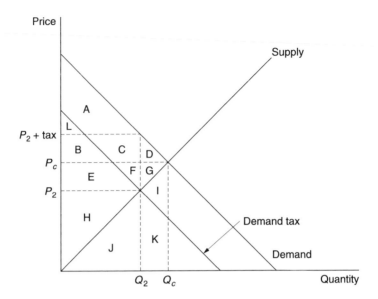

Figure 5.2 Tax on consumers

consumers. The market will redistribute some of the harms from those paying the tax to the other party through changes in price and quantity. In either case, consumer surplus and producer surplus are reduced, while a positive government surplus is created from the tax revenue. This conclusion is often misunderstood by legislators and the public.

Other forms of government involvement

While taxes are the most frequently discussed form of government involvement, other forms of government involvement also create inefficiencies, though the winners and losers may vary. Some examples of government policies include subsidies, maximum or minimum prices, and quotas. Each will be briefly explained.

Subsidies

A subsidy is in many respects the opposite of a tax. While taxes bring money from the market to the government, subsidies transfer money from the government to the private sector. Therefore, the government loses financially from a subsidy while others tend to gain. Figure 5.3 shows the effects of a constant per-unit subsidy. This subsidy is easiest to analyze if we consider it as a second source of revenue for producers in addition to the spending of consumers.[3] Assume that without the subsidy the equilibrium will be at P_1 and Q_1. The subsidy will shift the supply curve outward to **S + subsidy**, and move the equilibrium price and

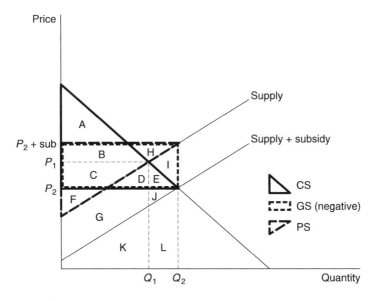

Figure 5.3 Producer subsidy

quantity to P_2 and Q_2. For each of the Q_2 units produced, consumers will pay the price P_2 and producers will receive P_2 plus the subsidy.

Subsidies are politically popular because they benefit both consumers and producers. Only the government suffers a net loss from the subsidy payments. In Figure 5.3, consumer surplus increases from triangle A + B to triangle A + B + C + D + E. Similarly, producer surplus rises from C + F to C + F + B + H. Because firms receive more for each unit than consumers are paying (another way in which subsidies and taxes are opposite), the producer and consumer surplus triangles overlap. Finally, since government is paying money to the private sector, the government surplus from a subsidy will be negative (recall that GS = revenue – spending). In Figure 5.3, GS equals the rectangle –B – C – D – E – H – I. Adding the three surpluses gives us the total net gains.

Net gains with subsidy = CS + PS + GS (GS has a negative value)
= (**A** + **B** + **C** + **D** + **E**) + (*C* + **F** + **B** + *H*)
+ (–*B* – *C* – *D* – *E* – *H* – **I**).

Canceling the letters in italics, net benefits equal A + B + C + F – I. Note that without the subsidy the total net gains from this market equal consumer surplus plus producer surplus, or A + B + C + F. The difference between the total net gains before and after the subsidy is the negative area I, the only part of the subsidy payment that does not increase consumer or producer surplus. Therefore, area I is the deadweight loss from the subsidy. It is a typical deadweight loss for a market that overproduces relative to the competitive equilibrium quantity.

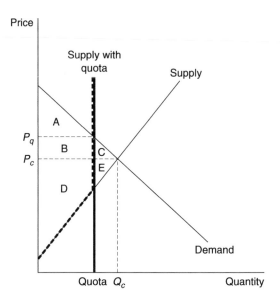

Figure 5.4 Quota

Quotas

A quota is a maximum allowable quantity of output. Quotas are sometimes used to restrict imported goods or to limit agricultural production in order to raise prices. Graphically, a quota appears as a vertical line that defines the maximum quantity, as shown in Figure 5.4. This has the effect of creating a vertical segment in the supply curve at the quota. In Figure 5.4 the quota reduces the quantity and increases the price to P_q. As a result consumer surplus is reduced from A + B + C to area A only. With the quota the producer surplus loses area E due to reduced production but gains area B from consumers due to higher prices. The net effect on producer surplus of these two changes is theoretically uncertain, but probably positive. Finally, a deadweight loss is created due to underproduction. The effects of a quota on the net gains from a market are basically the same as those of a monopoly.

Price floors and price ceilings

Other familiar examples of government-imposed maximum or minimum values relate to price rather than quantity. For example, a price ceiling sets a maximum legal price in a market. A fully enforced price ceiling will prevent equilibrium from occurring if the equilibrium price is above the maximum price. However, if the equilibrium price is below the price ceiling, the equilibrium will stand and the price ceiling will have no effect.

Examples of price ceilings include rent controls and the regulation of prices charged by electric utilities. In the case of a relatively competitive market like

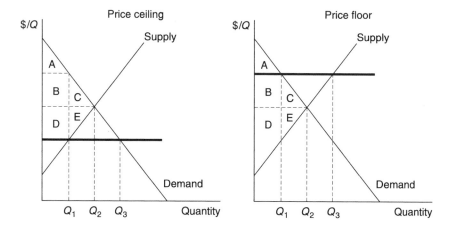

Figure 5.5 Price floors and ceilings

big-city real estate, price ceilings are generally criticized by economists. In some types of monopoly markets, such as public utilities, a well-designed price ceiling can improve efficiency. The public utility situation will be discussed later in the chapter. In a competitive market the direct effect of a price ceiling is to create a quantity shortage for the good. Since the amount actually bought and sold falls as a result of the price ceiling, the deadweight loss is typical of underproduction equilibrium. In Figure 5.5, the price ceiling produces a consumer surplus of A + B + D, a producer surplus of area F, and a deadweight loss equal to area C + E.

A price floor such as a minimum wage or agricultural price support will create a somewhat different set of effects. First, because the quantity supplied at the price floor is greater than the quantity demanded, excess supply is created. Like the price ceiling, the amount bought and sold with an effective price floor will equal the smaller of the two quantities, in this case the quantity demanded. In Figure 5.5, with a price floor in place only Q_1 will be purchased. Therefore, the consumer surplus equals area A, the producer surplus equals B + D, and the deadweight loss is equal to C + E. While the net benefits are distributed differently under price ceilings and price floors, the deadweight losses for both are consistent with an underproduction equilibrium.

A case study: agricultural subsidies

Agriculture is in most respects a highly competitive industry. There are many buyers and sellers, raw agricultural products are generally homogeneous, prices for grain and other commodities are highly flexible, and information about product quality and market conditions is widespread and accurate. However, agriculture is also risky, and farmers who might be driven out of business due to regional drought, low prices, or other causes could face significant costs while adjusting to a different livelihood. This cost of exiting the agriculture industry, a violation of the assumption of perfect mobility, is the primary market imperfection that might justify a modest degree of government intervention in the farming sector.

Another market imperfection which provided an important justification for early federal government intervention in the agriculture market is monopsony. A **monopsony** is a market with a single seller, while a monopoly is a market with one buyer. Like its definition, the effects of a monopsony are in some ways the opposite of a monopoly. Buyers pay a lower price and purchase a lower quantity than under competition, and sellers receive a lower level of producer surplus. The monopsony rationale is no longer widely discussed in the context of agriculture.

U.S. agriculture policy began in 1922 with the passage of the Capper–Volstead Act, which allowed the formation of agricultural cooperatives (cartels) and exempted them from anti-trust laws. However, federal policies that directly affected farmers' prices and income levels didn't begin until the New Deal. The Agricultural Adjustment Act of 1933 set price floors for major crops such as wheat. The Act also created a government loan program which used the farmers' crops as collateral, meaning that the farmer had the choice of repaying the loan or letting the government take the crops. This loan program had the effect of forcing the government to buy any surplus grain that existed at the price floor. In practice, the government could store this grain until the market demand rose, but another common outcome was that the grain would rot or be discarded.

The policy of maintaining a price target through government purchases is seen in Figure 5.6. In this case the price is set by the government at P_2. Since this price

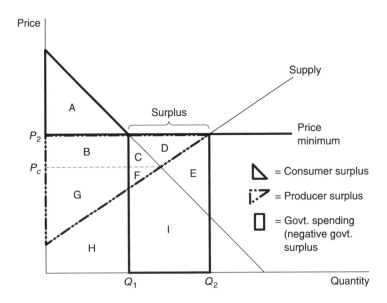

Figure 5.6 Price floor plus government purchase of surplus

is above the equilibrium, a quantity surplus will tend to exist. In Figure 5.6 the excess grain equals $Q_2 - Q_1$. In order to maintain this price the government must supplement consumer demand by buying the surplus, paying P_2 times $Q_2 - Q_1$ for that purchase. Since government spending produces a negative government surplus, the GS will equal $(-C - D - E - F - I)$. The consumer surplus is limited to area A by the higher price P_2. The farmers sell a total of Q_2 units to both parties combined at the price P_2 and attain a producer surplus equal to areas B + C + D + G + F. Adding the CS, PS, and GS together, the total net gains from trade are **A + B** + $C + D$ + **G** + $F - C - D - $**E**$ - F - $I. Canceling C, D, and F, one is left with net gains of A + B + G − E − I. This pattern differs considerably from the usual results of overproduction due to the extra government costs of buying and storing or discarding the excess grain.

The deadweight loss from this policy is also unusual, and must be viewed carefully. A **competitive equilibrium** at price P_c produces net gains from trade of A + B + C + G + F, with A + B + C equaling consumer surplus and G + F being the producer surplus. The deadweight loss from the government price support program equals, as always, the competitive net gains from the market minus the net gains under the price support program. This difference equals (A + B + C + G + F) − (A + B + G − E − I), or $A + B + $**C**$ + G + $**F**$ - A - B - G + $**E + I**. Canceling A, B, and G leaves us with a deadweight loss of C + F + E + I, which means that most of the government grain purchase ends up as pure waste. From the rectangle representing government purchases, only area D provides a transfer from the government to the landowner. The rest is deadweight loss.

Obviously this form of price support policy produces unusually high amounts of waste, both in terms of deadweight loss and the literal waste of crops. More recent policies have avoided the production of surplus grain either through the use of quotas or similar quantity restrictions (Figure 5.4), or through direct subsidies (Figure 5.3). With either of these two approaches the deadweight loss takes the usual triangular shape, and far less inefficiency occurs than with the original crop purchase program.

U.S. peanut policy

A relatively recent change in the U.S. government's method of supporting peanut farmers provides a direct comparison of the quota and subsidy approaches. Prior to 2002, a national quota of 1.5 million acres existed for peanut production. Permits to grow peanuts could be bought or sold, and non-agricultural owners of permits could rent the growing rights to farmers. This quota and permit system raised prices, as shown in Figure 5.4. U.S. prices were well above world levels under this policy. However, NAFTA (the North American Free Trade Agreement) led to an influx of peanuts from Canada and some imports from Mexico. This increase in imports drove prices down despite the quota on domestic production, and also substantially lowered the market value of the peanut permits. In response to pressure from growers and permit holders Congress passed a law that required the government to buy all outstanding peanut permits at a relatively high price and to introduce a direct subsidy program similar to that in Figure 5.3.

Your Turn 5.2: After reviewing Figures 5.4 and 5.3, identify whether consumers, producers, and government gain or lose as a result of this policy change from a quota to a subsidy.

In terms of inefficiency, agricultural quotas lead to underproduction while subsidies lead to overproduction. Either approach is far superior in terms of efficiency to the original policy of price supports and government purchases of excess grain. In Figure 5.7, the price support program produces a deadweight loss equal to the notched area outlined in the dashed line (C + E + F + I + L), which is far greater than the overproduction deadweight loss triangle of the subsidy (area E) or the underproduction deadweight loss produced by the quota (C + F).

Clearly the consumers are better off under the subsidy approach than either form of price support policy because the subsidy leads to a lower price and higher quantity than a competitive equilibrium. Producers will benefit equally from the price support and subsidy programs in Figure 5.7 since both programs produce revenue per unit of P_2 (under the direct subsidy P_2 equals P_1 plus the subsidy), and a total quantity of Q_2. Producer surplus is lower under the quota than either of the other choices due to the lower quantity produced. It is not obvious whether the government is better off under the price support or subsidy programs, since under the price support approach government pays for **all of the cost of part of**

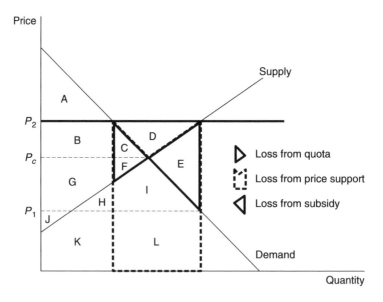

Figure 5.7 Deadweight losses for alternative agricultural policies

the grain (areas C + D + E + F + I + L) and under the direct subsidy approach it pays for **part of the cost of all of the grain** (B + C + D + E + G + F + H + I). Marketable production permits under a quota system cost the government little or nothing, and could actually produce revenue for the government during an initial sale.

However, all of these agricultural support policies introduce inefficiency, and are subject to criticism and occasional efforts at elimination. With the exception of crop insurance programs to control financial risk and agricultural extension services to provide information, most government agricultural support policies are inefficient, and efforts to reduce government spending in this area are likely to continue.

Government intervention in imperfect markets

The next step in our overview of the efficiency effects of government intervention involves analyzing the effects of public policy when markets are imperfect, as in the case of monopoly, externalities, or imperfect information. In each of these cases the deadweight loss produced by the original imperfection creates a window of opportunity for government to improve the efficiency of the market. A well-designed policy can do exactly that.

Pollution control

As an example let's consider a tax on a polluting industry. As noted in Chapter 4, pollution often acts as a negative externality that may harm members of society who are not direct participants in the market. If not controlled by some type of government intervention or other mechanism, a polluting industry will produce more than the ideal level of output for society and a deadweight loss from overproduction. Figure 5.8 shows the effects of overproduction in a market with pollution.

The goals of policy in such a market are: (1) reduce the gap between private and social costs by reducing the pollution and (2) reduce private production to the socially optimal level. In combination, these two goals imply that pollution control should involve imposing some cost burden on the polluting industry, most directly in the form of pollution control requirements, pollution taxes, or pollution permits that involve a cost to the polluter. This chapter presents the example of a tax on polluting firms. Other policy options are considered in Chapter 13.

Figure 5.9 shows the predicted effects of a fixed per-unit tax on producers in a market with external costs. The tax will increase producers' private marginal cost by the amount of the tax and shift the private supply curve upward to $MC_{private}$ + tax. Because taxes rather than higher private or social production costs cause the shift, there is no reason to shift the social marginal cost curve. As a result of the tax, the quantity will fall to Q_s, the socially optimal level. The consumer surplus will fall to area A because of the higher price, producer surplus will fall to areas K + L + M (the lowest solid triangle), external surplus,

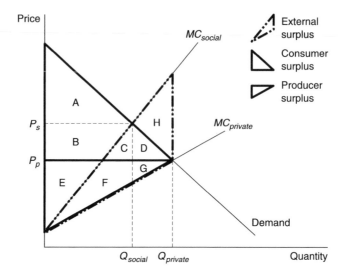

Figure 5.8 External costs

which is negative due to the harms of pollution, will fall to −(C + F + M) (the dashed triangle) and government surplus from tax revenue will equal the rectangle B + C + E + F. Combining all of the surpluses and canceling where possible, the net benefits from this market will be A + B + E + K, a Pareto-optimal result with no deadweight loss.

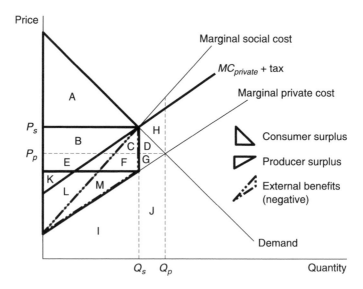

Figure 5.9 Tax on polluters

An extended example: a pollution tax with numbers

Toward the end of Chapter 4 supply and demand equations were used to compare the private and social equilibria in a market with external costs. To review, the equations were:

Marginal private cost = $10 + Q$

Marginal social cost = $10 + 1.5Q$

Demand $P = 100 - Q$

In this example the private equilibrium quantity was 45 units and the socially ideal quantity was 36 units. We also found that the private equilibrium produced total net gains of $1,518.75, while the socially ideal quantity produced total net gains of $1,620. The deadweight loss was the difference between the two net gains, or $101.25. This example will show that a tax on producers that raises producers' costs just enough to create an equality between demand and the private marginal cost curve at the socially ideal quantity will produce a Pareto-optimal result.

Step 1: Determining the tax

The goal of the pollution tax is to raise the producers' private marginal cost enough to reduce their quantity supplied to the socially optimal level. For this we must find the difference between the private and social marginal costs at the socially ideal quantity of 36.

$MC_{private} = 10 + 36 = \$46$

$MC_{social} = 10 + 1.5(36) = \$64$

The difference between the private and social marginal cost curves at Q_s ($64 − $46) gives us the ideal tax rate of $18.

Step 2: Finding the new equilibrium

With an $18 tax on producers, private supply rises to: $P = \$28 + Q$ (see Figure 5.10). The new equilibrium can be found by setting this supply equal to demand.

demand = *supply*

$100 - Q = 28 + Q$

$72 = 2Q$

$36 = Q$

$P = 28 + Q$

$P = 64$

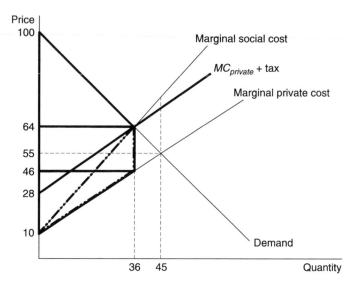

Figure 5.10 Tax on polluters with numbers

Step 3: Calculating net gains

The total net gains equal the sum of all the surpluses. The external surplus is more challenging than the others.

CS, PS, and GS

$$CS = \frac{1}{2} \times 36 \times (\$100 - 64) = \$648$$

$$GS \text{ (tax revenue)} = \$18 \times 36 = \$648$$

$$PS = \frac{1}{2} \times 36 \times (\$46 - \$10) = \$648$$

External surplus (ES) equals area C + F + M + I minus area I in Figure 5.9

$$\text{External surplus} = -[\frac{1}{2} \times 36 \times (64 - 10) - \frac{1}{2} \times 36 \times (45 - 10)] = -\$324.$$

Total net gains $= CS + PS + GS + ES$
$= \$648 + \$648 + \$648 - \$324 = \$1{,}620.$

Step 4: Measuring improved efficiency and other effects from the policy

Comparing this polluting market with the tax to the private equilibrium demonstrates several effects from this policy. Total net benefits have increased by $101.25, the socially ideal quantity has been produced, the deadweight loss has been eliminated, and the efficiency of the market has been maximized. However, winners and losers were created. Compared to the private equilibrium both consumers and producers are worse off, while government and those suffering the external costs are better off. Therefore, this policy meets the Kaldor–Hicks criterion for efficiency but can only achieve a Pareto improvement if consumers and producers are compensated for their losses.

Price caps and natural monopoly

Another example of government intervention that may improve efficiency is in the regulation of prices for natural monopolies. A **natural monopoly** exists when significant economies of scale cause the average total cost of production to decrease over most or all of the range of production for that industry, so that the minimum average total cost is less for a single firm than for any two or more firms. If a monopoly can produce its product at lower cost than multiple firms, creating competition in that industry would be at least partially counterproductive. For example, visualize a world in which a dozen telephone companies exist in your area, each of which has its own set of wires and poles. The private and external costs of these multiple networks could be very large.

On the other hand, allowing a single firm to monopolize the industry could lead to high prices and limited service, as displayed by the price and quantity P_m and Q_m in Figure 5.12. The goal of government policy when facing a natural monopoly is to impose a lower price and higher quantity than would exist with a private monopoly. Government may pursue this goal through price regulation or public ownership. In the case of electrical utilities, price regulation is the most common approach. In the case of transportation, public ownership is the most common solution, although regulated private ownership of bus and commuter rail systems also exists.

As noted earlier, a price cap on a competitive market is likely to produce shortages, reduced production, and deadweight losses. However, the effects of a well-placed

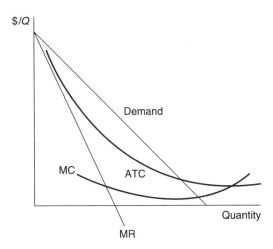

Figure 5.11 Natural monopoly

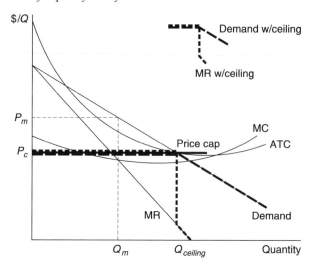

Figure 5.12 Natural monopoly with price ceiling

price ceiling on a monopoly are very different from those of a price ceiling in a competitive market. The most important aspect of a price ceiling placed on a monopoly is that the price ceiling limits the monopoly's ability to choose any price along its downward-sloping demand curve. Instead, the price cap replaces the part of the monopoly's demand curve above the cap with a flat segment (see Figure 5.12).

The effects of the price ceiling on a monopoly are not obvious, so some further explanation might help. Because the price cap prevents the firm from charging more than P_c, any quantity from zero to $Q_{ceiling}$ will bring a constant price and marginal revenue to the firm. Therefore, as long as the demand curve is above the price ceiling, the firm acts as though it is in a competitive market. Once the demand curve drops below the ceiling, however, the monopolist's original trade-off between price and quantity returns. The effect of the price ceiling on the monopoly's marginal revenue is a little more complicated, and is best explained with the help of your calculator.

Your Turn 5.3: Tables 5.1 and 5.2 allow you to see for yourself how a $6 price ceiling affects marginal revenue.

Table 5.1 No price ceiling

Price	10	9	8	7	6	5	4
Quantity	2	3	4	5	6	7	8
Total revenue							
Marginal revenue	xxx						

Table 5.2 Price ceiling at $6

Price	6	6	6	6	6	5	4
Quantity	2	3	4	5	6	7	8
Total revenue							
Marginal revenue	xxx						

Notice that where the price ceiling is in effect the demand becomes flat and the marginal revenue equals the price. However, once demand falls below the price ceiling the MR falls immediately to its original value. This occurs because once the price falls below the ceiling all units that could have been sold at $6 now bring only $5, re-establishing the original tradeoff between quantity and price for the monopoly.

Now the final step in the problem can be completed. The effect of the price ceiling on output requires finding the profit-maximizing quantity where marginal revenue (MR) equals marginal cost (MC). In Figure 5.12, with the price ceiling in place this equality between MR and MC occurs on the vertical portion of the MR curve. Therefore, the quantity produced by a profit-maximizing monopolist rises as a result of a well-placed price ceiling. This rise in output produces higher consumer surplus and lower or zero deadweight loss.

Price regulation is commonly applied to public utilities such as electricity or natural gas. In the U.S. all 50 states have agencies that regulate such utilities. One important question is where the price cap should be set by such agencies. In Figure 5.12 the price cap is set where demand crosses the average total cost curve. This is known as **average cost pricing** and is similar to the actual price cap policies used in states' regulation of utilities. Effective average cost pricing eliminates monopoly profits because economic profits are zero where price equals average total cost. However, average cost pricing does not necessarily produce a Pareto-optimal outcome.

A more efficient but less politically or technically feasible alternative is called marginal cost pricing. A **marginal cost pricing** strategy sets the price cap at the lowest point where the marginal cost curve crosses demand. Setting demand equal to the marginal cost of production is the basis for the Pareto-optimal outcome in a competitive market. As Figure 5.13 shows, marginal cost pricing produces a higher level of consumer surplus (areas A through E) than the average cost pricing method. Marginal cost pricing is Pareto optimal, while average cost pricing produces a deadweight loss of areas E + H.

However, marginal cost pricing also has political and technical problems. The most obvious problem with marginal cost pricing is that it creates the possibility of negative economic profits in the industry. In Figure 5.13 the marginal cost price is below the firm's average total cost, which means the firm will earn negative economic profits and will wish to leave the industry in the long run. In order to keep the monopoly in business while preserving the marginal cost price cap, the firm would have to be subsidized for its losses or allowed to engage in price

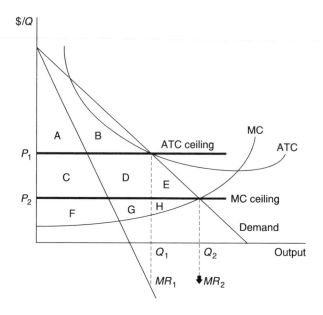

Figure 5.13 Marginal and average cost pricing

discrimination, both of which are likely to be politically unpopular. A technical problem with marginal cost pricing is that the marginal cost function for a complex firm is likely to be difficult to estimate and relatively easy for the monopoly to manipulate. Regulators without a background in economics or industrial engineering are likely to find the average cost calculation (total cost divided by output) much easier to understand.

The general conclusion of this section is that the intervention of government in an imperfectly competitive market has the potential to improve efficiency, and perhaps to eliminate any deadweight loss and achieve Pareto optimality. The theoretical possibility of improved efficiency through government intervention is not a guarantee that such intervention will be successful, however. The final section of this chapter will discuss several possible barriers to socially efficient public policy.

Public choice and government failure

The most common approach to analyzing the role of government in economics texts is to present evidence and argument about market imperfections, then to propose government intervention as a recommended solution to the problem. That is the usual approach of this book as well. However, there is an additional question that should be asked of this process: **Will government succeed in designing,**

implementing, and enforcing effective policy responses to market imperfections? According to some economists and others, the answer to that question is often likely to be no.

In economics, the analysis of government behavior is the primary subject of a field known as **public choice**. Public choice theory uses the concepts of self-interest and competition to analyze the behavior of voters, politicians, interest groups, and bureaucrats. According to most public choice economists, self-interested voters, politicians, and interest groups create multiple layers of problems that limit the ability of government to translate a society's preferences into effective policy. This critical analysis of government behavior is often labeled the "Virginia School" and began with the work of Buchanan and Tullock (1962). More positively, other public choice theorists argue that government policies tend to evolve into rational responses to market imperfections and injustice despite the pressures of interest groups, self-motivated politicians, or ineffective administrators. This positive economic view of government behavior is sometimes labeled the "**Chicago School**," and is represented in the work of Peltzman (1976) and Becker (1983). For a more thorough review of this literature, see Schugart and Razzolini (2001) or Mueller (2003).

The translation of the public will into public policy requires several steps, each of which can be subjected to criticism. These steps include identifying the public interest through voting or other methods, creating policy through the legislative process, and administering policy through a public bureaucracy. Each of these steps contains problems and challenges that are in some ways similar to those of imperfect markets. The goal of this section is to provide a brief overview of these challenges to the effective implementation of government policy.

A positive view of government behavior

A highly positive view of government behavior is sometimes labeled the **public interest theory of government**. This theory assumes that the goal of government is to improve or maximize the well-being of society. It further assumes that the desires and needs of the public, often referred to as the will of the people, can be determined through the democratic process, and that public policies are generally effective in promoting society's well-being. In this view, elected officials serve the interests of the general public in their legislative decisions, while laws and regulations are efficiently designed and effectively enforced. For example, a market with a negative externality such as pollution is likely to see its efficiency improved through a well-designed public policy such as a pollution tax. The public-interest theory of government is often adopted as an assumption in undergraduate microeconomics courses without much proof or careful observation.

Social welfare functions and collective decisions

The first step in designing policy that will improve society's well-being is to determine the needs and desires of the public. One theoretical tool and one political activity that attempt to measure public preferences will be discussed in this section. The first is the **social welfare function**, and the second is **voting**.

The social welfare function directly connects individual preferences and societal well-being. In general form, the social welfare function defines society's well-being as a function of the utility of its individual citizens. In equation form, the social welfare function is

$$SWF = f(U_1, U_2, \dots, U_N), \text{ where } U_1 \text{ is the utility of individual 1, etc.}$$

The social welfare function was introduced in Chapter 2 as part of our discussion of ethical theories. One inherent limitation in the social welfare function is that different ethical theories imply different forms for the social welfare function. For example, utilitarianism implies equal weights for each citizen's utility, while the Rawlsian difference principle implies that all weight should be given to society's least well-off person. However, even when the discussion is limited to the utilitarian social welfare function, this theoretical tool has limited applicability, primarily because any numerical value assigned to individual utility is arbitrary, and therefore cannot be added to others without additional unrealistic assumptions.

Arrow's impossibility theorem

In order for society to assess its preferences regarding a distribution of goods or a policy choice, it must be capable of adding individual preferences in order to determine the preferred outcome of society as a whole. However, economist Kenneth Arrow proved that under reasonable assumptions aggregating individual choices into an efficient collective choice is impossible. Arrow (1963) proposed the following criteria for an effective rule for collective decisions:

1   **The rule leads to a decision regardless of the form of voters' preferences.** People who prefer both extremes to a moderate position can interfere with the stable ranking of possible outcomes, and violate this rule.
2   **The rule can provide a societal ranking for all possible outcomes.**
3   **The rule must be consistent with individual preferences.** If everybody prefers one choice, society must also prefer that choice.
4   **The rule is transitive.** If society prefers choice A to choice B and choice B to choice C, then it must prefer choice A to choice C.
5   **Society's ranking of any two choices must be independent of other alternatives.**
6   **Dictatorship is not permitted.** The choice must be democratic, and no one person may determine public decisions.

Dr. Arrow then provided a formal proof of the proposition that it is impossible for a collective decision rule, including elections, to meet all six of these conditions. This proposition is known as **Arrow's impossibility theorem**. An important corollary to this theorem is called Arrow's paradox.

Arrow's paradox: The only collective choice mechanism that is always transitive and allows for consistent preferences over all choices is dictatorship (Munger 2001: 215).

It is obvious that dictatorship, or rule by one, is not a true collective decision process.

Arrow's paradox is not meant to support dictatorship, but to emphasize the limited consistency of collective decisions. The impossibility theorem implies that one cannot accurately combine individual preferences into a rule for determining social choices. This finding effectively rules out economic theory as a method of determining the collective will of the people. Therefore, indirect methods of measurement based on consumer and producer surplus offer the least problematic economic tools for estimating the tastes and desires of the public.

Voting

Voting for political candidates is our most familiar social choice mechanism. Unfortunately, voting for political candidates offers very limited information about public preferences toward specific policy issues. Individuals who favor some positions held by candidate A and some by candidate B will have a difficult decision under any "one person, one vote, one representative" system. Also, the intensity of one's preferences for a particular candidate or policy cannot be represented in a typical one person, one vote election. Intensity of preferences is part of one's individual tastes, and therefore would be considered in a fully efficient election process.

Another limitation of voting comes from the tendency of the dominant political parties in some nations to move to the center of the political spectrum. Despite the fervor of political partisans, there are reasons for candidates to move to the political center and minimize their differences. One model that demonstrates this tendency is the **median voter model**. This model states that elections will be determined by the preferences of the voter that has half of the voting public on each side of her preferences. For example, if the public was voting on an amount of funding for national defense, the voter who has preferences such that half of the population prefers a lower level of funding and half of the population prefers a higher level of funding will determine the outcome.

In a simple yes or no or two-party vote the outcome of the median voter model reduces to majority rule. However, if an election involves a range of preferences regarding an issue, the rule has deeper implications. Assume that a local election involves a set of candidates with different positions on taxes and school construction. Also assume that the public's preferences are distributed as shown in Table 5.3. In this table the median voter is among those who favor no spending increase.

Table 5.3 A distribution of spending preferences

Proposal	50% spending increase	20% spending increase	No spending increase	20% spending cut	50% spending cut
Number of voters (total = 10,000)	3,500	1,000	1,000	2,500	2,000

In a two-candidate election the candidate whose only goal is to get elected should favor no spending increase, because an opponent who takes any other position will not receive a majority. If candidate Jones favors a spending freeze and candidate Smith favors a 20 percent decrease, then the majority of voters who prefer either higher or fixed spending will favor Jones and he will be elected 5,500 to 4,500. Of course this also means that 9,000 of 10,000 will not have their preferences met, and that the most popular single choice (the 50 percent spending increase) will not be adopted.

Your Turn 5.4: Using the information in Table 5.3, assume that each candidate begins the race by favoring the extreme policies. For example, assume that Smith supports a 50 percent decrease and Jones a 50 percent increase. As Ms. Smith's chief political strategist, tell her why she should consider modifying her position. Also, predict what candidate Jones is likely to do.

The median voter model also implies that if individual voters are self-interested and not concerned with distributive justice, an incentive exists for elected officials to transfer income or other public benefits from the rich and poor to those near the median level of income (Stigler 1970). For all of the reasons discussed above, and several others, voting is an imperfect measure of the public will.

Interest groups and rent seeking

Interest group theories explore the influence of groups such as corporations, industry associations, environmental organizations, or labor unions on government decisions. The economics of political influence began with the work of Gordon Tullock (1967). The primary theoretical concept in Tullock's work is known as rent-seeking behavior. In a political context, **rent seeking** takes place when an organization uses political donations, public relations, or lobbying efforts to gather benefits from government. For a firm or industry, rent-seeking activity is rational if the net benefits of governmental activity outweigh the net benefits of investment in productive activity.

A political-interest group organizes membership through persuasion or offers of services, and then uses members' contributions to pursue political activities. The economist most associated with analyzing the formation of interest groups is Mancur Olson (1965), who suggested that interest groups raise funds and membership partly by offering products and services to members aside from their lobbying and other political activities. For example, the American Association of Retired Persons (http://www.aarp.org/) attains a large membership partly by offering a newsletter, organized vacations, group insurance programs, and member discounts. The American Rifle Association (http://www.nra.org/) also offers such services, as do many or most other organizations that rely on mass membership and dues as their primary sources of power. Rent seeking is considered inefficient in part because it wastes potentially productive resources and also because it biases public policy away from the general well-being of society.

Administration

The administration of public policy is an important but often ignored part of polit-ical debate and policy analysis. Passing a well-written and equitable law means little if that law is not adequately enforced or is repealed with the next shift in the political landscape. The administration and enforcement of laws and programs are the duties of the government's bureaucracy, and it too has been subject to some effective criticisms.

Critical models of administrative or bureaucratic behavior are commonly based on the self-interest of bureaucratic employees and effect of market imperfections such as imperfect information on the effectiveness of administrators. The produc-tivity of a self-interested bureaucrat may be affected negatively by the fact that she usually does not share financially in any cost savings, production increases, or revenue gains she produces for government. One important model of bureaucracy hypothesizes that the goal of the bureaucrat is to maximize her agency's **discre-tionary budget**, which is the difference between total revenue and the minimum cost of producing the agency's expected output. This goal is much like profit maximization, and in the absence of active oversight by legislators and the public or effective competition among different agencies, these bureaucratic monopoly profits are likely to be positive. This means that, like other monopolies, govern-ment services are likely to be too small in scale and too expensive relative to the efficient ideal.

Government regulation of industry is also subject to potentially significant inefficiencies due to pressure on or partial control of regulating agencies by the regulated industries themselves. The most well-known theoretical explanation for this possibility is known as "**capture theory**" (Stigler 1971). According to this theory, regulated businesses can control the setting of prices or enforcement of rules by rewarding the regulator for actions favorable to the firms or by controlling information about costs in a way that leads to favorable judgments. However, oversight by the public and the legislature provides a possible controlling mechanism for interest group power. Regardless of the degree of pressure group influence on regulators, a policy analyst should not presume that regulatory policies will be effective without careful consideration of the role of public and legislative oversight in the regulatory process.

Enforcement

The enforcement of government policies such as the minimum wage, health and safety regulations, anti-discrimination laws, or income tax payments is crucial to effective government policy, yet enforcement is often overlooked in political discussions and policy debates. A regulation can be enforced most effectively if the public can easily observe and understand the regulation and has an adequate incentive to follow it. The incentive to follow a regulation is usually financial. The role of financial punishment in law enforcement can be viewed through a relatively simple concept known as the **expected fine**. The expected fine equals the odds of being found guilty of a violation times the fine if convicted. In symbols,

---

$EF = \pi \bullet F$; where EF is expected fine, π (the Greek letter pi) is the probability of being convicted and F is the fine if convicted.

If the fine or the odds of being convicted are very low, the expected fine will also be low, and the incentive to follow the regulation or law will be small. For example, speed limits are regulations that are extremely easy to understand but difficult to enforce. Fines for speeding can be fairly high, especially for repeat offenders, but the probability of being caught is often very low. If this is true, the expected fine is likely to provide an inadequate disincentive for most people to follow a highway speed limit.

Industrial safety enforcement

More complex examples can be found in the enforcement policies of the Occupational Safety and Health Administration (OSHA), Equal Employment Opportunity Commission, or other agencies assigned to enforce government regulations. For example, the OSHA, founded in 1970, has proven to be relatively lax in terms of the number and effectiveness of its inspections and penalties, but according to most studies has also accounted for a statistically significant improvement in the safety record of U.S. industry over the past 35 years.

Early evidence regarding the OSHA's enforcement is provided by Viscusi (1983). As of 1980 the OSHA conducted 63,400 inspections nationwide in all industries. The average firm had about 0.019 inspections per year (1 in 50), including follow-ups. The number of violations per firm averaged about 2.1. The average fine per violation was $193 per violation and $403 per inspected firm.

Your Turn 5.5: Using the expected fine formula, if the average firm has a 0.02 chance of being inspected and faces a $400 average fine, what is the average expected fine? (Hint: You probably have more in your wallet.)

Viscusi was highly critical of OSHA's early efforts, partly because of its thousands of detailed regulations, partly because of its inadequate enforcement effort, and partly because of its early failure to concentrate on the most harmful health and safety issues or on serious violators. Weil's more recent study of OSHA's effect on construction safety produces somewhat similar odds of an inspection per construction site, but still concludes that OSHA has been somewhat effective in reducing construction accidents (Weil 2001). The broader lesson from this example is that the issue of enforcement should not be ignored when passing a new regulatory policy.

The primary lesson of this section is that there are several steps involved in the journey from the public will to an effective policy response. In spite of the many pitfalls in this journey, some influential economists with otherwise conservative reputations argue that government policy can reasonably approximate efficiency. Others clearly disagree.

Conclusion

The main goal of this chapter is to review the economic rationale for the role of government in an economy. Even under Adam Smith's concept of *laissez-faire,* government has the responsibility for maintaining a system of national defense, an impartial system of justice, and some level of infrastructure or public goods production. Beyond that minimum, market imperfections create an efficiency-based justification for the expansion of government policy into such areas as price regulation and pollution control.

However, these arguments are balanced somewhat by noting that in otherwise competitive markets government policy will reduce efficiency. Only when markets are inefficient does a window of opportunity exist for improved efficiency through public policy. Ethical reasons for government policy also exist, of course, as discussed in Chapter 2, and many of these are not fundamentally affected by the efficiency of the market. Finally, the possibility of inefficiency in voting results, legislative decisions, and the administration of policy should be considered when weighing the wisdom of government intervention.

Mathematically, this chapter provided further examples of the market-based mathematical topics introduced in Chapters 3 and 4. In this chapter the positive and negative effects of government policy on market efficiency were emphasized, but the basic mathematics of efficiency was used in much the same way as in earlier chapters. In the next section of the text the tools of benefit–cost analysis are introduced and applied. The concepts of net benefits and efficiency introduced in the last few chapters will be important in interpreting these new concepts.

Review questions

Conceptual questions

1. Adam Smith believed in the idea of *laissez-faire* government. How would your city or town be different if the government limited its activities to those allowed under *laissez-faire,* but your national government did not?

2. One problem related to public goods is the "free-rider" scenario. List three examples of free riders within your own community, class, family, or friends. In each case, what is the cause, and what (if anything) is the harm caused to you?

3. The last two chapters have included discussions of market failure and government failure. Review examples of each type of inefficiency. Given your particular political preferences, do you think that the public sector or private sector is the more significant impediment to efficiency? Why? Do you favor more or less government regulation of the private sector than currently exists in your nation? Why?

4. Why do economists believe the burdens of a sales tax on consumers to be the equal to those of a tax imposed on the producer, all else equal? Why might either side (consumers or producers) want the tax to be paid by the other?

5. What is Arrow's paradox? Debate the proposition, which is not Arrow's point, that dictatorship is a more efficient form of government than democracy. Consider the basic point of the Chicago School and public-interest approach in your answer.

Computational problems

6. On the graph, identify the lettered sections that correspond to each of the following terms after imposing a tax:

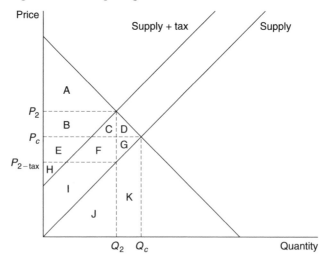

(A) Consumer surplus: _____
(B) Producer surplus: _____
(C) Government surplus: _____
(D) Deadweight loss: _____
(E) The tax rate per unit: _____

7. The graph displays the effects of a basic subsidy. Identify the lettered sections of the graph that correspond to the following:

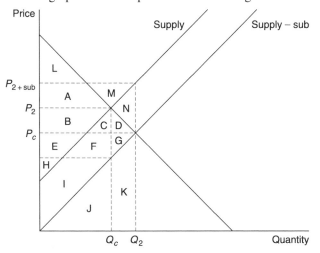

(A) Producer surplus: _____
(B) Consumer surplus: _____
(C) Government surplus: _____
(D) Deadweight loss: _____

8. Based on the graph above, are buyers or sellers receiving the subsidy directly? Compared to the original equilibrium (supply equals demand) are consumers better or worse off? Why?

9. Let's consider the welfare effects of agricultural support programs using a numerical example. Assume that the government is considering three general types of subsidies: (1) a price floor plus the government purchase of all surplus grain, (2) a price floor plus government payments to farmers to grow nothing, and (3) direct government subsidy payments to farmers. Assume that the **demand** curve is $P_d = 10 - Q_d$, the **supply** curve is $P_s = 2 + Q_s$, the price floor is at $7, and the direct subsidy is $2 per bushel.

    (A) Identify by letters in the Price floor graph on the following page the consumer surplus, producer surplus, government surplus, and total net gains for the competitive equilibrium and price floor programs (1) and (2) listed in this question (hint: they have very different deadweight losses). Do the same for the subsidy program in the Direct producer subsidy graph also on the following page.

(B)   Based on the equations above, find the equilibrium price and quantity, then the dollar values of the consumer surplus, producer surplus, and net gains for this market without government intervention.

(C)   Find the dollar values of the consumer surplus, producer surplus, and (negative) government surplus for all three programs. Find the key points in each graph first. What is the dollar value of the deadweight loss, compared to the net gains in part A, for each type of subsidy?

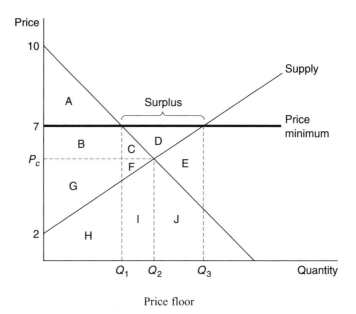

Price floor

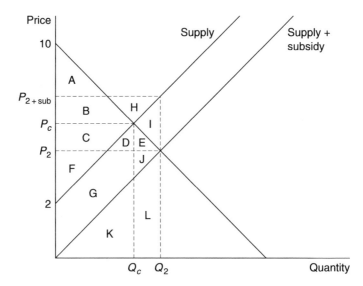

Direct producer subsidy

10. This question continues the externalities problem introduced at the end of Chapter 4. To review, the following graph represents a market with external costs. Assume that this graph can be summarized in the following equations:

Marginal private cost $= 10 + Q$

Marginal social cost $= 10 + 1.2Q$

Demand: $\quad\quad P = 120 - Q$

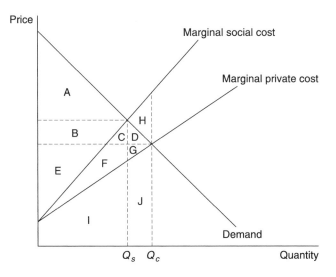

A market with external costs

(A) Find the price and quantity for a private equilibrium. Then find the dollar values of the consumer surplus (CS), external surplus (ES), and producer surplus (PS) for the private equilibrium using these equations. Be careful, external surplus will be tricky and indirect.

(B) The optimal pollution tax will add enough to the polluters' private costs to produce the ideal level of Q_s units of output from profit-maximizing firms. (1) Find the socially optimal quantity Q_s using the equations, then find the difference between the private and social cost at Q_s. This will equal the optimal per-unit tax. (2) Impose this per-unit tax on the private sector. This action will shift the private marginal cost curve up by the amount of the tax. What will the private equilibrium price and quantity be now? At this new price and quantity, find the numerical values for the CS, PS, Ex.S., and government surplus (GS).

(C) Find the total net gains from the private and social equilibria in parts A and B. How has taxing the polluting market affected the market's overall efficiency? To check your answer, find the area of the deadweight loss for the private equilibrium (area H). How does this compare to the net gains from the pollution tax?

11. In 2004 the European Economic Community agreed to phase out tobacco subsidies. Let's assume that the current subsidy is $20 per ton and that the original demand-and-supply equations (including the subsidy) are:

  Demand: $P = 200 - 1/10Q$

  Supply (S_2): $P = 1/10Q$

  (A) Find the equilibrium price and quantity for consumers with the subsidy, the current total amount of the subsidy from government, and the consumer, producer, and government surpluses in dollars. A sketch is recommended.

  (B) Now find the equilibrium price and quantity **without** the producer subsidy. Then find the consumer and producer and government surpluses when no subsidy is paid.

  (C) Calculate the total net gains to all parties in A and B. In which case was there a deadweight loss, and how large was it? Is this policy change a good one, in your view? Is the final result efficient, or are additional policy steps required in order to achieve efficiency? Briefly explain.

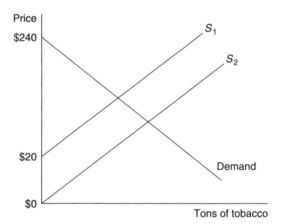

European tobacco

Part III

Tools for analyzing public policy

The cornerstone of policy analysis is the benefit–cost study. Benefit–cost analysis involves measuring and weighing the benefit and costs of any public policy, and recommending that policy if its benefits minus costs are greater than those of other alternatives. A full benefit–cost analysis requires that all benefits and costs be measured using a common scale such as dollar value. Chapter 6 introduces the benefit–cost model and applies the model to several different decision contexts. Alternative models and additional examples are also introduced. Chapter 7 presents the concept of present value, an important component of any policy analysis involving long periods of time. Chapter 8 summarizes the theoretical challenges underlying the choice of a discount rate. Chapter 9 introduces the concepts of risk and uncertainty to the analysis of public policy and private decisions, while Chapter 10 discusses the estimation of dollar values for non-marketed goods, including the controversial dollar value of human life. Finally, Chapter 11 introduces economic impact analysis. This controversial approach is used primarily by advocates of particular institutions or development projects for political purposes. The chapter presents an increasingly sophisticated set of economic impact models and case studies without endorsing the common uses of this concept.

6 An introduction to benefit–cost analysis

Information is a source of learning. But unless it is organized, processed, and available to the right people in a format for decision making, it is a burden, not a benefit.[1]

(William Pollard)

The Freedom of Information Act is the Taj Mahal of the Doctrine of Unanticipated Consequences, the Sistine Chapel of Cost–Benefit Analysis Ignored.[2]
(Antonin Scalia, Associate Justice, U.S. Supreme Court)

Benefit–cost analysis is a useful tool for organizing, measuring, and weighing the net benefits of alternative policy options. The primary goal of this analysis is to identify the policy option with the greatest social net benefit, and therefore the greatest efficiency. Benefit–cost analysis is the cornerstone of the economic analysis of policy, and is also closely aligned with the rational choice model from microeconomics. As such, benefit–cost analysis is subject to virtually all of the criticisms discussed in Chapter 1, including possible overemphasis on efficiency versus equity, rational pragmatism versus values, and markets versus government. It is also subject to criticism regarding its attempts to assign dollar values to socially valued goods that are not bought and sold in the marketplace, particularly human life and the assets of nature. This criticism is based partly on the difficulty of assigning such dollar values, and partly on the morally questionable nature of such valuation.

This chapter introduces the process and decision rules for benefit–cost analysis. It also introduces cost-effectiveness analysis, a decision model that can be useful when a full comparison of dollar-valued benefits and costs is not possible or not desirable. Finally, the chapter presents a related model labeled weighted benefit–cost analysis, which allows the analyst to assign different values to different affected groups, One application of these weights involves assigning higher values to the net benefits of the poor.

The process of benefit–cost analysis

The first chapter presented an outline of the policy analysis process. Reviewing this list may be useful before beginning the main topics of this chapter. Bardach's eight-step process includes the following: (1) define the problem, (2) assemble evidence, (3) select criteria for making the decision, (4) identify the policy alternatives to be considered, (5) predict the outcome of each alternative, (6) confront the tradeoffs, (7) make recommendations, and (8) tell your story. The primary focus of this chapter is on steps 3 through 7, but a brief review of the process of defining and quantifying a policy problem may also be useful.

Identifying the goals of the policy

Identifying policy goals generally involves two steps, one of which is often implicit. The first step is to identify the values and standards by which the policy is to be judged. For example, the values identified in the introductory chapter are efficiency, equity, and political practicality. Adherence to social norms can also be an important policy goal. The primary role of economic analysis is to evaluate efficiency, but knowledge of other core values is also important. Explicitly listing the values that define the goals of a proposed policy is a good first step in analyzing its probable success, although this step is often bypassed.

   The second step in establishing policy goals is to define and quantify the problem that is being addressed. In any type of policy analysis it is important to clearly define the nature of the economic or social problem to be addressed and any corresponding inadequacy in current policy. Any convincing policy analysis should have clear and detailed answers to a seemingly simple set of questions: **What is the problem? How serious is the problem? Where does the problem occur? What are the causes of the problem?** As simple as these questions sound, public officials and others are often quite unprepared to answer them. Moreover, advocates on either side of a hot political issue are likely to produce one-sided cases for their position based on selected evidence or biased interpretations. In rising above partisan argument, it is important that an analyst answers each of these questions in a balanced and thorough manner.

Assembling evidence

Various types of supporting evidence are needed to quantify and explain the problem and to aid in the formulation of policy alternatives. Defining a problem involves defining concepts used in the analysis and critically analyzing statistics and other evidence used to quantify the problem. However, even official government statistics are subject to arbitrary definitions and possible measurement errors. Examples of legitimately controversial government statistics include measurements of poverty, unemployment, and inflation. Some of these statistical problems will be discussed in later chapters. Others were discussed in Chapter 1.

   Identifying the seriousness of the problem involves quantifying both the number of people affected by the problem and the intensity of harm suffered by those people. Some problems such as violating speed limits are very widespread but on average not very harmful. On the other hand, some problems such as homelessness, airline fatalities, or childhood cancer are comparatively rare but are very serious for their victims. Estimating the frequency of a given problem usually requires broadly based statistics. For national problems the federal government is usually the first place to search for statistical data. One very useful on-line source for federal statistics from any department is http://www.fedstats.gov. Statistical data can also be produced by state and local governments as well as major private and public universities or research institutes.

Policy alternatives and decision criteria

The third and fourth steps in the policy analysis process are to identify alternative policy designs and to determine the criteria for choosing among these alternatives. Policy alternatives may be as general as pollution regulations versus pollution taxes, or as specific as alternative designs for a single highway interchange or sports stadium. In some cases only one alterative is considered in the analysis, and in others several alternatives may be analyzed.

The decision rules used to analyze policy alternatives depend to some degree on the problem being addressed. The most common rule for analyzing policy alternatives is the **Kaldor–Hicks criterion** or **fundamental rule of policy analysis** discussed in Chapter 4. This rule leads the analyst to rank projects according to their total net benefits, or total benefits minus total costs. However, several alternatives to this rule may be appropriate in certain circumstances. There are alternative mathematical formulas for comparing benefits and costs, such as the benefit–cost ratio, which are sometimes more easily understood by the public. In some policy areas, such as health and safety policy, a direct comparison of the dollar value of benefits and costs is particularly controversial. In such cases policy analysis models such as cost-effectiveness analysis, which does not rely on a dollar value for lives saved, are sometimes used. Finally, when analyzing policies for which the distribution of income or other net benefits is important, relying on ethical criteria or assigning higher weights to the net benefits of the poor may be appropriate. These alternative decision models will be discussed in this chapter.

Decision criteria for benefit–cost analysis

As noted above, most benefit–cost analysis is based on the Kaldor–Hicks criterion introduced in Chapter 4. To review, the definition is repeated below.

> **Definition: The Kaldor–Hicks principle** states that a policy should be adopted if the winners could *in principle* compensate the losers, which requires that the total benefits outweigh the total costs.

It is possible to compare the benefits and costs of a policy using at least three different formulas. The most common of these comparative formulas are **net benefits,** the **benefit/cost ratio,** and the **rate of return.** These three concepts are defined below.

Definitions:
- **Net Benefits** = Total Benefits – Total Costs
- **Benefit/Cost Ratio** = Total Benefits/Total Costs
- **Percentage Rate of Return** = 100% • (Total Benefits–Total Costs)/ Total Costs

---

In some situations these measurements are consistent, but in others they can produce different rankings for alternative projects. In cases where these measurements are not consistent, a clear preference exists in economics about which form of measurement is the most reliable. **Net benefits,** or total benefits minus total costs, provide the most reliable measure of the overall value of a given project.

Your Turn 6.1: One design for a new windmill-based electricity complex costs $9 million to construct, will produce $15 million worth of power, and will lead to $2 million in operating and maintenance costs. A second design will cost $6 million to construct, produce $10 million worth of power, and lead to $2 million in operating and maintenance costs. Find the net benefits, benefit/cost ratio, and percentage rate of return on each of these two projects.

Project 1: Net Benefits = _____ Benefit/Cost Ratio = _____ Rate of Return_____

Project 2: Net Benefits = _____ Benefit/Cost Ratio = _____ Rate of Return_____

If you can only recommend one choice, which option is best according to each measure?

Every policy analysis text, including this one, recommends the net benefit measure over the benefit–cost ratio. The primary reason for this preference is that net benefits are more consistent with the Kaldor–Hicks criterion. Net benefits directly measure the total net gain for society whether or not losers are compensated. There are also technical problems with the benefit/cost ratio and rate of return measures. The benefit/cost ratio and rate of return are sensitive to how one categorizes operating expenses. One can include them as part of the total cost, making the total revenue for the windmill project $15 million and the total costs $11 million. One may also define benefits as net operating revenue, or total revenue minus operating costs. Under this interpretation the benefits of the windmills would equal $13 million and the total costs $9 million. Both interpretations of operating costs produce net benefits of $4 million, but they produce different results for the benefit/cost ratio and rate of return.

> **Your Turn 6.2:** If you included operating costs as part of your total cost calculation for Project 2 above, now calculate net operating revenue by subtracting operating costs from revenue, then calculate the net benefits, benefit/cost ratio, and rate of return using net operating revenue versus total construction costs. Similarly, if you calculated net operating revenue and then subtracted construction costs, try it the other way. You will see that the net benefit total is not affected by the change.

Types of policy decisions

Benefit–cost analysis is interpreted somewhat differently for different types of decisions. Among the types of policy decisions an analyst may be required to investigate are the following:

1 **Should a single program be accepted or rejected?**
2 **Which one, at most, of a set of alternatives should be approved?**
3 **What is the optimal size of a budget covering multiple projects?**
4 **Which one or more projects should be approved within a fixed budget?**
5 **What is the ideal scale or scope of a particular project?**

Each decision will be considered below.

Accepting or rejecting a single project

This situation has two variants, accepting or rejecting one project or separately considering each of a series of projects. The decision rule in this case is very simple. Approve the project if the net benefits are greater than zero, so that society experiences a net gain in well-being. If total benefits are greater than total costs, then the benefit/cost ratio will be greater than one and the rate of return will be greater than zero. All these outcomes will lead the analyst to recommend approval of the program.

> **Your Turn 6.3:** Would you recommend building wind farm Project 1 above? Why or why not?

Choosing one of several possible projects

The second type of decision requires the analyst to choose at most one project among multiple alternatives. This type of situation occurs when determining the best use of a plot of land, or a particular choice among competing designs for a building or highway project. Assuming that all relevant costs including opportunity costs are included, the ideal choice in this simple case is to find the policy that will provide the most net benefits to society.

Your Turn 6.4: Assume that a particular plot of land could be developed as residential housing, an industrial park, or a factory outlet mall. Also assume there is a passable road adjoining the property, and that the property is about half a mile from a major highway. Only one alternative at most can ultimately be approved. Rank these choices in terms of their net benefits, and choose the one that places first. Then calculate the benefit/cost ratio and rate of return for each alternative. Note that the benefit/cost ratios for the industrial park and the outlet mall are not consistent with the net benefit ranking.

Table 6.1 Real estate alternatives

	Housing	*Industrial park*	*Outlet mall*	*Vacant lot*
Benefits	$1,000,000	$1,250,000	$1,600,000	$1,000
Costs	$1,100,000	$900,000	$1,200,000	$1,000
Net benefits				
B/C ratio				
Rate of return				

Choosing an optimal budget

Maximizing the well-being of society through policy involves approving all projects with positive net benefits for society as a whole.

Concept: An optimal budget is one that maximizes possible net gains to society as a whole. Therefore an optimal budget will fund all projects with positive net benefits for society.

In practice, funding constraints are often present at any level of government, so this goal is often politically difficult to achieve. It is also important to include a full accounting of opportunity costs when proposing funding of a set of projects or programs, a step which is often impossible. Finally, while this decision rule sounds like an argument for big government, it is quite likely that in some cases government exceeds its optimal budget as defined by this rule.

> **Your Turn 6.5:** What is the optimal budget for the set of projects in Table 6.1?

Choosing which one or more projects to fund given a fixed total budget

If a person runs a charitable institution that funds health research or a transportation agency that allocates a fixed budget for highway repairs, she will face this kind of decision on a regular basis. The goal of this decision rule is to maximize the possible net benefits of a fixed budget. The method for making this choice involves the following steps:

1 Calculate the benefit/cost ratio for each choice. Immediately reject any project which does not have a benefit/cost ratio greater than one.
2 Rank the projects according to their benefit/cost ratio.
3 Choose the highest benefit/cost ratio, then the next highest, and so forth until you cannot go further without breaking your budget.
4 If you must skip one or more projects due to budget considerations, choose the remaining programs with the highest benefit/cost ratios that fit into the budget.

> **Your Turn 6.6:**
> (A) Assume that you have plenty of available land but only $3 million to spend. Following the four steps above, choose the projects from the following table that should be approved within the $3 million budget. Then verify that these projects provide the greatest total net benefits.
> (B) Now assume that your budget has not been determined. Calculate the optimal budget for land development.

Table 6.2 Project choices given a budget

	Housing	Industrial park	Outlet mall	Golf course	Power plant	Vacant lot
Benefits	$1,000,000	$1,250,000	$1,600,000	$1,500,000	$4,200,000	$1,000
Costs	$1,100,000	$900,000	$1,200,000	$900,000	$3,000,000	$1,000
B/C ratio						
Net benefits						

Choosing the ideal scale of a project

A common question associated with many different types of policies is how large the policy or project should be. For social policies such as housing assistance or a job training program, the program's scale determines the number of dollars spent and the number of people served. For an infrastructure project, the physical size as well as the cost of the project may be an issue. For example, the number of lanes in a new road is very much an issue of scale.

The theoretical basis for determining the ideal scale for a single project is fairly basic. One calculates the marginal benefits and marginal costs of the project, and stops expanding when marginal benefits equal the marginal costs. We used the same story when discussing the basic decision of the rational consumer in Chapter 3. The optimal scale for a single project is pictured in Figure 6.1.

Another common administrative decision involves how much funding should go to various programs within a given department or program. The basic efficiency question involved in this relatively difficult decision is how one should allocate resources among the programs so as to maximize the net benefits of the entire budget of the department. Examples of this allocation issue abound. When a police department decides how many patrol officers to allocate to each neighborhood, or a transportation authority decides which highway construction projects to fund within their annual budget, the efficient allocation of funds should be considered. Of course, political factors are also likely to be involved in such decisions.

The analysis of this issue of allocation involves several steps, displayed graphically in Figure 6.2. First one needs to calculate the marginal benefits of each project for various quantities. One then adds the marginal benefit curves horizontally to find the marginal benefits of the total budget. This involves adding the quantities for each range of marginal benefits. One then finds the quantity where

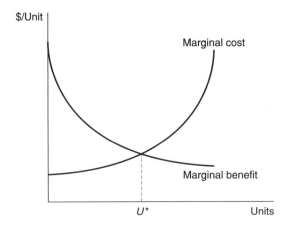

Figure 6.1 Optimal scale for one project

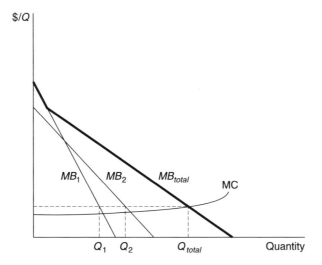

Figure 6.2 Allocating resources between two related programs

the sum of the individual marginal benefits meets the marginal cost (Q_{total}), as well as the value of the marginal benefit or marginal cost at this quantity. The final step is to set the marginal benefits of each program equal to this total marginal cost value and determine the quantity for each program associated with that marginal cost value. Finding the quantity for each program at which the marginal benefits of that program equal the overall marginal cost at Q_{total} gives you the efficient allocation of resources within your department. An example may be needed at this point.

Example: A new water system is being considered for Dry Gulch. The primary policy issue to be considered is how much water should be allocated to residential users and how much should go to commercial users. A previous analyst has estimated marginal benefit curves for residential and commercial users, along with a marginal cost curve.

Residential marginal benefits:	$MB_R = 1,400 - Q_R$ or $Q_R = 1,400 - MB_R$
Commercial marginal benefits:	$MB_C = 2,000 - \frac{1}{2}Q_C$ or $Q_C = 4,000 - 2MB_C$
Marginal Cost:	MC equals $\frac{1}{6}Q$

- **Step 1:** Add the marginal benefit curves horizontally to determine the total marginal benefit curve. This involves adding the quantities, then solving for the total marginal benefits. The resulting endpoint will be inaccurate because it includes negative quantities for the lower MB curve. However, as long as the dollar value of MB_{total} (see step 2) is less than all individual endpoints, no inaccuracy will occur in the calculations.

$Q_{total} = Q_R + Q_C = 1,400 - MB_R + 4,000 - 2MB_C = 5,400 - 3MB_{total}$
If $Q_{total} = 5,400 - 3MB_{total}$, then $MB_{total} = 1,800 - \frac{1}{3}Q_{total}$

- **Step 2:** After solving these sums for marginal benefits, set the total marginal benefit curve equal to marginal cost to determine the ideal total output to produce and the marginal cost at that quantity.

$$MB_{total} = MC$$
$$1,800 - \frac{1}{3}Q \quad = \frac{1}{6}Q$$
$$1,800 \quad = \frac{1}{2}Q$$
$$3,600 \quad = Q_{total}$$
$$MC_{total} \quad = \frac{1}{6}Q_{total} = \$600$$

- **Step 3:** Set each group's marginal benefit curve equal to the dollar value of the last unit's marginal cost ($600) to determine the quantity that should go to that group.

    Residential: $MB_R = 1,400 - Q_R = 600$, so $Q_R = 1,400 - 600 = 800$.
    Commercial: $MB_C = 2,000 - \frac{1}{2}Q_C = 600$, so $Q_C = 2,800$.

In this example the bulk of the water will go to commercial users. It is useful to check that the sum of the two sectors' water allocation equals the total water produced. In this case 2,800 + 800 equals 3,600.

Your Turn 6.7: Let's simplify the water system problem. Assume that the Marginal Cost is a constant $300 (*MC* = 300). Since the residential and commercial sectors are already added, start with Step 2 and calculate the total production and the amount that should be allocated to each group.

A scale decision with limited information

In 1942 the U.S. federal government established a 50 parts per billion (ppb) standard for the allowable amount of arsenic in drinking water. A 1999 report by the National Academy of Sciences concluded that the 50 ppb standard did not adequately protect public health.

Your Turn 6.8:
1 See Table 6.3 below. In 2001 the Environmental Protection Agency chose one of the following standards. Which one would you choose, if any, and why?

2 We haven't yet introduced the idea of dollar estimates for lives saved. However, current EPA policy is to assign a value of $6 million per life saved. If half of these cancer cases would result in death, what would the value of lives saved be worth in dollar terms? Use the high estimate of cancer cases avoided as an example.

Table 6.3 Alternate arsenic standard benefits and costs

Arsenic standard	3 ppb	5 ppb	10 ppb	20 ppb
Compliance costs (millions of 1999 $)	$698-792	$415-472	$180-206	$67-77
Estimated health benefits (millions of 1999 $)	$214-491	$191-356	$140-198	$66-75
Cancer cases avoided	57-138	51-100	37-56	19-20

Source: U.S. EPA (2001).

With limited information regarding demand or supply, deciding among a set of two to four alternatives is common practice.

Benefits and costs using efficiency concepts

So far this chapter has not discussed the relation between market imperfections and the benefits and costs of public policy. However, as we saw in Chapter 5, government policy initiatives are likely to offer net benefits to society as a whole only if they are designed to address some type of market imperfection. Moreover, measuring many of the benefits and costs in a policy proposal involves the use of concepts such as consumer or producer surplus.

The previous chapter contained an example of the effects of a tax on a polluting industry. In order to interpret that policy in a benefit–cost framework, one can simply compare the various surplus figures before and after the policy is enacted to find the effects of the policy on each party, and then on society as a whole. To review, Figure 6.3 shows the predicted effects of a tax on producers in a polluting industry. Because this policy leads to higher prices and lower output, consumer surplus falls. Because the firm experiences lower output and lower after-tax revenue per unit, producer surplus also falls. The government and those experiencing external harm benefit from the policy. The net benefits of this policy are most easily found by calculating the change in surplus for each group and then adding the net effects. See Table 6.4, based on numbers from the example in Chapter 5.

The total net benefits of imposing the pollution tax equals $101.25, which equals the original value of the deadweight loss eliminated by the tax. Notice also that the net benefits to both consumers and producers are negative, while the government and the outsiders suffering harm from the pollution gain. In principle, the winners could compensate the losers, but according to the Kaldor–Hicks criterion this is not required.

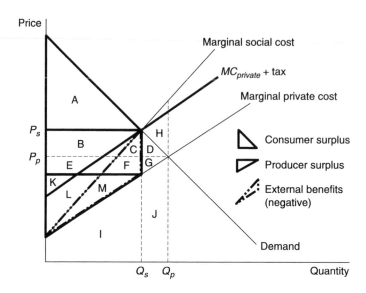

Figure 6.3 Tax on polluters

Table 6.4 Net benefits to different stakeholders

	Consumer surplus	Producer surplus	External surplus	Government surplus	Total net gains
Before tax	$1,012.5	$1,012.5	−$506.25	$0	$1,518.75
With tax	$648	$648	−$324	$648	$1,620.00
B–C of tax	−$364.5	−$364.5	$182.25	$648	$101.25

Cost-effectiveness analysis

For some policies, the benefits of a policy are not directly measured in terms of money either because no monetary values have been estimated or because the analyst cannot or will not use monetary values to measure the benefit. In such situations one can provide some potentially valuable information to policy makers by comparing the cost per unit of benefit of alternative programs. Weighing costs and benefits when benefits are not measured in dollars is referred to as **cost-effectiveness analysis.** The primary measurements in such studies are the cost/effectiveness ratio and the effect per dollar ratio. These ratios are direct inverses of each other.

> **Definitions: Cost-effectiveness ratio = total cost/total non-monetary effect**
> **Effect per dollar   = total effect/total cost**

The basic decision rule for this formula is to choose the alternative with the lowest cost per unit of effect, although this rule may not provide efficient recommendations under all circumstances.

A typical cost-effectiveness study might measure the number of lives saved per dollar spent on alternative cancer treatments or the number of lives saved per dollar spent on cancer treatment versus AIDS treatment. Because cost-effectiveness studies measure costs and benefits in different units, policy questions such as the optimal scale of a program or the optimal budget for a policy cannot be answered. However, cost-effectiveness analysis also has some advantages. First, it avoids some of the most controversial issues in benefit–cost analysis, such as measuring the benefits of saving a life in dollars. And in some circumstances where direct comparisons of the effects of different policies are possible, this type of analysis can provide some easily understandable and persuasive evidence.

Cost-effectiveness analysis under ideal conditions

Cost-effectiveness analysis can work reasonably well as a policy tool if it is used to compare policy alternatives with equal total costs or equal total effects. Either of these conditions reduces the problem to the comparison of a single dimension. The problem of having different measurements for benefits and costs is largely eliminated when one of the two measures is equal for different policy choices.

> **Example:** Assume that a President announces the goal of putting 100,000 more police officers on the street. This goal could be accomplished by offering grants to local law-enforcement agencies or by opening a national police training center. Assume that both programs include one year of federally paid salaries ($40,000 per officer) and training subsidies totaling $10,000 per officer. Therefore, salaries and training costs total $5,000,000,000 for each program. Assume further that the training center costs $100,000,000 to build and maintain, the grants include $10,000,000 in expected waste and fraud, and administrative costs will total $10,000,000. Given these assumptions the total cost of the training center is $5,100,000,000 and the total cost of the grants equals $5,020,000,000. Therefore, the cost per officer (the cost/effectiveness measure for this scenario) = $5,100,000,000/100,000 or $51,000 per cop for the training center and $5,020,000,000/100,000 = $50,200 per cop for the grants. The grants are therefore more cost effective and would be recommended.

Your Turn 6.9: Assume that starting salaries for police are $30,000 rather than $40,000. If all other costs are the same, recalculate the cost-effectiveness ratios for the training center and the grants. The policy recommendation will be the same.

Cost effectiveness under less than ideal conditions

If two alternative policies have unequal effects and unequal total costs, cost-effectiveness analysis is less reliable as a decision tool. Let's begin with an example.

Example: Assume that S. Lumlord owns 50 apartments that are currently infested with cockroaches. There are two methods of combating cockroach infestation: spraying and setting traps. Spraying costs $25 per apartment and is 80 percent effective in eliminating roaches in any single apartment. Setting traps costs $10 per apartment, but is only 40 percent effective in ridding each apartment of roaches. Which method should Mr. Lumlord use?

Assuming all apartments are treated, the cost of spraying is $25•50, or $1,250, while traps cost $10•50 or $500. The total effect is measured by the number of roach-free apartments. There will be 50•0.8, or 40 roach-free apartments after spraying and 50•0.4, or 20 roach-free apartments using traps. If we are measuring cost-effectiveness as dollars spent per roach-free apartment, the results are $1,250/40 ($31.25/bug-free apt.) for spraying and $500/20 ($25/bugfree apt.) for traps. According to this measure, traps cost less per roach-free apartment, and are more cost-effective.

One can also invert the cost-effectiveness measure and calculate the effectiveness per dollar. With this alternative rule the policy that maximizes the effect per dollar would be chosen. In the above example the number of roach-free apartments per dollar equals 40/$1,250 (0.032) for spraying and 20/$500 (0.04) for traps. Since traps de-infest more apartments per dollar, they are more cost-effective. As a practical matter, one can avoid results that appear as small decimals by expressing this ratio as the number of roach-free apartments per hundred dollars. In this example, 40/($1,250/$100) = 40/12.5 = 3.2 roach-free apartments per $100 is probably a more meaningful measure for the public.

Your Turn 6.10: Recalculate S. Lumlord's problem with two changes. Assume that spraying is 100 percent effective and that traps cost $20 per apartment.

This type of cost-effectiveness problem seems obvious enough, but some important issues are unresolved. First, there are 30 roach-infested apartments remaining after using traps but only 10 remaining after spraying. This should be a factor in the decision. Also, we have no way of knowing from cost-effectiveness estimates how much more valuable the apartments will be if they are roach-free, or how that value affects the total benefits of each method. It is quite possible that the added value of the extra 20 roach-free apartments after spraying would justify the added expense, but we cannot address this issue with cost-effectiveness analysis.

Weighted net benefits

It is relatively common to identify the effects of a given policy for various groups. For example, earlier in this chapter the effects of a pollution tax were identified for consumers, producers, government, and those affected by the pollution. In real-world situations political debates often include arguments about benefits or costs to the poor, to specific industries, or to local constituencies. As we have seen in the past three chapters, the common practice in cost–benefit analysis is to utilize unweighted net benefits for all groups in accordance with the Kaldor–Hicks principle. However, assigning higher weights to the net benefits flowing to disadvantaged groups can be easily justified on equity grounds and in a more limited way on efficiency grounds as well. One can also imagine policy makers privately assigning higher values to the net benefits flowing to their local constituents, political allies, or even favored racial, religious, or ethnic groups. Efforts to benefit one's constituents are particularly common. Such political or social favoritism is inconsistent with both efficiency and equity goals, especially on the national level.

The most important rationale for assigning higher weights to the net benefits of the poor arises from both efficiency and ethical arguments. Because the usual cost–benefit calculation measures net benefits in dollars rather than utility, it usually ignores the declining marginal utility of consumption. According to marginal utility theory an added dollar for the poor will lead to the purchase of goods with relatively high marginal utility, while a dollar of added income for the rich will often be spent on goods that the rich person already has in abundance. Such spending by the rich will add relatively little in the way of utility. Because social welfare is defined theoretically in terms of society's total utility, weighing net benefits for the poor more heavily helps to correct a bias in the unweighted calculation of dollar-based net benefits. This justification for assigning higher weights to the poor is consistent with utilitarian ethics for the same reason. Other ethical theories may assign very different weights to the net benefits of different groups. To take the most extreme example discussed in Chapter 2, John Rawls' difference principle, taken literally, would assign all of the weight to the net benefits of the least well-off person.

The graphical analysis of redistribution in Chapter 2 discussed the weighing of different persons' utilities using different ethical theories. These comparisons were made through an extended example with two people, Ritchie Rich and Paul Poorly. The two were assumed to have equal tastes, but only Ritchie produced income while Paul was completely unproductive. The same comparison is repeated below using individuals' incomes as our measure of well-being. This alternative provides a useful device for establishing the connection between ethics and cost–benefit analysis. As displayed in the graphical analysis of redistribution in Chapter 2, the assumption that Paul is totally unproductive means that he will have no income unless some redistribution occurs. In Figure 6.4, the income distribution between Ritchie Rich and Paul Poorly is displayed as a budget line with a slope of negative one. This is consistent with the neutral transfer case. To review, a **neutral transfer** of income has no effect on the behavior of either party.

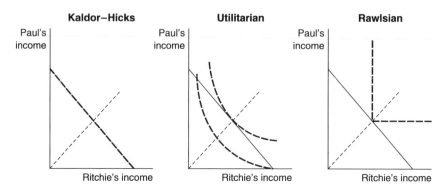

Figure 6.4 Income distributions with neutral transfers

It is an unrealistic simplifying assumption which allows us to compare the prescribed redistribution under the condition of fixed total income.

In Figure 6.4, the Kaldor–Hicks criterion weighs all incomes equally, so that the dashed line representing the K-H social welfare function is identical to the budget line of these two persons. This means that, according to Kaldor-Hicks, the distribution of net benefits doesn't matter. The utilitarian framework weighs the utility of different individuals equally, but not their income. Because the marginal utility of consumption declines as more goods are purchased, adding a dollar of income to the poor will provide higher levels of utility when that income is spent, assuming equal tastes across income groups. The two curved social indifference curves in Figure 6.4 show that social welfare increases as one moves toward total equality in the neutral transfers case. The Rawlsian case looks the same as in Chapter 2 utility possibilities graphs since Rawls' total concern with the well-being of the least well-off person applies to both utility and income.

Figure 6.5 displays the same alternatives with a bulging budget line that is consistent with non-neutral transfers (see Chapter 2), and more specifically with the assumption that Ritchie Rich's productivity will decline as his earned income is transferred to Paul. In this case no income redistribution is justified under the Kaldor–Hicks criterion, while a modest amount of redistribution is prescribed by utilitarianism and near equality is preferred according to the Rawlsian social welfare function.

Regardless of the justification for weighing dollar-based net benefits more highly for lower-income groups, the actual determination of weights is a very uncertain process, and no consensus has been established for weighing the net benefits of different income groups. Let us consider one basis for determining weights, the utilitarian model. The utilitarian approach requires an estimate of the relative marginal utilities of income for different income groups. Once such estimates are provided, the actual utility estimates would be equally weighted.

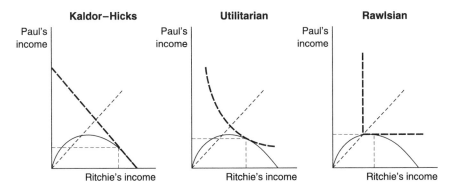

Figure 6.5 Income distributions with non-neutral transfers

Unfortunately, utility is generally not measurable, and any attempt to approximate its relationship to income is somewhat arbitrary.

An example of an explicit method of relating weights to income is provided by Feldstein (1974). A modified form of Feldstein's model is presented in the following equation:

$$Feldstein's\ weight = \left(\frac{Y_{median}}{Y_i} \right)^{\alpha}$$

where α = the marginal social utility of income and Y_i is the income level of a particular group.

Table 6.5 displays the weights produced by this formula for a few values of alpha (α).

Table 6.5 Distributional weights using the Feldstein formula

Unweighted income	Weight ($\alpha = 0$)	Weight ($\alpha = 1/2$)	Weight ($\alpha = 1$)
20,000	1	1.414	2
40,000 (median)	1	1	1
60,000	1	0.8165	2/3

A value of zero for α produces a weight of one for all levels of income, since raising anything to the zero power produces a value of 1. If $\alpha = 1/2$ the weight equals the square root of the ratio of median income to any given income level. For example, for the 20,000 income level the ratio of median income to individual income is 40,000/20,000, or 2, and the square root of 2 is 1.414. Therefore, according to the Feldstein formula the weighted value of net benefits going to someone with $20,000 of income would equal 1.414 times the actual dollar amount.

Your Turn 6.11: A training program for disadvantaged youth provides total net benefits of $100,000 to a group of youth. The program costs $120,000, and is funded by a tax on quiche. The median income in this society is $40,000. Before entering the program the youth had an average income of $10,000, while those paying the tax have average incomes of $80,000. Calculate the weights for the $10,000 income group and $80,000 income group using Feldstein's formula, then calculate the weighted benefits and costs for each group and determine the net benefits using each weight. Table 6.5 will be useful in guiding your calculations.

Table 6.6 A weighted net benefits example

	Weight ($\alpha = 0$)	Weight ($\alpha = 1/2$)	Weight ($\alpha = 1$)
$10,000 weight			
$80,000 weight			
Weighted benefits to poor youth			
Weighted costs to quiche eaters			
Weighted net benefits of program			

Notice that the unweighted net benefits are negative, so the program would be rejected using the Kaldor–Hicks criterion. However, higher weights for the poor increase the likelihood that a program with significant redistribution effects will be approved. Because the Feldstein weights are arbitrary, however, there is little justification for choosing one value over another. Most analysts recommend relying on the Kaldor–Hicks criterion for determining efficiency, and then using political or ethical arguments to justify redistribution in cases where net benefits are negative.

Conclusion

This chapter introduced the basic tool for the analysis of public policy, benefit–cost analysis, along with some related analytical tools. Most of the chapter concentrated on applying the Kaldor–Hicks criterion to benefit–cost analysis. The key elements of the chapter included the rules for various types of policy decisions, the introduction of cost-effectiveness analysis for situations in which either the benefits or costs cannot be quantified in dollar terms, and the consideration of different weights for the net benefits of different groups.

It is important to remember that benefit–cost analysis and all of its related models are best thought of as tools for organizing one's thoughts and evidence about a policy's effects, particularly its efficiency effects. It does not actively consider equity, political practicality, or other policy goals. Also, benefit–cost calculations are only as good as the information and numerical values that go into them. Since benefits and costs are often difficult to calculate, a substantial degree of humility is helpful when discussing your findings with experts, clients, or the general public.

Review questions

Conceptual questions

1. Discuss which of the following offers the most consistent criterion for judging the efficiency of alternative policies, according to economists. What are the problems with the other two, and what are their advantages over the economists' preferred choice?

   (A) Net benefits
   (B) Benefit/cost ratio
   (C) Percentage rate of return

2. Compare and contrast the ideas of cost–benefit and cost-effectiveness analysis. In a case where the benefits of a policy come in the form of non-marketed goods such as lives or wilderness, consider the advantages and disadvantages of a dollar cost–dollar benefit approach.

3. Discuss the strengths and limitations of weighted net benefits, ethical arguments, or the concept of leaky buckets as decision rules for programs that aid the poor.

Computational questions

4. Malcolm, the mayor of Schlafenberg, is being asked to choose the best among three proposals for a new water treatment plant. Plan A will cost $3 million to construct, purify $5 million worth of water, and lead to $1 million in operating costs. Plan B will cost $4 million to construct, purify $6 million worth of water, and result in $1.5 million in operating costs. Plan C, proposed by the mayor's son, will cost $7 million, purify $9 million worth of water, and result in $2.5 million of operating costs. Given this information, answer the following questions:

   (A) Fill in the following table:

Project	Net benefits	Benefit/cost ratio	Rate of return
A			
B			
C			

   (B) Suppose that the mayor proposed accepting the plan proposed by his son. Give a short argument as to why the mayor has made a poor economic decision.

5. The time has come for the formulation of Schlafenberg's annual budget. The town has allocated $2 million to spend on its various programs and community groups. The goal of the budget committee is to maximize the net benefits to the town from this budget. The alternatives are presented in the following table.

    (A) Complete the missing parts of this table:

	Theater company	Marching band	Road work	New signs	Public gardens	Soup kitchen
Benefits	$500,000	$650,000	$1,100,000	$300,000	$550,000	$150,000
Costs	$450,000	$500,000	$1,000,000	$300,000	$520,000	$100,000
B/C ratio						
Net benefits						

    (B) Is the $2 million sufficient for an "optimal budget," or should additional monies be allocated? If so, how much additional funding is needed?
    (C) Which programs should be approved within the $2 million budget? How much of a surplus does the government have once all feasible programs have been funded?
    (D) Now suppose a state grant for road work reduces the local cost of road work to $700,000. How would this change your answer to questions B and C?

6. Schlafenberg is now contemplating installing a new irrigation system and must determine how much of the water will go to agricultural users and how much will go to residential users. A policy student, home for the winter break, has estimated marginal benefit and marginal cost curves as follows:

    Residential marginal benefits: $MB_R = 1{,}800 - 3Q_R$
    Agricultural marginal benefits: $MB_a = 2{,}200 - 2Q_C$
    Marginal cost: $MC = \frac{1}{5}Q$

    Determine the quantity of water that should go to each group. The answer is not in whole numbers.

7. Suppose that 20 million Americans talk on cell phones while driving during the typical week. The U.S. government is seeking to reduce this number. Three options are being considered: (1) Ban cell phone use in cars. This policy would cost $2 million and be 40 percent effective. (2) Require car makers to install cell phone blocking technology, which costs $10 million and is 85 percent effective. (3) Launch a public service campaign educating drivers about the risks of cell phone use while driving. This would cost $3 million and be 30 percent effective.

    (A) Which of the three plans would be most cost effective? Calculate the number who stop calling per dollar spent to determine your answer.

(B) What additional steps should be considered in designing a more complete policy analysis of these choices?

8. This problem is based on question 7 in Chapter 4. In the sexy cigarette market, consumers think the total value of the product is consistent with demand D_2, but they have been fooled. The true value of the product is seen in demand curve D_1.

True demand is $P = 160 - 2Q$
Perceived demand is $P = 175 - 2Q$
Supply is $P = 10 + Q$

(A) If you haven't done so recently, find the price, quantity, and the **dollar values** of the consumer surplus, producer surplus, and deadweight loss when the consumers are being fooled.

(B) Now assume that government places a \$15 tax on the producers of sexy smokes, raising the after-tax supply to $P = 25 + Q$. The consumers are still fooled.

1   Find the new equilibrium price and quantity.

2   Find the Government Surplus and Producer Surplus values. Remember that the producer keeps $P - \$15$ after the tax.

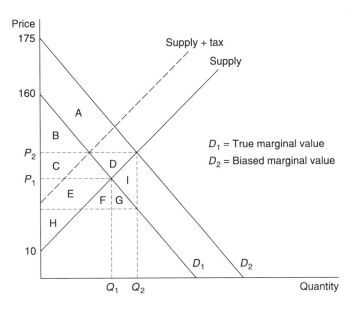

Market for sexy smokes

3 Now find the consumer surplus at this new quantity. Remember that they are still being fooled. Is the new CS less or more than the CS without the tax?

4 Now find the total net benefits (CS + PS + GS). Is this policy efficient? Is it fair?

(C) Calculate the net benefits of this policy by finding the changes in CS, PS, and GS from part A to part B. Compare these net benefits to the original deadweight loss. Is this new market equilibrium Pareto optimal? Why or why not?

7 Net benefits over time and present value

I don't believe in princerple, But oh I du in interest.[1]

(James Russell Lowell)

My interest is in the future because I am going to spend the rest of my life there.[2]

(Charles F. Kettering)

Many private and public sector decisions influence the well-being of the decision maker or others far into the future. A student's decision to attend college will affect her income and lifestyle for the rest of her life. A business's decision to build a factory or store will produce benefits and costs for at least as long as the facility is in use. Government investments in highways, education programs, nuclear waste storage, or other long-run policies also involve benefits and costs which extend over many years or even many generations. Analyzing a private or public sector decision with long-run benefits and costs is more complex and requires more information than a decision with only short-term consequences. Yet the goal of the decision-making process is the same. Theoretically, the rational individual or group will choose the course of action that creates the greatest positive difference between benefits and costs, subject to whatever constraints they face and using as much information as they can reasonably attain and process.

Let's start by briefly considering a basic individual choice involving time: How much of his income should a person save or spend? A common way to introduce this issue is to ask oneself the following question:

Would I rather have a dollar today or a dollar a year from now?

When I ask my students this question, most prefer to receive their dollar immediately. The reasons they give vary widely, but usually involve avoiding future risks such as possible inflation, forgetting about the promised dollar, or even facing a small risk of death. Some mention their personal preference for spending the dollar now, regardless of the risk or reward from waiting. Others mention the fact that if they took the dollar now and saved it for a year, they would collect interest in the meantime, and would therefore have more than one dollar a year from now.

All of these reasons for valuing a current dollar more highly than one received in the future have a certain degree of validity, particularly when considering an individual decision to spend or save.[3] However, only two or three factors seem to apply to public policy decisions. These are the rate of interest, the rate of inflation, and possible elements of risk. The rate of interest represents an opportunity cost of waiting for a given amount of income because, as stated above, waiting for future income involves giving up the chance to earn interest on that income between now and the time of the payoff. Secondly, inflation erodes the purchasing power of each dollar, so any future payoff involving a fixed number of dollars will be less valuable in the presence of inflation. The concept of risk, which will be introduced in Chapter 9, also has implications for the relative value of present and future income, although there is disagreement about the role of risk when benefits are spread across a large number of individuals.

Other versions of the earlier question about saving suggest the challenge facing a policy analyst or an individual when weighing this choice. Would I rather have $1 now or $1.20 (or $1.50, or $1.90) in two years? Would I rather have $1,000 now, or $1,200 (or more) in two years? Would I rather have $1,000 now or $2,000 in 20 years? By varying the amounts of time and money involved in the question one can get a feeling for one's own relative value of present versus future income. This relative value might vary for different lengths of time.

> **Your Turn 7.1:** If you had a choice of $100 now or $X in two years, how high would $X have to be before you would be willing to delay receiving the money? Discuss with classmates or roommates. Answer the same question for different lengths of time, such as five years and 20 years.

Decisions involving investment in long-lived assets raise similar questions. A new science building at your university could bring in additional students, more qualified faculty and research grants. Are these future sources of income worth the investment? The value of present versus future net benefits is one of several important dimensions in such a policy question. The same issue applies to highway or mass transit construction, new sports stadiums, and training and education programs for the poor. These types of issues will be discussed in more detail in later chapters.

Investment versus saving

The economic definitions of the terms investment and saving are somewhat different from their common meanings. In economics, **investment** is the purchase of long-lasting capital goods such as factories, shopping malls, machines, etc. This definition applies to private or public investments, and is equally true for human investment (education and training) or capital investment. When business, government, non-profit institutions or households decide to invest, they are usually spending money in the present or near future in order to attain net benefits which occur primarily in the more distant future.

Capital investment is one form of action that one can take with one's wealth. Another is saving. To the economist, **saving** means any action which stores wealth for future use. Saving includes any common form of personal financial investment such as the purchase of stocks, bonds, mutual funds, cash-value life insurance, or simple savings account deposits. This is a far broader definition of saving than the public would normally expect. Saving offers benefits in the form of interest, dividends, or financial capital gains. The income from saving represents an important opportunity cost of capital investment. Let's consider the benefits of saving, and then the corresponding opportunity costs of investment. For simplicity, the following discussion will concentrate exclusively on interest payments.

If you save: compound interest

Saving involves delaying the spending of one's assets in order to collect interest. For example, if the annual interest rate on savings is 3 percent, each dollar a person saves will produce 3 cents in interest after one year. Moreover, if a person allows the savings to remain in place, in future years she will begin to earn interest not only on the original deposit (the principal), but also on the interest accumulated during earlier time periods. This process of collecting interest on earlier interest as well as the principal is called **compound interest**, and can be computed for annual interest payments using the following formulas:

Future wealth next year: $W_1 = W_0(1 + r)$ (7.1)

Future wealth in t years: $W_t = W_0(1 + r)^t$ (7.2)

where W_0 = wealth today, W_1 = wealth after one year, W_t = wealth after t years, and r is an interest rate in decimal form.

Example: Don deposits $1,000 in a money market fund and leaves it there, along with any interest earned on the $1,000, for three years. If the annual interest rate on a money market fund is 5 percent, or 0.05, how much will Don have at the end of this time? To start, let's consider this process one year at a time. I will work out this example, and let you work out a similar example below.

How much interest will Don earn during his first year?
Don will earn $1,000 × 0.05, *or* $50 *in interest.*

How much will Don's savings account be worth after one year?
At the end of the year, his account will be worth $1,000 + 50, *or* $1,050. *Notice that* $1,050 *equals* $1,000 × (1.05), *where* 0.05 *equals the rate of interest.*

How much will Don's account be worth after two years?
According to the compound interest formula, after two years his account will be worth $1,000 × (1.05)², or $1,000 × 1.1025, or $1,102.50.

During the second year Don earns $52.50 in interest. This amount is made up of $50 of interest earned on the original principal plus $2.50 in additional interest earned on the $50 he earned during the first year. Earning interest in year 2 on the interest collected in year 1 is the basis for compound interest.

How much will Don's account be worth after three years?
According to the formula for compound interest, after three years his account will be worth $1,000 × (1.05)³, or $1,000 × 1.1576, or $1,157.63.

In year 3 his account grew by slightly more than $55, demonstrating that the total value of the account will increase at an increasing rate due to compound interest. To summarize this example, see Table 7.1.

Table 7.1 Don's compound interest

Year 0 (now)	After 1 year	After 2 years	After 3 years
$1,000 = 1,000	$1,000(1 + 0.05) $1,050	$1,000(1.05)² $1,102.50	$1,000(1.05)³ $1,157.63

In words, after the first year Don will have the original deposit (the principal) plus interest income which equals the interest rate times the principal. During the second year he will collect interest on the principal *plus* the first year's interest payment, which will make the second year's interest payment somewhat larger than the first, and so on.

Your Turn 7.2: Assume that Deirdre has $1,000 and access to an account that pays a guaranteed return of 10 percent (or 0.10) per year.
(A) How much interest will Deirdre earn during her first year? How much will her account be worth after the first year?
(B) What will her fund be worth at the end of two years? Why did her fund grow by a greater amount during the second year than the first?
(C) How much will Deirdre's savings account be worth after three years?
(D) Why is the difference between Deirdre's and Don's payoffs larger in the third year than in the first?

Now we can consider the implications of the previous examples more fully. If you completed Your Turn 7.2 correctly, you will notice that the value of the interest earned by Deirdre is twice as high as Don's in the first year due to the higher interest rate, but is *more than twice as high* as Don's in the second and third years. The annual payments resulting from the higher interest rate grow

Table 7.2 Examples of the future value of $1

	5 percent interest			15 percent interest	
Year	Formula	Future value	Year	Formula	Future value
0	$1(1 + 0.05)^0$	$1.00	0	$1(1 + 0.15)^0$	$1.00
1	$1(1 + 0.05)^1$	$1.05	1	$1(1 + 0.15)^1$	$1.15
2	$1(1 + 0.05)^2$	$1.10	2	$1(1 + 0.15)^2$	$1.32
3	$1(1 + 0.05)^3$	$1.16	3	$1(1 + 0.15)^3$	$1.52
10	$1(1 + 0.05)^{10}$	$1.63	10	$1(1 + 0.15)^{10}$	$4.05
25	$1(1 + 0.05)^{25}$	$3.39	25	$1(1 + 0.15)^{25}$	$32.92
50	$1(1 + 0.05)^{50}$	$11.47	50	$1(1 + 0.15)^{50}$	$1,083.62

more rapidly in future years for two related reasons: (1) Naturally, the higher interest rate will pay more money on any given amount of savings, as in the first year. (2) Because of the higher interest payments in early years, one earns interest on an increasingly greater amount of accumulated wealth as time goes by. In fact, wealth that is saved at a higher interest rate tends to move away from wealth saved at a lower interest rate quite explosively as the number of years grows. Table 7.2 demonstrates these two properties of compound interest.

In Table 7.2, two trends seem noteworthy. First, compound interest at any interest rate is most significant when allowed to accumulate for many years, because the amount of accumulated interest upon which compound interest can be earned is much higher. Secondly, higher interest rates bring increasingly substantial benefits in the more distant future. Notice that $1 saved for 50 years at 5 percent interest will be worth $11.47, while the same amount saved at 15 percent interest will be worth $1,083.62, or almost 100 times as much. At the 15 percent rate, $1,000 invested now will make you a millionaire ($1,083,620) in 50 years. It is no wonder that Albert Einstein once referred to compound interest as one of the most powerful forces in the world!

Your Turn 7.3: If your calculator can handle it, find the future value of $1,000 saved for 50 years at a 5 percent interest rate. Also calculate the future value of $1,000 saved for 100 years at 5 percent and $1,000 saved for 50 years at 10 percent.

If you invest: foregone interest and present value

Recall that to economists saving is the storing of assets for later use, often in an account which pays interest, and investment is the purchase of long-lasting capital goods. While savings generally earns compound interest, spending on capital goods does not. Similarly, no interest is earned on one's investment in college, a business's purchase of a factory or store, or the government's spending on roads, environmental protection, or job-training programs.

Therefore, compound interest is an opportunity cost of each of these long-term investments. In order to account for the opportunity cost of foregone interest, the future benefits and costs of investment spending must be **discounted** to their present value in order to account for the cost of foregone compound interest.

> **Concept:** The **present value** of a dollar received in some future year *t* is the amount which, if put in a savings account and allowed to collect compound interest, would equal $1 in year *t*.

The concept of present value can be displayed in the following example. If a person has a chance to collect $120 in two years, how much would that amount be worth in money available today? In this case we must reduce, or discount, this future amount of income by removing the compound interest which one could earn between now and two years from now. **If the future value (with compound interest) in year *t* equals the present value times $(1 + r)^t$, then the present value (PV) will equal the future value (FV) divided by $(1 + r)^t$.** In symbols,

$$FV = PV \cdot (1 + r)^t \quad \text{and} \quad PV = FV/(1 + r)^t \tag{7.3}$$

One can get from a compound interest equation to a present value equation by dividing both sides of equation (7.2) by $(1 + r)^t$.

> **Formula: The present value of $1 acquired in year $t = \$1/(1 + r)^t$.**

An example should prove very helpful at this point.

> **Example:** Tina gets her annual allowance on a delayed basis. Her insufferably cheap parents have given her the choice of $120 in two years or $100 today. If she accepts the $100, it will be invested in a fund paying 10 percent interest. Which choice should she make? The $100 is already in the present, so it does not need to be discounted. Therefore, finding the present value of the $120 and comparing the answer to $100 is one way to analyze this problem.
>
> **Present value of $120 acquired in two years**
>
> | In 2 years | Now | Now | Present value |
> |---|---|---|---|
> | $120 | $= \dfrac{120}{(1.10)^2}$ | $= \dfrac{120}{1.21}$ | = $99   (7.4) |

This present value problem says that $120 in two years is equivalent to about $99 today because if Tina deposited $99 at 10 percent interest, it would grow to $120 in two years. Therefore $99 is the *present value* of the $120 of future income discounted at the 10 percent interest rate. By comparing the present value of the $120 in two years with the $100 available now, we can see that Tina would be slightly better off choosing the $100 now. In this case, one could also calculate the future value of the $100 and compare it to the $120 available in two years. Because $100 \times (1.10)^2 = \$121$, taking the $100 is still the best option.

Conceptually, present value involves asking a modified version of the question asked earlier in the chapter: **How much would I accept today in order to give up a dollar I could receive at some point in the future?** For example, if the interest rate is 5 percent, how much would a person accept today instead of $1 two years from now? The concept of foregone interest says that the person would accept less than $1 today because that person could take today's income, put it in an interest-bearing account, and have additional funds in two years. More specifically, receiving $1 after two years involves foregoing two years of compound interest at 5 percent per year. Therefore the present value (PV) of $1 received two years from now would be

$$PV = \$1 \cdot \frac{1}{1.05^2} = \$0.907 \qquad (7.5)$$

In other words, a person would slightly prefer 91 cents today to a dollar paid two years from now given a 5 percent interest rate. Similarly, $1 to be paid in four years would be equivalent to 82.6 cents $[\$1/(1.05)^4]$ today because 82.6 cents invested at 5 percent would equal $1 after four years. Similarly, if the interest rate is 10 percent, $1 expected in two years would have a present value of 82.6 cents $[\$1/(1 + 0.10)^2 = \$0.826]$, and $1 expected in four years would have a present value of 68.3 cents. The present value of future net benefits is obviously quite sensitive to the interest rate used to discount the future sums to their present values.

This relationship between interest rates and present values is demonstrated further in Table 7.3. Table 7.3 is closely related to Table 7.2. Table 7.2 shows us

Table 7.3 Examples of the present value of $1

	5 percent interest			15 percent interest	
Year	*Formula*	*Present value*	*Year*	*Formula*	*Present value*
0	$\$1/(1 + 0.05)^0$	$1.000	0	$\$1/(1 + 0.15)^0$	$1.000
1	$\$1/(1 + 0.05)^1$	$0.950	1	$\$1/(1 + 0.15)^1$	$0.869
2	$\$1/(1 + 0.05)^2$	$0.907	2	$\$1/(1 + 0.15)^2$	$0.756
3	$\$1/(1 + 0.05)^3$	$0.864	3	$\$1/(1 + 0.15)^3$	$0.658
10	$\$1/(1 + 0.05)^{10}$	$0.614	10	$\$1/(1 + 0.15)^{10}$	$0.247
25	$\$1/(1 + 0.05)^{25}$	$0.295	25	$\$1/(1 + 0.15)^{25}$	$0.030
50	$\$1/(1 + 0.05)^{50}$	$0.087	50	$\$1/(1 + 0.15)^{50}$	$0.001

the possible future values of one current dollar, while Table 7.3 shows us the present values of $1 we might receive in various future years. Both logically and mathematically these tables have an inverse relationship. For example, receiving $1 in three years without the opportunity to earn compound interest at a 5 percent rate is equivalent to saving an initial deposit of $0.846 for three years. That is why $1 in the third year discounted at 5 percent has a present value of $0.846. As in Table 7.2, present values based on different interest rates in Table 7.3 diverge significantly in the distant future.

Your Turn 7.4: One of America's most common financial fantasies is winning the lottery. However, the way most States pay their lottery winnings makes the present value of the payoff less than its face value. For example, a person who wins $10 million in the Pennsylvania Lottery receives $250,000 immediately, $250,000 per year for 19 years, and then a $5 million payment at the end of 20 years. Assume that you are a winner. If the interest rate is 5 percent, find the present value of the $250,000 you will receive one year from now, two years from now, and three years from now. (Hint: Be sure that your answer is less than $250,000 in each case.) If your calculator can handle it, find the present value of the $5,000,000 you would receive in the 20th year.

By the way, if the discount rate is 5 percent, the present value of winning $10 million in the lottery paid in this manner over 20 years is $5,053,750, still a tidy sum.

The present value formula

Any public or private decision with net benefits extending into the future can be analyzed using the present value concept. The model for present value analysis follows a simple two-step process; (1) find the present value for each year's net benefits, and (2) add the present values of different years in order to determine the total present value of the decision. The formula for the total present value of an investment is

$$PV = \sum \frac{B_t - C_t}{(1+r)^t} = (B_0 - C_0) + \frac{(B_1 - C_1)}{(1+r)^t} + ... + \frac{B_N - C_N}{(1+r)^N} \qquad (7.6)$$

where Σ equals the sum of all years 1 to N, t equals the number of years elapsed since the beginning of the project, N is the final year of the project's net benefits, B_t = the benefits in year t, C_t = costs in year t, B_0 and C_0 equal the immediate benefits and costs, and r equals the discount rate. Notice that in the present value formula benefits in the present (year 0) do not have to be discounted, since net benefits received immediately have no time to collect foregone interest. According to the general formula, current benefits in year zero could be divided by $(1+r)^0$, but since anything raised to the zero power equals one, discounting current benefits amounts to dividing by one. Therefore, not discounting immediate net benefits is consistent with the present value formula as well as with common sense.

Applying the formula involves calculating the net benefits for each year, discounting each year's net benefit separately to present value and then adding the annual present values to determine the total net benefits. The order of these steps is very important. Do not add the benefits and/or costs across different years until the net benefits for all years are discounted to present value. Some examples will help to understand this process.

Example: In February 2003 Senator Barbara Boxer of California introduced a bill requiring that missile defense technology be installed on all commercial airliners.[4] Supporters of the bill cited several reported missile attacks on airliners over the past 25 years. Most attacks were against propeller planes in the Third World, but a few attempts have also been made against larger commercial jets. Technology for such a defense system is frequently used on military aircraft and has apparently been installed on some El Al planes (the Israeli airline). The primary benefits of this program are possible savings of lives and property. The defense equipment may also increase travel demand by decreasing fear among passengers. Opponents of the law cited its cost, the lack of proof of a domestic threat of this type, and some uncertainty about the best alternative technology for the project.

In order to calculate a simplified present value, assume that the full installation cost of the missile defense system is $10 billion and that all installation will take place in the first year. Each year $3 billion will be spent on maintenance and repair of these systems. As a result of this investment, an average of $7 billion a year in benefits occurs from increased safety and economic activity. For simplicity we will limit our analysis to the first three years of the project. A 10 percent discount rate is used. Here is the problem (numbers are in billions)

Now	Year 1	Year 2	Year 3	
$PV = -\$10/1.10^0$	$+ \$(7-3)/1.10^1$	$+ \$(7-3)/(1.10)^2$	$+ \$(7-3)/(1.10)^3$	
$= -\$10/1$	$+ \$4/1.10$	$+ \$4/1.21$	$+ \$4/1.331$	
$= -10$	$+ 3.636$	$+ 3.306$	$+ 3.005$	$= -\$0.05$

$$(7.7)$$

If the present value is negative, the policy should not be adopted. There is no reason to calculate the foregone compound interest separately. The opportunity cost of foregone compound interest is calculated through discounting.

If interest rates change, so will the opportunity cost of investment. An investment decision which would be rejected at high rates of interest may be accepted if the interest rate falls.

Your Turn 7.5: Find the present value of this policy decision regarding airline missile defense with a 5 percent (0.05) interest rate. All other values will be the same as in the previous example. Are the net benefits of the program positive now?

Present value with infinitely long net benefits

For investment decisions involving very long time frames, one can arrive at an easy and fairly accurate estimate of the present value of the net benefits by assuming that the stream of net benefits continues forever. If a project results in a constant net benefit each year, the present value of this stream of benefits can be summarized in a very simple formula:

$$PV_{\infty} = \frac{\$\text{net benefit}}{r}, \text{ where } r \text{ is the real discount rate.} \tag{7.8}$$

The derivation of this formula is similar to that of the spending multiplier you may have seen in introductory macroeconomics. It is presented in a note.[5]

Your Turn 7.6: Assume that preserving the Grand Canyon will provide $20 billion in annual net benefits forever. If the relevant discount rate is 5 percent, what is the present value of the benefits of preserving the Grand Canyon?

Alternatives to present value

While present value is the proper analytical tool for most types of long-lived public investments, it shares with the concept of net benefits the problem of being hard for some people to place in context. It is sometimes difficult to understand that a project with estimated net benefits of several million dollars might be a poor choice. If interpreted carefully, a smaller number such as the benefit/cost ratio or rate of return sometimes conveys the relative value of a project better than a net present value figure. As noted in Chapter 6, however, these alternatives are less consistent measures of efficiency gains than the net benefit measure. When one adds the time dimension to the earlier discussion of alternative measures, a somewhat modified set of alternatives arises. These alternatives to net present value include the internal rate of return and the discounted benefit/cost ratio. Each will be discussed below.

Internal rate of return

The most commonly discussed alternative to the present value of net benefits is the **internal rate of return**. This concept is easy to define and to understand, but is generally time consuming to calculate and sometimes gives misleading results. First the term must be defined.

Definition: The internal rate of return (IRR) is an interest rate that when substituted into the present value equation produces a discounted present value of zero. As a formula, the internal rate of return is:

$$PV = \sum_t \left(B_t - C_t\right) \Big/ \left(1 + IRR\right)^t = 0 \qquad (7.9)$$

Unlike the previous examples in this chapter, we know the present value (zero) but must find the interest rate (IRR). Unfortunately, there is no easy way to find this rate except through trial and error.

Example: Granny the graduate: Assume that Granny, a 63-year-old woman, decides to return to college for a one-year Master's degree, after which she will work until she retires at 65. She currently works at a job paying $20,000. Her tuition will be $2,000 for one year. After she graduates, she will earn $32,000 until retirement. Her benefits and costs are as follows:

Age (year)	63 (0)	64 (1)	65 (2)
Benefits	$0	$32,000	$32,000
Costs	$22,000	$20,000	$20,000

The steps for finding an internal rate of return are relatively easy to follow and, if you're lucky, not terribly time consuming. Start by finding the present value using any reasonable interest rate. If this first present value calculation is positive, choose a higher discount rate for a second guess. If the first guess produces a negative present value, choose a lower discount rate. In the Granny example, a 5 percent discount rate produces a positive present value of $312.92. After raising the discount rate to 6 percent the net present value is only 70 cents, which is close enough for me! Therefore, Granny's internal rate of return is about 6 percent. Comparing this rate to market interest rates on risk-free investments covering the same time period produces an easy way to judge the project. Government bond yields are a common example.

Decision rule for the internal rate of return: if the internal rate of return is greater than a comparable market interest rate, the project should be approved. If the internal rate of return is less than the discount rate, the project should be rejected.

For example, if Granny could earn 4 percent on a two-year certificate of deposit at a bank, the rate of return from her college investment is higher and her decision to attend is correct.

> **Your Turn 7.7:** Assume that Mega-Man is considering a two-year career in the National Football League as an alternative to his current job as a video game hero. His salary will rise from $200,000 to $320,000 for those two years. However, he must also train for one year without pay to develop the football skills he needs to complement his outstanding athletic ability. Through trial and error find the internal rate of return. (Hint: Start somewhere between 10 and 15 percent. Anything within a few hundred dollars of zero will be close enough.)

Problems with the internal rate of return

While the internal rate of return produces a number and a decision rule that are easy to understand, the internal rate of return can run into some serious problems if some of the future net benefits are negative. Negative net benefits in the distant future might lead to more than one internal rate of return, making the concept meaningless as a guide to policy decisions.

> **Example:** Assume that Cleveland is considering hosting an exposition on the history of the steel industry which involves constructing a model steel plant and a set of exhibits, running the exposition for three years, then demolishing the plant and cleaning up pollution from the project. Representative values for this project (in billions of dollars) are presented in Table 7.4. The first row gives the undiscounted net benefits.
>
> *Table 7.4* Inconsistent internal rates of return
>
> | Net benefits per year (millions) | Year 0 | Year 1 | Year 2 | Year 3 | Year 4 | Total PV |
> |---|---|---|---|---|---|---|
> | **0% discount rate** | −30 | 20 | 30 | 20 | −40 | **0** |
> | 5% discount rate | −30 | 19.0 | 27.2 | 17.3 | −32.9 | +0.06 |
> | **19% discount rate** | −30 | 16.8 | 21.2 | 11.9 | −19.9 | **0** |

If 5 percent is a reasonable discount rate for a net present value calculation, this project should be approved. However, there are two possible internal rates of return: 0 and 19 percent. If the IRR equals zero, the project should be rejected. At 19 percent, the project should be approved. Unlike the earlier example of Granny's education, there are conflicting policy prescriptions from the internal rate of return method for this case.

Discounted benefit/cost ratio

Another alternative to the present value model is the discounted benefit/cost ratio. This is similar to the benefit/cost ratio introduced in Chapter 6. With multiple time periods the gross benefits and costs should each be discounted before dividing to find the final ratio. The formula for the discounted benefit/cost ratio is presented below.

$$\text{Discounted } B/C \text{ ratio} = \frac{\displaystyle\sum_{t=0}^{n} \frac{Bt}{(1+r)^t}}{\displaystyle\sum_{t=0}^{n} \frac{Ct}{(1+r)^t}} \tag{7.10}$$

The decision rule for a single project using the discounted benefit/cost ratio is the same as with the basic benefit/cost ratio. If the ratio is greater than one, the project should be adopted. Like the internal rate of return method this model gives a relatively simple number that is easy to understand and defend. As with the basic benefit/cost ratio, this formula is sensitive to how one defines benefits and costs in a way that net benefits are not. See Chapter 6 for a discussion of this problem.

> **Your Turn 7.8:** Given the information in Your Turn 7.7, find Mega-Man's discounted B/C ratio given a discount rate of 7 percent.
>
> | | Year 0 | Year 1 | Year 2 |
> |----------|------------|------------|------------|
> | Benefits | $0 | $320,000 | $320,200 |
> | Costs | $200,000 | $200,000 | $200,000 |

Inflation and the discount rate

If inflation exists in an economy, saving involves both accumulating dollars through the payment of interest and lowering the value of each future dollar through inflation. In most nations, interest rates on mortgages, bonds, credit cards, or savings accounts are *not* automatically corrected for inflation. Interest rates that are not adjusted for inflation are known as **nominal interest rates**. Interest rates that are corrected for inflation are referred to as **real interest rates**. If a person invests $100 for one year at a nominal interest rate of 5 percent, she will earn $5 in interest and have a total of $105 at the end of the year. However, if there is a 5 percent inflation rate during that same year, each dollar will be worth 5 percent less at the end of the year. Therefore, logically, the $105 at the end of the year will be worth no more in terms of the actual goods it can buy than the $100 at the beginning of the year, and the real benefit to saving would be zero.

> **Definition: The real interest rate** is the rate of interest corrected for inflation.
> It is generally defined as the nominal rate of interest minus the inflation rate.
> If the real interest rate is r, the nominal interest rate is i, and the inflation rate is p,
> **the approximate formula for the real interest rate is $r = i - p$.**

This formula is actually a slightly exaggerated definition of the real interest rate, although the size of the mathematical inaccuracy is usually very small.[6]

Interestingly, it is not always necessary to choose a real interest rate as one's discount rate in the presence of inflation. Instead, the correct choice of a real or nominal interest rate depends on whether you are measuring your costs and benefits in real or nominal terms. If you are using real costs and benefits, a real interest rate is correct. If your costs and benefits are nominal, your discount rate should also be nominal. This claim is proven in a note.[7] A more detailed discussion of biases in common inflation measures and their implications for discounting is included in the next chapter.

Examples of federal government discount rates

Various government agencies often follow prescribed methodologies for policy analysis, including discount rates. For example, in 1992 the Office of Management and Budget (OMB) established a set of procedures for policy analysis which are widely followed in federal agencies. From that time on, the OMB has prescribed a basic discount rate of 7 percent (http://www.whitehouse.gov/ omb/circulars/a094/a094.html), but also allowed the use of the shadow price of capital method (to be discussed in Chapter 8) subject to approval by the agency. A separate set of discount rates is applied to decisions involving government ownership versus leasing of assets. (http://www.whitehouse.gov/omb/circulars/ a094/a94_appx-c.html). These rates are much lower than the benchmark 7 percent rate. It has been argued that this second set of rates is set deliberately low in order to bias government decisions in favor of ownership (Bazelon and Smetters 1999).

Other agencies tend to use lower and more variable discount rates. For example, the Environmental Protection Agency (EPA) issues annual reports prescribing discount rates which vary by the year, risk level, time frame, and class of the project, as well as the source of financing (http://www.epa.gov/airmarkt/epa-ipm/ chapter7.pdf). In the area of energy policy the 2000 EPA guidelines suggested discount rates ranging from 5.34 percent for privately funded capital projects to 6.74 percent for publicly funded high-tech energy projects (EPA website above, p. 7-4). In contrast, EPA policy uses a much higher interest rate of 10.6 percent or more when calculating the present value of the benefits to business from avoiding environmental clean-up costs. This choice of a high discount rate may be partially punitive rather than efficiency-based, and is a common source of legal debate in environmental compliance cases (see, for example, Judge Nissen's decision: http://ww.epa.gov/oalj/orders/stanche4.htm).

Much of the budgeting process in Washington and elsewhere does not involve an explicit discounting policy. For example, the federal government's five-year time horizon for many budget items includes no discounting for a five-year period and no consideration of net benefits beyond five years. Implicitly, this process sets the discount rate at zero for the first five years and infinity thereafter.

Choosing among alternative projects

In Chapter 6 we introduced multiple types of decisions to which benefit–cost analysis could be applied. These included accepting or rejecting a single project, choosing one or more projects given a fixed budget, finding an optimal budget, and choosing one among two or more alternative projects. For the most part these decisions are easily adaptable to a long-run context. One can simply judge among projects by comparing their net present values rather than their basic net benefits.

However, an important complicating issue arises when choosing one alternative among two or more projects on the basis of present value. **Projects that cover different lengths of time may not be directly comparable using present values**, since projects with shorter life spans can sometimes be repeated while a longer-lived project continues. In such cases choosing the project based only on its present value may not be correct. To give a simple example, let's assume that project A in Table 7.5 lasts for four years and that project B lasts two years. In this case the choice of a project will depend on whether the shorter project can be repeated in years 3 and 4.

Ignoring the differing life spans of the projects can lead to an incorrect choice. In Table 7.5 project A has a higher present value than project B ($7.98 vs. $6.12), but repeating project B in years 3 and 4 leads to a higher net present value than a single repetition of project A. Therefore, approving two repetitions of project B would be the correct decision if project B can be repeated.

Table 7.5 demonstrates one method for adjusting for the differing life spans of projects in a deceptively simple form. Repeating one or both projects until a common time frame is reached will correct for the problem of differing time frames. In practice, however, most projects will last longer than a few years

Table 7.5 Net present value for alternative projects

	Year 1	Year 2	Year 3	Year 4	Total
(1) Project A	−10	+10	+5	+5	xxx
(1) Discounted[a]	−9.52	9.07	4.32	4.11	**$7.98**
(2) Project B	−5	+12	0	0	xxx
(2) Discounted	−4.76	10.88	0	0	**$6.12**
(3) Project B repeated	−5	+12	−5	+12	xxx
(3) Discounted	−4.76	10.88	−4.32	9.87	**$11.61**

[a]The discount rate used is 5%.

and the longer project will not be an exact multiple of the shorter alternative. In such cases repeating both projects until a common time frame is found (for example, four repetitions of 12 years versus three repetitions of 16 years) can be very time consuming.

The common alternative method of analyzing repeatable projects is not as intuitive as finding a common time frame through repetition, but is likely to be far easier. This method is called the **equivalent annuity value (EAV)** or **equivalent annual net benefit** method. **Annuity** is a general term for any fixed payment that repeats over time. This method involves dividing the discounted net present value of each project by the discounted present value of an annuity that provides a stream of payments of $1 per year for the length of the project. The discount rate for the annuity should be equal to that of the project. The formula for the present value of an annuity of A dollars is straightforward, as seen in the following equation:

$$PV_{annuity} = \sum \frac{A}{(1+r)} \tag{7.11}$$

For long time periods this annuity can also be calculated from the following formula without explicitly calculating the full present value:

$$PV_{annuity} = A \bullet \frac{1 - \left[\frac{1}{(1+r)^n}\right]}{r} \tag{7.12}$$

where A is the annual payment and n is the number of years the project is expected to last.

Example: For the examples in Table 7.5, the equivalent annuity values of the two projects are calculated as follows for a 5 percent discount rate. Project B should not be repeated since doing so would be redundant when using the EAV method.

Project A

Four-year annuity value = $1/1.05 + $1/(1.05)^2 + $1/(1.05)^3 + $1/(1.05)^4
$$= 0.952 + 0.907 + 0.864 + 0.823 = \$3.546$$

Using the previous equation,

$$PV_{annuity} = \frac{1 - \left[\frac{1}{(1+0.05)^4}\right]}{0.05} = \frac{1 - \left[\frac{1}{(1.2155)}\right]}{0.05} = \$3.546 \text{ (avoid rouding error)}$$

The EAV of project A equals its present value from Table 7.5 divided by the PV of the annuity. In equation form, $EAV = \$7.98/\$3.546 = 2.25$.

Project B

Two year annuity = $.952 + 0.907 = $1.859. *EAV* for B = $6.12/$1.859 = **3.29**

The equivalent annuity values from this example mean that the net benefits of project A are equivalent to receiving an annual payment of $2.25 per year for each dollar invested, while the net benefits of protect B are equivalent to receiving $3.29 per year. Comparing the equivalent annuity values of the two projects allows the analyst to correctly choose project B without repeating one or both projects on paper.

Your Turn 7.9: Brian is starting a data storage business. He has two sources of servers to store data, used servers from eBay and new servers from Dell. The used servers will cost $1,000 and last two years. Additional used servers can be purchased in future years at the same price. The new servers will cost $3,000 and last five years. Each will produce net revenue of $800 per year. If the servers are purchased in year 0 and the relevant discount rate is 5 percent (0.05), which choice should he make? (Hint: The present value of $800 per year over five years is $3,464. You don't have to discount the purchase price.) Find the present value of the new and used servers, then calculate and compare the equivalent annuity values for both choices.

While there are other methods of correcting for differing time frames among alternative investments, the equivalent annuity value method provides a useful example of why such corrections are needed and how they can be accomplished.

Conclusion

The concept of present value provides the basic tool for any analysis of the efficiency of long-term private or public investments. Beyond decisions related to capital and infrastructure, it has also helped to organize and inform the analysis of long-run individual decisions such as college education, migration, and criminal activity. The primary lesson of the chapter is that for various reasons (including but not limited to the cost of foregone interest) a dollar of net benefits received in the future should be valued below a dollar received today. The reader should now be familiar with the mathematics of compound interest, discounting, and the role of present value in analyzing long-term policy decisions. The next chapter explores in much greater depth the crucial variable in present value analysis, the discount rate.

Review questions

Conceptual questions

1. The discounting of private capital investment makes sense because of foregone interest. Why might the present value discounting of public programs also make sense? (Hint: What are the possible opportunity costs of a public sector investment?)

2. Present value is sometimes criticized for being unfair to future generations. Assuming that real income increases over time, so that future generations tend to be somewhat wealthier, how would utilitarianism or the Rawlsian difference principle discount the well-being of future generations?

Computational questions

3. If the average annual return in the stock market is 8 percent per year, how much will $1,000 invested today be worth in two years? In 50 years? If the investment continues forever?

4. This question continues a case introduced in the questions for Chapter 6. Malcolm, the mayor of Schlafenberg, is being asked to choose the best among three proposals for a new water treatment plant. Plan A will cost $3 million to construct, purify $2 million worth of water per year, and lead to $1 million in operating costs. Plan B will cost $4 million to construct, purify $3 million worth of water, and result in $1.5 million in operating costs. Plan C, proposed by the mayor's son, will cost $7 million, purify $4.5 million worth of water, and result in $2.5 million of operating costs. Given this information, answer the following questions:

    (A) Assuming that each proposal will last for five years, find the present values of each using a 7 percent discount rate. Which policy would you recommend?
    (B) Find the internal rate of return for plan A to the nearest percentage point.
    (C) If plan A lasts for four years, plan B lasts for three years, and each can be repeated, find the equivalent annuity values for each option using a 7 percent discount rate. Which would you recommend?

5. In the U.S. major infrastructure investments such as bridges are often analyzed using a 50-year lifespan. The construction of an overpass to replace a road-level railroad crossing has a few significant benefits. A railroad overpass eliminates traffic delays, eliminates the need for trains to sound their horns when approaching the intersection, and also provides a minor improvement in safety. If the annual benefits from eliminating traffic delays are valued at $320,000, the annual estimated benefit of eliminating horn noise is $260,000, and the value of improved safety is $10,000, find the total discounted benefit using a 5 percent discount rate and the annuity value formula in equation 7.12. If the project costs $10 million in present value, is the investment worthwhile?

APPENDIX: THE FORREST CENTER FOR THE ARTS,[8] AN EXTENDED CASE STUDY

The Forrest Center for the Arts is a proposed state-of-the-art theatre in downtown Richardville, Pennsylvania. The goals of the Forrest Center are to provide a centralized location for Richardville performing arts companies and to provide the basis for a revitalized downtown business district. Your job is to analyze the costs and benefits of this proposed center, along with those of an alternative project, and to make a policy recommendation regarding construction. Discussion questions will follow the presentation of the case. Later chapters will also include questions referring to this case.

Last May, a group of local leaders met to lay the groundwork for a benefit–cost study of the Forrest Center project. These leaders included Steven Wood, the Mayor of Richardville, Richard Necking, head of the Transportation and Parking Authority, Natalie Voche, president of the Richardville Area Arts Council, Donald Suit, president of the Chamber of Commerce, Casey Jones, a construction engineer involved with the design of the Forrest Center, and Dr. Economicus (YOU), an economic consultant hired to conduct the actual benefit–cost study. The Mayor started the meeting off:

Steven Wood

Welcome to City Hall. I deeply appreciate your interest in downtown Richardville and the Forrest Center for the Arts, and hope today's presentation and discussion will prove fruitful. In order to bring our economic consultant up to speed on our project, let me begin by reviewing the plans for the Forrest Center for the performing arts.

The Forrest Center will be built on the former site of the Department of Construction building, which was imploded two years ago due to irreparable defects in workmanship. The current design of the Forrest Center calls for a 700-seat auditorium and facilities for education programs. The Forrest Center complex will be connected to the Capital Avenue Parking Garage and the upscale Harris City Hotel. Its location is between Capital and Free Market Streets on the north and south, and between First and Third Streets to the west and east. The structure will take approximately one year to build. Once complete, we expect to hire the equivalent of about 120 full-time employees.

Expected revenue

Mayor Wood continues

The benefits of a performing arts center come about in at least three ways. The first is performance revenue from resident companies and touring performers. The second is increased spending at local restaurants and parking garages. The third benefit is a potential increase in property values arising from the improved atmosphere in downtown Richardville.

We hope that the Forrest Center will become the official residence for several local performing arts companies, in addition to hosting touring performers in the main theatre. Bringing local performing arts organizations together under one roof will not only increase the space available for each group's performances, but will also increase attendance through greater familiarity with the central location and common ticket service provided by the Forrest Center. Also, two of the most popular local performing arts companies currently do not perform in Richardville, and all of the revenue they bring to the Forrest Center will represent a net gain to the city's economy.

Natalie Voche

I can fill in some information on the possible resident companies, and how the move to the Forrest Center might affect Richardville.

1 Richardville Theatre Company. This company performs about five works per year with five performances each. This company is currently housed in a 250-seat facility near downtown Richardville, which generally sells out, and expects to add at least 150 to its average audience by moving to the Forrest Center. It charges about $30 per ticket.
2 Richardville Opera Association. The Richardville Opera Association hires professional leads from major cities in addition to a community chorus. It currently performs at Bible University in Gap County [Richardville is in King County], and looks forward to moving to a more central location. It expects to sell an average of at least 90 percent of the seats in the main theatre for each of its 20 shows annually. It charges an average of $50 per ticket. It generally pays its professional performers a total of $10,000 per show. It currently draws about 400 people per show in its Gap County location, and hopes for at least another 100 per show in Richardville.
3 The Southern Pennsylvania Ballet Company currently performs in Candyville and in its home in Shlafenberg, which is also in Gap County. Its Nutcracker ballet is expected to sell out each of its eight performances at the Forrest Center, while the Company's other 12 performances at the Forrest Center are expected to sell about 400 tickets each. Nutcracker tickets cost $40 on average, and the others about $25.
4 The River Valley Chorus and the Chamber Players of Richardville also hope to call the Forrest Center home. Each currently performs at the Central Cathedral in downtown Richardville (a few blocks from the Forrest Center), and looks forward to an increase of at least 200 in their average audience. They charge an average of $35 for their 40 combined annual performances.

All of these groups are excited to be part of the plans for the Forrest Center, and see the central location of the theater as a major benefit to their companies.

Mayor Wood

We also hope that the main auditorium will become a venue for touring classical, folk, blues, and nostalgia performers. We project that the main auditorium will host an average of three touring performances per week with an average ticket price of $45 and average attendance of 500. We are talking about performers from outside the area that cost $10,000 to $20,000 per show. Major rock and popular shows would still have to be held at the Candyville arena or stadium.

While the primary goal of the educational program planned for the Center is to provide an active arts education experience for the region's children, fees paid by area school districts will provide some operating revenue for the Forrest Center. School districts will be charged a modest fee of $6 per child. Once the educational program is established, we expect to host about 100 children per school day. We expect to actively run the program for about 150 days per year. We will also host about 40 students for each of two four-week summer performing arts day camp programs. These programs will have a fee of about $400 per student. The cost of staffing this program is included in the general operating costs which will be introduced later.

Other local benefits

A survey conducted by the Chamber Players found that about a quarter of its audience ate in Richardville restaurants either before or after the performance. Those who ate in restaurants spent an average of about $20 per person. The local 1 percent sales tax means that the city will receive some direct benefits from this increased restaurant activity. The tax also applies to ticket sales at the Forrest Center.

Richard Necking

Also, only about a third of those attending Chamber Players concerts attempted to find free street parking in the evenings, preferring an enclosed lot with greater security. The rest parked in downtown parking garages. The attached Capital Avenue parking garage, a city-owned structure which charges a flat fee of $5 for evening parking, has 700 spaces, and is likely to be the lot of choice for those who prefer not to park on the street or cannot find a convenient street location.

Steven Wood

Finally, the longer-run development effects of a performing arts center can be substantial if combined with effective crime control and middle-class residential opportunities. The Forrest Center will encourage the development of a restaurant row near the site featuring restaurants and evening entertainment venues. Similarly, the development of galleries and shops for arts and specialty goods will be encouraged. Along with recent efforts to drive out pornography shops and lower the crime rate, the arts center could provide the second half of a one-two punch which will encourage development and raise property values in downtown Richardville.

Donald Suit

While any estimate of the Center's effect on property values will be somewhat uncertain, we do have some information which might be relevant. Pattieburg's downtown theater was estimated to increase downtown property values by about 5 percent the first year and an additional 2 percent for the next three years. After that time property values seemed to settle in at their new and higher level. The same thing may happen here. If so, it might be useful to know that the current assessed value of property in the 10-block area surrounding the Forrest Center site totals $300 million. At a property tax rate of 1 cent (10 mills) per dollar of assessed value, the city will share in the gains from this increase in local wealth.

Costs of the Center

Casey Jones

The total construction cost of the Forrest Center is estimated to be in the range of $50 million. Approximately $15 million of that will come from a state grant and $5 million more has been promised by a private foundation located in New York. The remaining $30 million will be funded by a Richardville bond issue. These bonds are expected to pay 3 percent interest for 10 years, with the principal to be repaid at the end of the 10 year period. Our best estimate of energy and operating costs for the Forrest Center is about $500,000 per year.

Donald Suit

It is also important to remember that while the Forrest Center may be politically popular, it is not the only choice we should consider. A major office building on the same property could bring in far greater government revenue than the Forrest Center, although without the same effect on evening activity in Richardville. We could easily construct a $30 million office complex with 80,000 square feet of office and retail space. When fully rented it would bring in about $10 per square foot every month. It would also offer more direct employment than the Forrest Center. Property taxes on the office complex would be about $2 million per year. Because the office complex would be a larger facility, its energy costs would be higher, perhaps $2 million extra per year.

Steven Wood

Yes, but the office complex would have to be entirely financed through the bond issue. Charitable donations and the State grant would be lost. Also, we can't be sure that the space would be rented. Currently, downtown office space is about 85 percent rented, which is fairly healthy but not indicative of a shortage. I would guess that an office building would be no more than 50 percent rented the first year, with a 5 percentage point increase each year after that *if* the economy continues to do well. If we fall into a recession, rental rates could stagnate or fall somewhat until the downturn is reversed. At no point would we expect more than 90 percent of the office space in the complex to be rented. We also don't know how much of that amount is diverted from other downtown office locations, but it could be as much as half. This building's 80,000 square feet would represent about a 10 percent increase in the total office space in the downtown business district. This big a jump in office space could have a negative effect on the average office rent. Also, there is a daytime parking shortage in the area that could make it very difficult on local commuters. Congestion in the downtown area during rush-hour would increase. The beauty of the downtown area would also be enhanced to a greater degree by the performing arts center. I'm just a lawyer, so the dollar values of these effects are beyond me. But they do seem important.

Donald Suit

Without a design for the office complex, a comparison of the beauty of the projects seems very premature. However, the rest of the points are well-taken. The office complex is not a guaranteed improvement over the Forrest Center proposal, but it should be considered because of its greater revenue potential.

Steven Wood

Dr. Economicus, I hope this discussion gives you some ideas for your cost–benefit analysis. We would like to know if we should build the Forrest Arts Center, the office complex, or perhaps neither. We are interested in the overall well-being of the Richardville economy. But we would also like to know which project would be best for the government of Richardville. We will be glad to cooperate in any way that we can.

Hints for students

This case study can be conducted in groups or as a single class project. The client is the City of Richardville, and the benefits and costs of the projects should be consistent with the goals of your client. The broader goal is to choose the project that offers the greatest net benefit to Richardville as a whole, but you also might also calculate the net benefits to the Richardville city government. It will be easier to keep these options straight if you complete separate benefit–cost calculations for the Forrest Center and the office complex. For convenience, I recommend using a **10-year time frame** for this study, although your instructor might suggest a longer or shorter time frame.

Be sure to follow the steps in a present value model carefully. As with any present value problem, the first and most difficult job is to gather the benefits and costs for each year. In order to calculate the restaurant and parking benefits you will first have to calculate the attendance at cultural events hosted by the Forrest Center, and the resultant increase in revenue. For those companies currently performing in Richardville, only the increase in attendance should be considered.

Similarly, when estimating the property value effect of the Center only the increase in property value should be included in the benefits. Benefits and costs to the city government require additional calculations based on the tax rates stated in the conversation. On the cost side, don't forget that the bonds for either project will be paid off at the end of the tenth year. Subtracting costs from benefits and finally discounting to present value will complete the calculations.

There is a lot of room for you to make your own assumptions regarding the benefits of the office complex. The effect of the office complex on overall rents and vacancy rates are left deliberately vague. Feel free to make any reasonable assumptions about these effects. Since different groups are likely to make different assumptions, the class will probably provide a type of sensitivity analysis regarding these assumptions.

The choice of a discount rate is up to you or your professor. If you wish to delay this project until after the next chapter you will be able to make a more sophisticated choice of discount rates. At this point the 3 percent real rate on government bonds or a somewhat higher rate such as the 7 percent real rate recommended by the Office of Management and Budget would be good starting points. Unless you are adjusting your net benefits for inflation, you should use a real interest rate in your calculations.

Discussion questions

1. Based on the present values of the two projects, which project is better for the community of Richardville? Which is better for the Richardville city government? Overall, which should be constructed?

2. If your groups used different discount rates, did the choice of discount rate affect your recommendations? Did higher discount rates tend to favor the Forrest Center or the office complex?

3. Who are the biggest winners from the Forrest Center project? The office project?

4. Discuss the benefits and costs from the two projects which were not quantified in dollar terms. How do they affect the relative attractiveness of the two projects?

5. How much difference would it make if the estimated increases in property values from the Forrest Center were excluded from your calculations?

6. The federal government is contributing a $15 million grant to the Forrest Center. Private foundations are contributing $5 million. If we were calculating the net benefits of the Forrest Center for all of society how would these two components be handled?

7. Is there a place like the Forrest Center in your home town? You might look up the website for any local performing arts theater and see what they offer. Is the Forrest Center more active in terms of frequency of shows than the theater you found on the web?

8 Choosing a discount rate

Few topics in our discipline rival the social rate of discount as a subject exhibiting simultaneously a very considerable degree of knowledge and a very substantial level of ignorance.[1]

(William Baumol)

A low rate of discount favors low yielding projects at the expense of others.[2]

(Raymond Mikesell)

♫ Sha-la-la-la-la-la, live for today, and don't worry
'bout tomorrow, hey, hey, hey.

(Author unknown, performed by the Grass Roots)

In a perfectly competitive world the choice of a discount rate would be very easy. A competitive market for loans would provide an equilibrium interest rate for each dollar loaned or borrowed, and this rate would be the appropriate discount rate. When complications such as taxes, risk aversion, and imperfect markets are included, finding an ideal discount rate becomes far more difficult, even for experts. While the economics profession has moved toward a near-consensus regarding the underlying theory of an optimal social discount rate, neither government agencies nor academics have established a consensus regarding a practical and equitable, as well as efficient, discount rate for public projects. In this chapter we will briefly review the discount rate in a perfectly competitive case, and then consider the implications of a few of the most important complicating factors. Unfortunately, there are many more.

The ideal market for loans

The interest rate in a market economy is the cost of borrowing money, and is determined by the supply of and demand for loans. The simplest model for loans assumes that the supply of loanable funds is provided by individual savings, while businesses demand (borrow) loanable funds in order to finance capital investment. This perfectly competitive model for loans appears in Figure 8.1.

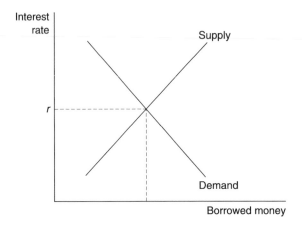

Figure 8.1 The market for loans

The supply of savings and individual time preference

Given the market interest rate, an individual chooses how much of her current income to consume and save. Income which is saved collects interest, leading to increased consumption in the future. Let's assume that Jill College has $100 now which she can spend as she wishes over the next two years. Each dollar can either be spent immediately or placed in an account paying 5 percent interest (see Figure 8.2). The straight line in Figure 8.2 represents her budget constraint given the current balance of $100 and the 5 percent interest rate. If Jill consumes $50 and saves $50 this year she will have $50 · (1.05) or $52.50 next year.

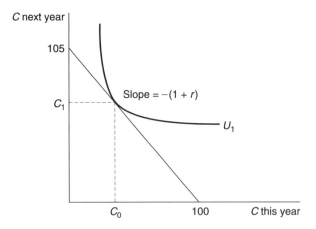

Figure 8.2 Utility-maximizing consumption and saving

More generally, saving a certain amount S_0 this year at interest rate r will produce a total of $S_0(1+r)$ dollars next year, which she will then consume. Her utility-maximizing choice, based on her indifference curve U_1, is to consume C_0 in the first year, and allow $S_0 = \$(110 - C_0)$ to earn interest until next year, when she will consume C_1. At her utility-maximizing point, where the slope of the indifference curve is also equal to $-(1+r)$, she is indifferent between $1 today or $1.05 next year. This is the graphical representation of Jill's time preference. While different individuals may choose different levels of saving versus current consumption in this model, in this perfectly competitive world they will be doing so on the basis of the same equilibrium interest rate. This interest rate can be called the **social rate of time preference**. In the formulas to follow, we will label the social rate of time preference in a competitive market r^*.

The efficiency of capital and the demand for loans

The demand for loans in Figure 8.1 represents the investment decisions of businesses. Rational and informed firms will choose to invest whenever the returns to capital investment, corrected for factors such as added risk, are greater than the returns to saving. This will occur whenever the present value of the investment is greater than zero when discounted using the market interest rate. The relation between investment and interest can be summarized in the marginal rate of return on investment (MRR) curve (see Figure 8.3), which ranks investment spending according to the internal rate of return of various projects. Ignoring the issue of risk, a market interest rate of 0.05 will lead to the approval of any investment with positive present value when discounted at 5 percent. Therefore, at the margin, the rate of return to investment will equal the market interest rate and the social rate of time preference.

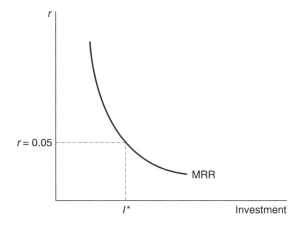

Figure 8.3 The marginal rate of return

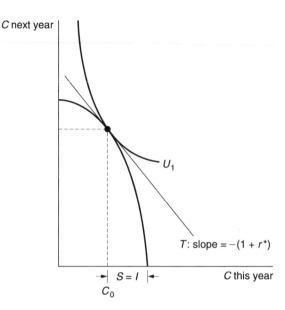

Figure 8.4 Competitive general equilibrium

The following general equilibrium model represents this competitive equilibrium more completely. In Figure 8.4 the bulging line is a production possibilities frontier (PPF) presenting a range of possible quantities of consumption over two time periods. The slope of the PPF equals $\Delta C_1/\Delta C_0$, the amount of consumption next year which can be added by foregoing a unit of consumption this year. Notice that starting from the horizontal axis the slope is very steep at first, but steadily flattens as one approaches the vertical axis. This flattening curve represents the declining marginal return to capital investment.

The curve labeled U_1 represents the highest possible social indifference curve that can be achieved given people's tastes and the limited productive resources of society. The straight line T represents the market price of trading current for future consumption. The slope of this line will be $-(1+r^*)$, where r^* is the competitive social rate of discount. At point A, the intersection between U_1 and T is the same in form and meaning as in Figure 8.2. Similarly, the slope of the PPF also equals $-(1+r^*)$, meaning that the marginal return to investment equals r^*. In this simple case an efficient result occurs at a single interest rate, r^*. In such a case r^* would be the correct discount rate for any public or private investment decision.

Distortions in the loans market

It is often argued that nations currently invest too little and consume too much. Three sources of inefficiently low savings and investment have been consistently referred to in the literature. These are shortsightedness or related behavioral limits

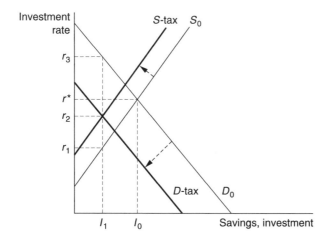

Figure 8.5 Taxes and interest rates

among the current population, risk aversion among investors, and government taxation and/or borrowing. All of these factors lead to excess current consumption and lowered efficiency. However, the effects of government taxes or borrowing are much easier to describe, and will be emphasized below.

As seen in Chapter 5, taxes create a gap between the full costs to the consumer and the after-tax revenue of the producer or supplier. In Figure 8.5 both the supply of loans (individual savings) and the demand (investment) are taxed. The result is to decrease investment and savings from I_0 to I_1. At investment level I_1 investors will receive a before-tax return of r_3 and an after-tax return of r_2. Similarly, savings brings a before-tax return of r_2 but an after-tax return of only r_1. In a market with taxes, r_1 is the social rate of discount because it represents the marginal benefit to a dollar of saving to individuals after taxes. However, r_1 is below the optimal social rate of discount r^* because of the tax effect.

In Figure 8.6 the equilibrium with taxes occurs at point A'. At this point the slope of the PPF equals $-(1+r_3)$ while the slope of T and the social indifference curve equals $-(1+r_1)$. Also, at point A' there is more current consumption and less investment and saving than at point A. The lower social indifference curve shows clearly the loss of efficiency from this inequality in the marginal rates of return.

A numerical example of the effect of taxes may help. Assume, for example, that the optimal social discount rate r^* is 5 percent, individual income is taxed at 25 percent, and business income is taxed at 50 percent. In this case the marginal individual receiving 5 percent interest on her savings would receive 3.75 percent after taxes. Similarly, a business would have to earn 7.5 percent on its investments in order to achieve a 5 percent return after taxes. This inequality between the after-tax rates of return on investment and savings creates the under-investment and loss of social welfare visible in Figure 8.6.

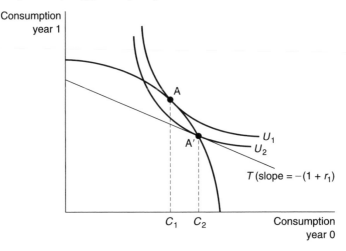

Figure 8.6 Taxes, interest, and investment

A range of possible discount rates

The difference between the social discount rate after taxes (r_1 in Figure 8.6) and the rate of return on capital after taxes (r_3) creates a range within which we can search for the optimal discount rate. Rate r_3 can be represented by the before-tax rate of return on capital corrected for risk, while r_1 could be represented by after-tax returns on savings accounts or low-risk government bonds. In current U.S. government policy analysis benchmark rates of 7 percent for the return on capital and 3 percent for the social rate of time preference are sometimes used. Current interest rates on U.S. treasury and corporate bonds can be found at the website of the Board of Governors of the Federal Reserve (http://www.federalreserve. gov/releases/H15/update/h15upd.htm).

Extreme cases

Over the past three or four decades, economists and other analysts have argued for various interest rates based on efficiency, and in some cases for a zero discount rate based on ethical concerns, an issue that will be discussed later in the chapter. In terms of efficiency, the debate has ranged between the relatively low social rate of time preference (r_1 in Figure 8.5) and a higher rate consistent with the marginal return to capital (r_3 in Figure 8.5). Some economists have argued that the low social rate of time preference should be used because a project with a positive present value at a low rate will produce enough future consumption to make the net benefits positive from the consumer's point of view. The primary measurement problem with the personal rate of time preference is that the range of personal interest rates on savings and personal loans is very wide, and estimating a reasonable average is difficult.

The arguments for a higher discount rate based on the rate of return to capital are also interesting. First, if a lower discount rate is used, public investment yielding 2 or 3 percent may displace private investment yielding a far higher rate of return, producing a net loss to society. The rate of return to capital provides an appropriate discount rate if the funding for the public project displaces private capital investment rather than personal savings and consumption. Given the low responsiveness of personal savings to modest changes in interest rates this assumption is often approximately true. In such a case the higher discount rate would be a reasonably accurate measure of opportunity cost. This is not a sufficient argument for claiming that the rate of return to capital approximates the optimal discount rate, however.

There are also implications for the size of government in this choice. Consistently evaluating public projects at a discount rate lower than the marginal rate of return to capital could have the effect of increasing the relative size of the public sector. As shown through the examples in Chapter 7, a lower discount rate will tend to lead to the recommended adoption of more public projects while a higher rate will tend to lead to fewer projects, all else equal.

One argument against using the rate of return to capital is based on the role of risk in the average firm's rate of return. The average firm faces greater risk in much of its activity than government, and therefore requires a higher average rate of return. Monopoly power may also artificially raise the private rate of return. Finally, some types of public spending for infrastructure or research may have a positive rather than negative effect on private investment. Therefore, a private rate of return on investment is probably an overestimate of the "true" discount rate.

Displacement of investment and consumption

The last thing most analysts want is to turn the discount rate into a political issue. Therefore, much effort has been put into trying to narrow the range of acceptable discount rates and to find a practical and theoretically acceptable form for an optimal discount rate. Efforts to compromise between the social rate of discount for individuals and the rate of return to capital involve weighing or combining the effects of a government project on investment and consumption. Since the marginal return to capital is greater than the social rate of discount after taxes, projects that displace investment will have a higher opportunity cost than those that displace consumption.

A brief graphical analysis of a project funded from either government borrowing or taxes will help you to follow the argument. Figure 8.7 displays the effect on savings and investment of government borrowing and through a tax on individual savings. A tax on investment would produce effects similar to those of a tax on savings. Government borrowing raises demand for loans and the equilibrium interest rate. This increases private saving and decreases private investment. The increase in private saving corresponds to a decrease in consumption, all else equal. Therefore, both private investment and consumption are displaced by a project funded by borrowed funds. Similarly, the tax on savings decreases the savings supply. This supply shift raises the before-tax interest rate, while lowering the

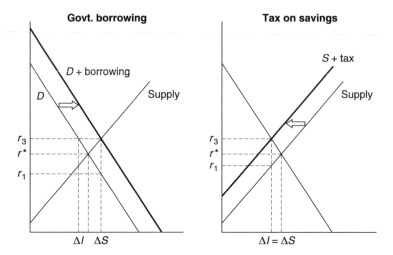

Figure 8.7 Savings and investment displacement

after-tax rate, and thereby decreases investment and savings. In this case the effect of borrowing on consumption in the short run is theoretically ambiguous since the lower return on savings decreases income and also decreases the opportunity cost of current consumption.

The shadow price of capital method

As noted earlier, the marginal return on capital investment (r_3 in Figures 8.5 and 8.7) and the social rate of discount (r_1 in the same figures) create a reasonable range for the debate concerning the preferred discount rate for public projects. Within this range an optimal discount rate has been suggested which is considered theoretically accurate but is difficult to measure or explain. This rate is based on a concept known as the **shadow price of capital**. The **shadow price** of any item is an estimate of the maximum willingness to pay for that item. According to this model the shadow price of a capital investment project is equal to the present value of lost future consumption from the investment. In theory, this present value of future consumption can be calculated in two steps. First, a dollar of investment provides a stream of future consumption determined by the marginal rate of return to capital (r_3 in our graphs). Then the present value of future consumption can found by discounting at the social rate of discount (r_1 in our graphs). Because r_3 is greater than r_1, the shadow price of capital generally will be greater than one. The shadow price of capital will equal r_3/r_1 if all of the interest earned from the investment is consumed, the original amount is reinvested, and no depreciation is considered. This is equivalent to having an infinite stream of annual consumption equal to r_3 for each dollar invested. Discounting this infinite stream using r_1 produces the final formula r_3/r_1. This approach is not realistic enough to be used in practice.

A more realistic and relatively understandable method of applying the shadow price of capital can be used for government-funded capital projects. The process takes four steps: (1) Estimate the policy's effect on investment versus consumption. (2) Annualize the capital costs over the expected lifetime of the capital equipment using the opportunity cost of capital. (3) Include these annualized capital costs in the net benefits of the project. (4) Discount the stream of net benefits at the consumption rate of interest. The following case study will explain this process.

An extended case study

Assume that the U.S. government is funding a major remedial education, training, and employment program called "No Adult Left Behind." The program is fully funded by the federal government through borrowing. The project requires an initial capital investment of $20 billion, will bring benefits of $6 billion per year, and will face operating costs of $2 billion per year after the initial training period in year zero. I will work through an example where the net benefits extend for 10 years. You can then do the same for a five-year time horizon.

Step 1: Estimate the project's effect on investment

The first step is to estimate the policy's effect on investment versus consumption. This step involves considerable uncertainty and debate, and may therefore be a candidate for sensitivity analysis (see Chapter 9). Harberger (1976)[3] has argued that because personal savings are quite unresponsive to interest rates, the supply curve in the loanable funds market will be nearly vertical, and that projects financed by borrowing will produce very little change in savings or consumption (see Figure 8.7). Therefore, according to Harberger nearly all borrowed funds can be assumed to displace investment. On the other hand, projects funded through taxes are more likely to displace consumption. On average only about 16 percent of total gross domestic product (GDP) is privately invested[4] while the rest is consumed by government or private citizens. This ratio of 16 percent foregone investment and 84 percent displaced consumption may be appropriate for projects fully funded by income taxes. In order to allow the reader to practice the full analysis with relative ease, let's assume that our example displaces private investment and consumption equally ($10 billion apiece).

Step 2: Annualize the capital cost

The fraction of total expenditure that displaces private investment will now be converted to an annual value. The annualized value of capital cost is found by solving the following present value equation for X:

$$PV_k = \frac{X}{1+r_3} + \frac{X}{(1+r_3)^2} + \cdots + \frac{X}{(1+r_3)^n} \tag{8.1}$$

where r_3 is the rate of return to capital and n is the number of years in the lifespan of the displaced capital. This equation can be converted to a more useful form that is similar to the annuity value equation in Chapter 7.

$$X = PV_k \frac{r_3(1+r_3)^n}{(1+r_3)^n - 1} \tag{8.2}$$

For example, a program with a 7 percent rate of return that displaces $10 billion in capital investment over a 10 year period would have an annualized value of

$$X = \$10B \frac{0.07(1.07)^{10}}{(1.07)^{10} - 1} \quad \begin{aligned} &= \$10 \text{ billion} \cdot 0.1377/0.96715 \\ &= 1.424 \text{ billion per year} \end{aligned} \tag{8.3}$$

This number is an estimate of the annual future consumption lost due to the displacement of capital investment. Using the social rate of discount after taxes (3 percent or some other estimate), the present value of this lost future consumption is $12.15 billion over 10 years, or about 1.2 times the present value of an equal amount of displaced current consumption. Therefore, 1.2 is the shadow price of capital in this example. Realistic estimates of the shadow price of capital are generally quite a bit higher.[5]

> **Your Turn 8.1:** If the project lasts only five years, find the annualized lost consumption from the $10 billion of displaced investment using a return to capital of 7 percent. Then find the present value of this lost consumption using a 3 percent social rate of discount.

If the initial investment takes more than one year to complete, the analysis involves the extra step of converting the two or more years of actual investment to present value, then annualizing over the life of the project using this formula.

Steps 3 and 4: Finalizing the present value estimate

Steps 3 and 4 break no new ground. Calculating the annual net benefits, including the annualized capital costs, should be easy enough. When discounting the net benefits remember to use the lower social discount rate of 3 percent.

Example: The $10 billion in displaced consumption can be assumed to take place at the same time as the project's initial spending. With the annualized investment costs included, the total net benefits for each of the 10 years of the project will be

$6 billion in benefits minus $2 billion in operating costs minus $1.4 billion in lost future consumption from the displaced investment, or $2.6 billion per year.

$$PV = -\$10\,\text{billion} + \frac{\$2.6B}{1.03} + \frac{\$2.6B}{(1.03)^2} + \cdots + \frac{\$2.6B}{(1.03)^{10}} = \$14.10\,\text{billion}$$

Your Turn 8.2: Perform the same calculation for five years only.

The weighted discount rate

An easier but less accurate method of dealing with the consumption versus investment issue involves discounting the project using a weighted average of the rate of return on capital and social discount rate on consumption.

$$\text{Weighted } r = a \cdot r_1 + (1-a) \cdot r_3 \tag{8.4}$$

where a is the fraction of the project's cost which is financed by displaced consumption and $(1-a)$ is the fraction which displaces investment. Another dimension of the weighted value which is becoming gradually more important in the U.S. is borrowing from foreign sources. While foreign lending to U.S. private and government borrowers is volatile over time, the early years of the twenty-first century have seen foreign lending to the U.S. rise to over 20 percent of total lending (Federal Reserve, Tables F.115-17). With foreign lending included, the weighted discount rate becomes

$$\text{Weighted } r \text{ with foreign lending} = a \cdot r_1 + b \cdot r_f + (1 - a - b) \cdot r_3 \tag{8.5}$$

where r_1 and r_3 are the social discount rate and return to capital, r_f is the interest rate on foreign lending, and b is the fraction of the project's cost financed by foreign lending. In general the appropriate interest rate for foreign lending would be the interest rate on the federal, state or local bond issue which is used to finance that part of the investment.

Your Turn 8.3: If r_1 is 3 percent, r_3 is 7 percent, a is 0.2, and b is 0.2, what is the weighted discount rate?

Other issues in choosing a discount rate

In addition to the difficult choice of a basic discount rate, there are a few other factors to consider when discounting. These factors include the rate of inflation, the riskiness of the project, and the lifespan of the project's net benefits. Inflation and risk involve relatively detailed issues, while the time frame question is much easier to explain. Inflation will be discussed in the following section. Risk is discussed in Chapter 9.

Inflation and the discount rate

While the basic definition of the real interest rate was introduced in Chapter 7, the issue of inflation is more complicated than that simple formula suggests. To review, the basic definition of the real interest rate is repeated here.

Concept: The real interest rate is the rate of interest corrected for inflation. It is generally defined as the nominal rate of interest minus the inflation rate. If the real interest rate is r, the nominal interest rate is i, and the inflation rate is p, **the approximate formula for the real interest rate is $r = i - p$.**

As mentioned in Chapter 7, the correct choice of a real or nominal interest rate depends on whether you are measuring costs and benefits in real or nominal terms. If you are using real costs and benefits, a real interest rate is correct. If your costs and benefits are nominal, your discount rate should also be nominal.

Whether inflating future net benefits in order to estimate future nominal values or calculating a real discount rate, the measurement of inflation is controversial. The most commonly used measure of inflation in the U.S. is the consumer price index (CPI) for all urban workers (CPI-U). This index measures changes in the cost of a fixed set of goods over time. This set of goods is established by a large survey of the spending habits of urban workers. This current fixed weight index is based on a spending survey taken during the period 1982 to 1984.

A price index that measures the cost of a fixed set of goods over many years exaggerates the costs of inflation for a number of reasons. The most commonly discussed reason is **substitution bias**, which refers to the tendency of consumers to substitute away from goods whose prices rise more than average. Other biases include **same store bias**, which exaggerates inflation by ignoring the gradual movement of consumption to discount stores, the introduction of **new products** and their tendency to experience steep price decreases in early years, and the increase in **quality** over time, particularly for technologically sophisticated products such as consumer electronics and automobiles. The Boskin Commission released a detailed study of these biases and concluded that the consumer price index was biased upward by about 1.1 percentage points per year.[6]

The primary government reaction to this argument has been to move toward greater use of chain-weighted price indexes rather than a fixed market basket index. Chain-weighted price indexes are based on annual spending data rather than a fixed market basket and therefore do not suffer from substitution, same

Table 8.1 Alternative inflation measures[a]

Inflation measure (%)	CPI-U	CPI-U (chain weighted)	Implicit GDP price deflator	GDP index (chain weighted)
2001	2.8	2.3	2.4	2.4
2002	1.6	1.2	1.7	1.7
2003	2.3	2.1	1.8	1.8
2004p	2.7	2.2	–	2.2

[a]For the GDP indexes, see the following Bureau of Economic Analysis website, Tables 1.1.4–1.1.9 (http://www.bea.gov/bea/dn/nipaweb/SelectTable.asp?Selected=Y). For CPI inflation data, see the Bureau of Labor Statistics website (http://www.bls.gov/cpi/home.htm).

store, or new product bias. The primary U.S. chain-weighted indexes are the chain-weighted CPI published by the Bureau of Labor Statistics and the chain-weighted GDP price index published by the Bureau of Economic Analysis.[7] Another chain-weighted price index with a longer history is the GDP price deflator, which is similar to the GDP price index. These alternative inflation measures are compared in Table 8.1.

The bias due to quality change, estimated by the Boskin Commission to account for a 0.6 percentage point exaggeration of inflation in the CPI-U (over half of the total bias) is the only one of the primary biases in the fixed weight index that cannot be directly observed in consumer behavior, and therefore isn't corrected for in the chain-weighted indexes.[8] Therefore, these chain-weighted indexes can be assumed to overstate inflation by roughly half a percentage point. Another dimension of choosing a price index is the scope of the index. The CPI-U measures the cost of living for urban workers and excludes costs relating to other sections of the economy, including government. For policies that involve benefits and costs to non-consumers, the broader GDP price index is probably a wiser choice.

Not surprisingly, for the analysis of future real benefits and costs an estimate of future inflation is necessary. Forecasting any future macroeconomic variable is at best educated guesswork, especially in the distant future. In practice, past averages are almost always used. Based on the above discussion, one might consider using a multi-year average inflation rate from the GDP chain-weighted price index, then subtracting five- or six-tenths of a point from the average in order to correct for quality bias. For example, a 10-year average of the inflation rate in the GDP deflator from 1994 to 2004 equals 1.79 percent (http://www.bea.gov/bea/dn/nipaweb/SelectTable.asp?Selected=Y). Subtracting half a percentage point for quality bias produces an average of 1.29 percent inflation. If one starts with a 7 percent nominal discount rate, the real discount rate based on this inflation adjustment would equal 7–1.29, or 5.71 percent. On the other hand, a 3 percent estimate for inflation would produce a 4 percent real discount rate, an underestimate of the real discount rate great enough to change policy recommendations for some marginal programs.

The project's time frame and the discount rate

The third issue in choosing an interest rate under competitive conditions is the time frame of the project. Interest rates vary with the length of time of the loan, and vary over time with variations in demand-and-supply conditions. Therefore, a long-term project should use a discount rate which represents the analyst's best guess at the average interest rate on a risk-free investment over the life of the project. Short-term interest rates are not appropriate measures of the opportunity cost of long-term projects. Therefore, **the discount rate should be based on an interest rate for low-risk assets such as government bonds that have a time frame similar to that of the investment project.**[9]

Long-term policies and intergenerational equity

Some policies have effects that extend far into the future and affect many future generations. Such policies confront a significant equity issue involving time and discounting, the relative importance of net benefits to different generations. According to utilitarian ethics, discounting long-range public projects at a constant rate will unfairly devalue the net benefits to future generations, particularly if the discount rate is significantly greater than the real growth rate of the economy. This section will review the effect of different discount rates on the distant future, discuss the implications of discounting for future generations, and briefly review two alternative approaches to discounting that are sensitive to inter-generational equity concerns.

During the later years of the George H.W. Bush administration (the early 1990s), the Congress was controlled by Democrats and the administration was Republican. During this time both the Congressional Budget Office (CBO) and the administration's Office of Management and Budget (OMB) had established discount rates for benefit–cost analysis. The OMB analysts had been using a discount rate of 10 percent since 1972, and in the late 1980s the CBO's recommended real discount rate was 2 percent, the approximate real cost of borrowed funds to the government at that time. How much of a difference would this disparity make in the analysis of the two agencies? First, consider the present value of a dollar of net benefits under each choice. Notice that the present values diverge as one moves into the future, until in year 100 the

Table 8.2 Present value in different agencies: 1980s

Year	CBO (2%)	OMB (10%)
Now	$1.00	$1.00
1	$0.98	$0.91
2	$0.96	$0.83
10	$0.82	$0.39
100	$0.14	$0.00007

present value of a dollar using the CBO rate is about 2,000 times as great as the OMB figure.

To put the distinction in somewhat starker terms, let's consider a hypothetical example.

Example: Assume we discover that a $100 trillion (or $100,000 billion) tragedy measured in real dollars will occur on Earth 200 years from now, and that we can prevent this tragedy by spending $10 billion this year. Should we spend this money, based on the present value of the costs and benefits? The present value problem is

$$PV \text{(billions)} = -10 + \frac{100,000}{(1+r)^{200}}$$

Using a 2 percent real discount rate, $(1 + 0.02)^{200}$ equals about 52.5, so the present value will be $-$10 \, billion + $100 \, trillion/52.5$, or about $1.9 \, trillion$. The CBO would clearly recommend the expenditure. On the other hand, $(1 + 0.1)^{200}$ equals $189,905,000$ (*much* higher than 52.5!), and the present value of the investment becomes -$10 \, billion + $100 \, trillion/189,905,000$, or $-$10 \, billion + $0.005 \, billion$, or $-$9.995 \, billion$. The astounding part of this result is that the $100 trillion cost occurring 200 years in the future has a present value of only $5 million using a 10 percent discount rate. While most policies do not have clearly identifiable benefits or costs that extend 200 or more years into the future, those that do, such as nuclear waste storage, must be analyzed with particular care. A simple present value model with a high discount rate such as 0.1 is simply not appropriate for such cases.

The goal of this example is to make it clear that the discount rate one chooses will have a significant effect on an analyst's policy recommendations, particularly in the long run. A low discount rate will tend to encourage some forms of private or public investment spending because the opportunity cost of foregone interest will be relatively low. High discount rates will tend to discourage such investment spending. Furthermore, a low discount rate will be particularly favorable to spending on projects with net benefits occurring in the more distant future, while higher discount rates will reduce the present value of future net benefits or costs, and will favor projects with more immediate benefits. This finding does not imply that low discount rates should be favored in all circumstances, despite the dubious results for our disaster scenario using a higher rate.

Intergenerational equity and discounting

For long-run projects with widespread public effects, the well-being of future generations becomes an important part of a benefit–cost analysis. For example, proposed policies to reduce possible global warming and climate change would

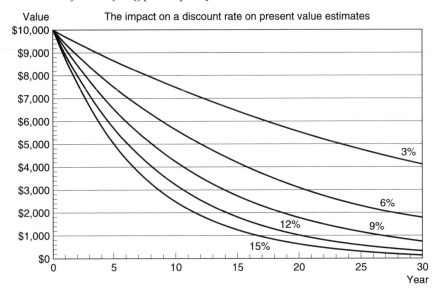

Figure 8.8 PV with alternate discount rates
Source: This chart was produced by the State of California (http://www.dot.ca.gov/hq/tpp/
offices/ote/Benefit_Cost/calculations/discount_rate.html)

be paid for primarily by relatively current generations and would benefit future
generations. While discounting is appropriate when valuing the future returns for
one generation's investments, the type of single interest rate discounting
discussed thus far also places a lower weight on the well-being of distant generations, a very different issue. Efforts to calculate a discount rate for long-term projects based on intergenerational equity have produced a great deal of discussion,
but no consensus.

In order to explain the dilemma, let's take a simple case that deals only with the
relative weights of current and future generations. The utilitarian social welfare
function discussed in Chapter 2 provides the most common starting point for this
issue. Assume that there are three generations whose utilities are given equal
weights according to utilitarian principles. For simplicity, we will also assume
that different generations have the same utility function. Even more simply,
assume that each generation's benefits take place over one time period. The utilitarian social welfare function for this example is thus:

$$SWF_U = U(B_1 - C_1) + U(B_2 - C_2) + U(B_3 - C_3) \tag{8.6}$$

In contrast, a social welfare function with discounting appears as follows:

$$SWF_D = \frac{U(B_1 - C_1)}{(1+r)^1} + \frac{U(B_2 - C_2)}{(1+r)^2} + \frac{U(B_3 - C_3)}{(1+r)^3} \tag{8.7}$$

These two equations are equal only if r equals zero, implying that the utilitarian ethic is inconsistent with the discounting of future generations' utility. However, this ethical rejection of the discounting of future utility does not mean that it is inappropriate to discount future **income**. If future generations are richer and the marginal utility of income falls as income rises, some discounting based on the falling marginal utility of income is acceptable according to utilitarianism.

One of the modern philosophers discussed in Chapter 2, John Rawls, also makes a somewhat relevant contribution to intergenerational equity. In the presence of long-term growth in per capita income, Rawls' difference principle would allow one to ignore the utility of wealthier future generations unless the policy in question reduces future incomes below that of the present. However, Rawls' **just saving principle** specifically rejects the difference principle in the intergenerational context and substitutes a moral requirement to save and grow until an adequate level of justice (or income) is achieved. According to Rawls, a rich society should save more than a poor one, but a fully affluent society has no reason to grow or save further. Overall, Rawls' position on generational equity is quite vague.

Discounting in a long-run context

At this time there are at least two types of models for dealing with the discounting of net benefits for future generations. One approach utilizes a **declining discount rate**. This method involves the use of one of several mathematical formulas in which the discount rate falls with the passage of time, and is generally referred to as hyperbolic discounting. Another approach discounts future net benefits based on the **expected growth rate** of the economy, which is partially related to the diminishing marginal utility of income argument mentioned above.

Declining (or hyperbolic) discount rate models use various discounting formulas that produce declining discount rates over time. Economists have produced several possible rationales for a declining discount rate, most of which are quite complex theoretically (Groom *et al.* 2005). In addition to the utilitarian argument that future generations are unfairly underweighted using the standard present value model, other arguments for a declining discount rate exist. The most understandable argument is that many studies of personal preferences have found that our time preferences behave consistently with a declining discount rate approach (Frederick *et al.* 2002: 360). Declining discount rate models can take several specific forms.[10] For example, one could define the present value of $1 in year t as

$$PV_{ddr} = 1/(1+at), \text{ where } a \text{ is the discount rate and t is time} \qquad (8.8)$$

Table 8.6 compares values for the declining discount rate and present value discounting formulas using a 5 percent rate of interest. It might be helpful to know that if the standard present value formula was used, a 2.47 percent discount rate would produce in a present value of 0.29 in year 50. Similarly, a discount rate of about 1.78 percent would produce a present value of 0.17 in year 100 using the

Table 8.3 Declining versus fixed discount rates

		Year 1	Year 4	Year 10	Year 50	Year 100
PV_{ddr}	$\dfrac{1}{(1+0.05t)}$	0.95	0.83	0.67	0.29	0.17
PV	$\dfrac{1}{(1+0.05)^t}$	0.95	0.82	0.61	0.09	0.008

standard present value discounting formula. So if one was using the standard present value model, successively smaller values for r would have to be used to produce the same time trend one gets from this PV_{ddr} formula. This example demonstrates that declining discount rate models are accurately named, and place greater weight on net benefits occurring in the distant future than the standard model.

The **expected growth rate** approach to discounting calculates a social discount rate by multiplying the expected growth rate of consumption in dollars by an estimate of the rate of decline of the marginal utility of a dollar of consumption. As a formula, if the expected growth rate equals g, the rate of decline in the marginal utility of consumption equals u, and the growth-based discount rate equals r_g, the discount rate formula is simply $r_g = g \cdot u$. If u equals one, the growth-based discount rate would equal the growth rate of consumption. If u equals zero, implying no decrease in the marginal utility of consumption over time, r_g also equals zero and no discounting takes place. A pure rate of time preference p is generally added to this equation, producing $r_g = g \cdot u + p$. An early study of this growth-based discount rate by Kula (1984) produced an estimate for r_g of 5.3 percent.[11] At this rate of discount, the use of a growth rate-based approach would differ very little from a shadow price of capital approach during periods of moderate interest rates.

It has become somewhat more acceptable to use lower discount rates or hyperbolic discounting formulas when analyzing long-term environmental policies in order to avoid dubious results such as the disaster scenario discussed earlier. However, as yet, there is no consensus on how or under what specific circumstances to do this.

Conclusion

The goal of this chapter was to provide a more detailed view of the theoretical challenges in determining an ideal discount rate for public projects. Determining the true opportunity cost of a project or an accurate measure of inflation are difficult theoretical and statistical tasks. The presentation of these issues was kept relatively basic, but the issues are truly complex.

There is no generally accepted discount rate for public projects, although economists have moved somewhat closer to a consensus over the past two decades. One's choice of a discount rate can be influenced by both efficiency and equity concerns. Efficient decisions based on present value discounting can expand the total wealth available to a society over time, thereby providing policy choices which can improve the total social welfare achieved with a given set of resources. Also, since in some contexts the choice of a discount rate directly influences the relative value placed on benefits and costs flowing to different generations, the choice of a discount rate can involve important equity concerns.

Review questions

Conceptual questions

1. Discuss the possibility that present value discounting is unjust to future generations. If you wish, consider the separate cases of capital investment and a long-term environmental policy such as the curbing of greenhouse gases.

2. Explain the difference between the shadow price of capital method and weighted discount rate method.

3. Should social security payments be adjusted for inflation using a chain-weighted index or by a fixed-weight consumer price index as they are now? Defend your answer.

4. If government borrowing tends to displace private investment as Harberger (1976) argues while taxes tend to have a significantly greater displacement effect on consumption, which method of financing would be more destructive to private sector growth in the long run? (This is a controversial issue.)

Computational questions

5. Figures 8.4 and 8.6 display the effects of savings and investment taxes on the utility and savings choices of a typical individual. Use the same type of graph to display the effects of a consumption tax:

    (A) How does a tax on consumption affect the social rate of discount, the return to capital, and the utility of the average individual amount of investment? (Hint: Assume that it applies equally to consumption in years 0 and 1, but not to savings or business income.)

    (B) If the new linear curve representing the tradeoff between current and future consumption goes through point A' in Figure 8.6, will the average individual be better off under the consumption tax or the original case?

6. Table 8.6 presented calculations of fixed and declining discount rate present values using a 5 percent discount rate. Fill in the following table using a 10 percent discount rate. Is the difference for future years greater or equal to those using the 5 percent rate?

		Year 1	Year 4	Year 10	Year 50	Year 100
PV_{ddr}	$\dfrac{1}{(1+0.1t)}$					
PV	$\dfrac{1}{(1+0.1)^t}$					

7. This question refers to the Forrest Center case study in the Appendix to Chapter 7. Assume that the social rate of discount (r_1) equals 3 percent and that the marginal rate of return to capital (r_3) is 7 percent. The Forrest Center's cost is financed by $30 million from local public borrowing, $5 million from taxes, and $15 million from private foundations. Ignoring the foundation contribution, assume that the local borrowing displaces $26 million in private investment and $4 million in consumption, while the $5 million in taxes displaces $4 million in consumption and $1 million in investment. Find the shadow price of capital appropriate for the Forrest Center project using a 10-year time period.

(A) Annualize the capital cost using the formula in Chapter 8.
(B) Subtract this annualized cost from the annual net benefit you calculated for the Forrest Center, then find the present value at the social rate of discount. How does this answer differ from your original present value calculation?

9 Policy analysis involving risk and uncertainty

The policy of being too cautious is the greatest risk of all.
(attributed to Jawaharlal Nehru, former Prime Minister of India)

Risk comes from not knowing what you're doing.[1]
(Warren Buffett)

Two increasingly important concepts in policy analysis are risk and uncertainty. These terms are often confused, as in the Warren Buffett quote above, but have distinct meanings and sometimes very different policy implications. One source of the confusion between risk and uncertainty is that the English language does not allow a clear distinction between their definitions, so we will have to consider the following definitions carefully.

Definitions:
- **Risk** exists when there is a known probability of random variance in the outcome of a given action. For example, we know that the flip of a fair coin involves an equal chance of seeing a "heads" or a "tails." We know the odds and the possible outcomes, but risk implies that there is a random chance that the outcome will vary from one flip to the next.
- **Uncertainty** is defined as imperfect information about the outcome of a given action, whether or not the outcome involves risk.

A second source of confusion between risk and uncertainty is that while they have different causes, they often have similar symptoms. Random errors in the predictions of policy analysts can come about because a lack of knowledge or evidence (uncertainty) or because of random movements in the variables being considered (risk). Another source of confusion is that at some levels the two concepts are analyzed using similar tools.

While the definitions and symptoms of risk and uncertainty may be similar, the policy implications of the two concepts are quite different. Policies to reduce uncertainty involve encouraging the discovery of new knowledge and the spreading of knowledge among the population. Examples of policies that reduce uncertainty include food labeling requirements enforced by the Food and Drug Administration, the subsidizing of health research by the National Science Foundation, or government sponsorship of public address announcements in the mass media.

Many dimensions of our lives are subject to risk, but most of the economic analysis of risk involves financial risk or risk to life and health. Policies for dealing with the risk of death or injury involve influencing human behavior or changing technology to reduce risk. For example, auto safety is enhanced through behavioral policies such as speed limits and seat-belt laws, and through technological requirements such as automobile air bags and "crumple zones" to absorb the force of a crash. Also, requiring drivers to purchase auto insurance reduces the financial risk of auto accidents.

Measuring risk and uncertainty

Risk and uncertainty can be represented in two general ways, as a continuous range of possible outcomes or as a few specific alternative results. Some types of risk involve only a few known outcomes, such as the results of a football match or a coin flip. Risk and uncertainty involving a continuous range of possible outcomes, such as future oil prices, global temperatures, or highway traffic deaths, can be represented by a probability distribution such as that in Figure 9.1. Even when a continuous range of possible outcomes exists, policy analysts sometimes simplify their studies by taking a small number of possible values, such as the low, mean, and high values in Figure 9.1, and use these values to calculate representative results for risky policies. In order to avoid the use of calculus in our analysis, all of the examples used in this chapter will be limited to a few specific alternatives.

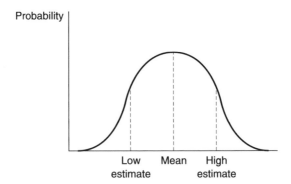

Figure 9.1 Normal probability distribution

Risk arises most often as a public policy issue when there is a possible catastrophic loss of wealth or possible injury, illness, or death. For example, we have reasonable statistics about the increased risk of lung cancer caused by smoking, but we can't predict which smokers or non-smokers will contract this disease. U.S. statistics for injury and illness can be found in several locations on the world-wide web, including the Bureau of Labor Statistics (http://stats. bls.gov/), the National Center for Health Statistics (http://www.cdc.gov/nchs/), the Occupational Safety and Health Administration (http://www.osha.gov/), the Consumer Product Safety Commission (http://www.cpsc.gov/LIBRARY/ data.html), and many others. Safety statistics are often reported in absolute numbers of injuries or deaths and are not easily converted to probabilities. The way these statistics are expressed will have some influence on the impression they give to the reader. A reasonably large absolute number of deaths or injuries cause by a type of event may be consistent with a low probability of death or injury from that event.

An even more challenging aspect of measuring risk is the interaction between different risks. For example, taking aspirin apparently decreases the risk of heart disease but may also increase the risk of stomach distress. Increased airline security efforts may lead to more use of automobiles, thereby causing more highway deaths. In cases where these offsetting risks can be identified and related, policy analysis should include both the negative and positive effects of the policy, producing a measure of the net benefits of risk reduction.[2]

Expected value

Analyzing risk involves the explicit inclusion of both the odds and results of random events. A basic concept in the analysis of risky decisions is **expected value.**

Definitions:
- **The expected value of a single outcome** equals the probability that the outcome will occur times the payoff received if it does occur. If the probability of outcome i equals p_i, and the payoff equals M_i, then the expected value equals $p_i \cdot M_i$.
- **Expected value (EV) of a risky decision** equals the sum of the expected values of all possible outcomes of the decision. In symbols, $EV = \Sigma_i \, p_i \cdot M_i$, where Σ_i equals the sum of all of the i outcomes, p_i equals the probability of outcome i, and M_i equals the money payoff (positive or negative) from outcome i. For a case with three possible outcomes ($i = 1$ through 3), this formula would equal $p_1 M_1 + p_2 M_2 + p_3 M_3$, where $p_1 + p_2 + p_3$ equals 1.

Let's consider expected value in two steps. First, **the expected value of a particular outcome** equals the probability that the outcome will occur times the payoff (positive or negative) which will result if the outcome occurs. For example, if you have a ⅓ chance of winning $150, the expected value of that outcome will equal ⅓ · $150, or $50. Similarly, if you have a ⅔ chance of losing $60, then the expected value of that outcome will equal ⅔ · (−$60), or −$40. **The expected value of a risky decision** is the sum of the expected values of all possible outcomes, where the sum of the probabilities equals one. If a person faces a gamble where she has a ⅓ chance of winning $150 and a ⅔ chance of losing $60, the expected value of the gamble is [⅓ · $150] + [⅔ · (−$60)], or $50 − $40 or +$10.

Example: The daily number

State lotteries in the U.S. usually include a daily number drawing. This bet typically involves buying a one-dollar ticket with a three-digit number. Each digit is chosen separately and can equal 0 through 9. The resulting number can equal 000 to 999. Let's assume that, if you win, the payoff is $500 minus your dollar, and if you do not win you lose your dollar. The odds of winning equal 1/1,000, and the odds of losing are 999/1,000. The expected value of this daily number bet equals $1/1,000 \times (500 - 1) + 999/1,000 \times (-1) = -0.5$. In English, you have a 1 in 1,000 chance of winning $500. This means that every time you place a $1 bet, you expect to lose 50 cents. To speak bluntly, the daily number is one of the biggest rip-offs in all of legalized gambling.

Example: Roulette

Roulette is an easy game that involves rolling a ball around a moving wheel and betting on where that ball lands. A typical U.S. roulette wheel includes the numbers 1-36 which are half black and half red, plus 0 and 00 slots which are green. The simplest type of bet involves a pair of choices such as high–low, even–odd, or red–black. For each of these bets the player loses if the ball lands on zero or double zero. For example, if one bets "low," she wins if the ball lands on 1-18, and loses otherwise. The payoff for winning is equal to the bet, so that if some-one bets $10 she ends up with $10 more. Let's use this information to answer the following questions:

1 **What are the odds of winning a single roll for our simple bet?**
    Answer: the odds of winning are 18/38, or 0.4737.
2 **What is the expected value of a $1 bet on "red"?**
    Answer: the expected value $= 0.4737 \cdot \$1 + 0.5263 \cdot (-\$1) = -0.0526$, or −5¼ cents.

Your Turn 9.1: A European roulette wheel has only one green slot rather than two, along with 18 red and 18 black slots. Find the expected value of a $10 bet on a European wheel. It wouldn't be surprising if roulette is a more popular game in Europe than in the U.S.

A **fair gamble** exists whenever the expected value of the gains equals the expected value of the losses. For example, if you could win $5 for a $1 bet that rolling a single six-sided die would turn up the number 3, you would have a fair gamble:

EV of rolling a die: $[\frac{1}{6} \cdot \$5] + [\frac{5}{6} \cdot (-\$1)] = \$\frac{5}{6} - \$\frac{5}{6}$, or 0

> **Concept: A fair gamble is a risky decision with an expected value of zero.**

This concept will be important in our analysis of insuring against risk.

Decision trees

So far our analysis of risk has been limited to simple two or three outcome problems such as a coin flip or the risk of one type of car crash. Many risky problems involve more outcomes and more layers of risk. A very useful device for representing and solving more complex decisions involving risk is the decision tree. A decision tree is basically a chart of the possible outcomes of one or more related risky decisions, arranged in a branching pattern. This device is most commonly used in game theory, which analyzes rational decision strategies given specific opponents, in the analysis of complex risky decisions, and in discrete mathematics, an important conceptual basis for computer science.

As with an expected value equation, diagrams of risky decisions must include the odds and the payoffs for each possible outcome. A decision tree must also identify any places where decisions are made along with various points of risk. Let's consider a simple example, the fair flip of a coin. Following common practice, the square at the left of the tree represents a decision point and the circles represent points where either probabilities or payoffs are identified. In Figure 9.2 payoffs are given as dollar amounts, so the tree provides a visual representation of an expected value problem. The tree is read from left to right. The choice presented is whether or not to flip a coin. If the person does not flip, the payoff is zero with complete certainty. If she does flip the coin, there is a ½ chance of winning $1.10 and a ½ chance of losing $1.

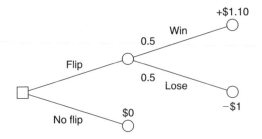

Figure 9.2 Decision to flip a fair coin

Solving a decision tree involves starting from the right and working backwards, eliminating any choices with lower expected values or utilities, until an answer is reached. This process is sometimes referred to as **tree flipping**. In the coin flip example, the final step in the problem is the expected value of the flip, so that is where one starts the solution. The expected value of this outcome is $1.10 \cdot \frac{1}{2} +$ −$1 \cdot \frac{1}{2}$, or $0.05. Replacing the final risk problem with its expected value produces the following simplified version of the problem. Since the expected value of the flip is positive, the choice to not flip can be eliminated.

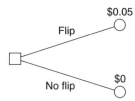

Figure 9.3 A partial solution to the coin flip

Example: Invading Iraq
Many more interesting problems can be analyzed using decision trees. The follow-ing example relates to a recent foreign policy problem that might be familiar to you. The decision is whether or not to invade Iraq in order to find and destroy weapons of mass destruction (WMD). This example assumes that before the decision is made there is only a 50 percent chance that these weapons exist. Also, the initial decision to invade will lead to further decisions depending on whether WMDs are found. A hypothetical multi-step decision tree regarding the invasion of Iraq is presented in Figure 9.4. Reading this tree may require some reminders. First, odds are present for each risk node (circles), but not for decisions (squares) where the policy maker

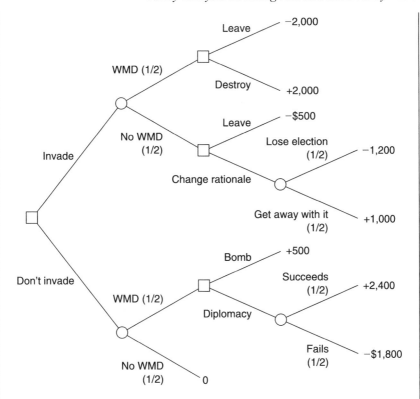

Figure 9.4 The Iraq game

must choose a path to follow. According to the tree-flipping approach, solving the problem requires you to start on the right and solve the expected values of each of the final risks. Then you should eliminate the final paths that have lower expected values. After eliminating some of the later choices, you move further left and repeat the process. Starting from the right and top, the final round of choices is analyzed as follows. If the U.S. invades and finds WMD, it will destroy them. If the US finds no WMD, it will prefer to change the rationale for the conflict rather than leave. If the US doesn't invade and WMDs are found, it will prefer bombing over diplomacy.

Once these latter choices are made the problem reduces to the following situation, displayed in Figure 9.5. If the US invades, there is a ½ chance it will find and destroy WMDs, and a ½ chance it will find no WMDs and change its rationale for the war. If the U.S. doesn't invade, there is a ½ chance that WMDs will be found and bombed, and a ½ chance that nothing will be found. The final decision nodes have been left in, but only the dominant later choices remain. Also, Figures 9.4 and 9.5

show that in this simplified example leaving Iraq is the most costly option once an invasion takes place even without the discovery of WMDs. This example could explain why neither major party candidate in the 2004 U.S. presidential election favored leaving Iraq.

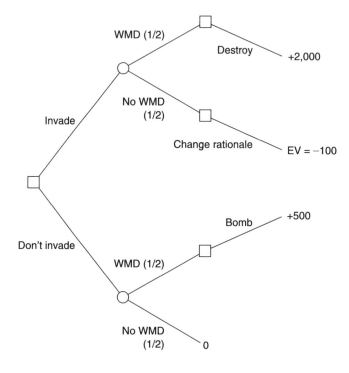

Figure 9.5 The Iraq game, partially solved

Your Turn 9.2: Find the final expected values for invading and not invading Iraq. Which decision should be made, according to this analysis? How would the analysis of Figure 9.5 change if the chance of finding weapons of mass destruction is zero?

This type of visual model can be very useful in organizing one's analysis of a risky or uncertain issue.

Your Turn 9.3: Assume that you have a choice of two study strategies in the three nights before your next exam: (1) study seriously for all three nights, or (2) cram the night before the test. If you study seriously, you have a 75 percent chance of an A grade and a 25 percent chance of a B. Assign your own values to these alternatives. If you cram, you will have two extra nights to party. There is a 50 percent chance you will get a B and a 50 percent chance you will freeze and get a grade of D.

(A) Draw a decision tree for this problem.
(B) Using the values you assigned for an A, B, and D grade, find the expected value for each choice. Add a value for the two nights or partying to the cramming choice if you wish.
(C) Which choice is best for you? Discuss how different partying values affect the choice that results.

The limits of expected value

Expected value is a useful analytical device in some circumstances, but it is a poor model for analyzing individual or collective decisions involving risk. There are two primary problems with expected value as a model of behavior. First, expected value ignores people's tastes regarding risk. The average person would prefer not to face added risk, all else equal. One way of considering added risk is to increase the size of a gamble. Many readers would be willing to undertake a simple gamble with even odds, such as flipping a coin, which pays $1.10 if they win and costs $1 if they lose. However, most would balk at accepting a gamble with a payoff to the winner of $1,000,000.10 and a cost to the loser of $1,000,000, again with equal odds of winning and losing. Yet a simple calculation will indicate that the expected values of these two gambles are exactly the same:

$$EV \ (\$1 \ \text{bet}) = \tfrac{1}{2} \cdot \$1.1 + \tfrac{1}{2} \cdot (\$-1) = \$0.55 - 0.5 = \$0.05$$
$$EV \ (\$1 \ \text{million bet}) = \tfrac{1}{2} \cdot \$1,000,000.10 + \tfrac{1}{2} \cdot (-\$1,000,000)$$
$$= \$500,000.05 - \$500,000$$
$$= \$0.05$$

In addition to attitudes toward risk, a person's willingness to accept a gamble is also affected by the amount of wealth they own before the gamble occurs. A billionaire is far more likely to accept a million-dollar gamble than a person of average wealth. For example, Ross Perot's decision to spend several million dollars of his own money on a presidential campaign in 1992, despite low odds of success, would not have been possible for most individuals. Because of these factors, individual decisions involving risk are often analyzed using a somewhat more complex version of the expected value model.

The expected utility model

The expected utility model adds two components to the expected value model. First, the values of each payoff are measured in terms of utility rather than dollars.

This allows the model to include some measure of the person's preferences toward risk. Secondly, it measures payoffs in terms of a person's total wealth after an outcome occurs, rather than the value of the winning or losing payoff itself. This allows wealth and affordability to enter the story. The next section will explain expected utility in more detail.

Risk attitudes and utility

A person's preferences toward risk may fit into one of three categories: risk averse, risk neutral, and risk preferring. A person's risk preference can be measured by determining whether she would be happier with a fixed sum or with a gamble with zero expected value. In Figure 9.6, a risk-averse person prefers a fixed outcome such as W_0 over a fair gamble even though the expected values are equal. This preference for avoiding risk occurs if the person has a diminishing marginal utility of wealth (the slope of the utility function in Figure 9.6). This means that the utility added by winning a certain amount is less than the utility subtracted by losing an equal amount.

One type of utility function which produces a risk-averse outcome is a simple square root.

$$A \text{ risk-averse utility function for wealth } U(W) = \sqrt{Wealth}$$

In this function utility is measured in **utils**, or units of utility. Such a measure is not directly observable, of course. Let's say that Rhonda Averse has $1,000 of initial wealth, and is considering placing a $100 bet that a fair coin flip will come up heads. The odds are ½ of winning and ½ of losing, and the payoffs are +$100

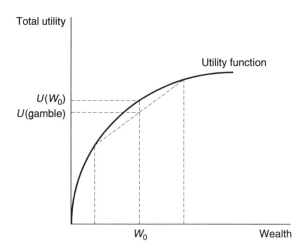

Figure 9.6 Risk aversion

and −$100. Putting all the pieces of the expected utility model together, the expected utility of this fair gamble would be

$$EU = \tfrac{1}{2}\sqrt{\$1,000+\$100} + \tfrac{1}{2}\sqrt{\$1,000-\$100} = \tfrac{1}{2}\sqrt{\$1,100} + \tfrac{1}{2}\sqrt{\$900} = 16.583$$
$$+15 = 31.583 \text{ utils (this outcome is in terms of utility, not dollars).}$$

In contrast, the utility of the original $1,000 equals $\sqrt{\$1,000}$, or 31.62 utils. Rhonda is risk averse because she receives more utility from her initial wealth than from a fair gamble.

Another implication of risk aversion is that smaller gambles are preferred to large ones. So let us assume that Rhonda is now considering a bet of $1,000, or all she has. Again, the expected value of this gamble includes the initial wealth and her utility function:

$$EU = \tfrac{1}{2}\sqrt{\$1,000+\$1,000} + \tfrac{1}{2}\sqrt{\$1,000-\$1,000}$$
$$= \tfrac{1}{2}\sqrt{\$2,000} + \tfrac{1}{2}\sqrt{\$0} = 22.36 \text{ utils}$$

This level of utility is far less than that of either Rhonda's initial wealth or the expected utility of the $100 bet in the previous equation.

Now let us consider a different type of attitude toward risk. Randy Wreckinger is a risk lover. His utility function for wealth might take the form

A risk-loving utility of wealth $=U(W)=(Wealth)^2$

The larger absolute utility numbers this function produces are not important. What is important is to compare the results of a fair gamble with those of Randy's initial wealth to see if he receives higher utility from the risk of a gamble.

Randy has initial wealth of $1,000, and is considering a $100 fair gamble on a coin flip. His expected utility for this bet is

$$EU = \tfrac{1}{2}(\$1,000 + \$100)^2 + \tfrac{1}{2}(\$1,000 - \$100)^2$$
$$= 605,000 + 405,000 = 1,010,000 \text{ utils}$$

Alternatively, the utility of his initial wealth is $(1,000)^2$, or 1,000,000 utils, less than the utility of the gamble. As seen in Figure 9.7, the utility of the initial wealth is less than the utility of the expected value of the gamble because the added utility from winning (the thrill of victory?) is greater than the reduction in utility from losing.

Your Turn 9.4: Assume you have $100 in spending money for the next week. A classmate offers a straight $20 bet on a coin flip. The expected value of the flip is zero.

(A) Would you take the bet? Does this mean you are risk averse, risk preferring, or risk neutral?

(B) Assume that you are risk averse, and that the same classmate offers $22 if you win the bet. You would still lose $20. Calculate the expected utility using the square root utility function. Would you take the bet now?

(C) Now assume that you are risk preferring, with a utility function *of* $U = (Wealth)^2$. If the same classmate offered you $18 if you win, would you still take the bet?

Risk aversion and the willingness to pay for insurance

The primary policy implication of expected utility is that risk-averse people are willing to pay somewhat more than the expected value of a loss in order to reduce their exposure to that loss. This added willingness to pay creates the opportunity for a profitable insurance industry and a demand for risk-reducing public policies, even when those programs involve a modest degree of productive inefficiency. Ignoring complicating factors, a simple market for insurance requires that the average cost per client must be less than the amount the average consumer is willing to pay for the coverage. Risk aversion creates exactly this situation.

Let's consider the insurance market from the seller's point of view before considering the consumer's demand for insurance. Public policy examples will follow.

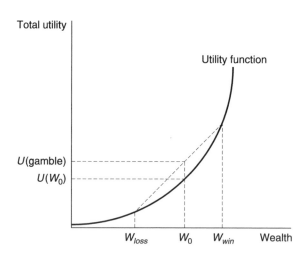

Figure 9.7 Risk preferring

The insurance provider's cost: expected loss

Some of those who are insured will not experience losses or file claims. Others will file claims for far more than the amount of their insurance bills. Therefore, the insurance company's average cost per customer is a form of expected value called the expected loss. **Expected loss** equals the odds of a loss times its dollar value. If a group of reckless drivers has a $\frac{1}{10}$ chance of suffering a $2,000 fender-bender, the company's expected loss would equal $\frac{1}{10} \times \$2,000$, or $200. Expected loss is part of an implicit expected value problem, where the full problem would include a larger probability that the loss would be zero. To continue the example, the expected value of this problem would be $\frac{1}{10} \cdot \$2,000 + 9/10 \cdot \$0$, or $200. Clearly the full EV problem is not required.

A consumer's willingness to pay for insurance

Assume that a risk-averse consumer faces a positive probability of an auto accident. He has a choice of buying an insurance policy that will cover all of his possible losses or paying for the losses out of his initial wealth.

Case 1: No insurance

If the individual doesn't have auto insurance, he or she faces a type of expected utility problem. For Rudy Averse (Rhonda's father), this problem would include his initial wealth of $10,000, the $\frac{1}{10}$ chance of suffering the $2,000 accident, and a risk-averse utility function. Using the square root function to represent risk aversion, Rudy's expected utility problem without insurance is

$$EU = \frac{9}{10}\sqrt{\$10,000} + \frac{1}{10}\sqrt{\$10,000 - \$2,000}$$
$$= 90 + 8.944 = 98.944 \text{ utils}$$

Having to face this risk leads to lower utility for Rudy since the utility of his initial wealth equals $U = \sqrt{\$10,000}$, or 100 utils.

Case 2: With insurance

His other choice in this simplified problem is to pay for insurance that would cover all of this expected loss. However, we do not yet know how much Rudy is willing to pay. If he buys the insurance, he will have to pay at least $200, the company's expected loss, and perhaps more, but he will benefit from the elimination of the financial loss due to an accident. From the problem above, we know that if Rudy doesn't buy insurance, he will have an expected utility of 98.944 utils. If he is going to buy insurance, he must end up with an amount of wealth after paying his insurance bill which will give him utility of at least

98.944 utils also. We can find this amount of wealth (W) by manipulating Rudy's utility function as follows:

$$\sqrt{W} = 910.944 \text{ utils. } By \text{ } squaring \text{ } both \text{ } sides, W = (98.944)^2 = \$9,789.92$$

Therefore, $9,789.92 is Rudy's *certainty equivalent*.

> **Concept: A certainty equivalent** is the amount of money with no risk which produces the same amount of utility as the expected utility of a gamble.

This means that the maximum Rudy would be willing to pay for insurance is $10,000 − $9,789.92, or $210.08. A bill of that size would leave him indifferent between buying the insurance and facing the financial risk of an accident.

> **Concept: Maximum willingness to pay for insurance:** The difference between a person's initial wealth and her certainty equivalent is the maximum she would be willing to pay for insurance.

If the company charged $200, which equals its expected loss, Rudy would buy the policy while the firm would earn zero economic profit.

Risk-averse people have a maximum willingness to pay for insurance that is greater than the company's expected loss. This result creates a window of opportunity for a profitable insurance industry to develop, and also creates a justification for public policies that reduce risk.

> **Your Turn 9.5:** Rhonda Reliable has a much more valuable car than Randy Wreckinger, but also has a much lower risk of an accident. Let's assume that Rhonda has a ⅟₆₀ chance of being in a wreck, and that her financial loss from the wreck would be $1,900. Assume that her initial wealth equals $10,000, and that she is also risk averse with a utility function of $U = \sqrt{W}$. The steps in this problem are as follows:
> (A) Find Rhonda's expected loss.
> (B) Find her expected utility without insurance.
> (C) Find her certainty equivalent.
> (D) Find her maximum willingness to pay for insurance.

The policy applications of the expected utility model are becoming more wide-spread and accepted. Conceptually, it is easy to translate willingness to pay for insurance into a willingness to pay for improved job safety, safer cars, healthcare, or social security.

Example: Social Security private accounts (highly simplified)
In 2005 the Bush administration promoted the creation of private investment accounts as a partial substitute for the guaranteed benefits of Social Security. While there are many devils in the details of such plans, one goal of this plan was to use private accounts to invest in a range of stocks and bonds rather than the federal treasury bonds purchased by the Social Security trust fund. This switch would pay a higher average return, but would also introduce increased risk into the payoffs.

Your Turn 9.6: Assume that under the current system Old Gloria's social security retirement income will equal $25,600. Under a private account there is a ¼ chance that it will be $12,100, a ½ chance that it will be $28,900, and a ¼ chance that it will be worth $34,596. There is no other initial wealth. Gloria's utility function is $U = \sqrt{income}$.

(A) Find the expected value of the private account.
(B) Find the expected utility of the private account. Assume there is no initial wealth to be added to the payoffs. Compare this to the utility of the current fixed payment. Which program offers the highest utility or expected utility?
(C) Find the certainty equivalent of the private account, and compare it to the fixed income payment under the current system. Will she prefer the private account? Verify that this approach produces the same decision as in part (B).
(D) If the government guaranteed that nobody would get less than $25,600 from their private accounts, how would Glory's expected utility change? Would her preference change?

One important lesson from this example is that a risk-averse public may weigh the added risk of private accounts more heavily than the added reward. However, the certainty equivalent in this problem is highly sensitive to the payoffs assigned to each choice. An extra $1,000 or so for each possible outcome would change the results of the problem. Also, the voluntary nature of the proposed private accounts does allow the risk-averse person to avoid any expected utility loss through choosing the present system. Overall, Social Security is an interesting but very difficult policy issue.

Option value and expected net benefits

Expected value can be applied to policy analysis, but because utility functions cannot be directly observed, other methods must be used to identify the public's certainty equivalents and willingness to pay for risk reduction. Also, policy analysis applies somewhat different labels to the expected value and expected utility models. In policy analysis texts these two models are labeled expected net benefits and option value. The expected net benefits concept is a form of expected value. The **expected net benefits model** arrives at a single net benefit estimate for a risky policy by calculating the net benefits of each possible outcome, and then weighing these net benefits using the odds that each outcome will occur. The result is an expected value measure of the policy's net benefits.

The term option value has more than one meaning in the economic literature. In its more basic version, the **option value** decision model uses the certainty equivalent concept to measure the net benefits of a risky decision. The second and more recent definition of option value is also referred to as quasi-option value, a term that will be used in this book. **Quasi-option value** is the dollar value of acquiring more information about a decision at some time in the future. New information has a monetary value if it reduces uncertainty, particularly if it simplifies or clarifies future decisions. While realistic applications of quasi-option value are very challenging for the intermediate student, a simplified version of the quasi-option value model will be introduced in the following section on uncertainty. In this section we will introduce the expected net benefit and option value models. Theoretically, the option value method is almost universally preferred to expected net benefits. However, because of the option value model's measurement difficulties the expected net benefit model is often used in practice. We will begin this section by discussing and providing examples of the expected net benefits and option value methods, and then comparing the two.

Expected net benefits

As with any expected value problem, the first step in analyzing expected net benefits is to identify the probabilities and payoffs for each possible outcome. In practice, most analysts rely on a relatively small number of representative outcomes whenever the actual number of outcomes is high or the actual probability distribution is continuous, as in Figure 9.1.

Concept: Expected net benefits = the net benefits of every possible policy outcome weighted by the odds of that outcome.

> **Formula: Expected net benefits** = $\Sigma_i\, p_i \cdot PV_i$, where Σ_i equals the sum of all of the i outcomes, p_i equals the probability of outcome i, and PV_i equals the present value of the net benefits from outcome i. For a policy with three possible outcomes ($i = 1$ through 3), this formula would equal $p_1PV_1 + p_2PV_2 + p_3PV_3$.

The careful reader will note that these are very similar to the definition and formula for expected value.

Option price and option value

In this section we will introduce the older definition of option value and compare it to the expected net benefits approach. There are two related concepts to be considered in the option value model: option price and option value. The **option price** associated with a risky product or policy is the maximum a person is willing to pay to purchase a risky product or adopt a risky policy without knowing the specific outcome. For example, a person might be asked about her maximum willingness to pay for a trip to the beach knowing that there is a risk of cold or rainy weather. That maximum willingness to pay is her option price. The **option price** is the certainty equivalent of the risky policy or product. The **option value** of the risky decision then becomes the maximum a person is willing to pay to avoid the risk, or the minimum a person is willing to accept in order to face the risk. For example, a person might be willing to pay for an absolutely accurate weather prediction before deciding whether to pay for the trip. A person who is averse to risk will be willing to pay to reduce risk, and therefore would have a positive option value for a risk-reducing policy. A risk-loving person would have to be paid in order to reduce risk, and therefore would have a negative option value.

> **Definitions:**
> - **Option price** = the maximum amount a person is willing to pay for a risky policy or product before knowing the outcome that will actually occur.
> - **Option value** = the difference between the option price and the expected value of the risky policy or product. This also means the maximum a person would pay to reduce risk.

Estimating the public's option price and option value for a given policy usually requires survey evidence. The use of surveys and other techniques for measuring the public's willingness to pay for non-commercial goods is covered in Chapter 10, but, for now, some consideration of the willingness-to-pay concept will help to clarify the option price and option value concepts. For example, a policy to provide reinforced shelters for hurricane victims along the Gulf Coast of the U.S. would have to be considered without the knowledge of when, where, how often, or with what power hurricanes will strike each area. An option value survey related to this shelter proposal would explain the likelihood of different categories of storms hitting their area, and then ask how much individuals would be willing to pay to implement the program. The analyst would then calculate the average person's willingness to pay from the sample and multiply this average by the relevant population to find the total willingness to pay for the area's population. This estimate of the total willingness to pay represents the dollar benefits of the program. If the program's costs are reasonably well understood, completing the net benefit estimate is quite easy.

Your Turn 9.7: Assume that your campus has a crime problem, particularly at night. Your college or university is considering expanding its security force to provide regular foot patrols between 9 p.m. and 3 a.m. How much would you be willing to pay for this service? What is the average willingness to pay for the men in your class? What is the average for women? Assuming that your class's answers are typical, use these average values and the total number of men and women living on campus to find the aggregate student willingness to pay for this expanded security service. If each new security officer costs $30,000 per year, how many officers could your college afford to hire for this program?

This case provides an example of the use of a simple survey to calculate maximum willingness to pay to reduce risk. However, because the actual improvement in safety (the expected value of the program) isn't easy to estimate, the separate estimate of the option price and option value isn't possible. A second example will add to our understanding of these terms.

Your Turn 9.8: Let's assume that 30 percent of each class at your school will drop out before they graduate, and that ⅓ of these dropouts, or 10 percent of the total, will drop out while a semester is in progress. Also assume that these mid-term dropouts lose one semester's worth of tuition. Either use your own school's average tuition payment per semester or assume that a semester's tuition costs $10,000. Finally, assume that your school is considering a tuition insurance program that reimburses mid-term dropouts for ½ of that semester's tuition.

(A) What is the expected value of this insurance?

(B) How much would your parents be willing to pay for this insurance if they are risk averse ($U = \sqrt{wealth}$) and have $100,000 of initial wealth? (Hint: They face some risk with or without the insurance. Compare the expected utilities and certainty equivalents of the two risk problems.)

(C) What is the option value ((B) – (A)) for this program?

(D) Would you or your family buy this insurance?

(E) Discuss how other factors, such as embarrassment or social pressure from home or friends, might affect your willingness to pay for this insurance.

Earlier in the chapter we considered the reader's risk preferences by asking about one's willingness to accept a $20 gamble involving a coin flip. If this insurance case only involves financial risk, those who refused the $20 gamble should have a positive option value for this insurance. If your answers for the two problems are not consistent, it may be the fault of non-monetary factors relating to this example. The analyst must be careful to identify and, if possible, correct biases in option value studies. These biases, along with the cost of conducting surveys, prevents the option value method of measuring risky net benefits from being as widely adopted as economists would prefer.

Risk and the discount rate

Chapters 7 and 8 introduced the concepts of present value and the discount rate to analyze net benefits that are spread over time. Choosing a discount rate accurately requires careful consideration of opportunity cost, inflation, the time frame of the project, the repeatability of the project, and possibly intergenerational fairness. This section adds one more dimension to this issue, risk. As with most of the other elements of choosing a discount rate, the primary goal in constructing an accurate discount rate in the presence of risk is to treat the numerator and denominator in a consistent way. The present value of a risky public project can be analyzed using either a risk-adjusted interest rate **or** certainty equivalent values or option prices for the net benefits. A risk-adjusted discount rate adds a risk premium to the denominator of the present value formula, while option prices or certainty equivalents deduct a risk adjustment from the net benefits in the numerator.

The **option value** method was described earlier. In a present value problem, one could use the option price to value the net benefits of a risky project, and then discount using the usual real interest rate. The other alternative is to calculate the expected net benefits of the project and adjust the discount rate upward to account for risk. The **capital asset pricing model** can be used to adjust discount rates for risk. The capital asset pricing model was developed as an analytical tool for financial markets, and relies on the concepts of diversifiable and non-diversifiable risk.

Definitions:
- **Diversifiable risk:** Risk that is specific to a firm, industry, or locality which can be eliminated through a diversified portfolio of assets.
- **Non-diversifiable or systematic risk:** System-wide or market risk that cannot be eliminated through diversification.

These two types of risk are relatively easy to identify in financial markets. In the stock market, the random movement of any broadly based stock index such as the Wilshire 5000 or the Standard & Poor's 500 averages can be used to measure systematic risk. The risk associated with any individual stock can then be divided into diversifiable and non-diversifiable risk by comparing its variance with that of the index. This is done by estimating the slope of a function relating the variance of the market index with the variance of the individual stock. This slope is labeled **beta (β)**. A beta greater than one means that the variance of the individual stock is greater than that of the market as a whole, while a stock with a beta less than one has a lower variance than the market. If an asset is negatively related to the movement of the market, the beta will be negative. A risk-free asset will have a beta of zero.

The capital asset pricing model is quite easy to work with given adequate information. In this model, the goal for investors is to accept the investment if its rate of return meets or exceeds a required rate of return calculated from the capital asset pricing model.

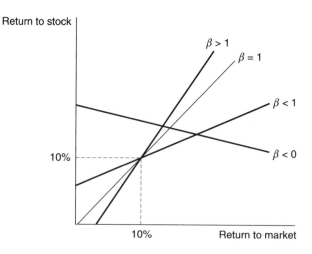

Figure 9.8 Illustration of beta

> **Capital asset pricing formula:**
> *Required rate of return = risk free rate + [β(market rate − risk-free rate)]*

For an asset with above-average volatility ($\beta > 1$) the required rate of return on the asset will be higher than the market rate of return. For example, if the risk-free rate is 2 percent, the market rate of return is 8 percent and the β of the asset is 1.5, then the required rate of return will equal $2\% + 1.5(8\% − 2\%) = 11\%$. Using 11 percent as a discount rate, rather than the market rate of 8 percent, adjusts for the relatively risky behavior of the asset.

Your turn 9.9: Use the capital asset pricing model to find the required return for the following assets:

Asset	Risk-free rate	Market rate of return	Beta	Required rate
Tech	2	8	1.8	
Food	2	8	0.8	
Gold	4	9	−0.2	
Telephone	3	6	0.6	4.8

Comparing the first two rows shows the relation between beta and the required rate of return, all else equal. The riskier asset has a higher required rate of return. Moreover, a beta greater than one means the required rate for the asset is greater than the market rate of return because it is riskier than the overall market. On the other hand, those assets with betas less than one are less risky than the market, and therefore have a required rate of return below the market return. Also, the asset with a negative beta has a required rate below the risk-free rate. This result means that including this asset in one's portfolio will counter some of the movement in the market, reducing the overall volatility of the portfolio.

The meaning of risk in a public policy context is not always clear. A debate persists over whether risk adjustment is necessary for policies affecting a broad range of the population. However, a few general statements about public sector risk can be made. Market or systematic risk in a public context generally means risk to society as a whole. A project's correlation to GDP is important in determining any risk adjustment to the net benefits or discount rate. Secondly, a project's specific risk often arises when its effects are concentrated in particular industries or locations. For example, a government loan guarantee to a foundering corporation involves taking on most of the risks of the corporation itself.[3] Similarly, the risks associated with urban development subsidies relate closely to the risks in the private markets for urban commercial or residential properties.

Your Turn 9.10: Loan guarantees to a struggling or bankrupt corporation transfer a large part of the risk of bankruptcy from the corporation and its stockholders to society as a whole. Two relatively well-known examples are the bailouts of Chrysler in 1980 and America West Airlines in 2002.[4] In return for these loan guarantees, the firms offered the government stock options and guaranteed payments. Assume that the America West loan guarantee has an expected value to the government of –$200 million. In return, America West offers payments of $50 million per year for four years and stock options with a present value of $40 million (these are not accurate figures).

(A) Recently, beta was estimated to be 3.0 for America West.[5] Using the OMB benchmarks of 7 percent for the market rate and 3 percent for the risk-free rate, find the required rate of return for America West.

(B) Calculate the present value to the government from this loan guarantee over a four-year period using the 7 percent market rate and the risk-adjusted required rate of return. (Hint: Only the payments have to be discounted.) From the government's point of view, is this a good policy decision?

Uncertainty and policy analysis

While tools such as expected utility and option value are useful for analyzing current problems with known risks, a more general issue in policy analysis is uncertainty, or lack of information. Uncertainty is often a major issue when considering the distant future or analyzing complex systems. There are two separate types of problems to be addressed in the discussion of uncertainty. One problem involves making predictions and policy decisions in the presence of uncertainty. The other is weighing the benefits and costs of new knowledge in order to analyze government support of basic research.

There are several methods for making decisions in the presence of uncertainty. The most straightforward method for dealing with uncertainty is sensitivity analysis. **Sensitivity analysis** involves assigning a set of different values to each uncertain variable and then calculating whether changes in these values change the policy decision. This method is used to determine whether a policy recommendation is sensitive to the assumptions about uncertain variables used in the analysis. The most common approach to determining the value of new information is often referred to as quasi-option value. **Quasi-option value** refers to the value of new information which might be obtained about an uncertain policy issue. This approach will be considered only in a highly simplified form.

Sensitivity analysis

A degree of uncertainty exists in virtually every policy decision, particularly decisions involving the distant future. Many studies limit their analysis to the most likely outcome, but often include some cautionary remarks regarding uncertainty in their discussion of these results. Sensitivity analysis adds to our typical benefit–cost analysis by comparing results based on different sets of assumptions. If the benefits outweigh the costs under every alternative set of values, the results are not sensitive to the study's assumptions. If costs outweigh benefits under some assumptions but not others, then policy makers have a more difficult decision. Being aware of a mixed result can be very helpful in avoiding potentially costly policy decisions.

Sensitivity analysis can be conducted by changing one variable at a time, or by establishing different net benefit estimates using alternative values for two or three variables. Both approaches can be visualized through the following example.

Your Turn 9.11: In 2001 Mathematica Policy Research released a study which found that participants in the Job Corps youth training program received $1,100 in increased income in the fourth year after the program (Burghardt *et al.* 2001). No further years were studied at that time. The cost of the training was about $14,000 for each trainee. One uncertainty in this type of result is how long the net benefits will last. Ignoring the four year delay, let's assume that the program will provide $1,100 in benefits for either 10 years or 40 years. The present value of each benefit stream can be calculated using the following annuity formula from Chapter 7.

$$PV_{annuity} = \$1,100 \cdot \frac{1 - \left[\frac{1}{(1+r)^n}\right]}{r}$$

where $1,100 is the annual payment, n is the number of years (10 or 40), and r is the interest rate (0.07 or 0.03).

(A) The results for the 7 percent interest rate are given below. Your job is to find the net benefits for each benefit stream using the 3 percent discount rate. Under which assumptions is this program worth the money?

Discount rates	40 years of benefits	10 years of benefits	Expected value
7%	$14,665	$7,726	
3%			

(B) If the odds are ½ for each of the two benefit time periods, what is the expected value of the 40-year and 10-year benefit streams for each interest rate? Is the expected value of the benefits greater than the cost for either interest rate?

The lesson of this example is that in some cases the policy recommendations produced by expected net benefit calculations can change when different assumptions are used. Ideally, policy analysts and policy makers will acknowledge this type of sensitivity when discussing their policy recommendations, but advocates for or against a particular type of policy may tend to use selective evidence in support of firmly stated conclusions, an inferior type of analysis. In this specific case, a final report by Mathematica found that earnings gains did not persist for most Job Corps participants, and that the social net benefits of the program were actually negative. It also found that the net benefits for the participants remained positive, and that older entrants (age 20-24) did see persistent increases in earnings (Schochet *et al.* 2003).

Quasi-option value

New information can change the perceived odds of a particular policy outcome, or in some cases can identify a certain outcome. Quasi-option value is a measure of the net benefits of new information about a problem. Option value and quasi-option value are similar concepts but are applied to different situations.

Option value = the maximum a person would pay to reduce risk, or the minimum a person would accept to face added risk.

Quasi-option value = the maximum a person would pay for new information that reduces uncertainty, or the minimum a person would accept to face added uncertainty.

There are two primary ways of paying for new information. One is to subsidize research into a policy area where uncertainty exists. New research can provide benefits in the form of reduced uncertainty about the problem or new technology to solve the problem. The other way of attaining new information is to wait before acting. Basically speaking, the longer one waits to implement a policy the more history one can use to analyze the effects of a problem. Quasi-option value is often interpreted as the value of waiting for new information before adopting a policy, but any method of increasing information can have a quasi-option value to the public.

The Iraq problem displayed in Figures 9.4 and 9.5 can be used to provide an example of the benefits of waiting for new information. One of the arguments raised by opponents of the U.S. coalition's invasion of Iraq was that United Nations weapons inspectors should have been allowed to finish their search for weapons of mass destruction before the invasion. As of 2006, all parties have acknowledged that Iraq's WMDs had been destroyed long before the invasion.

Waiting to find out this information before invading would have changed the problem from that presented in Figure 9.4 to that shown in Figure 9.9. In this case invading has an expected value of −100 and not invading has an expected

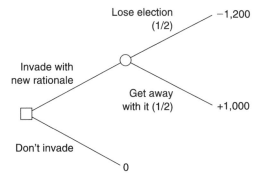

Figure 9.9 The Iraq game with new information

value of 0, so not invading would have been the correct choice given the new information. The **quasi-option value** of waiting for the WMD information equals the difference between the value of the best decision with the information ($0) and the value of the best decision without the information (−100, as in Figure 9.5).[6]

Quasi-option value has become a common tool in analyzing global warming policy. In this case there are multiple dimensions to the uncertainty involved. The amount of warming associated with current trends in the emission of greenhouse gases is uncertain. The harms associated with a given amount of warming are also uncertain. Another dimension of the uncertainty relates to technology. Because of possible improvements in energy efficiency and pollution control technology, we have the potential to reduce greenhouse gases at lower cost in the future. The reality of this issue is far too complex for any non-specialist to grasp completely, but a simplified example should be understandable.

Your Turn 9.12: Global warming: Assume that three rates of global temperature increase have been proposed. These are 1 degree per century, 3 degrees per century, and 8 degrees per century. Each has a probability of ⅓. Our first choice is to adopt a policy now that could prevent all future increases at a cost of $5 trillion. The dollar benefits of this policy would equal $0.5 trillion for 1 degree, $3 trillion for 3 degrees, and $9 trillion for 8 degrees.

(A) Find the expected net benefits of this policy.
(B) Assume that by investing in new technology we can decrease the cost of the cleanup to $3 trillion. Find the new expected value with this lower cost.
(C) The quasi-option value of waiting for this new technology is the change in the net policy's benefits produced by the new information. What is this value?

Conclusion

This chapter contains several analytical tools, most of which relate to two basic concepts: expected value and expected utility. Expected value appears in a simple form early in this chapter, but also appears as part of the expected net benefit model and in our introduction of decision trees. The concepts introduced in the expected utility model, particularly the certainty equivalent and willingness to pay for insurance, provide the basis for the option value and quasi-option value models used in policy analysis. Reviewing the connection between these models will help organize your thoughts regarding these sometimes difficult concepts.

This chapter also teaches us that it is wise to be aware of the limitations of our knowledge about the net benefits of a policy, both now and in the future. Some uncertainty is likely to exist in most policy analyses, particularly when estimating future effects. It may be acceptable in some cases to use only the most likely estimates of benefits and costs, but this choice should be accompanied by a degree of caution when interpreting the results.

Review questions

Conceptual questions

1. Differentiate between the following terms:

    (A) Risk and Uncertainty.
    (B) Expected Value, Expected Utility, and Expected Loss.
    (C) Certainty Equivalent and Maximum Willingness to Pay.
    (D) Expected Net Benefits and Option Value.
    (E) Option Price and Option Value.
    (F) Diversifiable Risk and Systematic Risk.

2. Individual decisions are often made in the face of risks and uncertainty. Both factors complicate individual decisions.

    (A) Give two general types of regulations that can decrease the risk of injury or death to humans.
    (B) Give two policies through which the uncertainty of product purchases can be decreased.

3. Do you consider yourself to be risk averse, risk loving, or risk neutral? Relate your choice to decisions you've made regarding risky activities.

4. In many places drivers are required by law to purchase and maintain car insurance. Explain why this might be the case. Why would some drivers purchase more than the required liability insurance (which covers only the damage caused to someone else's property or person for which you are responsible)? Why do other drivers continue to neglect insurance laws, even with the distinct possibility of state prosecution?

Computational questions

5. Jayne is playing a simple game with a fair 20-sided object. There are 9 blue sides, 9 red sides, 1 green side, and 1 black side. If the object lands with a blue side up, Jayne will win 5 points; if it lands with a red side up, she'll lose 10 points. Similarly, if it lands with the green side up, she will win 30 points, and if the black side is facing up, then she will lose 20 points. Based on this information, answer the following questions:

    (A) What is the probability that the chance cube will land with a blue face up on any given turn?
    (B) What is the expected value of each roll of the object?
    (C) Suppose it costs Jayne 1 point each time she rolls the cube. How much does this change the expected value?
    (D) Suppose Jayne is risk averse, with an initial wealth of 400 points and a utility function of $\sqrt{Wealth}$. Should she continue to play the game, or should she cash in her points for toys (a no-risk proposition)?
    (E) Zoe is more adventurous than Jayne. Zoe has a utility function $U = W^2$, where $W = Wealth$. If her initial wealth is 500 points, should she play the game?

6. Your Turn 9.6 analyzed a simple expected utility problem based on the 2005 proposal to reform Social Security. Let's consider this problem with different values, and see how sensitive an individual's choice is to those values. Assume that the current system would pay a retirement benefit of $25,600 per year with no risk. Also assume that the private account would provide the following possible benefits: a ¼ chance of receiving $14,400, a ½ chance of receiving $27,225, and a ¼ chance of receiving $36,100.

    (A) Draw the decision tree for this problem.
    (B) Calculate the expected value of the private account. For a person with no risk aversion, which retirement program should be chosen?
    (C) For a risk-averse person with a utility function of $U = \sqrt{I}$ and no initial wealth, find the expected utility of the private account. Would the person prefer this result to the certain $25,600 payoff?

7. Many countries have laws that prevent insurance companies from charging different insurance rates for men and women, even when the two have different probabilities of loss. Let's assume that there are equal sized groups of men and women. All persons have initial wealth of $10,000 and a utility function $U = \sqrt{I}$. The men have a ¼ chance of suffering $1,900 of auto damage per year, while the women have a ¹⁄₁₀ chance of suffering the same damage. Insurance companies will offer insurance at rates equal to the expected losses, unless otherwise noted.

    (A) Find the maximum willingness to pay for auto insurance for a typical member of each group. Also find the expected loss for each typical individual.

(B)   Assume that companies are now required to charge an equal amount to both groups, *and* that all individuals are required to buy insurance. How much must the insurance companies charge in order to break even? How much utility does the typical member of each group gain or lose compared to the utility of the original gamble? Discuss the fairness of this law.

(C)   Now assume that the firm must charge a single rate to both sexes, but individuals are not required to buy insurance. Who will buy and who will not? Also find the final expected loss for the insurance companies after all individuals have made their purchasing decisions.

8.   Complete the following table using the capital asset pricing model. Note how beta influences the relationship between the market return and required rate of return.

Asset	Risk-free rate	Market return	Beta	Required rate
A	1	7	1.4	
B	2	9	0.7	
C	3	6	−1.2	
D	4	8	0.5	
E	7	10	−0.6	

9.   Suppose the Springfield Penguins Ice Hockey Club is interested in developing the talents of local youth players. For that reason they found the "Redline to Redline Hockey Academy." Consider the following programs offered by the academy:

(A)   The skills of defensemen are relatively cheap to develop. The process requires an initial investment of $1,500. Players who complete the course will have improved their hockey value to the club by an average of $300 per year. Assuming an interest rate of 4 percent and a 20-year hockey career after the completion of the program, what is the present value of the course?

(B)   Unfortunately, there is a high injury rate among defensemen. There is a 20 percent chance that a player's career will last exactly five years, a 30 percent chance that the player's career will last 10 years, and a 50 percent chance that the player will play for the full 20 years. Given that additional knowledge, what is the expected net present value of the course?

(C)   Sam, a student in the academy, has received an offer to play for Team USA at an international youth tournament. He will not receive pay, but will improve his odds of earning a scholarship or a paying job on a professional team. However, there is also a chance that he could be badly injured and never play hockey again. Discuss the information you would need in order to make a rational decision for Sam based on the expected utility model.

10 The value of life and other non-marketed goods

The Answer to the Great Question of Life, the Universe and Everything … Is … Forty-two, said Deep Thought with infinite majesty and calm … I think the problem, to be honest with you, is that you've never actually known what the question is.[1]

(Douglas Adams)

All that a man hath will he give for his life.

(Job II.4)

♫ In daylights, in sunsets, in midnights, in cups of coffee, in inches, in miles, in laughter and strife. … How do you measure a year in the life?

(Jonathan Larson, *Rent)*

There are many important goods and services in our everyday lives that are not bought and sold. Danger, excessive noise, and polluted air are examples of non-marketed costs we all live with. Beautiful sunsets, views of snow-capped mountain peaks or historic buildings are examples of goods with non-marketed visual benefits. Because these non-marketed goods are common, benefit–cost analysis would be quite limited in scope if such goods could not be valued in dollar terms. Important policy issues related to all types of pollution, traffic congestion, health policy, and many others could not be analyzed in economically rational terms without some effort to assign defensible dollar values to these goods. The goal of this chapter is to explain how such values may be estimated.

Methods of valuing non-marketed goods

At least from the time of Adam Smith, people have been aware that some tasks involve unpleasant, dangerous, difficult, or boring working conditions. All else equal, most people would rather avoid unpleasant jobs unless they are offered higher pay or other benefits as compensation for these negative aspects of work. These tradeoffs between the monetary and non-monetary aspects of work are referred to as **compensating differentials** (Smith 1776: Chapter X, Part I).

The concept of compensating differentials provides one approach to estimating the dollar value of non-monetary costs and benefits, but there are other approaches as well.

There are two general categories of methods for measuring how much compensation people require in order to accept a non-monetary cost, or how much they are willing to pay in order to experience a non-monetary benefit. In simple terms, one can analyze how people **act** or how they **answer**. The first approach is to measure the effect of non-marketed costs or benefits on the choices people make. For example, many studies have explored how much extra money an average worker requires in order to accept a difficult or dangerous job. The benefits of recreation spots such as national parks are often measured by how much people pay in order to travel to those sites. The costs of highway or railroad noise can be estimated by calculating the lost value of nearby property. Property values can also provide estimates of the benefits of beautiful views. Studies of a consumer's willingness to pay for non-monetary benefits and costs through wages, property values, travel costs, or other market actions are referred to as **revealed preference (RP) studies**.

The other general method for measuring the value of non-marketed benefits or costs involves the use of surveys to assess people's maximum willingness to pay for a benefit or the minimum they are willing to receive in compensation for a cost. Such surveys are often referred to as **contingent valuation studies**, since the survey subjects are not required to actually pay the cost in question. A willingness-to-pay study can be performed in a laboratory environment or through sample surveys of the general public. In either case it is important to provide clear and unbiased information about the problem being considered and the type of valuation question that will be asked.

Willingness-to-pay questions can be formulated in a number of different ways, and are generally subject to some danger of misinterpretation or manipulation by the subject. The simplest form of a willingness-to-pay survey asks directly how much at most the respondent is willing to pay for a particular policy or effect. For example, the previous chapter included a survey question regarding the reader's willingness to pay for increased security at his or her college or university. This survey method is often criticized for having a large risk of biased responses, particularly when analyzing broad public policy issues. For example, those who favor a program and feel that they might be able to influence the results may exaggerate their responses. Another approach elicits willingness-to-pay estimates through various bidding methods. One form of bidding survey is to ask a large number of different people whether or not they would be willing to pay a randomly chosen amount for the good or service. The different acceptance rates can then be used to calculate dollar values. Another bidding method involves asking each person whether she would be willing to pay a small amount for a benefit, then repeating the question using progressively larger amounts until the subject refuses to pay. For a readable and much more complete discussion of this topic see Mitchell and Carson (1989).

Explaining the value of life

Possibly the most controversial application of the principle of compensating differentials involves estimating the dollar value of saving or extending a human life. Sometime between 1973 and 1975 (I don't recall the exact date) I wandered into a classroom to hear a well-known labor economist from the University of Rochester. The first two sentences of the talk were, "My topic for today is the value of human life. The answer is two hundred thousand dollars." The man's name was Sherwin Rosen, and he went on to become head of the economics department at the University of Chicago. Needless to say, at first I was astounded and disturbed by these seemingly bizarre statements. However, I kept listening as he went on to explain the theoretical and statistical basis for his answer and, more importantly, the policy applications of such a concept.

As with the quote from Douglas Adams that begins this chapter, it is premature to judge the answer without knowing the meaning and context of the question. It is important to keep an open mind as to what an analyst means when she says the value of life is $42, or $4.2 million, or some other figure. It is also important to know the policy issues to which such a figure might apply. After one understands the purpose of such estimates, then perhaps it will be easier to think about how such numbers are estimated, which numbers are most reasonable, and how these values might influence policy decisions for better or worse. At that point one can more reasonably assess the criticisms and limitations of this concept.

Is life priceless, or just highly valuable?

In answering such a question, it is important to define one's terms. The term "priceless" has at least two relevant definitions. First, priceless can mean some-thing that may not or cannot be bought and sold, and therefore has no observable market value. This is obviously true for human life, along with several other important benefits and costs of policy decisions, such as aesthetics, stress, and so forth. The first definition of priceless implies that searching for the value of any intangible benefit or cost will involve indirect estimates, which should be used with care and interpreted with humility.

A second definition of the word priceless is far more challenging to analysts like Dr. Rosen. Priceless also means infinitely valuable, or beyond measure. This definition is more challenging to the analyst because it implies a moral judgment that life should not be valued in explicit and finite terms. One test for a moral principle is whether and how it applies to actual human behavior. Therefore let's begin with a mental exercise. Assume for the moment that all lives actually have a value of infinity. Certainly, a life which is worth infinity is priceless according to the second definition.

Your Turn 10.1: If human life had a value of infinity, how would you answer the following questions?
(A)   What should the speed limit be on our interstate highways? Why? What should the typical fine be for speeding?
(B)   What is the most we would be willing to spend in order to save one life? What does your answer imply about spending on other goods, such as food?
(C)   How did you travel to class today? Were the benefits of the trip worth the risks, given an infinite value of life?
(D)   If life is infinitely valuable how many humans would sky-dive, fly, bungee jump, climb a ladder, cook dinner over a hot stove, cross a street against the light, smoke, drink, violate the speed limit, or drive *at* the speed limit?

The lesson of this exercise should be clear. Humans do not act as if their lives are infinitely valuable. We are all willing to face some risk in order to do things which offer pleasure, income, or other benefits. Defenders of the value-of-life concept argue that since we do not act as if life is priceless, it is not inherently immoral to place a finite value on life for analytical purposes.

Economists, in particular, would extend this response to the claim that life is priceless with another value judgment. Life is too valuable to be *ignored*. If a policy offers significant monetary benefits but also involves a degree of risk to human life, the failure to include the cost of lost lives may lead to the adoption of policies that would be rejected if the cost in human life were explicitly considered. More commonly, in the absence of a value for life, policy debates involving risks to life cannot move beyond impassioned but relatively empty rhetoric. As economic analysts see it, political rhetoric is a poor substitute for rational analysis. A reasonable range of estimates for costs associated with risks to life may protect against excessive claims from either side of a political debate over health and safety policy.

What do we mean by "life"?

In a policy context there are two quite different meanings of the term "human life." They are **identified lives** and **statistical lives**. **Identified lives** represent the lives of specific individuals. For policy purposes there are two somewhat different types of identified lives which may end prematurely: relatively unknown individuals who experience tragedy, and famous individual tragedies. Either situation is most often related to policy through wrongful death and injury suits and insurance claims. Awarding compensation for wrongful death involves placing an explicit value on the life that has been lost, along with other costs such as pain and suffering. Another type of identified life can be found in the newsworthy loss of a famous person, such as the death of Princess Diana, the Lindbergh baby, Archduke Ferdinand, Martin Luther King, or Gandhi. In one respect these cases are no different from the first group, in that an individual has died tragically, and we know the identity and can estimate the losses to society from the death of this person. On the other hand, the publicity and emotional responses associated with famous tragedies spreads far more widely than most individual tragedies. These cases can act as powerful catalysts for legislation or political action, including war and riots. However, as with other case studies, they can be dangerously inadequate and misleading as a source of policy action.

The other meaning of life in this context is often labeled a statistical life. **Statistical lives** are lives that may be lost or saved in the future due to the impact of public or private decisions relating to health and safety risks. We cannot predict precisely the identity or number of individuals who will suffer individual tragedy because of a particular type of risk. For instance, we know that some people will die each year in automobile accidents, but we can't predict in advance which or how many individuals will suffer this particular tragedy. Examples of policy problems that involve a risk of death include industrial and highway accidents, fire, war, and natural disasters. Policies designed to counteract such harms have opportunity costs as well as benefits, suggesting that a rational weighing of the benefits and costs requires some way of comparing lives saved to program costs.

What do we mean by the "value" of life?

First, let's make it clear that when analysts discuss this topic they are not discussing the explicit buying and selling of human lives. In order to address this misperception, we can consider briefly two of the alternative uses of money that are commonly discussed in introductory macroeconomics courses. Money can be used as a **medium of exchange**, which means that money can be used to buy and sell goods. Money can also be used as a **measure of value**, or as a means of comparing the values of various goods. In the case of non-marketed benefits or costs, these two uses of money are distinct and separate. Estimating a monetary measure of value for a non-marketed good does not imply that the good will be, or should be, bought and sold in the marketplace. Estimating a value for human life is meant to provide a measure of value which can be used in weighing danger against other aspects of policy, and nothing more.

Whose value of life?

According to economic theory and some ethical theories, the person usually best suited to judge an individual's value is **the individual himself**. As we will see in the following section, estimating how highly an average individual values her life is a challenging process, yet progress has been made in identifying reasonable methods of doing exactly that. Alternatively, the value of an individual to **others**, particularly one's employers and family, may also provide a basis for estimating the value of identified or statistical lives. A person may contribute to society through several types of actions, including employment, and contributions to one's family or community, along with one's basic consumption spending.

How to estimate the value of life

Because lives are not bought and sold in the market and have no explicit price, analysts must use creative means to estimate appropriate values. Three general methods are used to estimate the monetary value of life and safety. One of these two measures is based on the opportunity cost of lost income which arises from premature death. The second is based on the concept of compensating differentials discussed in the introduction. Survey methods have also been applied to this topic.

The first value-of-life measurement can be labeled **discounted future earnings (DFE)**. This is a type of revealed preference study because it is based on actual dollar payments. This method involves estimating an individual's expected future income and discounting it to present value. Variants of the DFE approach include one's contribution to his or her family, which in simple form equals earnings minus consumption. This approach is a common component of wrongful death and injury suits involving identified lives. Successful suits of this type also may include payments for pain and suffering of the victim and other affected parties, as well as punitive damages, so any inherent understatement of the value of life that may result from this approach is often compensated for through other sources of payment.

As a general measure of the value of life, particularly for statistical lives, the discounted future earnings method has serious drawbacks. First, by equating the value of life with the value of market work, the DFE approach ignores all other aspects of life, including leisure and the impact of a typical person on her family, friends, and society. Furthermore, such an approach values some groups less than others in a way that many would find unjust. Those with lower future incomes include the less educated, homemakers, some minority groups, and the elderly. To take an extreme case, a retired person with no future earnings would be technically worthless according to this measure. Therefore, as a measure of value related to general issues of risk, the DFE method is not recommended.

The second measure of life value is labeled the **required compensation (RC)** approach. The most common form of RC estimate of the value of life involves the statistical estimation of the relation between workers' wages and their risk of death on the job, holding other factors constant. We will refer to these as **wage-risk studies**. Such **wage-risk studies** are rather complicated in practice, but can be summarized in a few steps:

1 *Choose a large sample of workers.* Ideally, this sample should be representative of the population.
2 *Statistically estimate the relationship between added risk of death and earnings holding all other influences on wages constant.* This step results in an estimated value of the change in earnings for a given change in death risk.

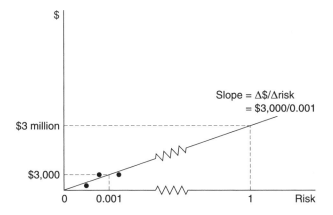

Figure 10.1 A value-of-life estimate

3 *Divide the added earnings per unit of added risk by the added risk.* This is equivalent to estimating the added earnings needed to face a risk of death of one. The answer is the estimated value of life.

Figure 10.1 displays an estimated linear relationship between income and death risk. The dots represent possible data points, all of which involve low risks of death. The value-of-life number appears on the graph only if one assumes a linear relationship between income and risk that extends all the way to a death risk of one (certain death). While not shown, a non-linear function with an increasing slope would allow one to calculate a value of life similar to that of the linear case within the range of actual risk without assuming any particular monetary value for certain death.

Formula: Value of a statistical life = Δ*income*(*all else equal*)/Δ*death risk*

Examples: If Evil requires $100 to face an additional 1/1,000 risk of death, his implicit value of life would be $100/0.001, or $100,000. If Ernie required $1,200 to face the same additional 0.001 risk of death, his value of life would be $1,200/0.001, or $1,200,000 dollars.

Your Turn 10.2: You have a choice of two jobs: extreme skier or instructor for beginning skiers. How much *extra* money would you require in order to take the extreme skiing job? If the risk of death for the instructor job is zero per year and the extreme job has a death risk of 0.001 per year, what is your value of life?

Value-of-life estimates from wage-risk studies vary widely. Fisher *et al.* (1989) surveyed the value of life literature from the late 1960s to the mid-1980s and found a range of estimates from $450,000 to $8,500,000 in 1986 dollars. These estimates have tended to rise in real terms as better data and more sophisticated methods of estimation have been developed. Newer wage-risk studies estimated the value of life at between $2.5 million and $6.8 million (Fisher *et al.* 1989: 90). Even the lowest of these estimates is far greater than Thaler and Rosen's (1975) early estimate of $200,000, which equals about $640,000 in 1986 dollars and $903,000 in 2004 dollars. Wage-risk studies should be used cautiously because of difficulties in measuring risk and its corresponding value. The wide range of estimates provided above is indicative of a significant degree of uncertainty regarding risk and its corresponding market value. (For a more critical review of these studies, see Dorman 1996: Ch. 3.)

The third approach is to ask people about their willingness to pay for various goods or services that reduce the risk of death. **Willingness-to-pay surveys** gather evidence about how much people value protection from death risk by asking them how much they are willing to pay in cash or increased taxes to fund a risk-reducing measure. These studies are far less common and far less consistent than wage-risk studies. Viscusi (1993: 1937-42) reviews a number of survey-based estimates of the value of life. Excluding an early study regarding ambulance services which found a value of life of under $100,000 (Acton 1973), other estimates from surveys range from $1.2 million in a New Zealand study related to auto safety (Miller and Guria 1991) to $15.6 million for a U.S. airline safety survey (Jones-Lee 1976).

There are two important conclusions to be drawn from a review of value-of-life estimates. First, there is a wide range of estimates of the value of statistical lives, and no established consensus regarding a common and reasonable estimate. This uncertainty means that analysts should generally include a sensitivity analysis using a range of reasonable values in benefit–cost studies of safety issues. Secondly, there has been an increase in typical value-of-life estimates since the early wage-risk studies, with modern estimates ranging from roughly $2.5 million to $8 million, or higher. As of 2003, different federal agencies recommended values such as $6 million at the EPA or $3 million at the Department of Transportation (Fialka 2003). Higher estimates of the value-of-life lead directly to greater support for health and safety standards. The following examples will help to explore the possible uses of this concept.

Case study: child safety seats in autos

Between 1978 and 1986 all 50 U.S. states passed laws mandating the use of auto safety seats for young children, with considerable encouragement from the federal government. Let us consider the efficiency of this requirement. According to a paper by William Evans and John Graham (1990), in 1986 an estimated 161 lives of infants and toddlers under five years old were saved by car seats. There were

18.3 million children five years old or less in 1986. The percentage of children using car seats increased from 17 percent to about 77 percent between 1978 and 1986, a 60-percentage-point increase (Evans and Graham 1990: 123). This increase was due to a combination of the new laws, education, publicity, and perhaps improved technology.

Your Turn 10.3: Assume that all 18.3 million young children ride in cars:
(A) If about 3/4 of the 60-percentage-point increase in seat use was due to the laws, about how many children were riding in car seats because of these laws?
(B) If 161 lives were saved by the law, what is the change in the risk of death due to these laws?
(C) What are the total benefits of the law if the value-of-life is assumed to equal $5 million?
(D) If car seats cost $30 per child in those days, what is the total cost of the law? (Hint: Every child using a seat because of the law pays this cost.)
(E) Do the benefits outweigh the costs? How would your answer change if you valued life at $200,000, as in Dr. Rosen's early estimate of the RC approach?

Another case study: child safety seats in airplanes

In July 1989, a severely crippled jet made an emergency landing in Sioux City, Iowa. Despite losing the plane's hydraulic controls, the pilot touched down on the runway, but at a slight angle. The plane flipped, rolled, and partially burned. Despite the violence of the crash and the deaths of 112 people, many survived. Tragically, one infant was torn from its mother's grasp as the plane rolled and died of smoke inhalation. Another infant was found in an overhead luggage compartment and survived. The crash fueled a call for legislation requiring the mandatory use of infant safety seats for all flights. Surprisingly, despite a letter of support signed by 56 House members, the strong support of safety advocates, and the eventual support of the airline industry, the proposed regulation was not passed at that time. Our task is to determine whether this regulation should be passed based on value-of-life analysis.

First, let's determine the benefits of requiring infant safety seats in airplanes. A Harvard Medical School study published in 1981 estimated that three lives might be saved over a five-year period, an average of 0.6 lives per year (*Wall Street Journal*, October 31, 1989). The Federal Aeronautics Administration (FAA) in 1990 testified that one life might be saved over 10 years, an average of 0.1 lives per year (*Wall Street Journal*, July 13, 1990). In order to find the percentage improvement in safety, we also need to know how many infants actually flew at this time. *Time* (March 5, 1990) stated that 5,000 to 10,000 infants boarded airplanes during an average day in the late 1980s, so the total number of infant flights per year would equal 365 days per year times a number from 5,000 to 10,000 flights per day. The highest number of infants flying would be $10,000 \times 365$, and the smallest would be half that number. The change in the annual risk of death for infants who fly would then equal the change in the number of lives lost divided by the total number of flights per year.

Given this wide range of estimates for both total infants flying and the number of lives saved through car seats, it is wise to consider high and low estimates of the percentage reduction in the risk of death ($\Delta deaths/total\ flights$). In this case, the highest possible estimate of risk reduction due to the car seat requirement for airlines would equal the highest estimate of lives saved per year (3/5) divided by the smallest number of flights (5,000/day $\times$ 365, or 1,825,000). This high-end estimate equals 3/5 of a life per year divided by (5,000 flights per day $\times$ 365), or 3/5) ÷ 1,825,000, or 0.000000329, or 3.3 ten-millionths. Obviously, this is a *very* small change in risk.

Your Turn 10.4: The low-end estimate of the change in the risk of death will equal the lowest estimated number of lives saved divided by the highest estimated number of infants flying per year. Based on the information from the FAA and *Time* magazine, calculate this estimated change in the risk of death.[2]

It may be helpful to consider why safety seats in airlines would save so few lives per year and change the risk of death by so small a fraction. Two reasons come to mind, though others may exist. First, airlines are quite safe, and relatively few infants die in plane crashes even without safety seats. Secondly, fatal plane crashes generally involve contact with the ground at high speed, fire, explosion, or smoke-related fatalities. Safety seats are unlikely to save lives under such circumstances.

The total nationwide annual benefits of requiring safety seats on airlines, in monetary terms, equals the number of lives saved per year times the monetary value-of-life. For the above estimates, a relatively high value-of-life of $12 million would lead to total national benefits of $1.2 million per year if 1/10 of a life is saved or $7.2 million if 3/5 of a life is saved. As for the costs of safety seats, parents are now allowed to carry infants on board and not buy an extra seat for them. Under the safety seat requirement, they would have to pay for an extra seat in most cases, perhaps at a reduced rate. Airlines would tend to experience some increase in demand from these extra paying passengers, so the average ticket price may rise slightly. These revenue gains would be partially offset by pressure for discount prices and the diversion of some families from airlines to cars because of the extra cost.

Your Turn 10.5: Cost questions

(A)   If the average airline ticket for each infant cost $200, how much in total would families have to pay in order to buy an extra seat for all infants in a given year? (Hint: Use the 5,000 to 10,000 infants-per-day figure to find the total number of infants flying per year.)

(B)   Given the total added cost for families, how much would U.S. families have to pay per life saved? Is this figure reasonably close to the estimated value of a statistical life? Since the average family is now free to choose to buy an airline seat for their infant (the primary effect of this tragedy), will they?

(D)   Try to explain how this regulation might have actually caused the total number of infants dying in travel-related accidents (not just airlines) to rise slightly.

Despite the political advantages of the proposed regulation requiring infant safety seats in airlines, the regulation ultimately failed, largely because the Federal Aeronautics Administration was opposed to the concept. The FAA presented several studies to Congress which found that, because some families would be diverted from airplanes to cars by the higher cost of flying, the number of infant deaths on highways would rise by more than the number of lives saved in airline crashes. One study found that nine *more* infants would be killed over 10 years in cars due to this regulation, as opposed to only one life saved in airplanes over the same time frame (*Wall Street Journal*, July 13, 1990). If these results are accurate the issue of the value of lives saved became irrelevant, since on balance lives would be lost rather than saved. With the possible exception of war, it is not reasonable to force families to pay money in order to lose lives, which is apparently what this regulation would have done.

Alternatives to the dollar value of life

Objections to the use of dollar values to measure the benefits of risk-related policies come in several forms. Some fundamental ethical principles, particularly those related to basic human rights, consider the discussion or practice of a trade-off between lives and dollars to be immoral, particularly in a public policy context where individuals have no choice about facing the risk. When one adds the very real technical challenges associated with measuring the monetary value of added risk, there are situations in which the dollar value of life and the use of cost–benefit analysis for risk-related policy cannot be used.

Cost-effectiveness analysis

Cost-effectiveness analysis was introduced in Chapter 6. It is reconsidered in this chapter because it has a particularly common role in the context of health and safety policy. For example, a comparison of the dollar cost per life saved is a common metric for judging alternative health and safety policies. If far more money is being spent per life saved in one area than another, some reallocation of money to the area with lower cost per life saved is likely to be cost-effective. Of course, the limitations of cost-effectiveness analysis discussed in Chapter 6 still apply.

Risk-risk analysis

The most basic reason for assigning a dollar value to life is to create a common unit of measurement for the comparison of the benefits and costs of risk-related policy. This cannot be done by comparing lives to dollar costs, as in cost-effectiveness studies. However, there is another alternative for creating a common unit of measure for some of the costs and benefits of health and safety policy, the comparison of lives lost from risk and lives lost from reduced income. This comparison allows the costs and benefits of the regulation of job risk to be considered in terms of death rates rather than dollars. More precisely, the mortality cost of a regulation equals the change in income times the change in mortality per dollar of lost income. Estimated lives lost can then be compared to estimated lives gained in order to calculate a net benefit figure.

Risk–risk analysis analyzes risk tradeoffs in a number of contexts. An important application of risk–risk analysis is the direct comparison of multiple risks that might be affected by a given policy. For example, the defeat of the airline car seat requirement discussed earlier was made far more likely by considering the added risk from auto deaths in addition to the reduced risk of airline deaths. Similarly, a proposal to ban the low-calorie sweetener saccharin in the mid-1970s due to evidence of cancer risk was defeated because of complaints that banning saccharin would increase obesity. At the time saccharin was the primary alternative to sugar.

One relatively understandable way of comparing value-of-life estimates with risk-risk analysis is to compare findings for each type of study. First, it is helpful to know that the value of life ($\Delta\$/\Delta death\ risk$) and the mortality cost of income loss ($\Delta death\ risk/\Delta\$$) are direct inverses. The primary difference in estimating the two is that the mortality cost of income loss is measured from different evidence. For example, Anderson and Burkhauser (1985) found from Social Security data that a $1 difference in hourly wages produced a 4.2 percent mortality difference over a 10-year period (see also Viscusi, 1994: 8). This converted to an annual change in mortality risk of 0.000000526 per dollar of earnings. Inverting this value produces a figure of $1.9 million, which in all respects (except name) is a value-of-life estimate. Viscusi (1994) reviews early versions of these studies and provides a useful policy example.

The lengthening of life and quality-adjusted life years

The term "saving lives" is somewhat misleading since at some point we will all lose our lives. Health and safety policies actually extend lives or prevent premature deaths. How and at what age one dies are factors of great importance in determining the value of delaying death. First, different methods of dying involve different degrees of suffering. Avoiding or delaying a protracted death due to a debilitating disease may be far more desirable (and valuable) than avoiding a quick and painless death in one's sleep. Another important question in determining the value of lives saved is how long those lives will last. Providing increased safety to the young may involve greater private and social benefits than an equal amount of increased safety for an older group.

> **Your Turn 10.6:** A space station is about to disintegrate. There is room for one person in an escape pod which will preserve that person's life until a rescue vehicle can arrive. There are three persons left on the station: a 20-year-old student, a 50-year-old scientist, and a young child. Who should be given the space in the escape pod, or should the three draw lots and decide randomly? To make it more difficult, assume that you are the student. Explain the reasoning of your decision.

A measure of life that includes both the length and quality of one's remaining lifespan is known as **quality-adjusted life years (QALY).** This concept is most commonly used in the analysis of healthcare policy. The basic principle of quality-adjusted life years is that a year spent in perfect health is more valuable to the average person than a year spent in some state of ill health. Therefore, the benefits of healthcare policy can be measured by determining people's preferences regarding the relative value of perfect health and various states of ill health, assigning lower weights to the less healthy states, and then measuring the value of either improving one's state of health or lengthening one's life. Estimating the values to be used in an analysis of quality-adjusted life years involves two steps: determining a set of categories of health status and then measuring persons' relative valuation of different states of health. Alternative approaches to each step will be discussed in this section.

In the QALY model the quality of life is measured by establishing a set of health categories, such as perfect health, relatively good health, relatively poor health, bedridden, or persistent vegetative state. When studying particular health problems, time spent suffering from particular ailments can be used in place of general health categories. A person is then assigned to a particular health category through statistical indicators such as days of work missed or medical visits, by survey responses regarding their opinion of their health status, or indirectly by assigning health risks associated with measured bacteria or pollutants (Adler 2005).

The second step in a QALY study is to determine how much less a year spent in any reduced health category is worth relative to a year in perfect health. The weights assigned to perfect health and other categories are determined through various survey techniques. For example, the "time tradeoff" survey approach attempts to determine a typical subject's point of indifference between living x years in perfect health and y (more than x) years in some condition of ill health.[3]

An example of such a question would be, "Would you prefer to live five years in perfect health or Y (10, 15, etc.) years in a bedridden state?" In this question, five years would be the value of X, and the minimum number of years one would choose to live in a bedridden state becomes the value of Y. The weight assigned to that level of ill health would then be x/y (Adler 2005: 1). For example, if 8 (y) is the minimum number of years the person would prefer to live while bedridden versus 5 (x) years in perfect health, then the weight assigned to that person's value of a year spent bedridden would be 5/8. Similarly, a year spent in perfect health would be 5/5, or one. Doing the same for each health category gives a full set of weights for different health levels. A person's quality-adjusted life years are the sum of all years spent in each health category.

> **Your Turn 10.7:** Assume that there are two health categories: (1) perfect health/active lifestyle and (2) healthy but inactive. If you had a choice of 30 more years of perfect health, what is the minimum number of remaining years you would accept in the healthy but inactive category? If the weight assigned to a year in perfect health is 30/30 or 1, what is the weight you would assign to the inactive category based on your first answer?

Dollar values are seldom assigned to these weights. When no dollar values are involved, this approach can be categorized as a form of cost-effectiveness analysis. However, some studies have assigned a dollar value to a healthy life year and then assigned lower values to lesser states of health based on the subjective weights noted above. An example will allow us to consider both non-monetary and monetary versions of this model.

> **Your Turn 10.8:** Anti-smoking initiatives in both the public and private sectors have been popular in recent decades, particularly in the U.S. In this highly simplified example, we will first provide a hypothetical set of quality-adjusted life year values for a typical smoker and non-smoker. Then the analysis will proceed in both cost-effectiveness and cost–benefit versions.

Step 1: Calculating quality-adjusted life years

A 30-year-old smoker is considering whether or not to quit. Assume that there are four categories of health: (1) perfect health, (2) healthy but relatively inactive, (3) ill and relatively inactive, and (4) bedridden. The weights for each health category are 1 for perfect health, 0.8 for inactive, 0.5 for ill, and 0.2 for bedridden. If she quits smoking, she will live to 82 (52 more years). If she smokes she will live to 74 (44 more years). Calculate the total QALY for each choice and

Table 10-1 Calculating quality adjusted life years

	Perfect health	Inactive	Ill	Bedridden	Total
Smoker (years)	20	14	9	1	44
Smoker (weighted life years)					
Smoker (weighted dollar value)					
Former smoker (years)	30	13	8	1	52
Former smoker (total weighted value)					
Former smoker (weighted dollar value)					

record the information in Table 10.1. For the dollar-value measure, assume that each healthy year is worth $15,000.

Step 2: Calculating the policy effects

Assume that two alternative sets of anti-smoking policies have been established. One proposal relies on information and incentives, and the other on legal restrictions and enforcement. To make the problem more interesting, each program will be analyzed in terms of multiple implementation steps. The information and incentive approach has fewer steps. This gives us the chance to consider the effects of scale on the policy choices. Calculate the missing marginal values based on the information presented in Table 10.2.

Step 3: Policy recommendations

Now consider the following questions assuming that you can choose steps from both programs as part of your recommendation. (Hint: Review the decision rules for benefit–cost analysis in Chapter 6 if necessary.)

Table 10-2 Benefits of anti smoking policy using QALY

Steps in program 1	Information and incentives			Steps in program 2	Regulation and enforcement		
	$\Delta cost$ (millions)	$\Delta QALY$	$\frac{\Delta QALY}{\Delta cost}$		$\Delta cost$ (millions)	$\Delta QALY$	$\frac{\Delta QALY}{\Delta cost}$
1	$4	28	7	1	$2	20	10
2	$4	14		2	$2	8	
3	$2	4		3	$2	6	
				4	$2	4	
				5	$2	2	

(A) If the total budget for this project is $10 million, which program steps should be adopted, and why?
(B) Now assume that the budget constraint no longer exists. If each quality-adjusted life year is worth $500,000, which steps from both programs should be adopted? Which steps should be adopted if each QALY is worth $250,000? To save time, do not discount to present value.

Quality-adjusted life years, in either monetary or non-monetary form, allow for a two-dimensional measurement of the benefits of health and safety policy. To review, the two dimensions are the quantity of years and quality of health while living. This is an important advantage when analyzing policies related to illness or injury.

Other non-marketed goods

There are many other non-marketed goods besides health and safety that relate to public policy issues. One example of a non-marketed good with policy implications is wasted time, a major factor in commuting costs, hospital waiting rooms, and other issues involving delay. This cost is considered in greater detail in Chapter 12. Another policy example involves unique natural or human locations such as the Grand Canyon or the Eiffel Tower. The benefits of such landmarks are not reflected in a market price, and are not limited to those who actively visit those locations. This issue is a part of the discussion of pollution policy in Chapter 13. While these non-marketed goods will be considered in greater depth in the applied chapters to which they relate, a brief overview of techniques for measuring other non-marketed values is included here.

The value of time

Waiting through a traffic jam or an airport check-in line can be an emotionally and financially costly experience. The costs associated with delay are real and significant, and are an important component of several specific areas of policy. Moreover, different types of delay may have different values depending on the opportunity cost of the time lost and the non-monetary costs due to frustration or risk. The key measurement issue is how much a person is willing to pay to reduce a particular type of time use. Travel time has been studied in many countries using various survey and non-survey methods. Studies of U.S. commuters have found values for travel time savings in the range of 40 to 60 percent of the commuter's hourly wage. The value of commuting time may be below the average wage if driving or riding is more pleasurable than work (consumption value), or if commuters use travel time to plan for or otherwise think about work (productive value). Regardless of the rationale, a value for travel time of about half the average wage provides a reasonable estimate for this important non-marketed cost. Time costs related to unexpected delays or waiting in line are probably much higher than those of regular driving (Mohring *et al.* 1987).

The value of recreational resources

As with other non-marketed goods, value estimates for recreational resources can be found by analyzing people's actions through revealed preference methods or by analyzing survey responses. The most common revealed preference method of valuing recreational sites such as national parks or forests is the **travel cost method**. In conducting a travel cost study one measures the cost in both time and dollars associated with traveling to a given type of site, and then averages this cost across the number of days spent in the activity. The resultant values vary considerably for different types of activity and different locations. Activities with longer average travel distances, such as deep-sea fishing, tend to have much higher travel cost values than hiking or picnicking. On average, a day of recreation was found to average about $34 as of 1987, which is equivalent to just over $56 in 2004. Also, travel time studies produced values for recreation that were 20 to 25 times higher than those found in contingent valuation surveys (Walsh *et al.* 1992: 711).

Existence Value

The values of unique natural or human attractions are important when analyzing policies related to wilderness or historic preservation. Such resources provide value to visitors, of course, and the willingness of tourists to pay to travel to and see such sites represents an important and non-controversial part of their value. However, such sites also have value for people who will never visit them, particularly in this age of mass media, and that this value should be included in the total benefits of the site according to some economists.

Existence value refers to the value of a resource to individuals who are not actively consuming or experiencing that resource. Existence value may occur for several reasons. First, mass media brings these locations to distant households through film, television, or the internet. Secondly, if a resource is preserved one has the option of visiting the site in the future. Existence value may also arise from knowing that others in the present or future can enjoy the resource. Finally, one may feel that a particular resource has value in an ethical sense. Preserving natural habitats or ethnic cultures may be considered good in and of themselves, aside from any current or future consumption value they may create. Goods which possess this moral value are sometimes referred to as **merit goods**.

Unlike the other non-marketed goods discussed in this chapter, existence value can be directly measured only by survey techniques, because revealed preference studies require that actual spending or other costly activity take place. Moreover, existence value is a relatively new concept with far less research evidence than the other non-marketed goods discussed in this chapter. However, as a potentially important factor in morally and politically charged issues such as preserving indigenous cultures or wildlife habitat, existence value will undoubtedly be further developed and applied in the future.

Conclusion

Health and safety risks are important factors in many types of policies, from high-way and auto design to damages from tobacco smoking. Rational analysis using the value-of-life concept is potentially useful in weighing the costs and benefits of safety regulations, pollution policies, nuclear waste storage, or many other issues. The emotional volatility of the value-of-life concept, along with the wide range of statistical estimates of its value, guarantee continuing controversy regarding this concept both within and outside of the economics profession. While less controversial, the valuation of other non-marketed benefits and costs through either survey- or activity-based estimates also provides the basis for important policy analysis in areas such as pollution control, recreation and preservation policy, and policy related to the arts. Some more detailed examples are provided in the last section of this book, which includes chapters covering transportation and environmental policy.

Review questions

Conceptual questions

1. Differentiate between the following terms:

    (A)   Identified Lives and Statistical Lives.
    (B)   DFE and RC.
    (C)   Wage-Risk Studies and Willingness-to-Pay Surveys

2. Discuss any instances you can remember in which *identified lives* have been used to promote a cause or a policy, other than the examples given in this chapter.

3. You may have noticed that there is a large disparity (in the range of millions of dollars) among the survey-based value-of-life estimates. What reasons can you think of to explain how researchers arrived at such different answers?

4. In most cases, the risk of death is seen as a cost for which compensation must be made. However, people continue to skydive, speed on the highway, and wrestle crocodiles for fun. Why? Does this mean that those individuals value their lives less than the more timid video-game player?

Computational questions

5. People occasionally engage in unwise and risky activities. In each of the following cases, fill in the missing part of the table:

Bad idea	Additional payment required	Additional risk of death	Value of life
Eat a large bug	$5	0.00001	
Run into a wall	$20	0.00004	
Hit your own head with a large stick		0.0003	$750,000
Jump off a small bridge	$500		$600,000
Play in traffic	$1,000	0.006	

6. Suppose that the government decides to require all school children to wear helmets when playing dodge ball. Assume that 40 million school children play dodge ball and that 50 percent more children wear helmets now than had previously done so. Given this information, answer the following questions:

    (A) If 4/5 of the 50 percent increase is due to the enactment of the law, how many children would now be wearing helmets because of the law?
    (B) If 3,500 nosebleeds are prevented per year, what is the change in the annual risk of nosebleeds caused by the new law?
    (C) Assume the implicit value of a nosebleed is $100. What are the total benefits of the law?
    (D) If a dodge-ball helmet costs $10, what is the total cost of the program? Do the costs outweigh the benefits?

7. Quality-adjusted life years might be applicable to the analysis of athletics. Athletes' productivity depends on avoiding a serious injury. Suppose that there are four categories of injury status: 100 percent healthy, 75 percent healthy, 50 percent healthy, and career-ending. Assume that each 100 percent healthy player is worth $1,200,000 in added revenue to his or her team. Other values can be determined from the weights in the table below. Fill in this table, and then answer the following questions.

	100% Healthy	*75% Healthy*	*50% Healthy*	*Career ending*	*Total*	*value per year*
Weight	1.0	0.7	0.4	0.0	–	
Player 1's years in each status	2	3	2	1		
Player 1's value						
Player 2's years in each status	4	2	1	1		
Player 2's value						
Player 3's years in each status	10	2	1	0		
Player 3's value						

    (A) Assume that the Fredrickton Football Club's roster is made up of equal numbers of players like those above (perhaps seven of each type). If the league requires a minimum salary of $800,000 per year, would this team make money in an average year?
    (B) Assume that player 1's 100 percent healthy years come first, followed by his 75 percent healthy years, etc. If the team's discount rate is 5 percent per year, what is the present value of player 1's career revenue?
    (C) Assume that a new surgical procedure could improve each 50 percent healthy player to 75 percent healthy status and add one year to

his career at that level of health. How much would the procedure add to each player's career value? If time permits, calculate both undiscounted and discounted values. If the procedure cost $500,000, should this procedure be required by law for each 50 percent healthy player? Consider the ethics and politics as well as the economics of this issue.

11 Economic impact analysis: macroeconomics in a micro world

> The private sector needs to determine the economic impact of the arts.
>
> (Harry Chapman-Chartrand, *Economic Impact of the Arts: A Sourcebook,* Chapter 1)

> The social value of one more arts impact study is nearly zero.
>
> (Bruce Seaman, *Economic Impact of the Arts: A Sourcebook,* Chapter 2)

Almost certainly, the most commonly used tool for local and regional policy analysis and advocacy in the U.S. is the economic impact study. It is also among the most controversial analytical methods for analyzing policy, and possibly the least popular among economists. **Economic impact** refers to the net increase in local or regional income, jobs, earnings, or tax revenue produced by a particular institution or investment project. Economic impact is estimated through two general steps. An economic impact study begins by calculating the direct net increases in income and employment produced by an institution or development project, and then calculates the indirect increase in jobs and income produced by the local or regional multiplier effect of this added direct spending.

Economic impact studies have become a common component of spending requests by state and federal government agencies as well as political debates over development projects. Common subjects for economic impact studies include military bases, sports stadiums, arts venues, and other urban or regional development projects. For example, the U.S. Base Realignment and Closure (BRAC) Commission, which periodically recommends military bases for possible closure and conversion to other uses, requires an economic impact study as part of each facility's submitted materials. State universities frequently use economic impact studies as part of the justification for their spending requests. Most famously, economic impact studies are often used to justify public investment in entertainment-related investments such as sports stadiums and performing arts centers. Examples of economic impact studies of the arts, sports, higher education, and military facilities are provided in this chapter.

Economic impact analysis has many critics among economists and policy analysts. One problem with economic impact studies is their exclusive concentration on local or regional effects. The net inflow of spending to one area often implies a net outflow of spending from another. By concentrating on only the local effects of a project or institution, one ignores the opportunity cost of that project or institution on other areas. This violates both the fundamental rule of policy analysis and utilitarian ethics, which require the consideration of a project's effects on all parts of society.

A more unique problem is that economic impact analysis includes outside funding for the construction or operation of a facility as a positive part of its local economic impact, rather than as part of its societal costs. If the construction costs of a facility are partly categorized as a net increase in local jobs and income (a benefit) and the facility's net revenue is also a benefit, there is no negative value on which to base a rational policy decision for a project that is funded by non-local sources. Given this problem, it subsequently becomes impossible to separate socially beneficial projects from socially inefficient "pork barrel" projects.

Finally, the results of an economic impact study are almost always reported as one or more big numbers that are difficult for the public and media to interpret. Any project that offers millions of dollars of new local income and hundreds of new jobs will sound attractive, regardless of its opportunity costs. Economic impact analysis is usually used as a tool of political advocacy rather than economic analysis. For these reasons economic impact studies are highly controversial among economists.

To the best of my knowledge, a chapter on economic impact analysis has never been included in a policy analysis text because it violates some of the basic rules of policy analysis. However, if properly constructed and compared to similar figures for alternative projects, an economic impact estimate can have a degree of validity roughly similar to that of cost-efficiency analysis. Also, because of the increasing popularity of economic impact studies there is value in knowing how to perform such a study and correctly interpret its results. This chapter will begin with an overview of economic impact analysis, and then provide a review of three types of regional economic models that provide the basis for impact studies. Finally, various examples will be considered.

An overview of economic impact analysis

Economic impact analysis is based primarily on macroeconomic rather than microeconomic analysis and therefore requires a new set of concepts. Macroeconomic terms used in economic impact analysis include exports, imports, and the spending multiplier. Because economic impact analysis usually applies to a locality or region rather than an entire nation, these terms require somewhat different interpretations. The economic impact of any institution or investment project is based on the net inflow of income to the community or region in which it resides, along with the secondary or multiplier effects of this net income gain. Any such net inflow of income to a local community should exclude spending that is displaced from other local sources, and should subtract any decreases in local income produced by the institution. Moreover, an institution that produces considerable overall economic benefits for a region may also bring costs, and these should be calculated and deducted from any gross impact estimate.

The economic impact of any institution includes three general components: (1) the increase in **direct spending** on local labor and other inputs which produces added local or regional income, (2) the secondary income produced by the spending of the institution's employees, known as **induced income**, and (3) the secondary income produced by the institution's spending on locally provided materials, energy, and other non-labor inputs. This income is often referred to as **indirect income**.

There are three general models for estimating the secondary effects of an institution or project: the Keynesian multiplier model, the export base model, and the input–output model. Each will be discussed in turn later in this chapter.

Steps in an economic impact analysis

The following list provides a more detailed overview of the process involved in conducting an economic impact study:

1 Calculate the net increase in local direct spending caused by the project or institution.
2 Determine the marginal propensity to consume locally and the local spending multiplier using data and an economic model. These terms will be defined later.
3 Use a multiplier or input–output model to determine the cumulative size of the induced, indirect, and total spending figures for the project.
4 Use available models and data to estimate total employment effects, which also include direct and multiplier effects.
5 In most cases, estimated effects on local government tax revenue and on the use of local public services such as schools can be calculated.

Each of these steps can be performed with various levels of detail. A complete economic impact analysis is a long and complex undertaking, but the use of commercially available computer models of an area's economy has greatly decreased the time and money required for such studies. No doubt the increased use of economic impact studies is partly based on these new efficiencies in production.

Estimating direct spending

Estimating the net increase in local direct spending from an existing institution or investment is the cornerstone of the economic impact study. Dealing with this issue involves answering the following question: **How would the local economy differ if this institution or investment project did not exist?** In the case of an existing institution such as a university, this question leads to others. Private universities receive funding from tuition and fees (minus any financial aid it gives from its own sources), annual gifts, and returns on its endowment. Public universities also receive funds from government. For the most part these sources represent net inflows of income into the local area. For example, the small college at which I teach has about 2,200 students, virtually none of whom would reside in our area if the college did not exist. In this case the measurement of direct spending begins with the estimated annual budget of the institution. If there is a budget surplus or deficit local spending, rather than revenue, should be used as the basis for both direct spending and the multiplier effects to follow.

The only serious dilemma in measuring direct spending from a college or university involves how one deals with students from local families and hourly workers who reside in the area. If these two groups would be working or attending school elsewhere in the immediate area if the college didn't exist, their spending and earnings are not net additions to the local economy. Analysts sometimes assume that these workers and local students would be unemployed or residing outside of the area without the college, an assumption that is much more reasonable in economically depressed areas. If one assumes that a college's non-professional staff would otherwise be working elsewhere in the area, one would then subtract hourly wages or budget items such as building maintenance from total direct spending in order to estimate added local spending from the college. There is no clearly correct interpretation of this measurement issue.

Estimating the added direct spending from an arts or sports facility is more challenging. Since a large proportion of the attendance at an arts or sporting event comes from the metropolitan area in which the event takes place, it is important for the analyst to estimate how many of the attendees come from inside versus outside the area, and how much each group spends during the outing. As a starting point, it is reasonable to assume that local residents do not increase their overall local spending because of a sports or arts performance. On the other hand, those traveling to the area for a performance are likely to bring an increased level of total local spending. For example, a study of the proposed New York Jets stadium in Manhattan divided potential attendees into local, regional, and overnight visitors (New York Independent Budget Office 2004). A simpler local versus non-local division of attendees is sometimes used. Regardless of the level of detail, it is important to note that much of the revenue from entertainment events does *not* provide a net increase in local income or a net economic impact.

In addition to ticket revenue or other direct revenue for the institution being studied, those who visit the area in order to attend an event are also likely to spend money on lodging, meals, or additional activities. Spending on these items is often referred to as **ancillary direct spending**. Local spending by university students is also a type of ancillary direct spending. Audience surveys are often used to gather information on the proportion of local versus non-local residents, ancillary direct spending, and additional information for the sponsor of the study.

The Keynesian multiplier and secondary economic impacts

While estimating direct spending involves the most difficult measurement issues in economic impact analysis, the estimation of the secondary income caused by the spending of the institution and its employees (earlier labeled indirect and induced spending) involves some complex theoretical issues. Economic impact studies are based on local or regional versions of macroeconomic models. Three models will be reviewed in this section: the Keynesian circular flow model and multiplier, the basic/non-basic regional growth model, and the input–output model. While each model offers useful concepts for conducting at least some types of economic impact studies, the input–output model is both the most sophisticated and most commonly used method of estimating a project's total economic impact.

Keynesian multiplier model

The circular flow model provides the most common representation of the Keynesian model of the economy. Figure 11.1 presents a version of the Keynesian model of a local economy's income flow. There is a corresponding flow in the reverse direction representing the actual exchange of goods and services. Starting on the right, firms provide local households with earnings. Firms also purchase some of their inputs from non-local sources. This non-local spending creates an outflow, or

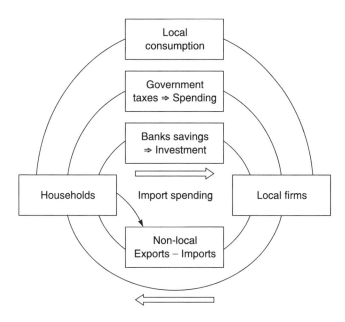

Figure 11-1 Local income flow

leakage, of income from the local area. These non-local goods can be labeled **imports**. Firms also export goods to other areas, producing an inflow of income to the community. Finally, some of the goods purchased by households are also produced outside the community, and also create an outflow of spending and income. The top half of the circular flow in Figure 11.1 is more typical of the Keynesian model. Household income is allocated to consumption spending (both local and imported), savings, and taxes. Savings are used to finance investment. If this investment is local, as Figure 11.1 assumes, it also adds to the local income flow.

Within this local economy growth takes place by injecting new money into the flow in one of a few different ways. The most obvious way of doing this is to increase the production of goods for export. Selling locally produced goods to other communities creates a corresponding inflow of income to the area. Local investment using non-local funds (not shown in Figure 11.1) offers a similar inflow, as does an increase in local consumption or local government spending.

Any new source of local income, such as a performing arts center or a factory complex, leads to new household income through employment and local spending on materials and other inputs. Part of this income is spent locally while the rest is saved, paid in taxes, or spent on non-local goods (imports). This second round of local spending in turn becomes a second source of local income, which because of the savings, taxes, and non-local spending is smaller than the first round. This process continues to add local income indefinitely at a decreasing rate, which leads to the Keynesian spending multiplier. The proof of the Keynesian version of the multiplier is included below.

Proof of the multiplier formula

The simple multiplier formula is based on an infinite series of declining rounds of added income. Using the letter m to represent the marginal propensity to consume locally, Y to represent income, C to represent the initial round of spending, and numbers to represent the different rounds of added income and spending, the infinite stream of increased income (ΔY) produced by an initial round of local spending (ΔC) appears as follows:

$$\Delta Y = \Delta C + m\,\Delta C + m^2\,\Delta C + m^3\,\Delta C + \ldots + m^\infty\,\Delta C \qquad (11.1)$$

For example, if m equals ½ and the initial change in local spending equals $100, the total change in income will equal $100 + $50 + $25 + $12.5, and so forth, decreasing by ½ each time. In theory at least, this process goes on forever. Later rounds of added income grow small quite quickly if the marginal propensity to consume locally is small, as is commonly the case.

Fortunately there is a shortcut which makes it unnecessary to separately calculate a large number of rounds of added income. Multiplying equation (11.1) by the marginal propensity to consume (m) produces (11.2).

$$m \, \Delta Y = m \, \Delta C + m^2 \, \Delta C + m^3 \, \Delta C + m^4 \, \Delta C + \ldots + m^\infty \Delta C \qquad (11.2)$$

Subtracting (11.2) from (11.1) leads to the following result where most items cancel. This cancellation occurs because there is no infinity-plus-one to add to the right-hand side of (11.2):

$$(1 - m) \, \Delta Y = \Delta C \qquad (11.3)$$

Dividing both sides by (1−*m*) produces the multiplier relationship:

$$\Delta Y = \Delta C[1/(1 - m)] \qquad (11.4)$$

Based on equation (11.4), if the marginal propensity to consume locally (*m*) = ½, the initial $100 in added local consumption will produce a cumulative effect of $100 [1/(1 − ½)], or $100 • 2, or $200. Dividing (11.4) by ΔC leads to **the basic Keynesian multiplier equation:**

$$\Delta Y/\Delta C = 1/(1 - m) \qquad (11.5)$$

Both sides of equation (11.5) are referred to as the Keynesian spending multiplier. The left-hand side ($\Delta Y/\Delta C$) is used to convert the direct spending from an institution or project (ΔC) into its total economic impact. The right-hand side of the equation provides the explicit connection between the marginal propensity to consume locally (*m*) and the multiplier value. Multiplier effects can be calculated for employment and earnings as well as total income through a similar formula.

Your Turn 11.1: Table 11.1 provides estimates of the direct, secondary (multiplier) and total effects for output, employment, and earnings for the Carlisle Barracks in Pennsylvania.
(A) Use the direct spending and total output figures in Table 11.1 to calculate the multipliers for spending and employment for the Carlisle area and for Cumberland county. There are four multipliers in total.
(B) Using the formula $\Delta Y/\Delta C$ = 1/(1 − m) and the spending multiplier values from step (A), solve for *m* to find the marginal propensity to consume locally.
(C) Use the direct spending figures from Table 11.1 and the spending multipliers you calculated in step (A) above to estimate the total impact of the Carlisle Barracks on local and county spending.

Economic base models

The second type of multiplier comes from an urban and regional growth model referred to as the economic base or basic/non-basic model.[1] Economic base

Table 11.1 Impact estimates for the Carlisle Barracks, 2004

	Carlisle area	Cumberland county
Spending effects		
Direct spending	$88,646,766	$109,461,405
Secondary spending	$29,253,433	$64,582,229
Total output	$117,900,199	$174,043,634
Employment effects		
Direct employment	1,580	1,932
Secondary employment	360	744
Total employment	1,940	2,676

Source: Bellinger (2004).

models arose in the urban and regional economics literature in the 1930s, and are related to the Keynesian macroeconomic model developed around the same time. **Economic base models** begin by dividing a region's production into two parts: (1) export goods and (2) local services. In this context the term "exports" refers to goods sold to another region or locality, not necessarily to another nation. Local services include retail services, education, entertainment, local government, and any other activity needed to support the local population. According to the economic base model, a region grows only by increasing its exports to other regions. Selling goods to other areas creates a corresponding inflow of income from outside the region. This income is in turn partly spent on local goods and services.

The economic base model is often expressed in terms of employment, the most easily measurable component of local or regional production. Total employment (L) is divided into basic or export employment (E) and non-basic or local service employment (N). The non-basic sector's employment is related to the area's total employment by a linear function, as in equation (11.7):

$$L = E + N \tag{11.6}$$

$$N = a + bL, \text{ where } a \text{ is a constant and } b = \Delta N/\Delta L \tag{11.7}$$

In (11.7), b equals the added local service employment for each unit of added total employment. Using Keynesian terms, b is the marginal propensity to employ locally. Substituting (11.7) into (11.6) produces the multiplier relationship between the export base and total employment:

$$L = E + a + bL$$

$$L - bL = E + a$$

$$(1 - b)L = E + a$$

$$L = (E + a)/(1 - b) \tag{11.8}$$

In this model the total employment in a region will be directly related to the employment in the export base. If the export base equals zero, the local economy will be limited to a relatively small, self-sufficient, agricultural community with total employment equal to the constant term *a*.

Your Turn 11.2: A community with 10,000 jobs in the export sector and values of 2,000 for *a* and ½ for *b* will have how many total employees? Use the last line of equation (11.9) to find the answer.

The simplest version of the export base model assumes that the endpoint *a* equals zero, meaning that no employment or economic activity would exist in an area without an export base. If the endpoint *a* in (11.8) equals zero, (11.9) reduces to a simple Keynesian spending multiplier formula stated in terms of employment, the export base multiplier will then equal total employment divided by export base employment, or L/E using the terms in the earlier equations.[2]

$$Export\ base\ multiplier = Total\ employment/ \\ Export\ base\ employment = L/E = \frac{1}{1-b} \qquad (11.9)$$

This multiplier can be used to predict the increase in total employment or economic activity associated with any change in the export base, though not always with great accuracy.

Your Turn 11.3: If a town has 20,000 total employees and a basic/non-basic multiplier of 2.5, how many employees work in the export sector?

The location quotient

This simple multiplier cannot be measured without dropping the assumption that production and employment can be divided into export industries and local service industries. In reality, most industries produce some of their goods for export and some for local consumption. Therefore, we need a concept for measuring the proportion of an industry's production that is exported from the area. This concept is called the location quotient. The **location quotient** for an industry is defined as the ratio of local production to local consumption of that industry's product. If this ratio is greater than one, the industry is a net exporter of goods. For the personal computer (PC) industry the location quotient would be defined as follows:

$$Location\ quotient = Local\ PC\ production/Local\ PC\ consumption \qquad (11.10)$$

In practice, local consumption cannot be accurately measured without costly survey data. Therefore, two alternative formulae are commonly used to approximate an industry's location quotient. One of these formulae compares an industry's local to national output, and the other compares the industry's local to national employment. Equation (11.11) includes both alternatives for the hypothetical case of the personal computer (PC) industry:

$$LQ_{prod} = \frac{\dfrac{City's\ PC\ production}{City's\ total\ production}}{\dfrac{Nation's\ PC\ production}{Nation's\ total\ production}} \quad LQ_{emp} = \frac{\dfrac{City's\ PC\ employment}{City's\ total\ employment}}{\dfrac{Nation's\ PC\ employment}{Nation's\ total\ employment}} \quad (11.11)$$

The denominator in the production location quotient (national PC production/all production) provides an indirect estimate of local personal computer consumption. This estimate is reasonable if residents in that locality have an average level of computer consumption and if the computer market is in equilibrium. The same assumptions apply to the employment-based location quotient. The numerators then provide the corresponding ratio of industry to total local employment. If the entire ratio is greater than one, the model predicts that the city will be a net exporter of computers.

Your Turn 11.4: Techville employs 400 of its 1,000 workers in the PC industry. Assume that for the nation 5 percent (0.05) work in the PC industry. Find Techville's location quotient (employment) for the PC industry.

Export base case study: the effects of Wal-Mart

While the export base model has serious conceptual and measurement problems, it is still used in some contexts. A variant of the export base model has been used by Kenneth Stone of Iowa State University to estimate the local and regional effects of Wal-Mart stores (Stone 1988; Stone *et al.* 2002). Stone's work utilizes a concept he calls a "pull factor," which is a modified form of the location quotient. A **pull factor** measures location quotients through an industry's sales revenue per person rather than through employment or total production. The only other change from equations (11.10) and (11.11) is that the pull factor compares county to state averages rather than national averages. The pull factor for a local industry is defined as follows:

$$County\ pull\ factor = County\ per\ capita\ sales/State\ per\ capita\ sales \quad (11.12)$$

For example, if the average person in Philadelphia, Pennsylvania (which is a county as well as a city), spends $100 per month in restaurants while the average person in Pennsylvania spends $50 per month, then the pull factor for Philadelphia restaurants equals $100/$50, or 2.

Dr. Stone's more recent Mississippi findings (Stone *et al.* 2002), along with other recent studies (Barnes *et al.* 1996), have found mixed economic effects from the introduction of a Wal-Mart store. Stone's study found that average county pull factors for general merchandise stores, a category that includes Wal-Mart, were steady and very close to 1 for the four years before the opening of a Wal-Mart store. In the four years following the opening of a county's first Wal-Mart, the average pull factor increased to 1.39 after one year and to 1.57 after four years. These results indicate that counties that added Wal-Mart stores became net exporters of general merchandise while counties with no Wal-Mart stores did not. Wal-Mart itself was the primary beneficiary of this change.

Competing stores experienced mixed effects. Food stores suffered significant drops in pull factors, dropping from about 1.2 to about 1.0 after five years. Miscellaneous retail stores other than Wal-Mart also dropped from 0.76 to 0.69 after five years. On the other hand, furniture and building materials stores experienced only random changes in pull factors and on average were no worse off. For all industries, counties with new Wal-Mart supercenters increased their pull factors slightly, rising by 10 percent in years 3 and 4 before dropping back somewhat, and counties with no Wal-Mart stores suffered roughly 10 percent declines in their overall pull rates, falling from 0.67 to 0.61. The primary conclusions of this type of study are that Wal-Mart draws consumers from outside its locality but also draws consumers away from local stores that directly compete with Wal-Mart's main products. According to Stone, the net impact of these two effects is apparently slightly positive for a Wal-Mart area in the short run.

Input–output models

The final method used to estimate local economic impact and the local multiplier effects is input–output analysis. **Input–output analysis** is based on an apparently simple mathematical table that measures flows of goods and services into and out of particular industries. This concept was developed by Nobel Prize winner Wassily Leontief of Harvard in the 1930s. Beginning with an input–output table, the calculation of industry-specific multipliers involves a few steps, which (as usual) are best explained through an example. Let's start with a hypothetical table of input–output coefficients for Steeltown, Pennsylvania.

In Table 11.2 the output levels by industry are presented as columns and the inputs to that industry are presented as rows. The coefficients appearing in each cell represent the fraction of each dollar of output that is spent on a particular input. For example, each dollar of steel produced requires 30 cents of local iron, 40 cents of local labor, and 30 cents of imports from outside the region. Obviously a full input–output table would be many times larger and more complex. However, the basic form would be the same.

Table 11.2 Input–output coefficients

Input sector/ output sector	Steel	Iron	Local services	Households
Steel	0	0.1	0.1	0.1
Iron	0.3	0	0	0
Local services	0	0.1	0	0.6
Household labor	0.4	0.4	0.7	0
Imports	0.3	0.4	0.2	0.3
Total	1	1	1	1

Assume that exports of steel from Steeltown increase by $1,000. This extra steel will create the following local multiplier effects through the first two rounds of spending (see Figure 11.2). Notice that spending on imports does not contribute to local income and is therefore not included in this chart. This pattern continues through further spending rounds as with the simple spending multiplier model.

Your Turn 11.5: Complete a graph showing two rounds of a local multiplier for a new iron mine expected to produce $10,000 of iron per time period. Use the "Iron" column in Table 11.2 to start the analysis.

A detailed input–output model cannot be easily reduced to a simple marginal propensity to consume locally. Fortunately, commercially available regional input–output models do this work for you. Using a regional input–output model produces multiplier values for each regional industry, such as those in Table 11.3. Given these multipliers an approximate figure for the marginal propensity to consume locally can be calculated using the Keynesian multiplier formula.[3]

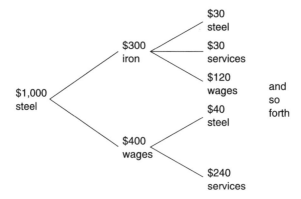

Figure 11.2 Input–output multiplier

Table 11.3 Hypothetical industry multipliers

Industry	Coal mining	Construction	Apparel	Chemicals	Retail trade	Health services
Farming	0.004	0.009	0.007	0.004	0.007	0.008
Mining	1.002	0.005	nil	0.005	nil	nil
Construction	0.016	1.011	0.015	0.016	0.023	0.019
Durables	0.139	0.161	0.016	0.029	0.025	0.022
Non-durables	0.043	0.070	1.264	1.088	0.079	0.077
Transportation	0.139	0.084	0.088	0.112	0.108	0.103
Wholesale	0.065	0.064	0.123	0.076	0.038	0.054
Retail	0.033	0.092	0.048	0.036	1.063	0.076
Finance	0.125	0.120	0.115	0.080	0.166	0.188
Services	0.139	0.231	0.211	0.143	0.236	1.298
Households	0.262	0.478	0.414	0.285	0.530	0.677
Total	1.967	2.325	2.301	1.874	2.275	2.522

Source: This is a hypothetical input–output-based multiplier table. The figures are randomly modified from an actual RIMS-II multiplier table for a multi-county region in the U.S.

Measuring indirect and induced spending

This section of the chapter explores how the measurement of indirect and induced spending differs for various types of impact studies. Studies of an existing institution such as a college or military base have a somewhat different set of components than those for a proposed investment such as a new sports facility, convention center, or performing arts center. These two general classes of studies will be compared in terms of direct spending measurement, multiplier effects, and other effects.

The multiplier estimate for a given project depends strongly on the location and size of the area being studied. Current practice is to base regional multiplier estimates on one of several commercial regional input–output models that can be purchased for any county or multi-county region in the United States. Three of the most commonly used models are the REMI model, the IMPLAN model, and the RIMS-II model, although others exist.[4] All three models are user-friendly computer programs that estimate the effect of a change in direct spending on all industries within the designated area.

These input–output models can be used with various degrees of accuracy depending on the detail of the direct spending data. If your direct spending information is limited to total budget figures for an institution, input–output multipliers for that institution's industry can be used to provide a rough economic impact estimate. For example, the regional model's multiplier for the higher education industry can be applied to the total spending of a university to come up with a rough economic impact estimate for that university. This approach requires one to assume that the institution being studied has a production process typical of that industry. Most impact studies have far more detailed information on direct spending.

More detailed impact studies require more accurate information on institutional purchases and employee or customer spending. A more accurate approach to estimating the indirect income from an institution's purchases requires detailed information about the location and type of these purchases. Most institutions interested in an impact study are willing to share detailed cost and spending information with the analyst. The institution's purchases can then be categorized by industry and the weighted average of the multipliers for each supplying industry can be used to calculate the institution's indirect spending.

The induced income produced by employee spending can be analyzed in two ways. First, regional models such as RIMS-II have a separate category for households. Combining payroll totals and the household sector multiplier for that region produces an estimate of induced spending. This approach assumes that the institution's employees have spending patterns that are typical for employees of that industry. The second method of estimating induced spending from employee income is to survey employees about their spending, categorize that spending by industry, use industry multipliers to determine the total impact in each sector, and then add these sector impacts together to calculate the total induced spending. Spending surveys allow one to avoid the simplifying assumption that the institution's employees have average or typical spending patterns.

Measuring an institution's effect on local government

Measuring the impact of an institution on government finances is a complex process. The spending of the institution and its employees on goods, services, and wages leads to increased income and sales tax revenue. On the other hand, any increase in population creates a greater demand for local services, including education. Estimating an institution's net effects on local government requires one to find state and local sales or income tax rates and multiply the institution's total multiplier effect on spending and income by these rates. For an institution's effect on education spending, employee surveys can find how many of the added employees have children attending public school. The average local variable spending per pupil can be found from the local school board's budget, leading to a simple calculation of the total spending effect. Spending on other services such as public safety or fire protection are also likely to be increased by an institution, and are usually estimated by assuming that spending on these services is constant across the population. An estimate of the number of employees (or students) residing locally can then be divided by the total town population. The resulting ratio can be applied to various local service budgets to estimate the impact of the institution on those spending categories. The geographic area of an institution can also be compared to the area of a town for some types of spending estimates.

The property tax is a common form of local government financing in the U.S. However, government and non-profit institutions such as private colleges are generally exempt from local property taxes. Therefore, lost property tax revenue is an important part of the local government impact of a tax-exempt institution. Lost property tax revenue can be valued in one of two ways. First, the actual assessed value of the property is often available in county tax records, particularly for colleges. Multiplying the assessed value by the local property tax rate leads to one estimate of lost tax revenue. This approach has the advantage of providing a very straightforward answer to one important question: **How much would the local government gain if this property were not tax-exempt?**

However, the opportunity cost principle requires the answer to a different question: **How much property tax revenue would local government receive if the college or military base did not exist?** This question can be answered by determining the average property value per acre or other area measure in the vicinity of the institution, multiplying that value by the number of acres occupied by the institution, and then multiplying the result by the local property tax rate. This method of calculating the lost property taxes generally produces far lower estimates of lost tax revenue, since the large and valuable buildings that often dominate colleges or government facilities would not exist in the absence of the institution. Overall, local governments and school districts are likely to experience negative budgetary effects from a college, military base, or other non-profit institution, while state governments are likely to gain.

The role of spending surveys

Survey evidence can provide three potentially useful types of information not available in regional multiplier models. First, local as well as county or multi-county impact figures can be derived from survey-based spending data. This is true because spending surveys allow the estimate of truly local, as opposed to county-wide, marginal propensities to consume locally. While multiplier values will be lower for local areas than for counties or regions, the percentage of the local economy impacted by any institution will be far larger. For example, the U.S. Army War College in Carlisle, Pennsylvania, was estimated to provide almost 10 percent of the total economic activity in the Carlisle area, but a very small percentage of county or regional economic activity (Bellinger 2004: 9-10).

Secondly, surveys can provide evidence of non-commercial effects such as community activity or charitable donations. Asking survey respondents about the hours they donate to local charitable activity, and then valuing those hours at an assumed wage rate, provides an average value of charitable services per student or employee. This average can then be multiplied by the total student or employee population to create an estimated total value for charitable activity. In general, charitable activity involves basic labor, and therefore it should usually be valued at or close to the minimum wage. Because no money changes hands, there are no multiplier effects. Also, since charitable activities are not marketed, some analysts do not include dollar estimates in the total impact figures. Instead, a description of the volunteer hours and dollar contributions of survey respondents can provide supplementary information above and beyond the dollar-based economic impact analysis.

Finally, surveys can be useful if the industrial categories provided by the regional input–output models are not completely accurate for a particular facility.

For example, survey evidence was useful in determining that the multiplier values for the U.S. Army War College were closer to that of a college or university than a more typical army post (Bellinger 2004: 28-32).

Economic impact case studies

In this section we will consider examples of economic impact studies for military installations, the performing arts, and entertainment venues such as sports stadiums.

Military base impact studies

Relatively permanent institutions such as colleges and military bases represent one class of economic impact subjects. In the case of higher education, one published work (Simmons 1992) listed 228 such studies since the mid-1960s. The large total impact figures provided by these studies provide seemingly impressive evidence for funding the institution or project, particularly for those who are not versed in policy analysis or critical thinking regarding numerical evidence.

Multiple rounds of military base closures have occurred in the U.S. in recent decades as the nation has slowly reduced military capacity built up in World War II. In order to reduce the political pressures on these cost-saving measures, the base realignment and closure process (BRAC) has operated through an established set of guidelines since the passage of the Defense Base Closure and Realignment Act of 1990. Information can be found at the BRAC website (http://www.defenselink. mil/brac/index.html). While the most recent BRAC guidelines rank military value as the primary basis for closure decisions, local and regional economic impact studies are also a required part of each base's BRAC documentation. Therefore, economic impact studies of military facilities have become very common in recent years. Most of these studies utilize the REMI or IMPLAN economic models for one or more counties, though some studies have encompassed entire states. Examples include Fort Drum, New York (http://www.edrgroup.com/pages/pdf/Ft-Drum-Econ-Impact.pdf), various South Carolina bases (http://www.commerce. state.az.us/pdf/commasst/Exec%20Summary.pdf), and the state-wide study of military economic impacts in Arizona (http://www.commerce.state.az.us/pdf/ commasst/Exec%20Summary.pdf).

All of these studies utilize a gross measurement of direct spending based on the base's budget and do not subtract the value of any alternative use of the properties. On one level this is relatively legitimate, since in the absence of the base most or all of the active military personnel and many non-military professional employees would locate elsewhere. However, the actual benefits of the institution should be compared to the best alternative use of its land in order to measure net benefits or impact accurately. In high-value urban areas, shutting down a military facility could lead to rapid and highly profitable alternative development. On the other hand, the impact of a base closing is likely to be more negative in otherwise lightly developed rural communities. Unfortunately, estimating the economic activity from a hypothetical alternative use of the property involves a great deal of uncertainty, particularly before any alternative development plans are devised. The BRAC commission handles this challenge by allowing gross economic impact estimates (excluding alternative use value of the property) and then stating explicitly that their published estimates assume no subsequent development. Given the secondary role given to a base's economic impact and the existence of gross impact estimates for all bases considered by BRAC, the use of consistent but exaggerated economic impact figures is probably reasonable as long as it is understood that future development of military property could reduce or even exceed any short-run losses.

Regional arts impact

The performing arts industry often utilizes economic impact estimates as part of its case for public subsidies. Performing arts economic impact studies come in two general categories: studies of the entire arts sector in a given region and studies of particular arts venues or performing arts companies. This section will review examples of arts industry studies. Studies of specific arts facilities or companies are similar to those for sports stadiums, which are reviewed later in this chapter.

Studies of the overall impact of an area's arts industry are generally funded by organizations supporting the arts, follow flawed methodology based on gross spending figures, and serve a primarily political purpose. A 2003 study provides a relatively detailed, and entirely one-sided, overview of this issue (Americans for the Arts 2003). However, we will consider an older and somewhat more specific study. The National Endowment for the Arts (NEA) published a report on the economic impact of arts and cultural institutions in Columbus, Minneapolis/ St. Paul, St. Louis, Salt Lake City, San Antonio, and Springfield, Illinois, in 1981. In each city the studies covered the major museums of art and science, the symphony orchestra, one or more theaters and dance companies, and an occasional opera or botanical garden, for a total of 49 institutions in the six cities.

The first step in this study was to estimate each institution's direct effect on local spending for goods and services, together with salaries and wages to local residents and the local spending by guest artists and arts audiences. Secondary effects were then estimated through an input–output model. The reported total impact data are the sums of the direct spending and secondary income figures. The ratios of total dollar impact to direct spending presented in the study allows us to calculate the multiplier values it used. These range from 1.44 for Springfield, Illinois, to 1.76 in Minneapolis-St. Paul, with a weighted average value for the total sample of 1.72.

Broadly-based studies of the regional economic impact of the arts are relatively rare due to their high cost and limited policy relevance. Their gross benefit methodology also limits their validity.

A more common type of arts- or entertainment-related economic impact study analyzes the effects of a particular public or private investment in an area. One goal of urban development efforts such as downtown stadiums or arts complexes is the reorientation of central cities into culture and tourism hubs. Performing arts

Table 11.4 Results of the six city arts impact study, 1981*

	Columbus	Minn./St. Paul	St. Louis	Salt Lake City	San Antonio	Springfield	Total
No. of Institutions	6	10	8	10	5	10	49
Direct spending ($ thousands)	$6,337	$28,600	$20,911	$6,080	$3,736	$2,998	$68,662
Direct spending (1998 $)	$11,584	$52,281	$38,225	$11,115	$6,829	$5,480	$125,514
Attendance (thousands)	699	2,765	2,504	348	467	410	7,194
Secondary income ($ thousands)	$4,044	$21,721	$15,899	$3,876	$2,345	$1,317	$49,202
Secondary income (1998 $)	$7,393	$39,705	$29,064	$7,086	$4,287	$2,407	$89,942
Total impact ($ thousands)	$10,381	$50,320	$36,810	$9,957	$6,081	$4,315	$117,864
Total impact (1998 $)	$18,977	$91,986	$67,288	$18,201	$11,172	$7,887	$215,456

*All estimates are for the cities' Standard Metropolitan Statistical Areas; 1998 dollar figures were calculated using consumer price index data for entertainment.

development projects have been undertaken in major cities such as New York, where the Lincoln Center provided a model for this development strategy, as well as in innumerable small towns. In addition to a facility's direct revenue, arts venues also bring ancillary direct spending to local shops, restaurants, and lodgings, and may help to draw new downtown residents, additional entertainment sites, restaurants, and other development to the area. Such facilities have a potentially positive role to play as an antidote for the suburbanization or globalization of manufacturing and retail activity.

Because of the local nature of these benefits, audience spending surveys must be used to determine the percentage of the audience that travels from outside of the area and the local spending of the average patron. Such surveys can identify ancillary spending patterns of arts patrons, as well as how much of the revenue received comes from those residing outside the area. However, the size and scope of the benefits of an arts facility are subject to great uncertainty, particularly prior to completion of the project.

The New York Sports and Convention Center

Economic impact estimates of sports facilities are among the most widely publicized and controversial of impact studies, partly because of the great public interest in sports and partly because of the high total cost and large government subsidies associated with sports stadiums. Stadium impact studies can be completed before (*ex-ante*) or after (*ex-post*) the project's completion. Such studies usually are completed prior to the facility's construction because their main purpose is to create public support for the project. Hamilton and Kahn (1997) provided a good example of an *ex-post* impact study for the Camden Yards baseball stadium in Baltimore, Maryland. They calculated the internal rate of return for the Stadium as well as the net inflow of non-local spending using a number of creative assumptions, and found that in its early years Camden Yards was a worthwhile investment.

The proposed New York Sports and Convention Center, the centerpiece of which would be a New York Jets football stadium, was a far more complex case in several ways, not the least of which is the fact that it had not been approved or constructed at the time of the main impact studies. Also, the project had an estimated cost of roughly $2.8 billion and included convention space as well as a stadium. However, economic impact studies of the project were commissioned and completed, and provide a good example of an *ex-ante* economic impact study. One study (New York City Independent Budget Office 2004) started by organizing the probable attendance at stadium events or expositions into three groups: city residents, regional same-day visitors, and overnight visitors. Average spending amounts were estimated for each group, and these averages were multiplied by estimated total attendance to produce the final total. The number of new events to be created by the Center included stadium events such as games and concerts, and expositions to be held in the convention center section of the facility.

The New York Jets estimated that the stadium would host 17 stadium events each year, including eight Jets football games and nine large concerts or college sports events. The study also assumed that there would be 20 multi-day expositions at the convention facility, of which 14 would be new to the city. Overall, added direct spending was estimated to be $314 million per year, of which $206 million was new visitor spending. The total economic impact of the facility was estimated to be $519 million per year. Government revenue and employment effects were also estimated and found to be positive. Based on these results and the cost estimate of $2.8 billion, the facility would offer a rate of return of over 18 percent (New York City Independent Budget Office 2004).

While this study followed common methodological steps, some major objections were raised. The direct spending was calculated for New York City only, but its multiplier was for the New York metropolitan area. This is problematic because the current home of the New York Jets is only a few miles away in New Jersey. There was also no consideration of ancillary spending in New York from the current New Jersey facility. Secondly, neither alternative locations for the stadium nor alternative plans for developing the Manhattan site were considered. So while the net increases in income were calculated with some care, the project's opportunity costs were not. Finally, issues of traffic and parking are not addressed in the study.

The Manhattan stadium proposal provides a good example of the potential for misinterpreting a large economic impact number. After the needed state funding for the stadium project was denied, alternative proposals for residential development of the proposed stadium site surfaced almost immediately. Prior to the effort to fund the stadium project, a $760 million offer was made for the same property (the Jets offered about $250 million).[5] A 2005 assessment valued the same property at $960 million (*New York Times* 2005). In overcrowded and hyper-expensive Manhattan, residential or mixed-use real estate development probably represented a better land-use option for the site. The large economic impact estimate for the stadium in no way contradicts this conclusion.

Conclusion

Economic impact analysis has a role in estimating the effect of a facility or investment on a local economy, but such studies are not entirely consistent with the goals or methods of efficiency-based benefit–cost analysis, or with the society-wide considerations required under utilitarian ethics. Any economic impact study that does not seriously consider the net rather than gross effects of a facility on the local economy, or does not actively consider alternative uses of the site, is likely to provide misleading results.

The more inherent problem with economic impact studies is their limited geographical range. While politics is often concerned with local issues, efficiency is a societal or even global issue. Money spent to encourage the location of a facility or business in an area usually competes with similar programs in other areas. The ultimate effect of policy decisions based on economic impact analysis is likely to be a great deal of government spending and little net change in the locational decisions of businesses, or sports teams.

The explicitly political role of most economic impact studies also raises concerns and questions that one should consider when reading about any economic impact number. Was the study funded by an advocacy group? Does the project being analyzed require a large public expenditure? What other alternative uses of the land or funding could be considered? Is the large economic impact number significant relative to an area's economy? Economic impact studies, particularly *ex-ante* studies of new investment proposals, are notoriously unreliable as guides to efficient policy choice, and should be interpreted cautiously by both analysts and readers.

Review questions

Conceptual questions

1. Thomas (Tip) O'Neill, former Speaker of the House of Representatives, once declared that "All politics is local." Discuss how local interests might create demand for economic impact studies, and why the well-being of society as a whole might not be enhanced by a local development program with a high economic impact value.

2. Discuss how your answers for the Forrest Center case study at the end of Chapter 7 would be different if analyzed as an economic impact study. Which costs would become local benefits, and what additional benefits would be included in the impact estimate?

3. Explain how your tuition might produce indirect and induced spending in your local community.

4. This question refers to the New York Jets study summarized in this chapter. Discuss ways in which the benefits of the Jets football stadium might have been greater than those of residential housing, and speculate on some local industries or interest groups that would have benefited or lost because of the choice of a non-stadium use of the site.

Computational questions

5. If possible, find the total annual budget of your college or university, have your instructor provide you with a county or metropolitan multiplier value for your area, and calculate a simple impact estimate. Discuss the implicit assumptions and limits of this simple form of economic impact estimate.

6. Let's consider the Forrest Center case in more detail. Review the Chapter 7 appendix and then answer the following questions:

    (A) Note that 2/5 of the $50 million in funding for construction is assumed to come from outside the area. Assume that the marginal propensity to consume locally for construction income is 1/3. What is the economic impact of this outside funding?

(B) Take the annual net increase in performance revenue calculated for the Forrest Center. If you didn't calculate this total, assume that it's $12,000,000 per year. If the local multiplier for the performing arts is 1.25, calculate the annual economic impact of the Forrest Center's performing arts offerings.

(C) Do the same for local spending on restaurants and parking assuming a 1.35 local multiplier. Adding the effects together, how does the annual economic impact compare to the added direct revenue calculated originally?

7. Assume that in Richardville 900 people are employed in the arts and that its total employment is 30,000. Nationally 2 percent (0.02) work in the arts. What is the Richardville arts industry's location quotient?

8. The U.S. Department of Labor offers a Location Quotient calculator at the following website: http://data.bls.gov/LOCATION_QUOTIENT/servlet/lqc. ControllerServlet. Choose any two counties under the Analysis Area links, check the box marked "sector," and then click on "Get Results." What are the primary export sectors for each county you selected?

Part IV

Public policy cases

The final four chapters of the text present more detailed overviews of selected public policy topics. Chapter 12 presents an overview of the problem of urban traffic congestion and several alternative policies for reducing congestion costs. Chapter 13 discusses pollution control policy with an emphasis on air pollution. Chapter 14 discusses the alternative meanings and measurements of poverty, and then analyzes U.S. income maintenance programs. Chapter 15 discusses additional policies for the working poor, including job training, the minimum wage, and the earned income tax credit.

One general lesson to be learned is that in most contexts several different types of policies might be applied to a particular policy problem. Another lesson is the difficulty that can arise in measuring, and sometimes defining, policy problems such as poverty or pollution. A third is that different problems can require very different areas of expertise. Engineers, scientists, and a broad range of social scientists play a role in understanding various policy problems. This requires the policy analyst to be capable of working in multi-disciplinary teams, to be able to learn the methods and language of a new field relatively quickly, and to communicate with some wisdom across a wide range of disciplines.

12 Urban transportation policy

Everything in life is somewhere else, and you get there in a car.[1]

E.B. White

The automobile has not merely taken over the street, it has dissolved the living tissue of the city. Its appetite for space is absolutely insatiable; moving and parked, it devours urban land, leaving the buildings as mere islands of habitable space in a sea of dangerous and ugly traffic.

(James Marston Fitch, *New York Times*, May 1, 1960.)

"Beam me up, Scotty"
(Common phrase associated with *Star Trek*)

Urban transportation is included in this book partly as an example of public investment in long-lived infrastructure, and partly to provide evidence of the wide range of alternatives available for dealing with externalities such as traffic congestion.[2] Of course, congestion is not the only negative externality that arises from the automobile. Others include air and noise pollution, unattractive views, human and non-human death and injury, the segmentation of neighborhoods, and the disposal of old vehicles (junk yards). Despite these social harms, the automobile has become the dominant form of transportation in many countries, particularly in North America and Australia. One reason why this trend is unlikely to be reversed in auto-dominated societies is that employment and housing have scattered across far wider areas than in nations where mass transit still dominates urban transportation.

Like all areas of public policy, several different fields of study contribute to our understanding of the costs and benefits of alternative transportation technologies and policy designs. The economic analysis of transportation investment often begins with interaction between economists and engineers. Civil and transportation engineers are responsible for the design and cost estimates of a given highway, rail, or airport project. Others who analyze the various effects of highway or rail projects include environmental scientists and urban sociologists, among others. Some exposure to these fields is useful in developing critical thinking skills regarding transportation policy.

The other lesson to be gained from a discussion of urban transportation policy is the wide range of policy alternatives that have been implemented in order to reduce urban traffic congestion. These include highway construction, fees on rush-hour commuters, taxes on autos or parking, regulations regarding highway use, the construction and subsidizing of alternative modes of transportation, and others. The wide range of alternatives for addressing traffic congestion provides a useful example of thinking beyond direct and obvious policy designs, and more generally for thinking broadly about any area of public policy.

This chapter begins with a brief review of three economic concepts that are relevant to the analysis of urban transportation policy: infrastructure, public goods, and natural monopoly. It will then analyze the demand for transportation services, including the automobile, review in some detail the externalities associated with commuting by car, and then discuss several policy alternatives for reducing traffic congestion.

Related economic concepts

Infrastructure is a term that can be defined in various ways. In its narrowest form, **infrastructure** refers to goods that involve large, interconnected networks. Goods delivered through network infrastructure include voice communication, electricity, water systems, sewage disposal, natural gas, and transportation. A broader definition of infrastructure could include any set of institutions that delivers public goods and services such as defense, healthcare, education, or culture. A common element connecting these forms of infrastructure is that they involve a regional or national market size, and have some of the characteristics of public goods.

Infrastructure is often owned or regulated by the government due to market imperfections that are consistent with infrastructure's characteristics. Because of these market imperfections, a purely private market will not be fully efficient in terms of maximizing the market's net gains from trade. As stated in Chapters 4 and 5, market imperfections do not ensure that government involvement will improve efficiency, but they create a window of opportunity for government to improve efficiency through effective policy choices. The first step in understanding the importance of government's role in infrastructure investment is to review these market inefficiencies.

An economic concept which overlaps considerably with infrastructure is the **public good**. As noted in Chapter 4, a public good has two unique characteristics. First, a public good has **no rivalry in consumption,** meaning that multiple persons can consume a public good at the same time. The second characteristic of public goods is **non-excludability,** which means that a person cannot be prevented from consuming a public good even if they have not paid. With the exception of toll roads, most highways are not excludable, and therefore meet the definition of public goods.

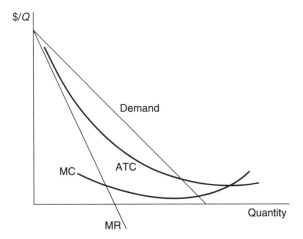

Figure 12.1 Natural monopoly

As noted in Chapter 4, the lack of excludability creates the incentive for people to become **free riders**. If people are not required to pay, the revenue potential of that product is obviously limited. Therefore, private demand for the good will be insufficient to provide the good at the socially efficient level. This is why highway construction and maintenance is almost universally a public sector activity. A second challenge created by non-excludable highways is the government's inability to directly control access to the highway in order to prevent traffic congestion.

In the case of network infrastructure such as roads or commuter rail systems, there is another rationale for government involvement. Due to the huge economies of scale associated with a highway or rail grid, network infrastructure can involve a concept known as **natural monopoly** (Figure 12.1), which was discussed in Chapter 5. The goal of government policy when facing a natural monopoly is to impose a lower price and higher quantity than would exist with a private monopoly. Government may pursue this goal through price regulation or public ownership. In the case of transportation networks such as highways or urban rail systems, public ownership is the most common solution, although regulated private ownership of bus companies and commuter railroads also exists.

Modal choice and transportation demand

The movement of goods or people can be accomplished through multiple forms of transportation which are sometimes referred to as **transportation modes**. These include rail, highway vehicles, aircraft, and ships. Supply issues in the transportation market involve the production costs, social costs, and accessibility of various transportation modes. The demand side involves the choice of transportation modes for freight, commuting, vacation travel, or any other use. This chapter concentrates on urban passenger transportation. For many urban residents, particularly in the U.S., this means reliance on the automobile.

In order to analyze the demand for urban passenger transportation, we should consider why individuals in the U.S. and some other countries so often choose to commute by car, and to what degree this choice can be modified through economic incentives or regulations. The choice of how to commute is known as **modal choice**, or the choice among alternative transportation modes. Analyzing this choice economically involves four steps: (1) dividing a commute to work into its component parts, (2) analyzing the costs of each part, (3) adding these costs to find a total cost of commuting, and (4) choosing the mode of transportation with the lowest total cost. A basic commute involves three stages: (1) getting from one's home to the vehicle (the collection phase), (2) traveling in the vehicle (the line haul phase), and (3) getting from the vehicle to the workplace (the distribution phase). Each phase involves costs through lost time, physical discomfort or stress, and money which vary among different modes of transportation.

Getting from one's home to one's vehicle (the collection phase) is usually far less costly in time and discomfort when traveling by car. For mass transit, with its limited number of collection points (bus stops, etc.), the collection phase generally requires greater time cost and physical exertion for the commuter. Therefore, the collection phase favors the automobile. The **line-haul phase** involves traveling from the collection point near one's home to a distribution point near one's place of work. This phase of the commute involves a set of tradeoffs that are highly dependent upon the commuter's specific circumstances. Rail mass transit is often faster than driving, but buses are usually slower. Furthermore, driving is generally more dangerous than public transit, involves greater effort and concentration, and in some locations may involve a greater risk of delay. Automobile amenities such as a good audio system or greater quiet and solitude offer some benefits relative to mass transit. Also, the car offers far greater flexibility for those who must run errands during the commute or during the day. The primary private benefits of mass transit are greater safety, the ability to work or socialize during the commute itself, and less effort and stress. The line-haul phase does not clearly favor either mode of transit.

The **distribution phase** involves getting from the vehicle to the workplace. If the workplace offers free and convenient parking, the auto is far less costly than mass transit during this phase of the commute. If parking a car is costly, risky (either in terms of finding a space or in terms of theft), or inconvenient, then the distribution phase may favor mass transit. Overall, the popularity of the automobile is easily understood. The car has substantial advantages at the collection phase and often at the distribution phase as well, in addition to having far greater flexibility. In nations such as the U.S. and Canada with relatively scattered urban populations, the automobile is often the only practical commuting mode. Any urban transportation policy will have to confront this challenge.

Your Turn 12.1: Analyze how your commute to class or work divides into these three phases. You might also do this for your typical daily bus ride to elementary or high school. How long did each phase take, and which was the most unpleasant per minute of time?

Highway congestion

Let's start our analysis of congestion externalities by considering how crowded highways lead to slow traffic. This slowing can be demonstrated as a graphical relationship between the total number of cars and the flow of cars over a given section of highway. Figure 12.2 demonstrates this relationship. If we begin with zero total cars, we have a flow of zero cars per hour. As the number of cars increases, the flow will increase as long as the added cars are not significantly interfering with other traffic. However, as the number of cars begins to approach the maximum capacity of the highway, traffic will slow down for three reasons: (1) because of shorter stopping distances, cars slow in order to preserve a margin of safety; (2) crowding lessens each car's ability to change lanes without disrupting others; (3) entry to and exit from the freeway are more likely to cause a slowing of traffic. In brief, traffic slows because the average car has less room ahead and less room to the side.

As the number of cars continues to increase, the relationship between the number of cars and the flow of traffic can then start to turn negative. Eventually,

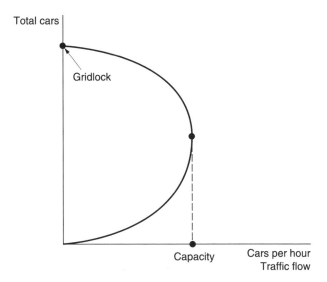

Figure 12.2 Cars vs. traffic flow

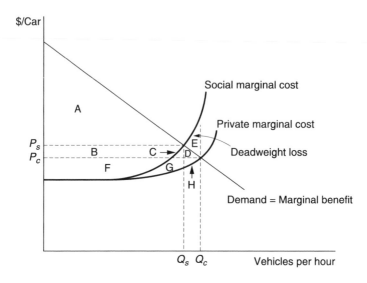

Figure 12.3 Traffic externalities

enough cars enter that a state of gridlock exists, in which case the flow drops to zero. Generally, gridlock occurs only when there is a blockage due to an intersection or accident, but the issue of congestion is not based on the extreme case of gridlock. The slowing caused by traffic congestion causes the rush-hour commuter to experience a type of external cost. Not only is the individual commuter's own trip slower, but her car will slow other cars in her vicinity. While her effect on the actual speed of traffic is small, that slowing will affect a large number of drivers. Therefore, the total external costs may be relatively significant. In Figure 12.3, the effect of crowding on the individual's time cost is shown by the rising private marginal cost curve. The cost of an added vehicle on all drivers combined is shown by the rising social marginal cost curve. Finally, the external cost for other drivers is the difference between the private and social marginal cost curves. Note that at low traffic levels there is no external congestion cost. This cost builds rapidly near capacity, and the slope of the social cost curve approaches the vertical if gridlock occurs.

> **Your Turn 12.2:** Identify the consumer surplus, producer surplus, and the negative external surplus in Figure 12.3 for a private equilibrium.

Transportation data

In the U.S. information on automobile use and other forms of transportation is available from various federal agencies. Data on auto use includes estimates of

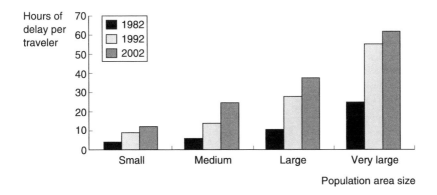

Figure 12.4 Congestion trends in U.S. cities
Source: The *2005 Urban Mobility Report,* http://mobility.tamu.edu

total vehicle miles, the number of vehicle registrations, and information about commuting from the U.S. Census and other sources. Downs (1992) argued that congestion worsened considerably in urban areas during the 1970s and 1980s, though his evidence is largely indirect. Government data suggest that urban congestion continued to worsen between the mid-1980s and mid-2000s in the U.S. (see Figure 12.4).

Congestion has increased in the U.S. because of a greater number of cars and a rise in the number of miles driven per car. The number of cars has risen because of growth in the number of households and an increase in total employment per household. The rise in the number of miles per car also results from more jobs per household, and therefore more commuting, but also from an increase in the average distance traveled due to residential and commercial sprawl (Downs 1992: Ch.1). Aside from total traffic flow, congestion can also be attributed to permanent features such as bottlenecks and the timing of traffic lights, which account for 45 percent of congestion, while temporary causes such as traffic accidents, weather, or work zones account for much of the remainder. While these catalysts may determine the time and place of severe congestion, total traffic volume greatly influences its severity (see Figure 12.5).

Another goal of urban transportation policy is improved safety. Safety is generally measurable by the number of lives lost, as well as damage to automobiles or other property. As was discussed in Chapter 10, the value of saving lives is an important aspect of estimating the costs of highway deaths and injuries. Since autos are far more dangerous than public transportation, safety is a potentially important argument in the debate over public transportation costs. Traffic safety is also a fundamental issue in law-enforcement decisions and car design regulations.

The number of U.S. highway deaths and injuries has remained reasonably constant over the past 30 years, with the annual death total ranging from a high of 52,500 in 1972 to 39,250 in 1992, the only year since the mid-1960s with fewer

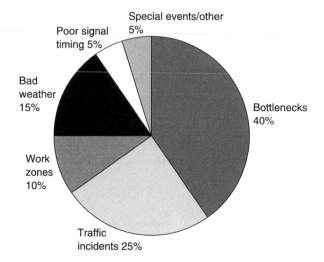

Figure 12.5 Sources of congestion
Source: Federal Highway Administration

than 40,000 highway deaths. However, this relative consistency masks two contradictory trends. On one hand, the number of vehicles has risen considerably, as has
the average number of annual miles per vehicle. On the other, the number of
deaths per vehicle mile has decreased substantially, from 5.5 deaths per 100 million
miles in 1965 to 1.6 deaths in 1997 (source: National Highway Traffic Safety
Council data).

The efficiency costs of congestion are similar to those of any negative externality. An unrestricted private market tends to produce too high a quantity and too
low a price given negative externalities, with a resultant deadweight efficiency
loss equal to a triangle facing leftward toward the socially ideal price and quantity. In Figure 12.3, this loss equals area E. However, while the general concept of
external costs may provide a guidepost for one's analysis of the harms of traffic
congestion, one would benefit from knowing in greater detail the specific harms
caused by traffic congestion. For the most part, that task is beyond the scope of
any single chapter on transportation policy.

Highway construction and congestion

There are a surprisingly large number of alternative policies for dealing with
traffic congestion. One may design policies to reduce the number of vehicles,
increase the capacity of roads, spread travel over a wider range of time, widen the
range of travel destinations, or encourage the use of alternative means of transportation. When one adds the other goals of transportation policy, including
increased safety, the reduction of sprawl, and reduced air pollution, certain of

these alternatives tend to drop out of the mix. For example, few people would support policies to encourage the diffusion of workplaces into suburbs or rural areas in order to reduce congestion, since doing so would tend to increase sprawl and related environmental costs. The most common policy options include highway construction, regulation and fees on automobile commuting, and the construction and subsidization of mass transit.

Highway expansion

One obvious and, at times, necessary part of the policy solution to congestion is the construction of additional highway lanes, either by building new roads or widening existing ones. Interestingly, while an effective system of roads and highways has significant economic benefits, expansion of the urban highway grid is not widely favored as a solution to rush-hour congestion, except in newly populated areas. This lack of acceptance is based on a principle often labeled **the law of traffic congestion**.

> **Definition: The law of traffic congestion** states that traffic expands to fill all available highway space until the maximum tolerable level of congestion is reached.

The general principle behind the law of traffic congestion is rational economic choice. Because highway expansion lowers the congestion costs of commuting, current commuters may travel in greater numbers, for greater distances, and more often during peak periods. This change will be shown as a movement down the original demand curve. More significantly, new commuters will be attracted to the expanded highways, causing a shift in the demand for highway miles. This two-fold expansion of traffic is shown in Figure 12.6. The movement along the demand curve from Q_1 to Q_2 is a reaction of current travelers to the lower opportunity cost of commuting. The shift in the demand curve from D_1 to D_2 and the subsequent increase in miles from Q_2 to Q_3 is caused by new highway commuters.

The lack of congestion on the highway at traffic volume Q_2 attracts new drivers looking for an opportunity to commute more quickly and efficiently. While the new highway commuters seem to pop up from nowhere, there are identifiable reasons why they will appear. The sources of these new highway drivers are summarized in what Downs (1992: 27-30) calls "triple convergence." First, some drivers will switch from alternative routes, such as non-highway routes or other highways. Secondly, other drivers will switch to their car from alternative modes of transportation, such as subways, buses, or car pools. Thirdly, other drivers will alter their time of travel toward the rush hour since they expect travel at peak hours to be quicker and less costly. As long as the new highway lanes offer a more attractive commuting choice, individuals will move their commute to the new highway.

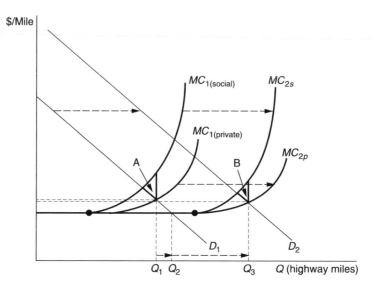

Figure 12.6 New highways

Only when the marginal cost of commuting on the new highway rises to that of other routes or transportation modes will the demand for that highway stop shifting to the right. The only reason why marginal commuting costs might be slightly lower after this adjustment process is complete is the effect of the new highway on total commuting capacity in the metropolitan area. The marginal cost at traffic volume Q_3 is slightly lower than at Q_1 for that reason.

In terms of efficiency, the results of this increase in capacity are less than ideal, since the deadweight loss caused by the external cost of highway commuting will not necessarily decline. In Figure 12.6, the deadweight loss will move from area A to area B. There is no reason to assume that area B is smaller than A. Increased highway capacity may decrease congestion costs, but this improvement may be offset by higher air and noise pollution, increased auto accidents, neighborhood disruption, and sprawl.

As with other public investments, projects are often analyzed in terms of benefit–cost or cost-effectiveness analysis. The benefits include increased capacity, decreased travel times, and related long-term growth in employment and economic activity. The costs of new highway capacity begin with the actual construction costs. Construction costs include the cost of obtaining and clearing the land plus the cost of all inputs used in highway construction. They should also include the opportunity cost of the land used for the highway and the external costs of noise, air pollution, neighborhood disruption, lost wildlife, and other non-marketed goods.

Highway case: Boston's "Big Dig"

Boston's Central Artery project (known as the "Big Dig") involves replacing an elevated six-lane highway with an underground multi-layer eight- to ten-lane route directly beneath the original road. The old Central Artery (I-93) had become highly congested and was likely to grow even more problematic without some significant expansion. As stated on the website:

> Traffic is at least moderately congested for as much as 10 hours or more each weekday. The accident rate is four times the national average for urban interstates. The same problem has plagued the two tunnels under Boston Harbor between downtown Boston and East Boston/Logan Airport. Without major improvements to the Central Artery and the harbor crossings, Boston can expect a stop-and-go traffic jam for up to 16 hours a day – every waking hour – by 2010. The annual cost to motorists from this congestion – in terms of an elevated accident rate, wasted fuel from idling in stalled traffic, and late delivery charge – is estimated to be $500 million.
>
> (http://www.masspike.com/bigdig/index.html)

In Boston's case there was little opportunity to widen the highway since adjoining land was densely developed. Landfill options such as those used for Manhattan's east- and west-side highways were also unavailable in Boston. The choice of elevated versus underground construction was the remaining policy decision. Three options were available for the vertical placement of the Central Artery's expansion. The expansion could be accomplished through the addition of an elevated highway above the original road, with one layer handling northbound and eastbound traffic and the other southbound and westbound traffic. Similarly, an underground layer could have been placed below the original roadway, which would have been converted to a single direction. The preferred choice was to place both layers underground.

Your Turn 12.3: Discuss possible benefits of placing an entire urban highway underground. Also discuss the added costs and technical difficulties of such a choice. Think about the issue from the drivers' point of view as well as that of those working or living near the highway.

The Big Dig project has been under construction since late 1991. As of July 2006, construction was about 98 percent complete. The cost for the Big Dig project will total approximately $15 billion, or nearly $2 billion per mile. In comparison, a hypothetical elevated highway in New York was estimated to cost as much as $333 million per mile (Wieman 1996), about one-sixth as expensive. An underground highway also requires complex ventilation and water-pumping backup systems, and creates risks of flooding or collapsing tunnels. The benefits of an underground highway are also substantial. They include the reduction of above-ground noise, substantial new open space for recreation or development opportunities, the use of the displaced earth for fill and capping material for solid waste sites, and some reduction in above-ground carbon monoxide levels.

Compared to the other urban transit policies considered in this chapter, new highways offer the greatest incentive for increased commuting by automobile. While the car offers a unique degree of flexibility to the individual, its social costs are significant. First, since cars create more pollution per commuter than other forms of transportation, policies that encourage automobile use will be costly to the environment. Secondly, since the car is far more dangerous than other forms of commuting, increasing auto use will increase commuting deaths and injuries. Furthermore, the highway takes up far more space than other commuting alternatives, and therefore can harm the social fabric of urban neighborhoods and the tax base of central cities. Finally, the flexibility of the auto will tend to increase the problem of urban sprawl. Finally, autos are relatively expensive, and may be beyond the means of poor working families. Therefore, reliance on travel by auto may deny the poor reasonable access to employment and consumption opportunities.

Policies to reduce rush-hour driving

Because of the social costs of cars and highways, many analysts see great benefits in adopting policies that discourage the use of automobiles for urban commuting. As was seen in Chapter 4, a market with external costs tends to produce more than the socially optimal level of output. Therefore, improving the efficiency of a market with negative externalities requires some effort to reduce output as well as the external costs themselves. In keeping with this efficiency goal, all other policy options to be discussed involve either directly discouraging auto use or subsidizing substitutes for the automobile.

Congestion fees

One approach with the potential to reduce the excessive use of highways is taxing the automobile in rush-hour situations. This may be done by charging a fee for highway travel during rush hour or taxing parking in congested areas. In terms of efficiency, congestion fees have some advantages over all the other alternatives we will consider, since they tend to reduce rush-hour traffic while preserving individual choice regarding alternative approaches.

Politically, however, commuting taxes have a few major disadvantages. First, they are taxes. Conservatives tend to dislike taxes, and progressives tend to distrust incentive approaches to policy. Secondly, congestion taxes fall heavily on middle-class commuters, a politically important group in developed nations. Thirdly, they also offer none of the benefits to construction and downtown business interests that are provided by highways or public transportation subsidies, so some local special interests are likely to oppose them. However, the social benefits of controlling commuting are significant, and despite the political challenges facing such a policy option, this approach shows promise.

The economic analysis of peak load pricing is not terribly difficult. In Figure 12.7, rush-hour demand has entered the quantity range beyond Q_A where significant external costs exist for commuters. Without the tax, drivers will choose a quantity of commuting miles where their demand equals the private marginal costs of commuting. In Figure 12.7 this quantity is labeled Q_p. However, because of the external congestion costs, the socially efficient quantity is at Q_s. Imposing a tax on commuting during the rush-hour period reduces the private demand curve by the amount of the tax (see the vertical axis) to the line labeled **demand-tax**. The commuter must now factor the tax into her decision about driving. Commuters will then choose a quantity of miles where the after-tax demand curve equals the private marginal cost.

Theoretically, the size of the rush-hour tax should be just enough to raise the private marginal cost to the level of the original social cost at the social equilibrium. In other words, the optimal tax should equal $MC_s - MC_p$ at quantity Q_s in Figure 12.7. If this tax is correctly chosen, the resultant traffic volume is Q_s, the socially optimal number of miles. In practice, these taxes may take several forms, including parking taxes, commuting licenses, and manual or electronic toll systems. In choosing among the various approaches, one should consider evidence regarding the effectiveness and costs of each approach, and to carefully think through the possible side effects of each option. A brief review of some commuting tax options will help organize our thoughts on this policy.

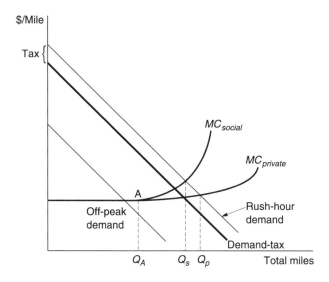

Figure 12.7 Peak load pricing

The Singapore Area Licensing Scheme

The approach that is closest to the theoretical model involves the use of licenses or electronic sensors to charge a fee for rush-hour commuting. Rush-hour fees have been in effect in Singapore since 1975 (Seik 1995; Toh and Phang 1997). The original plan involved requiring licenses to be displayed on windshields. Those entering a predefined section of the central business district between 7:30 and 9:30 a.m. any day except Sunday were required to display these licenses or face a fine. The licenses originally cost 3 Singapore dollars (S$) per day or S$60 per month. Since the inception of the program the schedule and fees have been adjusted several times. In 1998 Singapore replaced the Area Licensing Scheme with Electronic Road Pricing (Singapore Land Transit Authority), which combines an electronic sensor system with rush-hour fees.[3]

This program produced significant effects on rush-hour traffic. The initial reduction in rush-hour traffic was about 45 percent (Toh and Phang 1997: 25), far greater than the 25 to 30 percent goal. This led to arguments that the original fees were too high, and eventually a 33 percent reduction in the auto fee. Part of this reduction in traffic involved commuters switching to the passenger rail system, which increased its share of commuter traffic from 33 to 69 percent. The fixed time limit and area of the rush-hour fee also led to what are called **edge effects,** meaning that the times just before and just after the peak time period experienced significantly greater traffic, as did areas just outside of the restricted area. Overall, however, the combination of financial incentives and attractive substitutes created a successful traffic control program.

Another approach to taxing commuters is to tax downtown parking. This approach generally takes the form of metered street parking and taxes on parking lots. Used in combination, these parking fees have a few attractive features as well as some costs and indirect effects. Parking taxes are easy to administer and can be focused on areas that experience heavy commuter traffic. They also tend to transfer money from suburban commuters to urban governments. The primary social costs of parking fees are enforcement costs and their negative effect on downtown shopping. They also encourage the construction of private parking lots which can be more difficult to tax. Both political support and efficiency would be enhanced if the tax excludes short-term parking, which is more likely to be the pattern of shoppers than workers. The tax could also focus more on commuters by charging a higher rate for those arriving during predetermined hours, particularly the morning commuting period. Because of its less direct connection to commuting, a parking tax is likely to have more indirect effects than commuter tolls. However, it is a very common policy with its own set of net benefits.

Regulating auto commuting

Regulations are often more popular than taxes among politicians and the public because of their less obvious costs. In the case of congestion, the most common regulatory approach in the U.S. has involved limiting certain lanes of traffic to cars with multiple riders. These restricted lanes are commonly referred to as high-occupancy vehicle (HOV) lanes. In many cases, HOV lanes were created by painting diamonds on the left-hand lanes of highways, and in others extra lanes were constructed. In either case, only vehicles with a minimum of two or three passengers were allowed to drive in the HOV lanes during peak hours.

HOV lanes increase the benefits of car pooling by decreasing commuting time and congestion costs for multi-person vehicles, while increasing those same costs for single passenger vehicles. Ideally the resultant increase in multi-person vehicles will reduce total traffic volume and congestion. However, the effectiveness of HOV lanes is highly sensitive to demand. If too few vehicles use them, congestion may increase in the unrestricted lanes. If too many use them, the HOV lanes will experience congestion problems similar to those of other lanes. Enforcement has also been a problem in some cities.

A recent innovation combines the high occupancy lanes with an electronic fee system similar to that in Singapore. These lanes are called high-occupancy toll, or HOT lanes. In most cases one can legally drive in a HOT lane with three or more passengers without charge. Cars with fewer riders must carry a transponder such as those used in Singapore and pay a fee that varies by time of day. HOT lanes have been put into operation on Rte 91 in Orange County, California, I-15 in San Diego, California, and I-10 and US 290 in Houston, Texas (U.S. Federal Highway Administration 2003: 7). The specific operations and effects vary among these three cities.

In Houston, allowing single drivers access to the HOT lanes (subject to a toll) led to near gridlock conditions. As a result, Houston's HOT lanes now ban single drivers, allow two-person vehicles to use the lanes for a $2.00 fee during peak hours, and allow three-person autos free access at any time. In Orange County, HOT lanes were constructed privately, and from 1995 to 2003 were the only privately owned toll lanes in the U.S. Rush-hour fees for high occupancy vehicles began at zero, but were raised to 50 percent of the single passenger fee in the late 1990s. The effects of this first HOT lane system have been widely studied, and have been found to include more car pools, more use of mass transit, and more non-peak commuting (Small and Gomez-Ibanez 1998). By combining fees with regulation, HOT lanes have proven somewhat easier to manage than HOV lanes. Additional HOT lane projects have recently been instituted in Minneapolis, Minnesota, and Denver, Colorado.

Urban mass transit

Subsidized mass transit is among the most politically popular policy alternatives for urban transportation. Most mass transit in the U.S. occurs by bus, but mass transit also includes heavy rail subways and regional commuter trains and light rail alternatives such as trolleys, cable cars, and people movers. With the possible exception of highways, heavy rail mass transit is the most commonly analyzed form of urban transportation. Mass transit offers a set of private and external benefits that must be weighed against the construction cost and operating deficits of typical subway and commuter rail systems. Heavy rail systems are a form of network infrastructure requiring a substantial investment in the network before consumers can purchase the product. Moreover, subways are expensive to build and maintain, and a large ridership and revenue base are needed in order to cover the construction and operating costs of such a system.

The role of subsidies

Subsidizing mass transit raises the relative cost of commuting by car, much like the peak load pricing approach in Figure 12.7 above. The demand for auto travel will fall somewhat as a substitute good becomes cheaper. The primary difference between peak load pricing and subsidized mass transit occurs at the level of total transportation demand. Mass transit subsidies, like any subsidy, will tend to increase the total amount of the good traded. On the other hand, commuting fees are a form of tax, which will reduce the total amount of metropolitan travel somewhat. Therefore, subsidizing mass transit may offer political and economic benefits by encouraging, at least marginally, metropolitan employment and commerce.

Case study: MARTA and the Atlanta Inner Core Study[4]

MARTA stands for the Metropolitan Atlanta Rapid Transit Authority. Atlanta's current subway system is quite modest, with two lines meeting in the downtown business district. Given the relatively scattered population and employment base of the Atlanta area, one would expect rail ridership to be small and the system's financial condition to be poor. These expectations are correct. MARTA's operating revenue has covered between 30 and 35 percent of operating costs since 1997.

Atlanta is actively considering the addition of a ring or loop subway line that would create a mass transit version of a ring road. This addition to the system could offer significant increases in convenience and access to popular city venues for a relatively substantial number of commuters, shoppers, tourists, and students. Various planning reports on these proposals are available at http://www.itsmarta.com/newsroom/innercore.htm. *The Inner Core Feasibility Wrap-Up Report* (MAMRTA 2005a) at that website is particularly recommended. The three maps on page 306 present the main alternative designs (Concepts A and B) and one of several combinations of the two being considered along with a "no-build" option (MAMRTA 2005b: 4-6). The two original visions, the Beltline and C-Loop proposals, have somewhat different rationales. The Beltline proposal was based partly on the utilization of current track or abandoned rail beds, possibly reducing its cost. Because parts of the beltline proposal run through abandoned industrial sites, it also would encourage redevelopment of these areas. The C-Loop concept emphasizes the goal of connecting various high-use areas such as universities, entertainment areas, and shopping districts. The hybrid proposal is one of several

Figure 12.8 Current Atlanta subway system

suggested hybrids of the two original proposals. It attempts to blend the feasibility and redevelopment emphasis of the Beltline plan with the greater demand for the C-Loop route.

There is considerable value in reviewing the many steps involved in analyzing a major transportation project such as the MARTA inner-core loop project. These steps are complex and multi-disciplinary, involving public relations, political science, engineering, and economics. Therefore, a brief overview must suffice.

Cost assessment

For engineers the primary cost components of a mass transit project are construction costs and operating costs. Large projects funded through borrowing involve additional financial costs. External and opportunity costs are also involved. Engineers often develop construction cost estimates from the project's design on

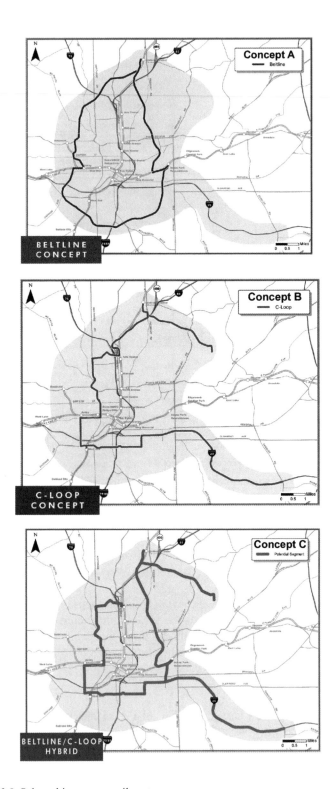

Figure 12.9 Selected inner-core rail routes

a cost-plus basis, meaning that a specific design is developed, then the per-unit cost is estimated with a markup to account for labor and profit, and then the total cost is estimated. For individual items such as bridges, the construction cost estimate can be quite specific, based on each component of the design. For larger projects, per-mile estimates are more likely. Additional costs such as land acquisition, temporary roads to minimize travel disruption and the construction or relocation of other infrastructure such as electrical wires, traffic signals, or underground pipes are also included when necessary. Possible external costs such as noise, traffic disruption, or accident risk are also included in more detailed studies, although these are seldom valued in dollar terms.

The MARTA estimates for total construction cost are based on estimates for the length of various types of construction such as "track feet for new imbedded track slab" (MAMRTA 2005a: 3-8 to 3-9), estimates of street widening, right-of-way acquisition, traffic signals, etc. Cost estimates are then calculated using previously developed cost figures for alternative types of technology, and a range of construction cost estimates is then provided. For the MARTA project, the Beltline cost estimate totaled $577 million, the C-Loop estimate was $111 million, and the hybrid design above was estimated to cost $178 million. Added operating costs for the three main alternatives were estimated to be $11.5 million annually for the Beltline, $10.8 million for the C-Loop, and $15.8 million for the hybrid design.

The primary direct environmental impact of rail operation is noise. The potential effects of noise are estimated in non-dollar terms by counting residential or commercial structures within 1,000 feet of the proposed routes. Another external cost is possible traffic disruption due to train crossings and some at-grade rail lines following street routes, which is also measured in detailed but non-monetary terms.

The estimation of construction and operating costs is one area where economists generally bow to engineers, with four exceptions. First, economists are more likely to note that all such estimates are subject to random variance from market conditions, which can significantly affect the bids offered by contractors. Second, economists are likely to be more cautious about assumptions regarding inflation and ridership. Current macroeconomic forecasts may offer a more informed view than the usual engineering assumptions about these economic variables. First, economists are more likely to note the alternatives and opportunity costs beyond the choices analyzed by engineers, which are generally limited to alternative designs for the same general type of project. For example, these Atlanta construction alternatives do not include express bus lanes or commuter fees, alternatives that are likely to be more cost-effective than rail. Finally, economists are likely to expand the use of dollar values to the non-monetary benefits and costs of the project, including external effects such as noise.

Benefit assessment

Benefits of a mass transit system include travel time savings, in part through the reduction of congestion, and a series of economic and environmental impacts.

These impacts include possible increases in land value, production, and employment due to increased access. Ridership estimates are the basis for most other benefit estimates, but are subject to considerable uncertainty and possible upward bias, particularly if estimated *ex-ante* for a proposed future transit line.

The MARTA study used an internal transit demand model to compare estimated ridership in 2030 under the current system and each alternative. For the MARTA inner-loop project, estimates of increased ridership were far greater for the hybrid proposals with access to major employment centers and points of interest than for the two original plans. These estimated increases in ridership were 14,000 per day for the Beltline route, 17,000 for the C-Loop route, 30,000 for the Concept C hybrid, and over 40,000 for two other hybrid routes (MAMRTA 2005a: 3-3). These increases in ridership translate into total travel time savings of between 1.1 million and 2.7 million hours per year (ibid.: 3-4). Other benefits were discussed in a more qualitative fashion. Vacant land near the proposed routes provides a measure of potential development. Vacant acreage ranged from 3,900 to 5,100 acres for the various proposals. The hybrid proposals offered larger and more diverse development options.

Cost-effectiveness assessment

The final results of this preliminary study came in the form of estimated total cost per added rider. This cost-effectiveness measure produced a range from $3 to $16 per rider, depending on the route chosen (MAMRTA 2005a: 3-8). Two of the hybrid proposals, including the hybrid plan shown earlier, were the most cost-effective alternatives. Since the social benefits of the plans were not calculated, it is not clear whether even the least expensive approach will provide a net benefit to the Atlanta area. As of August 2006, additional alternatives were still being considered and no final decision had been made.

Location and development options

Longer-run options with the potential to affect congestion and mass transit demand include policies to encourage the clustering of housing and employment, local limits on growth, and efforts to encourage technological change in the auto or other forms of transport. These development and locational policies are likely to involve a combination of development subsidies and land-use regulations. The general principle of such policies is straightforward. To the degree that housing and employment can be clustered near mass transit stops, the collection and distribution phases of the commute to work become less costly for mass transit commuters. Such policies are highly complementary to mass transit development, and have been included in the plans for most modern transit systems.

Efforts to control growth have a mixed effect on congestion depending on the context of the policy. Suburban efforts to preserve open space tend to increase sprawl and the average miles traveled to work. On the other hand, efforts to limit sprawl could decrease the average miles traveled. They may also lower the average collection and distribution times for bus systems or subways. However, anti-sprawl policies may also increase the concentration of traffic within the city in the absence of an effective public transit system. On balance, the effects of anti-sprawl policies are somewhat mixed with regard to congestion, although they have significant advantages in terms of the preservation of open space on the periphery of the city and at least minor benefits in terms of air pollution from transportation. Further evidence is needed on these points.

Conclusion

The primary lesson of this chapter is that some policy problems have a large number of possible solutions. The problem of traffic congestion can be improved at least temporarily by increasing the supply of highway lanes, decreasing rush-hour demand through fees and taxes, encouraging car pooling through regulations, increasing the availability of substitutes for the automobile by subway or express bus investments, lowering the cost of these alternatives through subsidies, and encouraging greater clustering of residential and business development near mass transit stops.

The ideal policy analysis would involve comparing the net benefits of several alternatives, and possibly enacting multiple policies. For example, subsidizing mass transit and imposing fees on automotive commuting would combine to decrease demand for auto commuting while providing a mixed effect on citizens' disposable income and long-term metropolitan growth. The policies could also prove complementary by offering the auto commuter greater access to other transit options.

Review questions

Conceptual questions

1. The encouragement of car pooling has proven relatively unpopular as a public policy:

   (A) Discuss why car pooling has not attracted much support. The modal choice model might offer some guidance.
   (B) Consider the benefits and costs of allowing private subscription ride services using mini vans or other small-scale vehicles. Again, use the modal choice model to compare small-scale transportation services with mass transit such as buses and subways.

2. In addition to congestion, the automobile also has other major effects. One such effect is air pollution, another negative externality. Highways and the automobile have also increased the relative value of land further from the center of a city. Finally, highway transportation has also lowered transport costs.

   (A) Discuss the effects of the congestion tax, the subsidization of public transit, and the construction of additional highway lanes on each of these other effects.

(B)   On balance, are any of the three main congestion policies less attractive after considering these other effects? Discuss.

3.   Discuss the advantages and disadvantages of electronic monitoring and fee
payment systems compared to toll booths. Should transponders be required
equipment on all cars in order to encourage greater use of fee-based congestion policy? Why or why not?

4.   Rail mass transit systems are very poor financial investments in all but the
most crowded U.S. cities. What can be done to improve demand for rail
systems? In your opinion, will the Atlanta loop-rail proposal discussed in this
chapter significantly improve the finances and ridership of the MARTA
system? Why or why not?

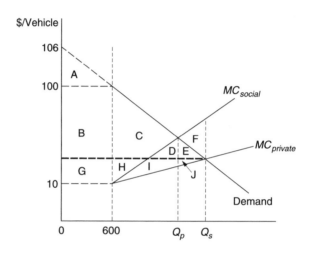

Linear externality problem

Computational problems

5.   We can analyze a congestion externality graphically and numerically without
much difficulty if we identify the maximum congestion-free volume and
assume that the increasing private and social costs beyond that level are
linear. In the graph, rush-hour demand is high enough to significantly
increase private and social marginal commuting costs.

(A)   Identify the external cost, consumer surplus, and deadweight loss graphically for the private equilibrium. (Hint: Benefits and costs are both experienced by drivers, so there is no separate producer surplus in this case.)
(B)   Using the following equations, find the social and private equilibrium
quantities and costs, and then find the consumer surplus, external
surplus, and deadweight loss for the private equilibrium. (Hint: Setting the

demand endpoint at 100, its value at $Q = 600$ (rather than 106) makes finding the equilibrium values much easier.)

Demand: $P = 106 - 1/100Q$.

Private MC $= 10 + 1/100$ (max $Q - 600,0$),

Social MC $= 10 + 1/50$ (max $Q - 600,0$).

(C)   Find the optimal congestion tax for this problem, and verify that (with the tax in place) the traffic volume will be equal to the social equilibrium.

6.   Parking taxes and constant highway tolls are two examples of commuting fees that are not limited to rush-hour:

(A)   Consider the effects of a non-peak fee on the non-peak demand curve using Figure 12.7, which is repeated here. How does it affect consumer surplus, external surplus, and any dead weight loss?

(B)   Compare parking fees and constant highway tolls. What are the limits of each, and which comes closer to achieving the goals of peak load pricing policy?

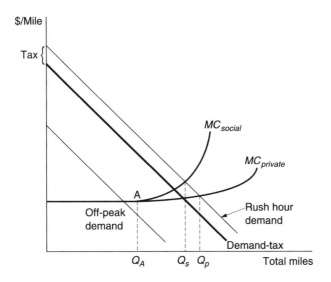

Peak load pricing

13 Pollution control policy

If we intend to provide a better life, and a better world, for future generations, we can't ignore the quality of the environment we leave them.[1]

(John Kasich, former Congressman from Ohio)

If the federal government had been around when the Creator was putting His hand to this state, Indiana wouldn't be here. It'd still be waiting for an environmental impact statement.[2]

(Ronald Reagan, former President)

♫ Pollution, pollution, they got smog and sewage and mud.
Turn on your tap and get hot and cold running crud.

(Tom Lehrer, *Pollution*)

Think Globally, Act Locally[3]

(René Dubos)

Few policy areas involve as wide a range of backgrounds and areas of expertise as environmental policy. The list of those actively involved in environmental policy includes representatives from every level of government, academia, public-interest groups, the private sector, and local citizens. Examples include scientists developing predictive models that explain the dynamics of complex ecosystems, government bureaucrats allocating their limited pollution control budgets, and local children's groups working to rid their neighborhoods of litter. Environmental policy also involves a wide range of analytical expertise, including several scientific fields as well as ethics, economics, and other social analysis. The basis for environmental policy analysis, however, is the scientific analysis of the production, distribution, and harms of pollution. Without some exposure to environmental science, an environmental analyst or advocate will have great difficulty understanding the nature and scope of the problem, an important first step in any informed analysis of public policy.

Knowing the sources and components of any type of pollution is also required for sound policy analysis. Air pollution is produced by both nature and man. For example, lightning is a common cause of forest fires, volcanoes are an occasional source of global dimming and cooling, and an asteroid collision is now widely believed to have contributed to the extinction of the dinosaurs and cooling of the planet. Most of these natural pollution sources tend to be occasional rather than constant, meaning that even the most serious cases generally do not cause high levels of cumulative harm. Human pollution is a more common source of policy concern because it often occurs on a relatively constant basis, tends to occur closer to human population centers and, most obviously, is something we have a greater capacity to control. Human-produced air pollution includes gases and suspended liquids and solids. Smoke, for example, is a combination of all three substances. Gases account for about 90 percent of smoke's pollutants by weight, but suspended solids produce some of its most harmful effects.

Economics has multiple roles to play in pollution policy. The primary tasks of economists are to estimate dollar values of the non-marketed costs of pollution and to provide benefit–cost or cost-effectiveness analysis of pollution-reduction policies. The primary goals of economic analysis in this context include how much (if any) pollution to eliminate, the optimal distribution of the pollution reduction, and the preferred policy design for pollution reduction.

In this chapter we will discuss various economic concepts related to the environment, the nature and measurement of harms from common forms of pollution, various policy options for dealing with excessive pollution, and examples of air pollution problems and policy responses. While the main focus of the applied sections of this chapter will be on air pollution, the steps in analyzing pollution problems and policy options are similar for any pollution problem. One must identify the source and distribution of the pollutant, identify the pollutant's effects on humans and other parts of the ecosystem, determine pollution-reduction goals, and assess policy alternatives for achieving these goals. More broadly, this chapter attempts to provide the student with enough general background to critically consider the scientific as well as economic and political components of pollution policy. However, it will not make the reader an environmental expert.

Economic views of nature and pollution

There are a few conceptual connections between economics and the environment that provide the basis for the economic analysis of environmental and resource policy. These concepts relate to economic production, property rights, market imperfections, and rational decision making. More than most policy areas, however, the tradeoffs between benefits and costs associated with economic analysis are often unpopular with both non-economic environmental analysts and environmental advocates. A selection of these alternative viewpoints will also be considered in this chapter.

Natural resources as part of the economic flow

Natural resources are an inherent part of the production process. Basic goods such as wood, other plants and animals, stone and metals, and fossil fuels provide important components for our production of goods and services. Adding natural

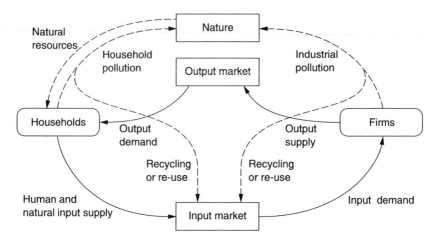

Figure 13.1 Resource and output flows

resource inputs and pollution to a typical flow chart of an economy identifies key links between nature and the production and consumption of goods and services. It also identifies the links between productive activity and two different but related branches of economics: environmental and natural resource economics. Environmental economics addresses the issues of pollution, while resource economics concerns itself with the use of resources in production and the net benefits of resource conservation.

As Figure 13.1 demonstrates, the key links between nature and the economy occur in three places. Nature provides inputs to the production process, as well as the final resting place for the waste and byproducts of our production and consumption. Nature itself has similar flows indicated with dashed lines, including naturally caused pollution and resource depletion. However, the primary focus of this chapter is on human pollution and alternative methods of pollution control.

Your Turn 13.1: Sustainable development is perhaps the most fundamental environmental goal. Discuss possible improvements in the production of housing and automobiles that might aid in achieving this goal. Also identify where such improvements would influence the resource and economic flow in Figure 13.1.

Pollution as an externality

The root word of externality is "external." If pollution is categorized as an externality, one might reasonably ask what pollution is external to. The answer was provided within the groundbreaking work of Ronald Coase (1960). According to Coase's analysis, externalities lead to market failure due to a lack of fully defined property rights. In this sense pollution and other externalities are outside of the legal system because of a failure to define a right to pollute or, alternatively, to define a right to be free from pollution. The role of property rights in dealing with externalities is fairly basic. If a neighbor fouls your property, you can file a criminal complaint or sue for damages. In the absence of some right to protection from and compensation for these harms, polluters have little incentive to refrain from the practice.

Pollution of the air or other common spaces creates several types of external costs, including human health effects, reduced visibility and unnatural odors, reduced agricultural and industrial productivity, and harms to plants and animals. In the case of air pollution, there are multiple dimensions to the problem. A single source of pollution might emit several harmful substances into the air. Similarly, a single pollutant or related group of pollutants can contribute to several different environmental problems. For example, nitrogen oxides (nitrous oxide, nitrogen dioxide, and others) contribute to smog, acid rain, and global warming (http://www.epa.gov/air/urbanair/nox/). In the absence of private property rights or public policy, markets will discourage producers from considering these external costs when making capital investments or production decisions.

Figure 13.2 reviews the inefficiency created by an industry with uncontrolled pollution. See Chapters 3 and 4 for a review of the various concepts in this graph. According to economic theory, external costs are unlikely to be accounted for in the decisions of competitive producers, leading to overproduction and a deadweight loss.

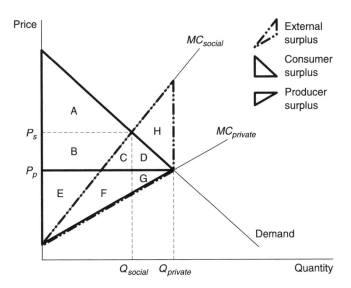

Figure 13.2 External costs

There are two related solutions to this overproduction. One is to decrease production in the polluting industry, and the other is to reduce the external costs. The two goals can be produced simultaneously by requiring polluting firms to bear the cost of pollution reduction, thereby achieving some combination of lower externalities and lower production in the polluting industry. For the most part, this is the case in our pollution control policies.

Resources and pollution as public goods

Because the air and many bodies of water are not owned by any public or private party, they take on the characteristics of public goods. In the case of environmental and resource economics, the primary public goods issue involves unowned property, often referred to as **the commons** or an **open access resource**. For example, public waters may be dumping grounds for trash or sewage, public land may be subjected to overgrazing, and unregulated fishing or hunting can lead to severe population declines or extinction (Hardin 1968). The lack of ownership of public lands provides an area of overlap between public goods and externalities. The key policy issue regarding common lands and resources is to assign the right to restrict the harvesting of common resources. In most cases this right is claimed by government and used as the basis for regulations or other pollution control policies.

The benefits of pollution control

The crucial challenge for environmental analysts is to estimate the costs and benefits of pollution control. Determining the benefits of pollution abatement requires identifying and quantifying the harms of pollution, estimating human or other exposure to pollution, quantifying pollution's harms, and in some cases assigning dollar values to these harms. Each of these steps will be discussed in this section.

Assessment of pollution risks

The first step in estimating the benefits of pollution control policy is to measure the harms of the pollution. This process is often labeled **environmental risk assessment**. Air pollution has the potential to create a number of harmful effects, including human health problems, loss of plant and animal life, destruction of property, and unpleasant (or occasionally pleasant) views and odors. It also contributes to broader problems such as acid rain, ozone depletion, and global warming. Also, some air pollutants tend to have relatively localized effects, while others can be carried far from their source before affecting the Earth. Carbon dioxide, for example, is not toxic to humans in moderate amounts, but is a significant contributor to global warming. Finally, harms from pollution depend on the amount of exposure to the pollutant. At low levels many pollutants are not harmful to human or non-human health.

The goal of environmental risk assessment is to provide information about the possible harms of pollution for human health, as well as other effects, and to provide guidance for environmental standards and other policy options. Risk assessment acts as the basis for cost-effectiveness analysis of various policy alternatives, and as the first step in a dollar-based benefit–cost analysis. Risk assessment involves the following steps:

1 Identifying the possible harm. This is known as hazard identification.
2 Estimating the relationship between harm and the amount of exposure. This is known as dose–response assessment.
3 Measuring aggregate human exposure.
4 Integrating theory and evidence to determine the aggregate risk.

Each step will be discussed in this section.

The first step in identifying a pollutant's effect on health is to identify possible harmful substances. This step will be labeled **hazard identification**. Environmental hazards can be identified through laboratory experiments using animals or various types of direct human evidence. The primary role of animal laboratory studies is to provide a fully controlled study of the effects of a single substance, something that cannot be done outside the laboratory. However, there are also limits to the results of animal studies. First, the animal response may not correspond to a human health response. Secondly, studies that use high doses only will not provide direct evidence of the effects of low-level exposure on either humans or animals. There are also serious ethical issues involved with animal experimentation.

There are two primary types of non-laboratory studies. **Epidemiological studies** test the general population for pollution-related health effects while controlling for other health factors. This approach requires a great deal of data about other health-related factors such as age, income, and lifestyle issues such as smoking. The second type of non-laboratory study is known as **case cluster analysis**. This type of study involves identifying areas with unusually frequent health problems that may be related to pollution exposure. Cancer clusters have been a powerful tool for both analysts and advocates of the control of toxic chemicals, for example. Because case clusters and epidemiological studies may not fully control for other causes of disease, laboratory studies often provide a firmer causal link between the pollutant and the health problem. For example, the majority of the reported deaths from London's killer smog of 1952 were from pneumonia, an infectious disease. The connection between smog and susceptibility to infection was established by laboratory tests on animals.

The effects of a pollutant may vary significantly with the amount of exposure. **Dose–response assessment** involves estimating the statistical relationship between the amount of exposure to a substance and the harm to human health. Laboratory studies usually involve the exposure of animals to high doses of suspected toxic substances, measurement of the health effects of the substances on animals, and finally estimates of how a range of exposure levels will affect humans. When measuring a single effect such as cancer risk, the estimation procedure involves measuring the shape and endpoint of the exposure–health effect relationship (see Figure 13.3).

When multiple health effects are caused by a single pollutant, one must estimate the threshold between lesser and greater effects. For example, low levels of exposure to carbon monoxide may produce drowsiness. Higher exposure levels may produce brain damage and even death. Estimating the exposure level above which a substance can be fatal is one part of this complex process. In the U.S., the Environmental Protection Agency keeps a database of known risks known as the Integrated Risk Information System (IRIS) (http://www.epa.gov/iris/intro.htm). This website discusses the basic process of risk assessment and presents data on known hazards and dose–response relationships for hundreds of chemicals and other toxic substances.

The third step in the process of assessing harm to human health is to estimate the amount of **human exposure** to these harmful pollutants. Like applied economics, the science of air pollution relies on models and data samples to estimate human exposure to harmful pollutants. The basic steps in pollution exposure involve measuring or estimating its production, its dispersal through the environment, and its harms to humans, other living things, property, and the ecosystem. Measurement of pollution can take place at the source. For example, some nations require annual auto emissions testing programs. Pollution is also measured through networks of monitoring equipment, particularly in more heavily polluted urban areas. There are many different types of devices for measuring pollution (Boubel *et al.* 1994: 195-203; Godish 1997: Ch. 7), and their accuracy and cost-efficiency have improved over time.

A source of U.S. data on pollution exposure is the Environmental Protection Agency's Toxics Release Inventory (http://www.epa.gov/tri/). Another potentially valuable data source is the National Human Exposure Assessment Survey (NHEXAS) (http://www.epa.gov/heasd/edrb/nhexas.htm), which is in the early

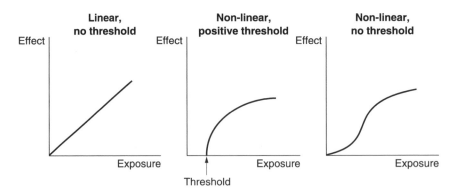

Figure 13.3 Dose response examples

stages of development, but promises relatively direct detailed measurement of human exposure to many forms of chemical pollutants. Additional air pollution monitoring is available for metropolitan areas and regions, including grids of measurement devices and survey data. Other U.S. data sources are available at the EPA website. The Envirofacts data warehouse is one such source.

Your Turn 13.2: Visit the EPA's Envirofacts website (http://www.epa.gov/enviro/), click on a topic such as water or air, enter a town, city, or zip code, and see which firms emit pollutants in that area.

Modeling air pollution exposure

Models of air pollution exposure are important in estimating the distribution of pollution once it leaves the source. These are complex models involving variables such as wind direction and speed, smokestack height, vertical and horizontal dispersion rates of the pollutants, and geographical factors. Two relatively basic models will be discussed here. The first is a simple concentric circle model, which despite its serious limitations is still occasionally used in environmental research. The second is a basic form of the Gaussian diffusion model, which will strike most readers as interesting because of the variables it uses rather than its functional form.

Concentric circles around a pollution source measure proximity to the source rather than actual exposure. This type of model is still seen on occasion in studies of racial or income-related differences in pollution exposure (Pastor *et al*. 2004). However, without some consideration of wind direction and the distance the pollutant travels before affecting the ground, actual exposure cannot be determined from this model. Moreover, those still relying on this approach argue that proximity to a pollution source suggests various types of costs, including health risks, dust, and poor visibility.

The Gaussian plume model assumes that pollution is proportional to the emission rate, inversely related to wind speed, has a normal distribution both horizontally and vertically, and flows with the direction of the wind.[4] Additional factors such as the buoyancy of the pollutant and air turbulence can then be included (Boubel *et al*. 1994: Ch. 19). While these models are well beyond the level of this book, the idea that pollution is distributed in a three-dimensional cone around a line based on stack height and wind direction provides a good starting point for reasonable estimates of pollution exposure.

Once the distribution of a pollutant has been determined, human exposure can be determined through detailed census data. The U.S. decennial census provides population counts to the individual block (http://www.census.gov/). At this or somewhat higher levels of aggregation, additional factors such as race, age, and income can also be determined. It is this combination of science and social statistics that provides evidence of pollution's human effects.

Benefit–cost analysis of reducing pollution

Executive Order 12866 (http://www.whitehouse.gov/OMB/inforeg/eo12866.pdf), issued by President Clinton in 1993, directed federal agencies to conduct benefit–cost analyses of proposed regulations, as well as alternative policies, and to determine policies that maximize net benefits. Three of the goals in this document are particularly significant:

> Each agency shall identify and assess available alternatives to direct regulation, including providing economic incentives to encourage the desired behavior ...
>
> (*Federal Register,* Section 1:b:3)

> Each agency shall assess both the costs and the benefits of the intended regulation and, recognizing that some costs and benefits are difficult to quantify, propose or adopt a regulation only upon a reasoned determination that the benefits of the intended regulation justify its costs.
>
> (Ibid., Section 1:b:6)

> Each agency shall base its decisions on the best reasonably obtainable scientific, technical, economic and other information concerning the need for, and consequences of, the intended regulation.
>
> (Ibid., Section 1:b:7)

In the case of environmental policy, this order requires an effort to quantify the non-marketed benefits of environmental policy along with a comparison of the net benefits of various policy alternatives. An executive order cannot replace or contradict a law passed by Congress. Therefore, earlier legal requirements that environmental standards be set to achieve the greatest technically feasible level of pollution reduction still stand. With this goal in mind, cost-effectiveness analysis has a role to play in determining the most efficient method of achieving these goals. However, the tools introduced earlier for evaluating risk, the value of human life and other non-marketed goods, and present value are also used to evaluate the benefits and costs of environmental policy.

Valuing benefits

Chapters 6, 7, 9, and 10, which covered benefit–cost analysis, present value discounting, risk, and the value of life and other non-marketed goods, provide the basis for a benefit–cost analysis of environmental policy. Applications of these principles require some organization of past information and a hypothetical example. The first step in valuing the benefits of pollution abatement is to provide a complete list of these benefits. For simplicity we will limit our list to four factors: (1) improved human health, (2) improved visibility, (3) improved agricultural production, and (4) reduced erosion of buildings.

Placing a dollar value on each of these benefits requires somewhat different methods. Improved human health can be valued using at least two measures. The more precise method is "quality-adjusted life years" (Chapter 10), which values both the increase in average lifespan and the improved health conditions resulting from pollution control. The more common method is an expected value-of-life estimate. This involves multiplying a common figure for the value of life by the change in the number of deaths due to the policy. For example, assume that 150 lives will be saved per year by imposing new bans on smoking in restaurants. Using the EPA's recommended figure of $6 million per life, the total benefits in terms of lives saved would equal $900 million.

Visibility is another non-marketed good that is significantly affected by smog and haze. Reduced visibility can be treated somewhat differently if it relates to a tourist destination versus a more typical urban area. The most generally applicable method of valuing visibility involves contingent valuation surveys. Contingent valuation studies based on responses to photographs have proven useful in estimating a dollar value for visibility at the Grand Canyon and other National Parks (Lesser *et al*. 1997: Ch. 11). Existence value, or the value of a resource to those who do not experience it directly, may also be a factor in measuring the benefits of improving the visibility of a natural wonder or major urban skyline. This value is also estimated through contingent value surveys. Property value estimates can be useful when residents have access to a view of an urban skyline or natural object. Travel cost studies (Chapter 10), which use estimates of travel time and expense to value recreational activity, can also be applied to any location whose primary attribute is a beautiful view or recreational activity. A useful website with additional information on these and other valuation methods is http://www.ecosystemvaluation.org/. The section on dollar-based valuation includes clear explanations of each method and multiple case studies.

Measuring costs

The social costs of pollution control include the opportunity cost of the policy to both the public and private sectors. As a reminder, opportunity cost includes implicit costs as well as expenditures. The direct costs of pollution control to the private sector include capital spending on pollution control equipment or revised production methods, while added operating costs include the purchase of cleaner but more expensive fuels or added labor or materials needed to operate pollution control systems. For example, the initial response of U.S. electricity generators to required sulfur dioxide reductions was split almost evenly between the installation of scrubbers to clean the smoke and a switch to low-sulfur coal (Schmalensee *et al*. 1998: 59). Public sector costs of a direct regulation involve monitoring and enforcement, while additional public costs may arise when operating a permit trading market or collecting a tax. Subsidies for pollution abatement transfer some of the capital and operating costs from the private to the public sector.

Pollution control cost estimates generally use one or both of two methods (see Callan and Thomas 2000: Ch. 9). The first is the **engineering method**. This approach, which was also introduced in the previous chapter on transportation, begins by offering a few alternative pollution control designs based on current technology. The capital and operating costs of each design are then estimated. The total cost of design is then estimated by multiplying the cost per pollution source of each alternative by the total number of sources. A final design is then chosen based on net benefits or cost-efficiency.

The **survey method** for assessing pollution control costs begins by asking private and public sector polluters about their pollution spending under the previous policy, their expected spending under any new policy proposal, and their preferences among alternative pollution control options. On the one hand, polluting firms have far more practical experience in pollution control than most engineers or regulators. On the other, firms may not be aware of recent technology. They also have an incentive to exaggerate the costs of any future program they might oppose. In practice, both types of information can be used in a well-funded cost study.

A benefit–cost example

In January 2004, the EPA issued a report analyzing alternatives for a new set of regulations to control mercury emissions from electric power plants. In this report (U.S. Environmental Protection Agency 2004), the EPA considered a uniform technological requirement and a cap and trade option, and recommended the cap and trade approach. In response to a request from several U.S. Senators, the General Accounting Office produced an analysis that found the EPA's cost–benefit analysis to be seriously flawed (GAO 2005). Four major problems were identified. First, the EPA did not analyze the cap and trade policy separately from other proposed policies, as it did for the technological requirement. Also, the EPA did not estimate the dollar value of the direct benefits from mercury reduction or estimate the effects of a change in the mercury standard on the cap and trade policy's net benefits. Finally, it did not use sensitivity analysis to account for some major uncertainties in the results. These criticisms provide guidance for any policy analyst, and are consistent with the lessons of earlier chapters of this book.

Policy goals: how much and where to reduce pollution

Obviously, the basic goal of environmental policy is to reduce pollution. What is not as obvious is by how much various types of pollution should be reduced. Both the overall quantity of pollution reduction and the distribution of pollution involve fundamental disagreements. There are two basic, and often very different, goals regarding the ideal amount of pollution abatement. One goal is to achieve the maximum technically feasible level of clean-up, and the other is to achieve the economically optimal level of clean-up. The first alternative, which is the official goal of pollution policy in much of the developed world, involves attaining the highest technically feasible level of abatement regardless of opportunity cost. The usual justification for this approach is ethical. Supporters of this goal often argue that humans have a basic right to a clean and healthy environment. The political advantages of the no-cost approach to goal setting are clear. It involves a clear statement of a basic value judgment that a clean environment is more ethical than money, a statement that few in the developed world would find objectionable.

The economically efficient level of pollution abatement occurs where the marginal benefits and marginal costs are equal, as in Figure 13.4. This simple graph can also be used to consider some more subtle issues. One implication of this simple model is that uncertainty regarding the benefits of pollution abatement leads to a range of estimated optimal clean-up levels. For example, assume that the range of predicted global warming under current policy ranges from two to ten degrees over the next century, with a median predicted increase of three degrees.[5] The seriousness of the harms created by warming are hotly debated at any level of warming. When combined with a wide range of predicted temperature change, the actual harms, and therefore the benefits of abatement, are very different. As with any case involving significant uncertainty, further research is a natural policy recommendation. However, if the predicted harms are positive and potentially significant, there is no rationale from Figure 13.5 for doing nothing. While further research may refine one's knowledge of the problem, an active policy response is almost certainly required, regardless of any new information.

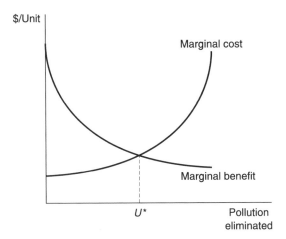

Figure 13.4 Optimal pollution abatement

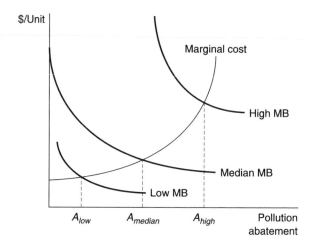

Figure 13.5 Optimal abatement with uncertain benefits

Where to clean-up?

Another implication of the marginal benefit/marginal cost basis for an optimal clean-up level is the value of individual flexibility. In Figure 13.6, two firms face significantly different costs of pollution abatement. If both are required to clean-up to the average level, both firms will have inefficient results. Firm 1 is forced to clean-up beyond the point where marginal benefits equal marginal costs, and

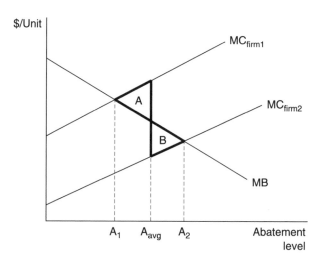

Figure 13.6 Different abatement costs

firm 2 has not yet reached its efficient level of clean-up. Achieving efficient clean-up requires that each firm clean-up to its efficient level. If firm 1 cleans up to level A_1 it will eliminate the abatement for which marginal costs outweigh marginal benefits. Similarly, if firm 2 cleans up to abatement level A_2, a greater than average level of abatement, it will provide additional pollution abatement for which the marginal benefits outweigh the marginal costs. The net gains achieved by dropping a universal clean-up level and adopting a more flexible approach equal areas A plus B in Figure 13.6.

There is another dimension of the flexibility argument, however, which often wins the day in political and policy debates. That dimension is the unequal effects of pollution on those with low incomes, including urban racial minority groups. In the U.S. this problem is often referred to (sometimes correctly) as environmental racism. The negative correlation between income levels and pollution exposure in urban areas is well-established (Pastor *et al.* 2004; Brajer and Hall 2005). However, the causal relationship between the two is not always clear. Polluted neighborhoods close to factories are likely to be more affordable than others, partly because of the factories' visual and pollution-related effects on property values, and partly because of the advanced age of many neighborhoods near high-pollution factories. Many such urban neighborhoods in the U.S. began as white working-class areas, and were later populated by minorities after the northward migration of African-Americans, and later Latinos, during the twentieth century and the white flight to the suburbs after World War II.

The location of new pollution sources such as waste disposal sites or newer factories provides a better test of this cause-and-effect relationship between race and pollution than overall pollution exposure. Ethical arguments against high and unequal exposure levels are clearly involved here. For example, Rawls (see Chapter 2) would argue that the well-being of the least well-off should be given priority, as opposed to a utilitarian view that flexible pollution policies should be judged primarily on their net benefits for all rather than their negative net benefits for a relative few.

Direct regulation and pollution control

As with many other policy issues, pollution control can be implemented using several different policy designs. These various approaches to environmental policy are often grouped into two categories known as **direct regulation** and **incentives** or, more combatively, **command and control policies** and **pay-to-pollute schemes**. Direct regulation involves setting pollution control standards administratively and enforcing them through regulatory agencies and the courts. Incentive approaches work by creating a financial incentive for the private sector to reduce its emissions. The primary incentive methods are pollution taxes, abatement subsidies, and pollution permits. Both categories of pollution control require effective monitoring of pollution and an effective enforcement system for violators. However, the differences in these policy designs are far more interesting than their similarities.

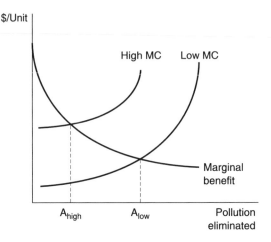

Figure 13.7 Optimal abatement with different marginal costs

Types of direct regulation

Direct regulation can be analyzed in terms of four general categories: ambient standards, effluent limits or point-source standards, required pollution control methods, and the banning of harmful substances or activities. **Ambient standards** (ambient means surrounding on all sides) include metropolitan, regional, or national maximums on certain pollutants. The U.S. government has established ambient standards for six "criteria pollutants" as a basis for federal air policy. These are particulate matter, sulfur dioxide, carbon monoxide, nitrogen dioxide, lead, and ozone. These pollutants are primarily related to urban smog and acid rain. For example, current national ambient standards are 9 parts per million (ppm) for carbon monoxide averaged over any eight-hour period, and 8 ppm for ozone (http://www.epa.gov/air/criteria.html). This group includes the most common and widespread pollutants. A second and much larger group is known as hazardous pollutants or **air toxics**. These pollutants are generally less common but more harmful than the criteria pollutants. There were 189 toxic pollutants identified in the 1990 Clean Air Act. The Act required that maximum standards be set within 10 years for each toxic pollutant.

While setting these standards is a federal responsibility, monitoring and enforcement takes place at state and metropolitan levels. Areas are categorized according to their ability to attain the ambient standards for the six criteria pollutants. Various degrees of non-attainment are also classified, ranging from marginal to extreme violations. Areas that are not in compliance are required to submit plans and implement policies to move toward the attainment of the required standards.

Effluent limits are maximum standards for individual pollution sources such as auto tailpipes, smokestacks, and sewer system outlets. Pollution sources that seriously affect nearby areas, as well as mobile sources such as autos, are usually subject to limits of this kind. One disadvantage of effluent limits is that they offer limited control over total pollution in the long run, since every new auto or factory is permitted to pollute up to the allowable maximum. Another problem is that without rigorous monitoring it can be difficult to identify or control individual violations.

The third common type of direct regulation is referred to as a **technological requirement**. This type of regulation requires particular anti-pollution actions or equipment without necessarily measuring the level of emitted pollution. When pollution monitoring is particularly costly or difficult, this approach may be optimal. For example, catalytic converters have been required on automobiles in the U.S. since the late 1970s. These converters are part of the car's exhaust system and act to eliminate carbon monoxide, hydrocarbons, and nitrogen oxides, all major causes of smog. However, more recent research suggests that these devices convert some of the nitrogen compounds to nitrous oxide, a powerful greenhouse gas that contributes to global warming.

The fourth type of direct regulation involves **banning** substances or processes that produce pollution. This relatively stringent approach can be appropriate under certain conditions. If the substance is extremely harmful, cannot be effectively monitored, cannot be adequately contained, and has reasonably cost-effective substitutes, then banning the substance is a reasonable alternative. For example, lead additives have been banned from gasoline (or petrol) since the 1970s. This ban has produced a substantial reduction in lead exposure. Relatively modest redesign of some engine parts proved sufficient to prevent any harm to engine life or efficiency.

Incentive approaches to pollution control

Incentive- or market-based policies attempt to control pollution through market forces and financial incentives. There are three types of governmental incentives to decrease pollution. These are emissions taxes or fees, pollution quotas (often in the form of pollution permits), and subsidies for pollution-reduction investments. The primary benefits of incentive approaches are the flexibility they allow regarding how and where pollution reduction occurs. Some also admire their ability to turn self-interest into public good. The primary problems with these approaches are possible inequality of pollution exposure and the usual political and rhetorical problems that arise when markets or self-interest are discussed in the same context as human health or the preservation of nature.

Emission taxes

Taxes on pollutants have the potential to reduce pollution by influencing the self-interest of the polluter. A basic pollution tax imposes a fee on each unit of pollution emitted. Assuming that effective monitoring and enforcement exist, the polluter has the choice of either reducing her pollution or paying the tax. If the marginal

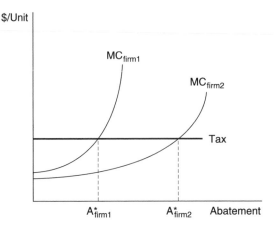

Figure 13.8 Pollution tax, two firms

cost of abatement is less than the tax, the firm gains profits by cleaning up. Firms with different abatement costs will be encouraged to clean up by different amounts, as seen in Figure 13.8.

Taxes placed directly on pollution emissions are rare, but taxes that raise the cost of polluting substances are more common, as seen in Table 13.1. Taxes on gasoline are particularly widespread, while broader taxes on fossil fuels, known as carbon taxes, are common in Europe and have also been implemented in Quebec. Australia recently rejected a proposal for a carbon tax program. Note that taxes on petroleum products in the U.S. are substantially below those of other developed countries. Japan has an excise tax on crude oil refined in Japan in addition

Table 13.1 Selected European and other carbon taxes

Country	Gasoline (petrol)		Diesel		Coal		Natural gas	
tax rates	$/1000 liters	$/ton CO_2	$/1000 liters	$/ton CO2	$/1000 kg	$/ton CO_2	$/1000 m^3	$/ton CO_2
France	590	245	370	129	0	0	1	1
Germany	495	205	313	109	0	0	33	17
Spain	490	203	356	124	0	0	8	4
UK	630	261	645	224	0	0	0	0
USA[a]	101	42	116	40	n.a.	n.a.	n.a.	n.a.
Japan[b]	320	133	124	43	n.a.	n.a.	23	12

Tax rates for European countries are for 1998 in national currencies and then converted with 1997 purchasing power parities (PPP) 1997 (PPP source: OECD *Main Economic Indicators*, July 1998, Paris)
a Figures for USA: 1996 (source: OECD/IEA: *Energy Prices and Taxes*, Paris, 1997).
b Figures for Japan: 1996 for petrol and diesel; 1995: gas oil; 1994 natural gas (source: OECD/IEA: *Energy Prices and Taxes*, Paris, 1997).

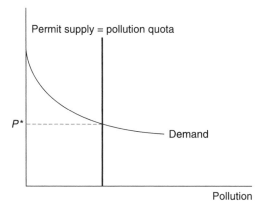

Figure 13.9 Market for permits

to the above taxes, so their relatively low rates are somewhat understated. Note also that none of these nations tax coal, a major contributor to acid rain and global warming.

A tax on the output of a polluting product or industry was first considered in Chapter 5. The goals are to reduce output toward the socially optimal level and decrease the pollution level. Taxes such as those in Table 13.1 raise the cost of fossil fuels and thereby decrease the equilibrium quantity. As with any good, of course, other policies that reduce the demand for fossil fuels can act as complements to the tax policy. Subsidies for public transportation, alternative fuels, and energy research aid the long-run effectiveness of taxation programs.

There are some limits to pollution taxes that make them less than ideal for controlling some types of pollution. First, taxes do not directly control the quantity of pollution, though a tax rate can be adjusted if the desired abatement level has not been reached. Second, compliance and enforcement will be at least as difficult as with direct regulation, since the tax is costly and the required payment depends on the same monitoring process as regulations. Third, because under some designs most or all firms may have to pay some tax, the tax may produce a negative impact on production and consumption even for relatively clean industries. However, because taxes provide an incentive to economize on more expensive sources of pollution, they have a role to play in the environmental policy mix.

Pollution permits

Over the past few decades economists have come to favor a different type of incentive system. This alternative is known as **pollution permits**, or a **cap and trade system**. Under a permit system government issues a limited number of permits to pollute according to predetermined standards. This initial distribution is usually free of charge and based on some measure of recent or current emissions. This limited number of permits acts as a quota on legal pollution emissions. Individual firms are allowed to buy and sell these permits in an open market.

Under a permit system firms may choose to reduce their pollution, buy permits, or some combination of the two. If abatement costs are less than the cost of the required permits, firms will be encouraged to clean up. If permits are the cheaper option, firms will have the incentive to buy them rather than invest in abatement.

The primary benefit of this approach is that it naturally concentrates abatement among firms with the lowest clean-up cost. If adequate monitoring and enforcement exist, permits create a flexible system that provides a predictable level of pollution reduction at a relatively low cost.

A firm's demand for pollution permits depends on its abatement costs, which represent the opportunity cost of purchasing the permits. Two brief examples will explain how a permit market works.

Example: Assume there are three polluting firms in a market and that pollution is currently free. Assume that each firm faces the constant per-unit abatement cost shown in Table 13.2. Columns (1) and (2) present the outcomes of a policy requiring a uniform one-half reduction in the original pollution level. Columns (3) and (4) represent the outcomes of a permit system offering 250 permits for one ton of pollution each.

As shown in Figure 13.10, firms 1 and 2 will be willing to outbid firm 3 for permits because of their higher clean-up costs. In this simple case with constant marginal abatement costs, the equilibrium permit price will be $16. At that price firm 1 will buy 100 permits and not clean up at all, firm 2 will buy the remaining 150 permits and eliminate its remaining 150 tons of pollution. Firm 3 will eliminate all of its pollution at $10 per unit. As shown in the last two columns of Table 13.2, the permit system will achieve equal pollution reduction at significantly lower cost.

Table 13.2 Equal abatement vs. permits

Firm	Pollution	Abatement cost/unit	(1) Pollution after uniform ½ reduction	(2) Total cost of ½ reduction	(3) Permits purchased (total=250)	(4) Abatement cost with permits
Firm 1	100 tons	$20/ton	50	$1,000	100	0
Firm 2	300 tons	$16/ton	150	$2,400	150	$2,400
Firm 3	100 tons	$10/ton	50	$500	0	$1,000
Total	500 tons	xxx	250	$3,900	250	$3,400

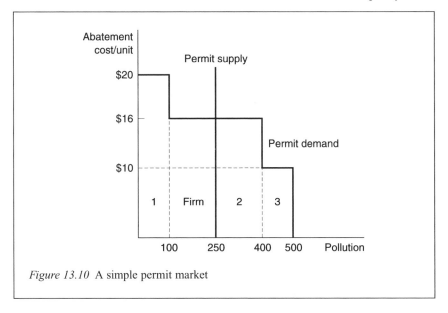

Figure 13.10 A simple permit market

Your Turn 13.3: Assume that the recommended level of pollution abatement is 25 per cent rather than one-half. Recalculate the values and compare the total costs of the two alternatives.

Table 13-3 Equal abatement vs. permits, 25 % reduction

Firm	Pollution	Abatement cost/unit	(1) Pollution after uniform ¼ reduction	(2) Total cost of ¼ reduction	(3) Permits purchased (total=125)	(4) Abatement cost with permits
Firm 1	100 tons	$20/ton				
Firm 2	300 tons	$16/ton				
Firm 3	100 tons	$10/ton				
Total	500 tons	xxx				

For both political and economic reasons, permits have become more popular than taxes, particularly in the United States. Permits do have some important advantages over taxes. First, they involve an explicit maximum level of legal pollution. In that sense they are more of a quota than a license to pollute. Secondly, the prices of permits provide useful information regarding the pollution problem they are controlling. Low permit prices suggest that the initial number of permits was higher than necessary, or that enforcement of pollution limits set by the permits needs to be enhanced. Also, either government or relatively well-funded private organizations can reduce the permitted level of pollution by buying permits and retiring them rather than using them to establish allowable pollution levels. In fact, cap and trade programs generally include a gradual reduction of pollution levels either through the issuing of fewer annual permits or the purchase and retirement of previously sold permits.

Comparing direct regulation and incentives

There are several problems with direct regulations, but the problem most commonly noted by economists is their tendency to be rigid across pollution sources with different clean-up costs (Blinder 1987: Ch. 5, provides an interesting defense of incentives). Clean-up costs may differ substantially across firms due to the age of the pollution source or the type of production process used, among other reasons. Requiring equal clean-up for all sources may accomplish a given level of reduction far more expensively than a more flexible policy that concentrates clean-up where it can be done most efficiently. Also, while monitoring of major pollution sources has become commonplace, enforcement of standards for small or mobile sources remains a challenge. Additional problems exist with **technological requirements**. While governments usually make an effort to consider the cost-effectiveness of various technologies for reducing pollution, special interests and bureaucratic inertia may lead to the requirement of inefficient or outdated methods of clean-up.

Critics of incentive programs sometimes claim that standards are more democratic than a governmentally-run permit program. Since both types of policy involve publicly determined maximum pollution levels, there is limited truth to this criticism. While communities can aid in the enforcement of fixed standards, they can also influence permit trading in at least two ways. One is to buy permits in order to prevent them from being used for pollution. For example, the 2006 sulfur dioxide permit auctions included small purchases by several environmental and educational institutions (http://www.epa.gov/airmarkets/auctions/2006/06summary.html). The other method of influence is through private negotiations or public demonstrations aimed at encouraging companies to stop selling unneeded permits in order to retire them from the market.

Pollution policy examples

The final section of the chapter will briefly review three examples of pollution problems and policy alternatives. These problems are urban smog, acid rain, and ozone depletion. In the first two cases, combinations of direct regulation and permit systems have been used to reduce the pollution problem. In the case of the ozone layer, a more stringent policy option was chosen.

Photochemical smog in the Los Angeles basin

Smog is a common and serious urban pollution problem. There are two primary types of smog. The most common is **sulfurous smog**, produced largely through sulfur dioxide and particulate emissions from fossil fuels. This type of smog was first noted in Roman times, and is a primary result of the industrial age. In the United Kingdom, pollution control policy emerged as a result of a deadly smog episode in London in 1952 during which approximately 4,000 people died (Williamson 1973: Ch. 8). The other main type is **photochemical smog**. This type of smog is produced by the interaction of nitrogen oxides and certain hydrocarbons with sunlight. The primary cause of photochemical smog is auto exhaust. Los Angeles is both highly dependent on the automobile, which accounts for about 50 percent of all air pollution in the region, and surrounded by mountains on the east that trap exhaust and other air pollutants in the LA basin. Photochemical smog first became visible in the Los Angeles basin in the 1940s, and has since appeared in many other urban areas (Williamson 1973: Ch. 10).

The Los Angeles area's extreme potential for photochemical smog has led to an unusually stringent set of laws and regulations. A metropolitan example of a permit- and fee-based anti-pollution policy is the South Coast Air Quality Management District in the Los Angeles area (http://www.aqmd.gov/). Air quality is controlled through several different policy methods operating simultaneously. The 2003 air quality plan (http://www.aqmd.gov/aqmp/AQMD03AQMP.htm) will be replaced by an updated plan in 2007.

This plan includes a limited pollution trading program. The LA permit program for nitrogen and sulfur oxides began in 1994. It applies to any stationary pollution source using approved pollution control equipment that emits four or more tons of nitrogen or sulfur-based compounds per year. There are separate markets for nitrogen oxides and sulfur oxides, and also separate markets for firms located inland and near the coast. The program restricts inland firms' ability to sell permits to firms near the coast, which is upwind from the more polluted inland zone. The original program granted permits to firms based on their highest level of output between 1989 and 1992. The number of permits then decreased by 7.1 percent per year for nitrogen oxides and 4.1 percent per year for sulfur oxides. Permits are for a single year only and cannot be saved for later use. New firms must buy permits from the government for a fee. Trading is voluntary, and operates in conjunction with other state and federal laws and regulations. See Harrison (1999) for a description of the program's development.

According to the Pareto-improvement principle (Chapter 4) and the Coase theorem, the efficiency gains from trading do not depend on the initial distribution of property rights, but the distribution of gains does. Permits are generally distributed according to some measure of recent emissions of the controlled pollutants. Critics argue that this allocation approach rewards past pollution. On the other hand, it also minimized initial disruptions caused by the program.

Critics of the LA emissions trading program note that because of the relatively loose initial standards, there was little trading of permits or effect from the caps during the early years of the program. More recent evidence suggests that continuing growth throughout the area in the 1990s has led to the type of constraint on total emissions expected under a cap and trade program (Gangadharan 2004). There is still considerable controversy regarding the program's success, however.

Another possible efficiency flaw in the South Coast system involves the failure to allow permits to be used in different years. Some permit systems allow annual permits to be used for any period within a multi-year time frame. This time flexibility is often called **banking**. If a limited number of permits are available for a given year only, disruptions in the markets can lead to sharp price changes, disequilibrium in the permits market, and an increase in violations of pollution limits. These problems occurred during the 2000 California energy crisis.

Acid rain

Another familiar air pollution problem is acid rain. Acid rain is caused by reactions between water vapor and either sulfur dioxide (SO_2) or nitrogen dioxide (NO_2). These reactions create sulfuric and nitric acids which then fall as rain. The primary sources of acid rain in both the U.S. and Eastern Europe are coal-burning electric generators, although autos and smelters also produce these gases. Acid rain harms aquatic life in lakes and streams, and also damages trees and slows forest growth. In some cases, visibility is also reduced by airborne sulfate particles created by power plant emissions (Lesser *et al.* 1997: 630-4). Acid rain also damages buildings. There are debates about the relative importance of human versus natural acid pollution, as well as local versus long-distance acid pollution (Griffin 1994: 240-7). However, the common view is that humans have contributed significantly to acid rain effects, and that the problem is not limited to areas near the pollution source.

Acid rain policy in the U.S. took on a new dimension with Title IV of the clean air amendments of 1990. This Act introduced a permit system for sulfur dioxide emissions from power plants, the first such system in the U.S. This permit program replaced a set of effluent limits on new and pre-existing power plants, with older plants being less strictly regulated. The goal of the permit program was to reduce SO_2 emissions to one-half of their 1980 level by 1995. The market for sulfur dioxide permits was established at the Chicago board of trade, which conducted the first 13 annual auctions without charge. The EPA now operates the auctions (http://www.epa.gov/airmarkets/auctions/index.html). The immediate effect of the SO_2 permit system was better than expected. An unexpected drop in the cost of shipping low-sulfur coal, along with a somewhat exaggerated investment in scrubbers, created an initial disequilibrium in the permit market and fewer emissions than the maximum allowable level (Schmalensee *et al.* 1998: p. 58). Due to more recent economic growth, the price of permits has more than doubled since the early years.

Permits, and certain types of regulations, give polluters a free choice of how to reduce emissions. In the case of the SO_2 program, about 55 percent of the reduction was caused by switching to low-sulfur coal, and about 45 percent was due to the installation of scrubbers that remove SO_2 from smoke. The results of the program are worth noting: "Not only did Title IV more than achieve the SO_2 emissions goal for Phase I, it did so on time, without extensive litigation, and at costs lower than had been projected" (Schmalensse *et al.* 1998: 66).

Because of the promising results of the sulfur dioxide trading program, cap and trade programs have been implemented for nitrogen oxides in the eastern U.S. (http://www.epa.gov/airmarkets/cmprpt/nox03/noxreport03.pdf) and for carbon dioxide emissions in Europe (http://www.climnet.org/EUenergy/ET.html). Emissions trading has proven to be a relatively cost-effective policy for regional or global environmental problems.

Ozone depletion

The Earth's stratosphere contains an ozone layer that protects the Earth from solar radiation. This radiation can result in skin cancer and crop damage, among other problems. Ozone depletion during the twentieth century produced holes in the ozone layer, particularly over the southern polar region and to a lesser degree over the Arctic. As with any problem, identifying the cause is the first step in the process of determining the appropriate solution. The primary human cause of ozone depletion is a chemical reaction involving chlorofluorocarbons (CFCs), a relatively complex set of compounds used for much of the twentieth century as refrigerants, aerosol propellants, and for other uses.

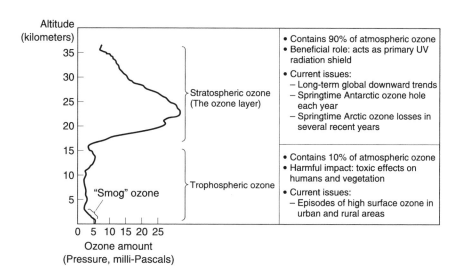

Source: U.S. Environmental Protection Agency

The chemical interaction between CFCs and ozone involves a few steps, but is not overly complicated. First, the chlorofluorocarbons interact with ultra violet light to release chlorine (Cl). The chlorine then interacts with the ozone (O_3) to produce chlorine oxide (ClO) and free oxygen (O_2). ClO also interacts with single oxygen molecules to produce chlorine (Cl) and O_2. These two processes produce a catalytic process where one chlorine atom can destroy several ozone molecules.

Discoveries about the causes and effects of CFCs led to the passage of the 1987 United Nations Montreal Protocol proposing a 50 percent reduction in CFCs by 2000. In response to new evidence, later agreements required the banning of CFCs by 1996. U.S. policy during the transition period included research efforts to find substitutes for CFCs, a mandatory recycling program, an escalating tax on ozone-depleting substances, and a CFC emission permit program in which the cap on permissible CFCs eventually declined to zero (Callan and Thomas 2000: 370-81). Effective replacement refrigerants and propellants have been found, and most nations have enacted this ban on CFCs. Recent evidence suggests that the decline in the stratospheric ozone is slowing, and that the ozone layer should begin to increase within the next decade and return to a normal level within 50 years (http://www.epa.gov/Ozone/science/sc_fact.html). In a case where the pollutant is seriously harmful in small quantities and relatively cost-effective substitute products are available, a ban may be appropriate. If the substance is widely used, a transition period with incentives may be required. CFCs provide an example of such a case.

A note on the politics and rhetoric of pollution control

Many nations have been relatively slow to adopt incentive approaches to pollution control. There are several political and bureaucratic reasons for this. Fixed standards offer less uncertainty regarding their effects, particularly on the local level. The possibility of local areas of high pollution under permit systems is very real for pollutants with relatively local effects. Also, both legislators and regulators are more likely to be trained in law than in economics, and will therefore be more familiar with writing and enforcing legal standards. See Stavins (1998) for a broad and readable overview of the political and economic lessons of the SO_2 permit experiment in the U.S.

The politics of environmental policy occasionally sinks into a rather troublesome rhetorical competition between supporters of incentive-based approaches and direct regulation. Opponents of incentive approaches frequently refer to them as "pay to pollute schemes." This entertaining phrase emphasizes the common view of an inevitable partnership between markets and greed, as well as implying to the casual listener that there is no actual limit on pollution under incentive policies. Regardless of one's view on the first issue, the second is clearly false. Pollution permit systems begin by setting a maximum quantity (quota) of permissible pollution, and then allowing individual firms or others to buy and sell permits based on their self-interest.

However, this rhetorical battle has two sides. Supporters of permits and taxes, including most economics texts, refer to direct regulation as a "command and control" approach, which is factual enough but has a somewhat fascist tone. Control, or enforcement, is an essential part of every effective pollution-reduction policy, including incentive approaches, a point that is sometimes de-emphasized in economics texts. One should be careful not to let inflammatory wording from either point of view interfere with one's ability to view the issue of pollution control with an open mind.

Conclusion

This chapter has provided a review of the process of environmental policy analysis with some emphasis on the role of scientific study in determining the benefits of pollution control. The goal of this overview is to provide the student with some concepts and tools for working with environmental scientists and critically thinking about their findings. Alternative goals of pollution policy were discussed, along with a review of various regulation and incentive approaches to pollution control. Of course, environmental policy is frequently available as a major field of study for undergraduate and graduate students. Therefore, a single chapter leaves much ground uncovered.

Review questions

Conceptual questions

1. The potential harms of air pollution are relatively easy to list. Its occasional benefits are less obvious to most people. Develop a list of possible harms and benefits of particulate matter (smoke). Is it reasonable to de-emphasize harms that don't involve direct costs to human health? Why or why not?

2. Are the costs of pollution control morally less important than the benefits? Is the cost–benefit criterion less morally acceptable than a more stringent technical feasibility standard? Considering all factors, which type of goal would you recommend? Interpret these questions in terms of the ethical goals and theories in Chapter 2, along with your own views.

3. The two methods of measuring environmental compliance costs are the engineering method and the survey method. Discuss the advantages of each, and the possible benefits of combining both methods when designing pollution control policy.

4. Since banning CFCs seems to be proving successful as a policy regarding the ozone layer, should the banning of greenhouse gas emissions, including carbon dioxide emissions, be the basis for our policy for controlling global warming? Why or why not? What would you need to know in order to be more certain of your choice?

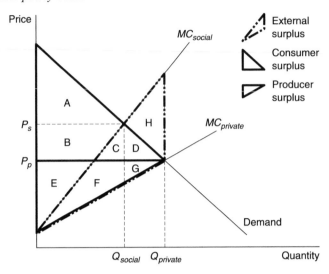

Computational problems

5. If the demand equation in Figure 13.2 is $100 - 2Q$, the private MC is $10 + Q$, the external marginal cost equals $\frac{1}{2}Q$, and the social MC is $10 + 1.5Q$, find each surplus, the total net gains, and the deadweight loss in dollar terms. (Hint: Find the private equilibrium price and quantity first.)

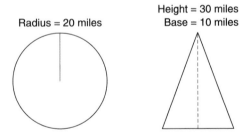

Graphs for problem 6

6. If the areas in the graphs have 100 persons per square mile, how many people would be exposed to a pollutant using each distribution pattern? (Hint: In case you don't remember, the area of a circle is πr^2.)

7. Calculate a basic dose response for each of the cases below assuming that the exposure level (X) is 50 parts per million and the effect (Y) is measured as the added risk of one more human death per year:

    Linear: $Y = 1/10,000X$

    Linear with threshold: $Y = -1/10 + 1/10,000X$

    Non-linear: $Y = 1/1,000 \ln X$

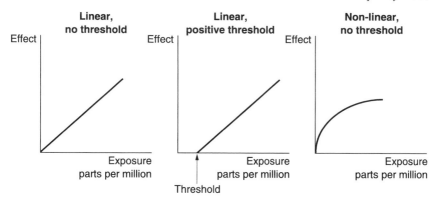

8. Let's consider pollution control alternatives for two polluting firms with different pollution control costs using the following table:

Quantity of pollution abatement	Total pollution harm in $	Marginal benefit of abatement	Total abatement cost (firm 1)	Marginal abatement cost (firm 1)	Total abatement cost (firm 2)	Marginal abatement cost (firm 2)
0	200	xxx	0	xxx	0	xxx
1	120	80	20		5	5
2	70			50	13	
3	40		140			14
4	20		240		47	
5	10			140	97	

(A) Fill out the remaining blanks in the table.
(B) If the maximum technically feasible clean-up level is five units of abatement, what are the total benefits and costs for each firm, and for both combined?
(C) Now assume that each firm will clean-up to where the marginal benefits equal the marginal costs. How much pollution will each firm eliminate? What are the total benefits and costs of abatement for both firms combined?
(D) If the government modifies the standard in part (B) to three units of pollution abatement for every firm, find the total costs and benefits of pollution abatement. How do your answers compare to those in part (C)?
(E) If the government passed a $20.01 tax of pollution emissions, how much pollution would each firm eliminate? Find the total abatement costs and benefits under this policy.

14 Poverty and income support policies

Poverty is hunger. Poverty is lack of shelter. Poverty is being sick and not being able to see a doctor. Poverty is not having access to school and not knowing how to read. Poverty is not having a job, is fear for the future, living one day at a time. ... Poverty is powerlessness, lack of representation and freedom.[1]

(World Bank)

The government's War on Poverty has transformed poverty from a short-term misfortune into a career choice.[2]

(Harry Browne, former Libertarian Presidential candidate)

There was never a war on poverty.
Maybe there was a skirmish on poverty.[3]

(Andrew Cuomo, former Secretary of Housing and Urban Development)

Of the many topics discussed in this book, poverty is one of the most difficult to define and explain, as well as being one of the most difficult to solve. The concept of poverty is similar to ethical goals like freedom or equality. These terms involve multiple dimensions, multiple definitions, and alternative measurements. As the first quote above indicates, poverty is not necessarily a lack of real income. The lack of access to publicly provided services such as education also provides evidence of poverty. Even if poverty is interpreted as inadequate income, its meaning remains controversial. According to some common measures, income poverty is virtually non-existent in the affluent countries of North America and Western Europe. According to other common measures, U.S. poverty ranges from 12 percent to as much as 20 percent of the population. There is also a conceptual dispute about the relationship between poverty and inequality that affects our interpretation of poverty. Finally, most poverty measures divide a nation's population into two groups: the poor and the non-poor. For example, a single American under 65 earning $195 per week is officially poor but another single American earning $196 per week is not. Yet it is quite clear that poverty is not a yes or no problem, since some officially poor households are far better off than others. If we can't agree on what the problem is, any debate over possible solutions to the problem becomes particularly difficult to resolve.

The perceived causes of poverty also vary widely across different cultures and ideologies. As we will see, differences in attitudes toward the causes of poverty can have a significant effect on the design and generosity of anti-poverty programs. Schiller (2004: 4-7) offers three alternative views of the causes of poverty. The **flawed character** view blames poverty on the poor's lack of motivation or skills. The **restricted opportunity** view blames poverty on society's barriers to opportunity. According to this view the poor are often trapped in poverty by inadequate education and services as well as class and race barriers. Finally, the **big brother** view blames the disincentive effects of government policy for at least some of the income and employment problems of the poor. Views of the poor appear to be considerably more negative in the U.S. than in Europe. One set of survey evidence found that 60 percent of Americans but only 26 percent of Europeans considered the poor to be lazy, while 29 percent of Americans versus 70 percent of Europeans believed that the poor are trapped in poverty (Alesina and Glaeser 2004: 184). Based on these attitudes, one might predict that U.S. anti-poverty programs would tend to be more restrictive, more concerned about work incentives, and less well-funded than anti-poverty programs in Europe. In most cases this is true.

To make the policy challenge of poverty even more serious, the goals of anti-poverty programs are relatively numerous and often contradictory. Of course, the primary goal of any anti-poverty program is to reduce poverty and increase the well-being of the low-income population. However, as with other policy areas there are many types of policies that can contribute to this overarching goal. The alternative views of poverty mentioned above, along with the leaky bucket principle discussed in Chapter 4, suggest that other goals may be important when choosing among various programs. Other goals include the minimization of disincentives or barriers to work, the minimization of administrative costs, the minimization of diversions of funds from the intended recipients, a simple and user-friendly program design, and several others.

Given the lack of consensus regarding the meaning of poverty, the causes of poverty, and the goals of poverty-reduction programs, it is clear that little or nothing discussed in this chapter will be entirely non-controversial. With that strong caution in mind, we will nevertheless attempt to present a fair overview of the alternative meanings and measures of poverty and inequality, an overview of a selection of U.S. programs providing aid to the poor, and a more detailed analysis of the effects of the primary U.S. cash assistance programs for the poor. In Chapter 15, additional programs that target the working poor will be considered.

What is poverty?

Before starting our discussion of the meaning and measurement of poverty it is important to consider why some households with equally low incomes might be better off than others. Low income may be temporary and therefore less harmful to one's well-being, or common in a nation or culture and therefore less harmful to one's status or self-image. Also, some families that are poor in terms of income may still have a measure of security through property ownership, as in the case of small farmers, or through access to public services. Aside from income or wealth, poverty may also be defined in terms of non-monetary factors such as hopelessness or powerlessness, which can also vary across low-income households.

Regardless of the broader meanings of the term, income poverty is the most frequently discussed and measured form of poverty. Income poverty statistics are based on one of two general concepts. **Absolute poverty** refers to insufficient income relative to some standard measure of need. Official U.S. poverty measures are of this type, and will be discussed in more detail later in the chapter. **Relative poverty** measures compare a household's income to some measure of the nation's average income. Relative poverty measurements are more commonly used in Europe than in North America or less-developed countries. More generally, while absolute measures emphasize the basic inadequacy of income, relative measures also emphasize inequality.

Absolute poverty in less-developed countries

The standards used to measure poverty in underdeveloped nations are extremely low relative to those of the developed world. Measures of extreme income poverty estimate the percentage of the population who cannot afford regular access to basics such as food, shelter, clothing, basic transportation, or healthcare. While nations define poverty differently, common standards such as $1 or $2 per day have been developed by international agencies to compare extreme poverty levels across nations. As shown in Table 14.1, a comparison of the $1 per day measure across regions and time identifies the primary economic event of the past 25 years: the explosive economic growth of East Asia, including China. A check of the development literature will reveal a great deal of criticism of China's growing inequality. The data in Table 14.1 indicate that this inequality has been caused by unequal improvement in living standards rather than a lowering of living conditions among China's poor. Table 14.1 also demonstrates that for most of the rest of the world, particularly Eastern Europe and sub-Saharan Africa, the past quarter century has seen little progress in the fight against poverty.

Table 14.1 Percent living below $1/day

Region	1981	1990	1996	2001
East Asia & Pacific	57.7	29.6	16.6	14.9
China	63.8	33.0	17.4	16.6
Europe and Central Asia	0.7	0.5	3.7	3.6
Latin America & Caribbean	9.7	11.3	10.7	9.5
Middle East & North Africa	5.3	2.3	2.0	2.4
South Asia	51.5	41.3	36.6	31.3
Sub-Saharan Africa	41.6	44.6	45.6	46.4
Total	40.4	26.1	22.8	21.1

Source: World Bank.

The United States' absolute poverty measure

The United States did not officially define or measure poverty until the early 1960s. The method it adopted at that time, and uses with few modifications to this day, is both ingeniously simple and highly controversial. It is an absolute poverty measure in that its goal is to define an income level consistent with a particular level of need. Also, U.S. poverty is measured by household income rather than individual earnings. That is why most college students are not officially poor despite a low level of individual income. The primary challenge in defining an absolute measure of household poverty is establishing an acceptable level of need. Defining income is also somewhat controversial.

Your Turn 14.1: Consider your own preliminary answers to the following two questions: (1) In your view, what is the minimum level of income a family of four needs to sustain itself? (2) Is subsistence (enough to survive) a high enough minimum standard for household income in an affluent society?

These questions cannot be answered without debate, and debate is a constant part of policy discussions regarding poverty. These two questions are difficult to answer for different reasons, however. The first question involves finding answers to two subsidiary questions: (1) What items does a family need in order to survive? (2) How much do those items cost? There are many different kinds of food, shelter, and clothing that will provide the means for survival, and both the specific goods and their price can vary across cultural groups and locations, even within a given nation. The cost of shelter, particularly, varies widely between urban and rural areas and among different cities. The second question relates more to one's values regarding equality than to any measurement issue.

The original U.S. poverty estimate was not based on a detailed list of necessary items. Rather, in the early 1960s the Council of Economic Advisors adopted a much simpler approach that involved the following two steps: (1) find a measure of the annual cost of food needed for a poor family; (2) divide by the fraction of a poor family's income spent on food. The first step utilized a U.S. Department of Agriculture study which found that (as of the mid-1950s) three meals a day would cost a family of four a minimum of $2.736 per day, or just over $998 per year.[4] The second step used consumption data indicating that the average low-income family spent about one-third of its income on food. Therefore, rounding the food expenditure to an even $1,000 and dividing by one-third, the first officially sanctioned poverty line was set at $3,000 per year. Almost immediately, problems became evident. Most importantly, there was no adjustment in the original line for the size of one's family. For example, $3,000 in the early 1960s may have been adequate for a single individual living in a small town, but a family of eight in a major city would have been severely destitute at the same income level.

Table 14.2 2004 poverty thresholds by family size and number of related children under 18 ($)

Household size	0 Children	1 Child	2 Children	3 Children	4 Children	5 Children	6 Children
1	9,827						
2	12,649	13,020					
3	14,776	15,205	15,219				
4	19,484	19,803	19,157	19,223			
5	23,497	23,838	23,108	22,543	22,199		
6	27,025	27,133	26,573	26,037	25,241	24,768	
7	31,096	31,290	30,621	30,154	29,285	28,271	27,159

Source: http://www.census.gov/hhes/www/poverty/threshld/thresh04.html.

The Council of Economic Advisors Index was replaced in 1964 by the Social Security Administration Poverty Index constructed by Molly Orshanski. This index slightly modified the basic poverty line for a family of four to $3,130 as of 1963, and also constructed different poverty lines for families of different sizes, farm versus non-farm dwellers, the sex of the family head, and the number of children versus adults. A total of 124 different poverty lines now exist for various combinations of the above factors. Since that time the various poverty lines have been corrected for inflation using the consumer price index. For the most recent figures visit the following website: http://www.census.gov/hhes/www/poverty/poverty.html.

Table 14.2 identifies a set of poverty lines for various family sizes and compositions as of 2004. The full table includes categories for families of eight and nine or more members, as well as a separate category for households that have a primary member at least 65 years old. The negative relationship between the number of children and the poverty line for large families is probably based on higher food, clothing, and housing costs for adults. Table 14.3 compares U.S and European poverty using the U.S. poverty measure. The authors (Smeeding *et al.* 2000b) caution that exchange rate issues make this comparison difficult.

Table 14.3 International poverty rates using U.S. method

Nation	Year	Poverty rate (%)
Australia	1994	17.6
United Kingdom	1995	15.7
United States	1994	13.6
France	1994	9.9
Canada	1994	7.4
Germany	1994	7.3
Sweden	1995	6.3
Finland	1995	4.8
Luxembourg	1994	0.3
Overall average		8.6

Source: Smeeding *et al.* (2000b: 32).

Another measure based on the absolute poverty concept is the **poverty gap**, which measures the average and total difference between the poverty line and the actual incomes of poor households. For example, in 2001 the U.S. poverty gap averaged $2,800 per poor individual, and totaled $92 billion for all poor Americans. In comparison, spending on all the cash programs for the poor in 2002 totaled about $83 billion, and social security spending for the elderly was far higher than all cash programs for the poor combined.[5]

Criticisms of the U.S. poverty line

Any poverty line is somewhat arbitrary. For example, it is obviously arbitrary to categorize a single 30-year-old person as poor if her income is $10,100 but not poor if her income is $10,200. However, the distinction between the just-poor and near-poor is not the primary source of controversy. The larger debate revolves around how the government defines a typical household's needs, and how this measure has been affected by inflation and other trends since the 1960s. Some critics argue convincingly that the current poverty line is too low, and others are quite persuasive when arguing that it is too high. Our next step is to review both sides of the argument about the imperfections of the poverty line.

The U.S. poverty line is too low

There are some strong arguments in favor of raising the U.S. poverty line. Some are based on technical flaws in the original measurement of poverty, and others are based on the rather wide disparity in people's attitudes about minimum income requirements. The primary technical issue is that the ratio of food expenditures to total expenditures used in the original measurement was too large. As discussed above, the original poverty line used data from the 1950s that concluded that the average poor family spent about one-third of their income on food. However, in the current version of the consumer price index food expenditures account for about one-fifth of total expenditures for the average person, suggesting that the figure of one-third is too high. For example, a $2,000 food budget would translate into a $6,000 poverty line using the current ratio of one to three ($2,000/0.333 = $6,000), while a food/total ratio of one to five would produce a poverty line of $10,000, a 40 percent increase.

Other arguments favoring a higher set of poverty lines include their failure to include increasing costs of work such as childcare and transportation. For example, the Economic Policy Institute (EPI) has established a family budget-based set of poverty lines (http://www.epinet.org/issueguides/poverty/poverty_issueguide.pdf). While this measure also varies by geographic area (an excellent improvement), the primary difference between the EPI's family budget lines and the official measures is that the family poverty lines are much higher and produce poverty rates over twice as large. Also, surveys of the public's opinions of the minimum adequate level of income tend to produce a much higher level of income than the official measure (Schiller 2004: 38). Another basis for complaint is that any long-running absolute measure will tend to fall further behind the average standard of living in a growing economy. This argument is most commonly used in support of a relative poverty measure.

Alternative measures have been published by the U.S. government in the last 10 years, along with the official measures. A 1996 report published by the National Academy of Sciences suggested several changes in the method of calculating the poverty line. (http://www.nap.edu/readingroom/books/poverty/). The main recommendations of the committee were to use a different survey to collect data for calculating the poverty lines, include a more detailed set of goods rather than the food times 3 measure, include all sources of income in the poverty line, and subtract certain basic expenditures such as healthcare from total income. In 2004, the official poverty rate for a family of four was 12.7 percent. The modifications suggested by the Academy's report would raise this rate to 13.9.

The U.S. poverty line is too high

On the other side of the issue, there are some strong arguments suggesting that the poverty line is too high. First, the current poverty level does not include the value of non-cash assistance such as food stamps, Medicaid, housing subsidies, or aid from private charities. The government has calculated poverty rates under different income assumptions for many years, so the impact of these non-cash benefits is well known. See Table 14.4 for a comparison. Secondly, some estimates have found that the spending levels of the poor are well above their stated income levels. For some temporary poor this could be a result of drawing down one's savings, but the more common explanation is that many of the poor systematically understate their income. A final argument is that the inflation measure used to adjust the 1960s poverty lines is biased upward by roughly 1 percent (see Chapter 8's discussion of inflation bias). Since the U.S. index was established in 1963, this bias could produce a significant upward bias in the inflation-adjusted poverty line over the past four decades.

Relative poverty

The active debate over relative versus absolute poverty measures tends to begin when a nation or region lowers its extreme poverty rate to low or negligible levels.

Table 14.4 U.S. poverty rates with different income definitions

Year	Without transfers and before taxes	With cash transfers (official definition) (%)	With cash and non-cash transfers (%)	With imputed return on home equity (%)
2002	20.0	12.1	9.4	8.6
2000	18.7	11.3	8.8	8.0
1995	21.8	13.8	10.3	9.4
1990	20.4	13.5	10.9	9.8
1985	20.9	14.0	11.7	9.9
1980	20.7	13.0	10.1	8.2

Source: U.S. Census Bureau.

The primary relative measure of poverty classifies a household as poor if its income is below some fraction of a nation's mean or median. One form of relative poverty measure categorizes a family as poor if its income falls below 50 percent of median household income. Another relative measure sometimes used in Europe defines poverty as 60 percent of mean household income. These two measures are relatively close in value. This definition has the disadvantage of being unresponsive to long-term economic growth, and also cannot be compared easily across countries or other political boundaries. It is more a measure of inequality than of inadequate income, which is a somewhat different issue ethically as well as politically.

The study by Smeeding *et al.* (2000b) included two relative poverty rates with lines set at 40 percent and 50 percent of median household income, respectively. As with their absolute poverty comparison, the U.S. has the highest relative poverty levels in the developed world (see Table 14.5). In some respects the choice of relative or absolute poverty measures is less important than the primary conclusion of both. The U.S. has the highest poverty rate in the developed world, despite having one of the highest average levels of real income.

Broader measures of inequality and poverty

Income inequality involves some measure of the range or dispersion of income levels within a society. A common measure of income inequality is provided by the Lorenz curve and Gini coefficient. The **Lorenz curve** is a graph that measures the cumulative population on the horizontal axis and the cumulative income on the vertical. In Figure 14.1, the straight line represents total income equality, since the proportion of the total population always equals the proportion of total income. The curved line is the Lorenz curve, which represents the actual cumulative distribution of income in a society. The larger the area between the two curves (area A in Figure 14.1), the more inequality exists in that society.

Table 14.5 Relative poverty rates

Country	Year	40% poverty rate	50% poverty rate
United States	1997	10.7	17.8
Italy	1995	8.9	13.9
Australia	1994	7.0	14.3
Canada	1994	6.6	11.4
United Kingdom	1995	5.7	13.2
Sweden	1992	4.6	6.5
Germany	1994	4.2	7.5
France	1994	3.2	7.4
Finland	1995	2.1	5.0
Luxembourg	1994	1.3	3.9
Overall average		4.7	8.6

Source: Smeeding *et al.* (2000b: 40).

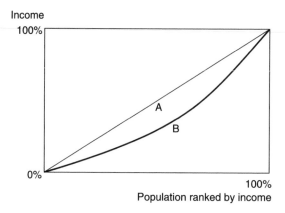

Figure 14.1 The Lorenz curve

The **Gini coefficient** is a fraction that measures the degree of inequality displayed by the Lorenz curve. It is the ratio of area A over areas A + B in Figure 14.1. In a nation with perfect equality, the Gini coefficient would equal zero since area A would not exist.

$$\text{Gini coefficient} = \frac{A}{A+B} \quad \text{(see Figure 14.1)}$$

Not surprisingly, estimated Gini coefficients are far lower (more equal) in Europe than in the U.S. According to the *World Development Report* of 2002, Gini coefficients were 0.408 for the U.S., 0.361 for the UK, 0.3 for Germany, and 0.25 for Sweden and Japan. Less-developed countries often have higher Gini coefficients than these.

The U.S. has become less equal over the past 25 years by these measures. Table 14.6 displays the distribution of U.S. household income by fifths for 1968 and 2002, while Figure 14.2 displays the U.S. Lorenz curve for 2002.

Example: The 2002 Gini coefficient can be calculated without calculus by identifying the various rectangles and triangles in area B, summing the areas, then subtracting from ½ (the area of A + B) to determine area A. The Gini coefficient is then a simple division problem. Rounding-off the income shares, the four rectangles below the Lorenz curve in Figure 14.2 are 0.2 × 0.03, 0.2 × 0.09, 0.2 × 0.15, and 0.2 × 0.23.

Table 14.6 U.S. income distribution by quintile

	Lowest 5th	Second 5th	Third 5th	Fourth 5th	Top 5th
1968	4.2%	11.1	17.5	24.4	42.8
2002	3.5%	8.8	14.8	23.3	49.7

Source: http://www.census.gov/hhes/www/income/histinc/incfamdet.html.

Your Turn 14.2: Calculate the areas of the four rectangles and five triangles below the Lorenz curve and then calculate the 2002 Gini coefficient.

In the past decade a multi-dimensional measure of poverty known as **social exclusion** has become a valuable source of information about European poverty. (European Commission 2006: 7-15). Social exclusion refers to the inability of some households to gain access to adequate income and services based on that nation's values. For European nations, this measure involves a combination of relative income deprivation and separate measures of inadequate housing, education, employment, health, and other services. Aside from the relative versus absolute poverty debate, the abandonment of the idea of a simple poverty rate in favor of a series of separate measures may be very appealing to those who find one-dimensional poverty measurements inherently flawed.

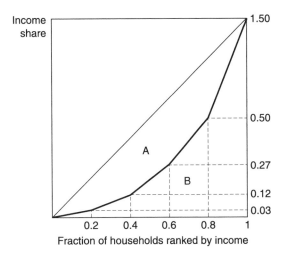

Figure 14.2 2002 U.S. Lorenz curve

Who are the U.S. poor?

Poverty in the United States does not fall equally on all groups. Different races, ethnic groups, ages, and genders have different probabilities of being poor. Characteristics such as single parenthood or low educational levels also greatly increase one's chances of being poor. All of these factors can vary over time, and some groups have significantly different poverty rates today than they did several decades ago. For example, the elderly had a high poverty rate in the 1950s, but now are less likely to be poor than the average household.

   Table 14.7 provides an overview of trends in poverty rates for different racial and ethnic groups as well as the elderly and single adult households headed by women. The trends in poverty rates are quite different for various categories. Overall and for whites, the 1960s saw an extremely large decrease in the poverty rate but no meaningful change since. African-Americans experienced significant declines in poverty during the 1960s and 1990s, and to a lesser degree this pattern also holds for female-headed households. The elderly have experienced a steadier decline in poverty rates over this period.

Analyzing U.S. public assistance

The Social Security Act of 1935 is almost certainly the most important piece of social legislation ever passed in the United States. The Act's early programs can offer some evidence about the attitudes that informed the law. The Social Security Act created several programs that can be grouped into two categories: social insurance and cash assistance. The social insurance programs are Social Security (retirement and survivor's insurance), Unemployment Insurance, and Workers' Compensation (disability insurance). Although these social insurance programs have minimum and maximum payment levels which introduce a degree of redistribution, households with higher former income levels get higher government payments. Therefore, it is somewhat misleading to refer to these policies as

Table 14.7 U.S. poverty rates by ethnic group and family status

Year	All	Over 65	White-Anglo	Hispanic	African-American	Family – no husband present – all races	Family – no husband present – black
1959	22.4	35.2	18.1[a]	—	55.1	49.4	70.6
1970	12.6	24.6	9.9[a]	—	33.5	38.1	58.1
1980	13.0	15.7	9.1	25.7	32.5	36.7	53.4
1990	13.5	12.2	8.8	28.1	31.9	37.2	50.6
2000	11.3	9.9	7.4	21.5	22.5	28.5	38.6
2004	12.7	9.8	8.6[a]	21.9	24.7[b]	30.5	39.5[b]

Source: U.S. Census Bureau.
[a] White, without reference to Latino heritage.
[b] Black only.

anti-poverty programs. Also, Social Security is unique among the main U.S. cash assistance programs because it is a single federal program with equal payments for people in different states. In general, Social Security Act programs give states some flexibility in payment levels and eligibility requirements. The other set of programs established by the Social Security Act offer cash payments to specific groups of people with low incomes and minimal wealth. The original programs included Aid to the Blind, Aid to the Permanently and Totally Disabled, Old Age Assistance, Aid to Dependent Children (later changed to Aid to Families with Dependent Children, or AFDC), and a voluntary program for the states labeled General Assistance. These categories suggest an important principle behind federal cash assistance to the poor. Under the original legislation, only those judged to be unemployable by the standards of the 1930s were allowed to receive public assistance. Cash assistance programs for the elderly, blind, and disabled were later merged into the Supplemental Security Income program (http://www.ssa.gov/notices/supplemental-security-income/) and continue to be an important source of support for the elderly or disabled poor.

Goals of anti-poverty programs

The main U.S. cash assistance program for the poor, Aid to Families with Dependent Children, underwent a radical revision in 1996. The 1996 law was entitled the Personal Responsibility and Work Opportunity Reconciliation Act, and the new cash assistance program is entitled Temporary Assistance to Needy Families (TANF). Ten years after the radical revision of cash assistance in the U.S., there is still value in a two-step evaluation of the effects of this type of program. The first step is to review general evidence regarding the effects of cash assistance on the well-being and behavior of recipients. Much of this evidence predates the 1996 reform. The second step is to review the changes caused by the TANF program.

The basis for judging the effectiveness of anti-poverty programs lies in a series of goals that differ in emphasis depending on one's ideological or theoretical viewpoint. For example, Kimenyi (1994: Ch. 15) lists the following objectives for public assistance programs:

1 **Adequacy**: The poor should receive an adequate income level.
2 **Target efficiency**: Benefits should go to those most in need. Payments to the non-poor or evidence of cheating or inaccuracy violate this goal.
3 **Administrative efficiency**: Services should be provided with minimum overhead costs.
4 **Horizontal equity**: People in similar situations should be provided with similar benefits.
5 **Vertical equity**: Those with greater need should receive greater benefits, and those with more earnings should receive higher total incomes, including benefits.
6 **Work incentives**: Recipients should have a reasonable incentive to work.
7 **Family stability**: Family break-up should not be encouraged.

8 **Independence**: Public assistance should discourage long-term dependence on benefits.
9 **Coherence and control**: Public assistance should be easy to understand and administer.

This list can be interpreted as a more detailed form of Okun's leaky bucket principle, discussed in Chapter 4. In addition to adequacy and other equity measures, Okun offered several sources of inefficiency (leaks) from either the funding sources or spending patterns of social programs. These included administrative costs, work disincentives, disincentives to save and invest, and socio-economic costs such as family break-up. Another source of leaks that Okun does not mention is the payment of benefits to those who are eligible for the program but not poor. I label this leak **misdirected funds**.

Coherence and administrative efficiency

Aid to the poor in the U.S. is generally considered to perform poorly with respect to these two criteria. Coherence is a particular problem for a large federal system of government. The U.S. social safety net, as it is sometimes called, is constructed primarily from several programs representing specific areas of need. For example, in addition to cash assistance through Temporary Assistance to Needy Families, separate programs exist for children's nutrition, housing, food, health, training, and adult education. Some programs such as public housing and housing vouchers have relatively broad eligibility requirements but limited budgets and long waiting lists. Others have specific clienteles, including TANF, Supplemental Security Income (SSI), and Social Security. Some poor households qualify for and collect benefits from multiple programs. Others qualify for few and collect benefits from none. This fractious system of benefits presents a barrier to coherence and administrative efficiency.

Adequacy and **vertical equity** have somewhat overlapping meanings and measurements. Adequacy is best measured by an absolute poverty measure, while vertical equity relates to relative poverty or inequality measures such as the Gini coefficient. Given the large number of programs available, adequacy is best viewed by the effect of the combined programs on poverty. As seen in Table 14.4 above, cash and in-kind programs reduced the U.S. poverty rate from 20 percent to 9.4 percent in 2002. The official poverty measure of 12.1 percent included cash assistance but not in-kind benefits.

Another criterion for judging social programs is **horizontal equity**, or the equal treatment of equally situated people. Because of the segmentation of cash assistance into multiple programs, households with equal incomes and family sizes often have very different levels of benefits. On average, the elderly receiving Social Security are far better off than the disabled receiving SSI, and SSI recipients are better off than TANF recipients. Social Security payments vary quite widely, but averaged roughly $900 to $1,000 per month per recipient in 2002, while SSI averaged about $400 per recipient and TANF about $160 per recipient (Schiller 2004: Chs. 12 and 13). Another dimension of horizontal inequity in the U.S. arises because some programs allow substantial differences in payment levels across states. In 2002, average TANF monthly benefits for a three-person family ranged from over $630 in Alaska to $140 in Mississippi (Schiller 2004: 213). The multiple programs mentioned earlier create another layer of horizontal inequity, paying far more to those who are aware of the full range of available programs than to those who are not.

The negative income tax model and work incentives

Despite the apparent importance of equity in judging the effects of anti-poverty programs, possible work disincentives seem to dominate economic and political discussion of these programs in the U.S. A modified form of the utility-maximizing consumer model introduced in Chapter 3 can be used to analyze the effect of public assistance benefits on work hours and recipient utility. This model is referred to as the negative income tax model, after the proposed welfare reform of Milton Friedman (1962: 190-5). The negative income tax itself involved replacing multiple government aid programs with a simple fixed rate income tax that paid money to those with incomes below a certain level of income. While several variants of the negative income tax were proposed in the 1970s, none was ever implemented.

The basic model of a negative income tax is useful for analyzing the effects of any income transfer program. A simple negative income tax contains two components: a **base payment** for someone with zero earned income, and an **implicit tax rate** or **benefit reduction rate** that reduces the amount of government aid as earnings rise. The basic formula for the implicit tax rate is $t = \Delta$welfare/Δearnings. Since welfare payments usually decrease as private income rises, the implicit tax rate is usually negative. For example, an implicit tax rate of $-1/2$ means that the recipient will lose one dollar of welfare for each two dollars of earnings she gains.

The income for a welfare-eligible family can be summarized in the following equations.

$$\text{Earnings} = \text{Wage} \cdot \text{Hours} \qquad (14.1)$$

$$\text{Welfare} = \text{Base} + t \cdot \text{Earnings} \qquad (14.2)$$

$$\text{Total income} = \text{Earnings} + \text{Welfare} = \text{Base} + (1+t) \cdot \text{Earnings} \qquad (14.3)$$

Example: Assume that the wage equals $6 per hour. Hours means hours worked per week, welfare's base payment equals $75 per week, and the implicit tax rate equals $-2/3$. If the welfare recipient does not work (zero hours), she will earn nothing and collect $75 per week in public assistance. If she works 10 hours per week, she will earn $60, collect $75 - 2/3 \cdot $60, or $35 per week in public assistance, and have total income of $60 + $35 = $95. Notice that her added income from 10 hours of work totals $20, the difference between her earnings and her reduction in welfare.

Your Turn 14.3: Assume that a welfare recipient works 10 hours at $6 per hour. Also assume that the best payment is $75, and that the implicit tax rate equals negative 1. Find her earnings, welfare grant, and total income. How much income does she gain by working? Note that for much of its history, AFDC had an implicit tax rate of –1 on most earnings.

Graphical analysis of work incentives and well-being

In order to analyze the effects of assistance programs on work effort and well-being, the individual's budget line must be modified. The horizontal axis in Figure 14.3 is measured from left to right in hours of leisure. Assuming that time use is limited to either work or leisure, work also can be seen on the horizontal axis as any time not consumed as leisure. Since one can't buy an hour of leisure at a store, the cost of leisure is an implicit cost that includes the foregone wage the person might have earned during that hour. Therefore, as a simplifying assumption, the price of an hour of leisure is often assumed to equal the marginal change in income the person would receive from an added hour of work.

The budget line is different from the usual consumer budget in one other way. In the basic budget line income is assumed to be fixed and acts as a constraint on the quantities of goods one can buy. In this labor hours model income is a variable that is determined by one's wage and choice of leisure versus work hours. So what *is* the constraint in this case? The constraint is provided by one's wealth. This wealth includes the value of one's savings or other assets and the potential dollar value of one's time. If the person has no income from financial assets, the person's wealth would equal the wage times the total number of hours the person could possibly work. In Figure 14.3 this would be $24 \cdot w$, the wage. If income

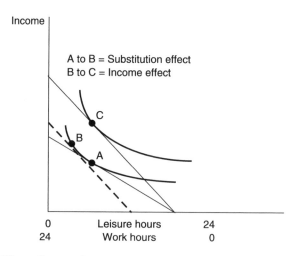

Figure 14.3 Effects of a wage increase

equals $24 \cdot w$ and the price if leisure is w, then the X endpoint on the budget line will equal $24 \cdot w/w$, or 24. If the person also has unearned income, the budget line will begin at some vertical distance above 24 hours of leisure.

The primary difference between the wage increase in Figure 14.3 and public assistance in Figure 14.4 is the change in the slope of the budget line, and therefore the substitution effect. Wages increase the cost of an extra hour of leisure (the foregone wage) and therefore create a substitution effect in the direction of more work. When combined with the predicted reduction in work hours due to the income effect (assuming that income is a normal good), the net change in hours worked due to a wage increase is ambiguous.

Figure 14.4 shows the effect on labor hours of a public assistance program with an implicit tax rate between 0 and -1. Because the implicit tax rate lowers the net gain in income from an hour of work, the substitution effect predicts fewer hours worked. The income effect of this program also implies fewer hours worked if leisure is a normal good. Of course, both public assistance and higher wages increase the utility of the individual who receives them.

Many studies have explored the effect of cash assistance on work effort. In general the findings are consistent with the predictions of the theory, but are not large. For example, cross-state studies prior to TANF found that for each $100 increase in monthly benefits the average recipient would work two hours less per month (Blank 1997: 146), or somewhat more than one full-time week per year. This type of study measures only the income effect of the program, since the implicit tax rate was constant across states prior to TANF, so the full effect of the program on work hours would probably be a bit higher.

Another issue related to work incentives is welfare dependency. Critics of the AFDC program frequently argued that near-permanent reliance on AFDC was commonplace. Evidence on this issue was mixed. First, it was common for women

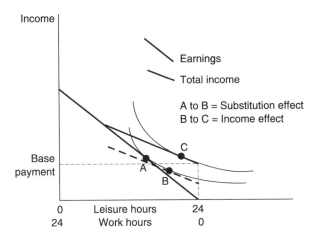

Figure 14.4 Effects of welfare

to enter and leave the welfare system periodically based on family and work factors. The average recipient collected benefits for less than two years consecutively (Blank 1997: 153). However, a relatively small percentage collected public assistance for far longer. About 7 percent of all recipients collected for over 10 consecutive years, and over 20 percent collected for more than 10 years during their lifetimes (ibid.). This group and other long-term recipients are the most directly affected by the TANF lifetime time limits.

Finally, studies have considered the effect of AFDC benefits and eligibility rules on family break-up and childbearing. To review, for much of its history AFDC applied only to female-headed families, primarily due to its original inclusion of only children. The AFDC-UP (unemployed parents) program was optional for states. Only after the Family Support Act of 1988 did this program become mandatory. Since family break-up was virtually mandated by AFDC regulations prior to the Family Support Act of 1988, this effect has been widely accepted. However, the causal link between the two has proven difficult to establish statistically (Moffitt 1992: 27-31). The effect of public assistance on the decision to bear children is also a matter of some controversy, and again the evidence to support the claim of a direct effect is weak (Blank 1997: 148-51).

The 1996 U.S. welfare reform law

In the U.S., proposals to reform AFDC have been dominated by concern about welfare dependence, work disincentives, or the total cost of the program. The work incentive program (WIN) of 1967 included a reduction of the implicit tax rate from -1 to $-2/3$ and some relatively ineffective work and training requirements. On the other hand, the 1981 revisions returned the implicit tax rate to -1 for most recipients and imposed more stringent national eligibility requirements in order to reduce the program's total cost. Various efforts to encourage work effort and job training have also occurred, along with two periods of state experimentation with variants of the federal program.

But by far the most radical restructuring of the cash assistance program came in 1996 when President Clinton signed a bill to replace the Aid to Families with Dependent Children program. This law changed public assistance in several ways, among which three are most notable. The most widely reported change in public assistance under TANF is the imposition of a lifetime maximum of five years' eligibility for federal TANF funds. States were allowed to impose shorter time limits, exempt 20 percent of their caseload from federal time limits, and support families for additional time using state funds. Secondly, the TANF program imposed additional work requirements on both individuals and states. TANF required recipients to engage in work-related activity within two years of entering the program. The policy also required the states to place an increasing percentage of beneficiaries in work for at least 30 hours per week. Work requirements, if enforced, offer relatively strong work incentives, as seen in Figure 14.5.

TANF also gave more freedom to the states to design their own assistance programs. With the exception of performance standards related to work, and a

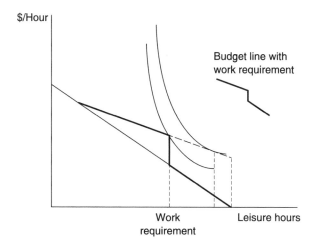

$/Hour

Budget line with
work requirement

Work
requirement

Leisure hours

Figure 14.5 Welfare with work requirement

requirement that states maintain total welfare spending of at least 75 percent of their final AFDC grant, states were free to set their own payment levels, implicit tax rates, and program designs. Finally, federal financing of TANF was provided through fixed block grants. These replaced cost-sharing arrangements under which the federal government paid greater amounts to states with higher benefit levels. Some changes were also made in complementary programs. Medicaid, the U.S. health insurance program for the poor, was separated from the cash assistance program and expanded to include all children in poor families as well as one year of coverage for all women who left welfare for employment. Also, childcare assistance was consolidated and expanded under this new program.

Since states have much more flexibility regarding most provisions of their public assistance programs under TANF, one cannot easily summarize its effects on specific policy design issues such as the implicit tax rate or employment incentives. However, many states included a significant reduction in the implicit tax rate as part of their program design. Implicit tax rates in the 50 percent range are now relatively common.

Your Turn 14.4: Graph the effects of a reduction in the implicit tax rate from −1 to −1/2. Are these effects more like those of a wage increase (Figure 14.1) or a welfare program (Figure 14.2)? Discuss the positive and negative aspects of this policy change.

Most states also significantly revised the role of welfare caseworkers, changing their main task from determining eligibility and payment levels to counseling
recipients on employment and training options (Nathan and Gais 1999). The most
common employment strategy in most states has been "work first," which, as the
name implies, offers advice on job search and job application skills but little in
the way of training or education. This approach, when combined with the time
limits and work requirements of TANF and expanded childcare and healthcare
eligibility, offered strong incentives to leave welfare and attempt to find part-time
or full-time work. Whether the households making this switch would actually find
permanent and gainful employment remained an open question.

Effects of the TANF reform

The majority view is that the effects of the seemingly draconian TANF program
have been less harmful to the poor than most critics expected. Among the most
significant effects of the program was a huge decrease in welfare caseloads, a
decline which began before the TANF program was implemented but accelerated
because of the program (Blank 2002: 1115-16). The total number of families
receiving welfare payments declined from 4.6 million in 1996 to 2.1 million in
2002. The percentage of eligible families receiving benefits dropped from 80 to
48 percent over the same time period (The Urban Institute 2006). The crucial
question then becomes: what became of these former public assistance recipients
and their dependents? There is considerable controversy about this issue, partly

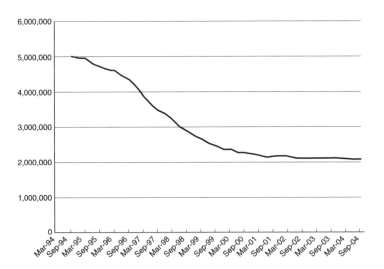

Source: National Conference of State Legislatures.

Figure 14.6 U.S. Welfare caseloads 1994-2004
Source: National Conference of State Legislatures. "Welfare caseload Watch," March 9,
2005 (http://www.ncsl.org/statefed/welfare/caseloadwatch.htm#overall).

because of mixed research findings and partly because of the continuing ideological debate regarding U.S. anti-poverty policy.

The positive view of this reform has come to dominate in recent years. According to evidence gathered by state surveys of former welfare recipients, the early effects of the TANF program are relatively positive. Labor force participation and employment rates among former welfare recipients have been quite high. Surveys of former recipients found employment rates in the first quarter after leaving ranging from 47 to 68 percent, with a figure in the mid to upper 50 percent range most typical (Acs and Loprest 2004: 28). In comparison, in 2005 the national employment/population ratio was about 62.5 percent for all adults and 56 percent for adult women. The percentage employed was similar in the fourth quarter after leaving assistance and earnings were generally higher, but only 20 to 40 percent of leavers worked in all four quarters of the first year after leaving the program. On average, these women worked over 35 hours per week with average hourly wages of $7.50 to $8.50 (Acs and Loprest 2004: 35).

However, the total income of this population has not necessarily improved and a substantial number of former recipients have not found steady and gainful employment. The National Survey of America's Families (http://www.urban.org/center/anf/nsaf.cfm) found that half of those who left welfare between 1997 and 1999 were employed and not receiving TANF in 1999. The other half included TANF recipients (22 percent), individuals living with a working partner (8.6 percent), and individuals with no partner and no employment (18.6 percent). Only a third of this last group had worked in the past year (Acs and Loprest 2004: 60). According to the same survey, 53 percent of former TANF recipients were officially poor in 1999. Adding the value of food stamps received lowers this to 41 percent (Acs and Loprest 2004: 76). A large percentage of this group would have been poor without the change of policy, but the overall well-being of the former AFDC population remains clouded as of 2006. For a more complete overview of the effects of the TANF program see the Urban Institute's website relating to the issue (http://www.urban.org/toolkit/issues/ welfarereform.cfm).

Multiple programs

The poor are often eligible for several types of public or private services or subsidies in addition to cash assistance. These include subsidized housing, food stamps, health insurance through the Medicaid program, child nutrition through the Women Infants and Children (WIC) and school lunch programs, and childcare assistance through state TANF programs. Participation in multiple subsidy and service programs changes the earlier equity and efficiency analysis of public assistance in two ways. First, these programs improve the real standard of living of some of the poor and reduce the true rate of poverty below the official figures, all else equal. Secondly, some of these subsidy programs have implicit tax rates of their own that further reduce the marginal benefits of an hour of work. For example, a person who had collected AFDC for more than four months in 1985 would have faced an implicit tax rate of −1. Adding a housing voucher program

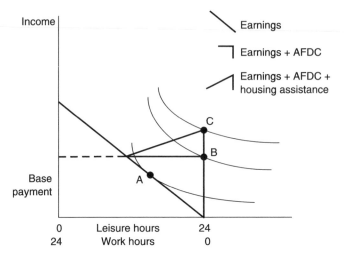

Figure 14.7 Multiple implicit tax rates

with an implicit tax rate of −3/10 produces a negative relation between work and income for a participant in both programs shown in Figure 14.7. If one adds the 0.25 implicit tax rate on Food Stamps, each dollar of added earnings could cost the individual collecting benefits from all three programs $1.55 in benefits, for a significant net loss per hour. Even with the reduced benefit reduction rates under TANF (approximately −1/2 is relatively common), the marginal change in income from an hour worked is still likely to be slightly negative. The rational consumer model predicts that the typical utility-maximizing individual will choose zero hours of work given these incentives. Those who blame government policy for creating a leisure class of AFDC recipients during this time can find support in Figure 14.7. Those who blame the poor directly cannot.

Other in-kind programs have cut-off points for eligibility after which the value of the program falls immediately to zero. In the U.S., Medicaid is an example of this type of policy. There is no gradual reduction in benefits received or increase in co-payments required. When one loses eligibility through increased income, the entire benefit of the program is lost. Such programs create cliffs or notches in the budget lines of recipients, as seen in Figure 14.8.

As noted earlier in this chapter, attitude surveys indicate that the majority of Americans believe that poverty is due primarily to the laziness of the poor while most Europeans believe that the poor are trapped in poverty through no fault of their own. In some respects the TANF program presents a major challenge to both views of poverty. The substantial reduction in welfare caseloads and increase in labor force participation among the eligible poor indicate that the U.S. poor are not lazy. On the other hand, the reduction in poverty rates among minorities and female-headed families during the 1990s suggests that poverty need not be a

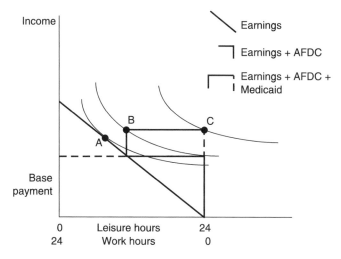

Figure 14.8 AFDC + Medicaid

permanent condition, particularly when policy change occurs during a period of unusual economic prosperity and low unemployment. Shiller's "big brother" category, which assigns part of the blame for poverty to the adverse incentives of government policy, apparently deserves at least a marginal place among the explanations of poverty.

In-kind versus cash benefits: the food stamp problem

Policies for the poor exist in many forms. Many of these programs provide benefits in the form of subsidies for only limited types of goods. Food stamps, housing vouchers, childcare subsidies and heating oil assistance are just a few U.S. examples of these **in-kind** or **directed benefit** programs. These specific benefit programs are relatively popular among the general public because they force the poor to use assistance for a narrowly defined set of necessities such as food or housing. However, economic theory provides an argument in favor of less restrictive cash grants.

Because cash grants allow greater freedom of choice, they also lead to equal or higher utility among the poor for a given amount of aid. The reasoning behind this claim can be clarified by a graph. In Figure 14.9, two persons with different tastes – Hal Green (solid indifference curves) and Dottie Rose (dashed indifference curves) – originally maximize their utility at points A and C, respectively. Two alternative policies are presented. The first is food stamps, which allows each person to receive a limited amount of food using government coupons

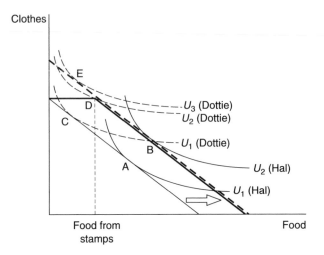

Figure 14.9 Food stamps vs. cash

without giving up any of their own money. This policy is represented by the kinked budget line in Figure 14.9. However, if the person wishes to spend some of her own earnings on food as well, additional units of food can be purchased at market prices. The effect of the program is to shift the budget line rightward by the value of the stamps without increasing the maximum affordable quantity of clothing or any non-food good. That is why the food stamp line is flat while the stamps are being used but returns to its original slope when the food stamps are gone. Both Sue and Hal are better off with the food stamps than without them, of course. Hal moves from point A to point B, while Dottie moves from point C to point D. At D she is using all of her food stamps for food, but is spending all of her original earnings on clothing.

The other policy option is a cash grant equal to the value of the food stamps. It is represented by the dashed line in Figure 14.9. Because cash can be spent freely on either food or clothes, both endpoints increase as with any rise in income. The cash grant is equally as valuable as food stamps for Hal because he can afford the consumption bundle at point B under either policy. For Dottie, however, cash provides more utility (point E versus point D). The general conclusion from this example is that only two outcomes are possible when comparing an in-kind benefit such as food stamps with cash. Either the person will be equally well off with either cash or stamps (Hal) or the person will be better off with the cash (Dottie). There is no third alternative. Specific benefit programs coexist with cash assistance in every developed country, so this theoretical argument is apparently not persuasive to policy makers.

Your Turn 14.5: Discuss additional reasons for favoring either cash benefits or food stamps as forms of aid to the poor. Which do you prefer, and why?

Conclusion

Poverty may be the most controversial policy issue discussed in this book. Even the basic meaning of poverty is the subject of irresolvable debate. The causes, frequency, and harms of poverty are also far from achieving a consensus. This chapter has attempted to show that critical thinking regarding even the most value-laden issues can benefit from the analysis of statistics and research-based evidence.

The substantial change in behavior among the U.S. poor in response to the TANF program and the accompanying economic boom of the late 1990s is capable of confounding those with almost any ideological point of view. Certainly the substantial response toward work indicates that the majority of recipients proved not to be lazy. The reaction of the welfare bureaucracy to the change, as well as the substantial increases in other forms of aid such as childcare subsidies and the earned income tax credit, also should be considered when analyzing the causes of this movement to work among the poor. On the other hand, the long-term effects of this program remain to be fully determined, and the continuing poverty and intermittent employment experienced by many former welfare recipients suggests that the TANF program has not been a complete success, except perhaps in the view of those who do not include poverty reduction or the well-being of the poor among the goals of anti-poverty programs.

There are other dimensions of the poverty problem that were not discussed in this chapter, such as health effects or the intergenerational transmission of poverty. Further reading from some of the sources provided in this chapter can fill these gaps in coverage. Also, though only a brief discussion of the relationship between ethics and anti-poverty policy was included in this chapter, one would benefit from reconsidering the implications of each of the main ethical theories discussed in Chapter 2 in the context of poverty.

Review questions

Conceptual questions

1. Discuss and compare the meanings of absolute and relative poverty. Then discuss the advantages and disadvantages of each concept as a measure of income inadequacy. Then include the multiple measures of access to income and basic services in your discussion. Which of the three do you prefer, and why?

2. Discuss how an absolute poverty measure might react to a deep recession or long period of growth, and why a relative measure might react differently.

3. In your view is the U.S. poverty line for a typical family size too high, too low, or about right? Why?

4. In his book *Losing Ground*, Charles Murray proposed eliminating all federal aid to the poor. Discuss this proposal in terms of the criteria for welfare programs listed in the chapter, and in terms of our ethical theories from Chapter 2.

Computational problems

5. Your Turn 14.2 presented a Lorenz curve and asked the reader to calculate the U.S. Gini coefficient for 2002. Now draw the Lorenz curve and calculate the Gini coefficient for 1968 from the following rounded income distribution figures. Has U.S. equality increased or decreased between 1968 and 2002?

U.S. income distribution, rounded

	Lowest 5th	Second 5th	Third 5th	Fourth 5th	Top 5th
1968	4%	11%	17%	25%	43%
2002	3%	9%	15%	23%	50%

6. The Work Incentive Program (WIN, not WIP) of 1967 reduced the implicit tax rate for AFDC from −1 to −2/3, and also established work effort requirements that turned out to be ineffective.

   (A) If the base payment is $50 per week and the person's wage is $6, calculate the amount of welfare, earnings, and total income he will receive after 20 hours of work.

   (B) Graph the income and substitution effects of this reduction in the implicit tax rate. Is this person working more or less based on your graph? Is the person better off?

   (C) Now assume that the recipient must work 30 hours per week to remain eligible for the program. Graph this budget line and compare it to your answer from part (B). Is the person working more with this requirement? Is he better off?

7. Question 4 above mentioned Charles Murray's proposal to eliminate public assistance programs.

   (A) Analyze graphically the effect of Murray's proposal on the work effort and utility of a former welfare recipient.

   (B) In a more recent book, *In Our Hands*, Mr. Murray proposed a universal aid program giving $10,000 per year to virtually every person

21 years of age or older. More specifically, assume that Murray's universal cash grant pays $800 per month with a zero implicit tax rate, while the combination of public assistance, housing allowances, and food stamps pays $1,200 per month with a combined implicit tax rate of −1.

1   Using income and substitution effects compare the well-being and work effort of those with very low work hours as they move from welfare to the universal cash grant program.
2   Now analyze the same issues for those who initially are not collecting public assistance.

15 Policies for the working poor: training, worker subsidies, and the minimum wage

There is nothing training cannot do. Nothing is above its reach. It can turn bad morals to good; it can destroy bad principles and recreate good ones; it can lift men to angelship.[1]

(Mark Twain)

The U.S. minimum wage of $5.15 an hour has not been raised in nearly a decade, and we believe it is out of date with the times.[2]

(Lee Scott, Wal-Mart CEO)

This chapter continues the analysis of anti-poverty programs with a review of three types of policies for low-income workers: job training, the minimum wage, and the earned income tax credit (EITC), a form of subsidy for working poor households. Public job training programs and the minimum wage produce mixed results and controversy regarding their effects on the working poor, while the EITC is almost universally lauded by economic analysts despite its limitations in providing for the basic needs of the poor.

As usual, this chapter begins by introducing economic concepts that allow us to interpret the training process and the social benefits and costs it produces. A brief history of federal training policy is then presented, followed by a guide to the evaluation of job training programs, a brief overview of past evaluations of job training programs, and case studies for the student. The minimum wage and earned income tax credit programs will then be discussed somewhat more briefly.

The problem: skills and the labor market

Those who lack marketable job skills also lack the opportunity for fully gainful employment. As noted in Chapter 14, many poor households include one or more full-time workers with insufficient earnings to lift the household out of poverty. The working poor are a primary target group for public sector training programs. Training programs also have been designed to benefit workers displaced by technological change or foreign imports. In the U.S. displaced workers are measured directly by the Department of Labor through data on total displaced workers and their labor market experience, as well as indirectly through data on mass layoffs by single employers (http://www.bls.gov/mls/home.htm), while poverty statistics can be found at http://www.census.gov/hhes/www/poverty.html.

Job skills concepts

Economists analyze the connection between skills and the labor market through human capital theory. This set of theoretical concepts, generally associated with Theodore Schultz and Gary Becker,[3] adapted the analysis of capital investment to several types of individual decisions involving long-run net benefits. Examples of these decisions include educational investments, job search, migration, property crime, and healthcare spending, as well as job training. These decisions are analyzed using the present value model presented in Chapters 7 and 8. In the case of job training or education there are a few additional concepts that allow us to relate public and private training decisions to the present value model. These concepts are general and specific skills, and private and social net benefits.

Human capital theory divides skills into two general categories: general and specific. **Perfectly general skills** are skills that can be applied to any employment situation. Basic education and good work habits are examples of general skills. **Occupational skills** such as auto repair or economic analysis can increase one's productivity at many different firms, and therefore are also properly categorized as general skills. Because general skills increase one's productivity for many employers, they also increase the market's demand for one's services, providing higher expected wages to the worker. According to human capital theory, the cost of acquiring general skills should be paid by the worker, since the worker receives the benefits. **Perfectly specific skills** increase a worker's productivity at one firm only. Examples include knowing the location of equipment in a particular firm or how to perform a task which is unique to a specific employer. Because specific skills do not increase a worker's productivity at other firms, they don't increase his or her market value, and therefore should be paid for by the employer.

> **Your Turn 15.1:** Discuss whether the skills learned in your major field are perfectly general or specific to a limited set of occupations. Also, discuss whether it seems rational to have students pay for the acquisition of general skills but not specific skills. Should university and post-graduate education be heavily subsidized despite this argument? Why or why not?

The rationale for government training programs

One U.S. anti-poverty policy whose theoretical justification is far stronger than its measured results is government-funded job training. The rationale for job training as an anti-poverty policy is straightforward. Increasing a worker's skills adds to his or her productivity and increases demand for the trainee's labor. If training accomplishes this basic goal, several direct or indirect benefits occur for the individual and for society as a whole. For example, trainees benefit from increased earnings and decreased risks of unemployment or arrest, government gains from decreased social spending and increased tax revenue, and the rest of society benefits from decreased crime costs and an overall increase in productivity.

Government support for job training can be justified on ethical grounds as well. Two very different ethical arguments combine to provide an unusually strong moral underpinning for job training as a policy for the working poor. One is the injustice of having a large group of full-time workers who are poor. The other is the positive dimension of industriousness provided by full-time work, a social good in many cultures that is likely to be enhanced through the availability of subsidized training. A third factor is the tradition of free or heavily subsidized public education in most of the world. Ineffective or highly unequal educational opportunities and limited access to higher education provide commonly accepted arguments for some type of government support for adult vocational education.

Efficiency arguments for government support of job training arise from imperfections in the labor market and possible external benefits from enhanced individual skills. The competitive assumptions of homogeneous products, perfect information, and perfect mobility have limited accuracy in the labor market. As workers or employers we are not identical, are seldom fully aware of our full range of employment opportunities, and cannot costlessly move to any available job. In combination, mobility costs and diverse skills create a number of different sub-markets for labor – for example, the market for carpenters in London. Imperfect information creates a costly and somewhat risky job search process for workers, and an imperfect hiring process for employers. These market imperfections create a window of opportunity for a series of government services such as employment agencies, unemployment compensation, and remedial and vocational education programs.

Job training institutions can have imperfections similar to those of the labor market as a whole. Training and education can vary greatly in quality, and information about the quality of training or education is often limited for the employer or the prospective student. In the United States, vocational training is provided through a highly decentralized system of private and public sources. This type of vocational training system faces problems due to low levels of information about individual training programs and a lack of product rating services. Furthermore, in the U.S. there is a lack of nationally accepted certification standards in many of the skilled trades.[4] These factors create a lack of reliable information about workers' skills.

Your Turn 15.2: Discuss your strategies for searching for work as you approach your degree. Discuss when you will start your search, which information sources you will explore, and how you will choose among (hopefully) multiple offers.

Another problem with training relates to property rights. Firms that train their employees often provide skills that are industry- or occupation-specific, rather than firm-specific, and may increase the worker's market value. Therefore, firms have a limited incentive to train workers, particularly in a nation like the United States where workers often move between firms several times during their working lives. Similarly, private sector training opportunities are expensive, and workers with limited budgets and access to capital also experience barriers to training. Therefore, unless both firms and workers have some ability to capture the benefits of their training investments, the private sector may under-invest in worker training.

Other nations reduce these market imperfections in various ways. For example, Germany and the Netherlands are among the nations that offer vocational training through apprenticeship programs that train a large majority of industrial workers in general and occupational skills during early adulthood (Lynch 1994: 78-86).[5] France and Australia have imposed a training tax on employers, requiring the firms to either engage in training or pay the training tax. Larger firms in Japan traditionally have followed a strategy of training and job rotation, particularly during slack production periods, as an alternative to layoffs. Also, Japanese workers often face a significant wage and benefit reduction if they voluntarily change jobs. Therefore, the employer is more likely to capture the benefits of their training expenditures. Many nations offer national certification in skilled trades, another policy that improves information in the labor market.

A brief history of U.S. public sector job training

In the U.S., government involvement in job training was very limited prior to the 1960s. The New Deal employment programs of the depression era provided work and a minimal wage, but seldom included explicit provisions for training. Federally funded job training for adults began in the Kennedy administration with the passage of the Manpower Development and Training Act in 1962. This Act funded two categories of programs: institutional training and on-the-job training. Institutional training involved remedial education and vocational training in a school-like setting, while on-the-job training provided employer-based experience and skills development.

Voluntary training programs

The Johnson administration's War on Poverty of the 1960s featured a free-for-all period of experimentation with job training approaches and programs. This era resulted in a plethora of programs under several different agencies, the majority of which were administered through the Department of Labor and the various state employment services. Among these early programs were the Job Corps, the Neighborhood Youth Corps, Operation Mainstream, the Job Bank, Upward Bound, the Work Incentive Program (WIN), the National Alliance of Businessmen's Job Opportunities in the Business Sector (NAB-JOBS), the Concentrated Employment Program, and several others. Educational and employment services offered through these programs included remedial education, training in specific occupational skills, subsidies to employers who hired program participants, subsidized work experience at government or non-profit agencies, and job search assistance. These services remain at the core of job training design today. Figure 15.1 displays an organizational chart of War on Poverty training programs as of 1972. The details of the chart are far less important than its overall impression. The War on Poverty was an era of experimentation and action. Its organization and efficiency left something to be desired. Not surprisingly, the War on Poverty's job training efforts produced critics even among liberals, who found the numerous federal programs to be repetitive, wasteful, overly bureaucratic and difficult to access.

The first major overhaul of the training bureaucracy was provided by the Comprehensive Employment and Training Act (CETA) of 1974. This Act attempted to rationalize the War on Poverty training programs in two ways: consolidation and decentralization. Under this program local organizations applied directly to the federal government for grants to run training and employment programs for the disadvantaged. Few of the War on Poverty initiatives survived as independent programs. One section of the CETA program provided funds for public sector employment. This part of the program became more significant during the Carter administration, and came to be seen as dominating the training component of the program. The CETA program was replaced in the first Reagan administration.

The next phase in training policy was the Job Training Partnership Act (JTPA) of 1982. This program revised CETA by distributing money to state governors rather than local agencies, and by giving veto power over state programs to private industry councils. These adjustments were adopted in order to decrease the federal bureaucracy that had apparently built up around the approval and oversight of local sponsors, and to include business more explicitly in program design. Total funding for training and employment programs was also cut significantly during the Reagan years. The most recent reorganization of job training took place in 2000 with the passage of the Workforce Investment Act. The primary policy revision in this Act was also administrative. It emphasized the formation of unified local centers for the delivery of education, training, and counseling services.

Public assistance and training requirements

The programs described above were primarily voluntary for individuals. Other job training programs which have also undergone revisions over time involve required work and/or training for those receiving public assistance. Beginning in 1967, the **Work Incentive Program (WIN)** changed the implicit tax rate from −1 to −2/3, as discussed in Chapter 14, and with some exceptions required welfare recipients to register for WIN training, employment, and or job placement services. As with many other training programs, lack of funding and participation were problems. Welfare recipients were required to register but not participate, and funding was far short of what was needed to provide services such as daycare or transportation assistance for welfare recipients.

Manpower Programs and Funding Patterns

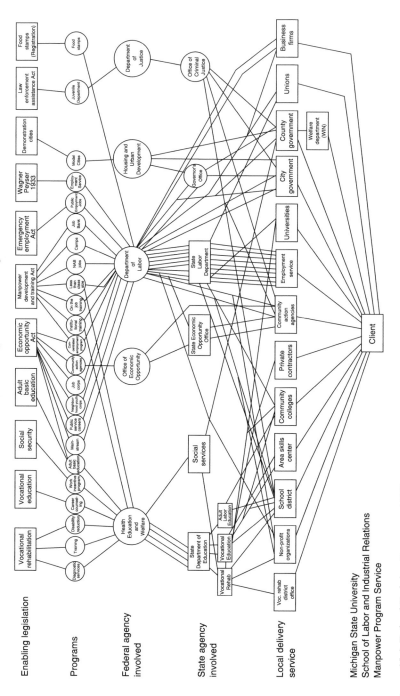

Figure 15.1 Federal Training Programs: 1972

Note: This chart was part of my class notes for a graduate course taught by Daniel Kruger at Michigan State University in 1972. I was unable to find a published source for this chart.

Michigan State University
School of Labor and Industrial Relations
Manpower Program Service

The WIN program was modified with the passage of the **Job Opportunities and Basic Skills (JOBS)** program in 1989, which among other things was the second program to use the JOBS acronym. This program added participation requirements to the WIN formula, and also required states to provide at least two of four possible services: on-the-job training, job placement assistance, public service jobs, or wage subsidies. States were provided with a maximum of $1 billion in federal matching grants. The welfare reform of 1996 ended this specific program. However, states were given block grants and strong incentives to reduce the number of recipients and to provide job placement and support services, including training and education.

The frequent revisions of training program design suggest at least two dilemmas for training policy. First, target groups and preferred policy designs vary across time and the political spectrum. Secondly, there have been recurring problems with overlap and disorganization in the administration of federal training programs. Despite the apparent improvement in the administrative structure of federal training policy since the adoption of CETA, program overlap and duplication is still a problem (GAO 2000). Underlying these frequent changes are the mixed results attained from benefit–cost studies of various training programs.

Evaluating training programs

This section of the chapter includes a review of the methods for conducting benefit–cost analyses of training programs and multiple case studies. The goal of this section is to give the student a firm enough background to critically review alternative training policies and understand benefit–cost studies of this type of program.

The fundamental goal of a training program is to increase the skills and employability of trainees. Improving employability through training can result in measurable benefits to recipients such as increased earnings and decreased unemployment, as well as effects on non-recipients such as reduced crime and reduced government social spending. Because of ethical concerns and the voluntary nature of many training programs, it is important to consider the net benefits for program participants independently from the net benefits for society as a whole. A voluntary training program that benefits society but provides a net loss for program recipients is unlikely to attract many volunteers, in addition to failing most ethical tests.

Several of our earlier efficiency and cost–benefit tools come together in the analysis of training programs. Because the benefits of training are expected to persist over several years, present value discounting is an important part of the analysis. Also, because training might reduce the likelihood of negative occurrences such as unemployment or crime, expected value (see Chapter 9) is also important. Because program effectiveness will be analyzed separately for program participants and for society as a whole, a modified version of our analysis of the net gains or surpluses for various groups will also be used.

Estimating earnings effects

The most direct benefits from a training program are increased employment and earnings for the trainee. The most difficult challenge in measuring the effect of training on earnings is controlling for other factors besides program participation that affect earned income. Variables such as prior schooling, school quality, family background, age, race, and sex affect earnings and employment, and must be controlled for in order to isolate the effects of training. There are two general ways of controlling for these other factors: experimental and non-experimental methods. **Non-experimental studies** attempt to control for other factors affecting income through advanced econometric methods. **Experimental studies** establish two groups as part of the study, an experimental group that participates in the program, and a control group that does not. These two groups must be as similar as possible. An early study of the Upward Bound program by Garms (1971) utilized a control group made up of older siblings of the same sex as the participants. Most experimental studies randomly assign individuals who are eligible for the program to experimental and control groups, a method that is also common in human drug testing. More recent literature suggests that experimental methods using control groups are more reliable than non-experimental methods (Friedlander *et al.* 1997).

While a detailed discussion of statistical methods for estimating a program's effects on earnings is beyond the scope of this book, the basic process for analyzing the net benefits of a training program is not. The steps for analyzing training programs will be outlined and explained. Examples will follow.

Steps in estimating training benefits and costs

The basic steps in conducting a benefit–cost analysis of training are as follows:

1 List all possible private benefits and costs to program recipients and external net benefits to other members of society. Other members of society include government and the general public. Social net benefits, or benefits to all of society, are the sum of the two.
2 Quantify all private benefits and costs, including non-marketed benefits such as reduced theft and drug use, for several years into the future. The net benefits for trainees are measured as the difference between the experience of the training group and the experience of the control group. Future net benefits are then discounted to present value.
3 Quantify the external net benefits for other private individuals and government for several years into the future.
4 Add the net benefits for trainees and for the rest of society to find the social net benefits. Discount future social net benefits to present value.
5 Report the discounted net benefits for trainees and for society as a whole. If both figures are positive, the program should be retained. If both figures are negative, the program should probably be repealed. If the trainee's net benefit is negative, both practical and ethical reasons exist for canceling the program. If society's net benefits are negative, the program could be canceled on efficiency grounds.

Private net benefits, or benefits to program participants, include increased after-tax earnings during and after training due to increased hourly wages, a higher probability of employment, more hours of work, and increased benefits such as health insurance or paid vacations. Labor compensation is a measure which includes both wages and the dollar value of benefits, and therefore provides a convenient measure of the benefits of employment. Ideally this benefit should include any increases in compensation extending throughout a person's lifetime, although this is nearly always impossible. **Private costs** include any expenditures or lost income to the experimental group occurring because of program participation. Foregone wages from previous employment are an important component of private cost, along with any out-of-pocket expenses, reduction in revenue due to reduced criminal activities, and lost unemployment insurance or other government payments.

External net benefits equal the net benefits for other members of society and government. The general public benefits from the reduced costs of crime, among other factors, while government benefits through decreased social spending and increased tax revenue. Of course, government also bears much or all of the administrative and operating costs of the program.

Social net benefits are the sum of private and external net benefits. When one combines a program's effects on participants and the rest of society, some flows between the program participants and the rest of society tend to cancel each other. For example, reduced property crime leads to reduced illegal income for the program recipients and a somewhat greater reduction in crime costs for the rest of society. This occurs because illegal goods have lower value than legally owned goods. In benefit–cost analysis any reduction in income must be subtracted from the total net benefits even if the income source is illegal activity. Similarly, reduced public assistance or unemployment insurance payments are a cost to program participants but a roughly equal benefit to the rest of society, and may not appear in the final social net benefit figures.

Most training studies track program participants for a few years after their participation ends. Evidence of increased employment and earnings or decreased crime is provided only for these few years. Evidence about the persistence of benefits beyond the relatively few years of a typical study is quite scarce, but a couple of tentative conclusions are possible. Follow-up studies have found persistent income gains for programs that emphasize the development of general or occupation-specific skills. Programs that emphasize job placement and experience rather than training or education have shown short-term cost-effectiveness but less persistent income gains (Friedlander *et al.* 1997: 1836). In light of this relatively inadequate evidence, using sensitivity analysis to provide high, low, and intermediate estimates of future earnings is a wise choice. At this time a reasonable high-end estimate would be to continue the net benefits found for the final year studied throughout the working life of the individual, while a low estimate might assume that net benefits end within a few years of the conclusion of the study.

Job training studies

After a brief review of the evidence regarding federal job training programs, two examples will be provided. The second example provided in the Appendix to this chapter is quite challenging. Hundreds of benefit–cost evaluations of job training programs have been completed over the past four decades.[6] The majority of early studies found that job training programs provide modestly positive net benefits for adults, particularly adult women, but generally fail for the young. These results also indicate that on-the-job training may have somewhat higher net benefits than basic adult education. Relatively recent experimental studies have found more positive results for men and youth and high internal rates of return for the voluntary training programs funded through the Job Training Partnership Act. The residential component of the Job Corps program has received mixed reviews.

Mandatory training and job placement programs for welfare recipients have existed since the 1960s through the Work Incentive Program, the Job Opportunities and Basic Skills Program, and as part of the work requirements included in the Temporary Aid for Needy Families Act (TANF) of 1996. However, mandatory training, education, or work requirements do not always translate into actual participation. Some welfare recipients may accept financial penalties or leave the program rather than undertake training. However, experimental studies of actual training participants have found generally positive effects on earnings from both the WIN and JOBS programs (Friedlander *et al.* 1997: 1839-46).

Job Corps

A more detailed example should help to explain the evaluation process and some of the effects of training. The **Job Corps** is a U.S. residential training and education program for disadvantaged youth which began in 1964 as one of the myriad of training programs under the War on Poverty. It is unique in having survived several reorganizations of federal training policy as an independent and largely unchanged program. The Job Corps was designed to provide intensive education, training, socialization, and placement services to disadvantaged youth. According to a 2001 study of the Job Corps program, about 80 percent of participants are high school dropouts, 70 percent are members of minority groups, and 27 percent have been in trouble with the law prior to entry (Burghardt *et al.* 2001).

Most Job Corps program participants dwell in residential centers. Separation from poor home and neighborhood environments was one of the key elements in the original program design, and while the original rural centers have been supplemented by urban residential programs, the residential program remains Job Corps' most unique characteristic. There is no fixed time schedule for attendance. While the average length of stay at the residential centers is about eight months, almost 25 percent resided at the centers for over a year while between 25 and 30 percent stayed less than three months (Burghardt *et al.* 2001: 10).

The primary services provided for Job Corps participants are counseling, remedial education, job training, and work experience. Education programs prepare participants for the General Educational Development (GED) high school equivalency certificate. Many participants receive remedial education before enrolling in actual GED preparation classes. Job skills are provided for a range of occupations which varies across individual Job Corps centers. Most job training prepares recipients for jobs in clerical, mechanical, construction, or service occupations.

Evaluations of the Job Corps program have produced conflicting results over the years. However, larger experimental studies (Long *et al.* 1981; Mathematica Policy Research 2001) have tended to produce positive net benefits for both participants and society as a whole. Benefits to participants include higher literacy rates, employment rates, higher average wages, and more hours worked per week. Benefits to the rest of society include lower crime rates and reduced spending on public assistance and other social programs. No change has been found in the likelihood of attending or completing college. Costs for the Job Corps program are quite substantial, averaging about $14,000 per participant according to the Mathematica study (2001: 5).

Mathematica reported in 2001 that measured increases in earnings began in the third year after the program and averaged $1,150 in the fourth and final year studied. However, if measured increases in earnings persist over the participant's lifetime, the present value of private benefits would total an estimated $31,000, with benefits to society as a whole of $17,000 per recipient (Burghardt *et al.* 2001: 5). Clearly the positive findings in the Mathematica study are highly sensitive to the assumption of persistent lifetime earnings gains. In this specific case, a final report by Mathematica found that earnings gains did not persist for most Job Corps participants, and that the social net benefits of the program were actually negative. It also found that the net benefits for the participants remained positive, and that older entrants (age 20-24) did see persistent increases in earnings (Schochet *et al.* 2003). This finding was discussed in Chapter 9 as an example of uncertainty. In this case it serves a more specific purpose.

Your Turn 15.3: A relatively basic training problem

As an analyst for the Congressional Budget Office, you have been given the task of analyzing a training program entitled the Housework Initiative for Men (HIM), which trains men to do housework, thereby improving their employment and marriage prospects. This program has total training costs of $120,000, all of which is spent in the first year (year 0). During this time the program trains a total of 10 men. During their year of training each recipient receives a $5,000 wage from the government in addition to training. After training, all 10 find jobs as cooks, housekeepers, or childcare workers with an average salary of $20,000. The control group also consists of 10 men. Five are working at part-time jobs in retail or lawn care, earning an average of $6,000 per year. They also collected $2,000 per year in food stamps. The other five work as truck drivers, earning $20,000 per year. Assume that all of the program's effects last for three years after the training period and then disappear.

Step 1:
Table 15.1 will help you organize the effects of the HIM program prior to discounting. The change in government payments includes training costs and the reduction in food stamp payments for recipients. In this example, "government" also represents the rest of society.

Table 15.1 Net benefits for the "HIM" program

	Year 0	Year 1	Year 2 (same as year 1)	Year 3
(1) ΔGovernment payments				
(2) Income for trainees				
(3) Income for control group				
(4) Net benefits for trainees				
(5) Net benefits for rest of society				
(6) Net benefits for all of society				

Step 2: Discounting
(A) In the late 1980s as standard policy the Congressional Budget Office used a discount rate of 0.02, or 2 percent. Find the discounted net benefits for recipients and for society as a whole, and make a recommendation regarding its adoption.
(B) Also in the late 1980s the Office of Management and Budget used a discount rate of 0.10, or 10 percent. Would they support this proposal? Recalculate the discounted net benefits for HIM participants and for society to find out.

Step 3: Should this program be retained or eliminated? Why?

Job training and placement services have become increasingly important under the TANF programs of most states. In light of the somewhat mixed findings from previous training program studies, the ultimate success of the TANF employment programs cannot be guaranteed.

The minimum wage

In the U.S. the national minimum wage was created under the Fair Labor Standards Act of 1938. Its main purpose was to provide a "minimum standard of living necessary for health, efficiency and general well-being of workers" (U.S. Code: Title 29, Chapter 8, Section 202) by creating a wage floor above the labor market's lowest equilibrium wage levels. The original Fair Labor Standards Act

set the minimum wage for covered workers at 25 cents per hour. The federal minimum wage has been raised many times in the following years, and as of now is
set at $5.15 per hour for covered workers. The Act has also been amended several
times to raise the number of workers covered under the law. Approximately
88 percent of non-supervisory employees in private industry are now covered by the
federal minimum wage. The primary groups of workers not covered are executive,
administrative, and professional personnel, household workers, workers in certain
recreational industries, those who regularly receive tips, and agricultural workers.

Most American workers are not directly affected by this federal wage floor
because they earn well above the minimum. In 2005, only 2.5 percent of American
workers earned the $5.15 minimum wage or less (Bureau of Labor Statistics 2006).
Of the approximately 1.9 million minimum wage earners, about one-half were
under age 25 and about one-quarter were aged 16 to 19 (ibid.). Minimum wage
workers typically work part-time in the service sector of the economy.

A minimum wage model

The minimum wage is a form of price floor (see Chapter 5), and a simple price
floor model can be used to display the predicted effects of the minimum wage.
Figure 15.2 displays the simple introductory version of a minimum wage model.
In this model a minimum wage above the equilibrium raises the wage, but also
lowers employment from L_1 to L_{min}, raises the quantity of labor supplied, and
creates a labor surplus (unemployment). Theoretically, a minimum wage could
either increase or decrease the total earnings (wage • labor hours) of labor,
depending on the elasticity of demand for labor (see Chapter 3). If elasticity of

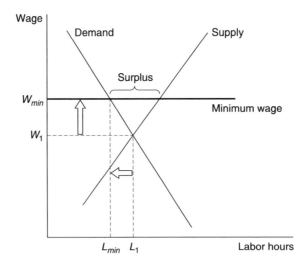

Figure 15.2 Minimum wage

demand for labor is greater than one, an increase in the minimum wage would reduce total earnings. If demand is inelastic, total earnings would rise.

Most studies of the minimum wage have found that a rise in the minimum wage will lead to a relatively small decline in employment, as the perfectly competitive model predicts. An early consensus was that a 10 percent increase in the minimum wage reduces teenage employment by 1 to 3 percent (Brown 1988). A smaller increase in the minimum wage typically has little or no negative effect on employment, although it may reduce hours per worker. Studies also found that the greatest effect is felt by the teenage working population.

A two-market model and other minimum wage effects

Two related questions involving the effects of the minimum wage are not answered by the one market model: (1) What happens to workers who are displaced by the minimum wage? (2) What happens to workers not covered by the minimum wage? These and other questions can be answered by considering a model that divides the low-wage labor market into covered and uncovered sectors (Welch 1974). The uncovered sector includes legal workers not covered by the minimum wage, workers in illegal sectors such as sweatshops, and others such as food servers who are covered by a far lower minimum wage. These workers comprise the labor supply in the uncovered market seen in Figure 15.3.

As drawn in Figure 15.3, the two markets have identical demand and supply curves and an initial equilibrium at wage W_1 and employment level L_1. The minimum wage causes a decrease in employment to L_d and an increase in labor supply to L_s in the covered market. Based on the height of the supply curve, workers originally employed in the covered market are willing to work for a wage of W_1 or lower, while those who enter the covered market after the minimum wage is imposed are not willing to work for a wage of W_1. Workers displaced by the minimum

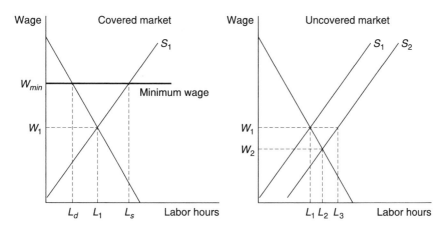

Figure 15.3 Minimum wage, two-market model

wage will seek work in the uncovered market at the original wage of W_1. This will shift the supply curve in the uncovered market to the right by the amount of the covered market's employment loss (L_3–L_1 in the uncovered market equals L_1–L_d in the covered market). Because of the supply shift the wage in the uncovered market will fall, and some of the displaced workers will drop out of the labor force.

When combined, the two sectors in Figure 15.3 have smaller and more ambiguous effects than the single market model in Figure 15.2. If labor demand is highly inelastic at low wages, total earnings will rise in the covered market but fall in the uncovered market. The overall effect of the minimum wage on the earnings of low-income workers becomes a statistical question that is very difficult to answer given the role of illegal employment in the uncovered market. The total number of jobs lost due to the minimum wage is also reduced by the existence of an uncovered market. Using the two-market model, all workers displaced by the minimum wage are willing to seek work in the uncovered market, but as the uncovered wage falls, the labor supplied falls from L_3 to L_2. It is this loss of quantity supplied in the uncovered market that represents the total net loss of jobs in the two markets.

In the presence of the uncovered market, our list of gainers and losers can be refined somewhat. Those who retain minimum wage jobs are clearly better off. Those displaced workers who find jobs in the uncovered sector have lower wages, but lose less than indicated in Figure 15.2. Those originally employed in the uncovered sector are worse off because of the lower wage. Finally, displaced workers who cannot or will not work for the lower uncovered market wage (W_2 in Figure 15.3) end up outside of the labor force and without earnings. These side effects of the uncovered market cushion some of the negative effects from the minimum wage.

A debate over the minimum wage

Supporters of the minimum wage argue that it offers higher incomes to working poor families, has little or no negative effect on employment, reduces the exploitation of labor by management, and is particularly important as a minimum ethical standard for the fair treatment of workers. Opponents argue that the minimum wage cuts employment opportunities for low-skill workers, raises prices for consumers, and distorts the market.

In the 1990s the finding that an increase in the minimum wage decreased the quantity of labor demanded was challenged. Card and Krueger (1994) found that an increase in the state minimum wage in New Jersey did not decrease employment, but actually increased it slightly, relative to a control group in Pennsylvania. An increase in employment could result from a minimum wage if the labor market is imperfect in some ways. Suppose, for instance, employers have **monopsony** power as buyers of labor. A monopsonist is a single buyer in a market, the opposite in some respects of a monopolist. A monopsony would maximize profits by hiring where the marginal cost of labor equals demand, at labor quantity L_1 in Figure 15.4. A minimum wage replaces part of the market supply curve with a

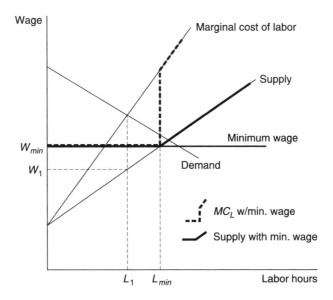

Figure 15.4 Monopsony with minimum wage

flat relationship between the wage and quantity of labor supplied, thereby creating the possibility that more workers would be hired at a higher wage. In Figure 15.4 the minimum wage raises the quantity of labor hired to L_{min}, as well as increasing the hourly wage. Secondly, the higher minimum wage could have the same effects as an efficiency wage; the higher wage might motivate workers to work harder, thereby raising employment demand. The higher wage could also attract more productive, higher-quality workers to the market, thereby increasing the productivity of labor and labor demand.

Evidence of minimum wage effects

In 1992, New Jersey increased its state minimum wage to $5.05, while the bordering state of Pennsylvania remained at the federal minimum of $4.25. The standard minimum wage model tells us that employment would decline in New Jersey and stay the same in Pennsylvania, all else equal. In a study of fast-food restaurants, David Card and Alan Krueger (1994) found that employment went up somewhat, creating a conflict with standard theory. David Neumark and William Wascher (2000) later published a paper about the New Jersey case using different data and concluded that the rise in the minimum wage had reduced employment. Card and Krueger's reply (2000) defended and extended their original results, but also left open the possibility that while total employment had not fallen, the average hours per worker may have (ibid.). When this particular set of evidence is combined with early U.S. studies (Brown *et al.* 1982), which were nearly unanimous in their conclusions that the minimum wage reduced labor hours, the preponderance of evidence suggests that demand for low-wage labor is quite inelastic (if not zero), and that modest minimum wage increases will decrease labor hours by a relatively small percentage. The resulting effect on the total earnings of low-wage labor would be positive due to the low elasticity of demand, even if the employment effect is negative.

Since the goal of this chapter is to review alternative policies for the working poor, the effect of the minimum wage on poverty should also be considered. Interestingly, most U.S. evidence suggests that a large majority of minimum wage or near-minimum wage workers are not poor. This is possible if an individual is a secondary worker in a non-poor household, a common occurrence. Studying data from the early 1990s, when the minimum wage increased from $3.35 to $4.25, Burkhauser *et al.* (1996) found that 22 percent of those earning less than $4.25 lived in poor households, 20.3 percent lived in households with income between two and three times the poverty level, and almost 33 percent lived in households making more than three times the poverty level. Taking a different approach, Addison and Blackburn (1999) noted that poverty rates were higher for teens and young adults, that the minimum wage significantly reduced the poverty rates of teens (but not young adults), and was particularly beneficial for the young with the least education. Overall, the minimum wage suffers as an anti-poverty measure by frequently missing the poor population.

The earned income tax credit

A less well-known but important U.S. policy for the working poor is the earned income tax credit, or EITC. This policy is a type of refundable income tax credit for workers living in low-income households. The word "refundable" means that a working poor family receives a relatively substantial payment from the government even if it does not earn enough to owe federal income tax. To claim the EITC for 2004 a person had to meet the following income requirements:

1. The taxpayer must have earned income from employment or from self-employment.
2. The taxpayer's earned income and adjusted gross income (AGI) must be less than $34,458 if the taxpayer has more than one qualifying child, $30,338 if the taxpayer has one qualifying child, $11,490 if the taxpayer has no qualifying child ($12,490 if married, filing jointly).
3. The taxpayer's investment income (such as interest) must be $2,650 or less.

   (Source: http://www.irs.gov/individuals/article/0,,id=96456,00.html)

Nearly 21 million U.S. households received the EITC in 2003 and EITC spending totaled about $38 billion. Note that the cutoff point is far above the poverty line, particularly for families with one or more children, but does exclude those from high-income families.

Effects of the earned income tax credit

The EITC acts like a producer subsidy for poor workers and their families. As seen in Chapter 5, a producer subsidy tends to shift the supply curve outward, thereby lowering the consumers' price but increasing the quantity traded and the producer's total revenue per unit (the consumer's price plus the subsidy). Figure 15.5 shows the general effects of this type of subsidy. The subsidy is predicted to lower the wage paid by employers from W_1 to W_2, but raise the workers' full wage from W_1 to W_2 + subsidy. Employment will increase because of the subsidy.

A subsidy produces inefficiency through overproduction, but as a method of help-ing the working poor the EITC has several advantages over the minimum wage. First, employment is increased, not decreased. Secondly, the program aids only the work-ing poor, rather than middle-class teens or young adults. Thirdly, the EITC will tend to reduce production costs and consumer prices slightly, rather than increase them. Only the government is worse off because of a worker subsidy such as the EITC.

The earned income tax credit has not been studied in the same detail as the minimum wage or public assistance. However, its effects on recipients' incentives and well-being are relatively easy to display on our income–leisure graph. The budget line for the EITC recipient is very different from that of the TANF recip-ient. Figure 15.6 displays the budget line for unmarried EITC recipients with one child. Those earning less than $7,500 receive a subsidy of 34 percent of their earned income. At $7,500 they receive a maximum EITC subsidy of $2,550. Recipients can keep that total until their earnings exceed $13,750, after which they face an implicit tax rate of 16 percent and gain 0.84 times their wage for each addi-tional hour worked. The cutoff point for this program is quite high (over $29,600)

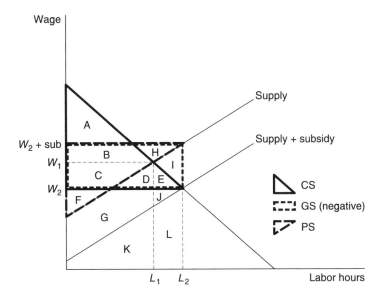

Figure 15.5 Labor subsidy

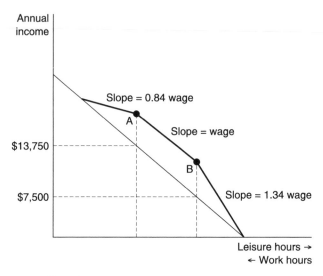

Figure 15.6 Budget line with EITC

given the low implicit tax rate on this flatter portion of the recipient's budget line. Since only the highest-income EITC recipients face a negative implicit tax rate, and that rate is far lower than any TANF rate, its work incentive effects are clearly less negative than public assistance.

Your Turn 15.4: Analyze the income and substitution effects of the EITC for each of the three segments in Figure 15.6. In which segment are hours worked most likely to decrease? Why? For which segment does the EITC act like a negative income tax? Unearned income? A wage increase?

Two aspects of the EITC make a graphical analysis of its effects inadequate. First, the work requirement is not included in the above graph, and would clearly encourage some level of labor force participation. Secondly, most EITC recipients receive their subsidy as a one-time payment rather than a regular source of income. The EITC subsidy is most often used for bill paying or large purchases rather than regular living expenses (Smeeding *et al.* 2000). Marginal work decisions are probably less likely to be affected by one-time payments than by regular income. Overall, however, this subsidy program is quite popular as a form of income support for the working poor.

Conclusion

This chapter provides an overview of the economic concepts and analytical tools involved in the analysis of public job-training programs, minimum wages, and employment subsidies, three main tools for helping the working poor. Training was analyzed using some of our earlier tools, including private and social net benefits and present value discounting. The experimental approach emphasized in the training analysis section can work in other contexts, including private training and educational decisions. The history of federal job training and brief review of past studies of job training programs indicate that job training has a positive role to play in anti-poverty policy, but that neither the efficient administration of the various training programs nor an ideal design for the actual training process has been accomplished.

The minimum wage and EITC reviews were less detailed, though the use of relatively basic market and individual choice models made the theoretical component of the analysis relatively straightforward. In this case the efficiency effects of the minimum wage seem to be less consistent with the well-being of the working poor than those of a subsidy such as the earned income tax credit. However, ethical arguments favoring the minimum wage, particularly those related to minimum moral standards, seem to provide a positive basis for the policy's political popularity. Also, the positive effect of the minimum wage on labor earnings, if not employment, appears to effectively counteract the efficiency and employment losses that may occur due to the policy. As for the EITC, the only disadvantage associated with this relatively efficient and beneficial subsidy program is the common payment of benefits as an annual lump sum rather than steady flow of assistance, which limits the program's potential for providing for the basic needs of recipients.

Review questions

Conceptual questions

1. List three externalities of government training programs. Are these positive or negative externalities?
2. Differentiate between experimental and non-experimental studies.
3. Explain how a decrease in criminal activity could lead to a decrease in marginal benefits for a training participant but a net benefit to society.
4. Some studies have found that the net benefits to trainees from on-the-job training are higher than for adult basic education. Explain why this might be true.
5. In the U.S. there are two national efforts under way to increase the minimum wage. The first is to increase the federal minimum wage from $5.15 to $7.25 per hour. The other is known as the "living wage" movement, which generally raises the minimum wage for government employees and the employees of government contractors in large urban areas to a much higher level, perhaps $9 to $12 per hour. Compare the probable employment effects of each, and discuss the ethical and political advantages or disadvantages of each approach.
6. Compare the minimum wage and the earned income tax credit based on the criteria for judging welfare programs listed in Chapter 14. Also compare them on the basis of the leaky bucket analogy (Chapter 4), and the ethical

theories presented in Chapter 2. Which do you prefer personally, and are there any changes you would recommend to your preferred choice.

Computational problems

7. Suppose that a recent U.S. government ban on telemarketing (annoying phone calls from sales representatives) has led to a program to retrain displaced phone representatives as equipment managers for sports teams. The program is labeled the Calls to Balls program. Calls to Balls has a total cost of $100,000, all of which is spent during year 0. There are slots for 15 former sales reps, and each manager in training receives a wage of $4,000 while in the program. Upon graduation from "Calls to Balls," all 15 are hired as equipment managers at an average salary of $18,000. There is also a control group of 15 telemarketers who did not receive the training. All 15 earn $10,000 per year in their new jobs as fast-food workers and receive an additional $2,000 in income support. Assume that the equipment manager certification lasts three years, after which all benefits disappear.

    (A) Use the following table to organize the effects of the "Calls to Balls" program. In this case, "government" represents the rest of society.

	Year 0	Year 1	Year 2	Year 3
				(same as year 1)
(1) Government payments				
(2) Income for trainees				
(3) Income for control group				
(4) Net benefits for trainees				
(5) Net benefits for rest of society				
(6) Net benefits for all of society				

    (B) Assume a discount rate of 5 percent. Find the discounted net benefits for the participants and for society in general. Should the program be eliminated?

    (C) Now use a discount rate of 10 percent. How does this change your answer to question 7(B)?

8. Assume that a living wage has been proposed for your college's cafeteria workers. Obviously this wage will not cover all jobs in your area. Using a two-market model, analyze graphically the probable effects of this proposal on (1) employment, (2) unemployment, (3) total income, and (4) employment in an uncovered market. Briefly describe your results.

    (A) Assume that there are two identical markets, Covered and Uncovered. For each the labor demand curve is $W_d = 14 - 2L_d$ and the supply curve is $W_s = 2 + L_s$, where L is millions of workers.
    1   Find the equilibrium wage and quantity of labor for either of these markets (they are the same).

2   If the minimum wage in the covered market was originally $5 (rounding a little from the actual U.S. rate) briefly discuss the amount of unemployment and lost employment that occurs in the covered market.

(B)   Now assume that the minimum wage is raised to $8 in the covered market as a result of the living wage proposal. Find the new levels of labor demanded and supplied in the covered market. Then calculate the change in total employment and the initial labor surplus in the covered market.

(C)   The supply curve above ($W_s = 2 + L_s$) is also equal to $L_s = W - 2$. After the living wage the uncovered market supply will be $L_s = W - 2 +$ the displaced employees from the covered market (careful of the signs). Find the new equilibrium wage and quantity of labor in the uncovered market after this supply shift.

(D)   Using your answers to parts (A), (B), and (C), find the total change in labor income (or the wage bill) for both markets combined, along with the net change in employment and unemployment for the two markets combined.

APPENDIX: A MORE COMPLICATED TRAINING CASE

This example allows a relatively detailed analysis of a hypothetical training program using participant and control groups. Let's assume that the National Basketball Association has developed an outreach program for prospective athletes called **Basketball Job Opportunities in North-East States** (acronym: **Basketball JONES**[7]). The NBA has conducted a pilot program consistent with the best-known research methodology. The study took place over four years, with a training year (year 0) followed three post-training years. Your job is to calculate the benefits and costs for the average program participant and for society as a whole, based on the following information. Your instructor may place you in groups of two or three to complete this exercise. Present value and expected value will be important concepts in this problem. In this case we are calculating the private and social net benefits for a single average participant. Unless your professor decides differently, assume that the net benefits disappear after the three post-training years.

Labor market experiences of the experimental group (participants)

1   The average JONES member's production during the training period equals $16,000. Half of this production goes to the JONES participants through camp improvements; the other half is general production which benefits the rest of society.

2   Training expenses of $10,000 per member are paid by government (part of the rest of society). The members also receive a stipend from the government of $5,000 while in the training program.

3   Salary during post-training periods (years 1 to 3) averages $26,000 per year. There is a 90 percent chance that JONES graduates will be employed.

4   Unemployment benefits are zero during the training period for JONES trainees. The post-training unemployment rate is 10 percent and government unemployment benefits for each unemployed person are $8,000. These payments are a gain to members and a loss to the rest of society.

Labor market experiences of the control group

1   Those *not* participating in the program earn an average salary of $20,000 each year, including the training period. There is an 80 percent chance the control group will be employed each year.

2   Unemployment benefits: the unemployment rate is 20 percent for the control group. Each unemployed person receives $8,000 per year in unemployment benefits.

The social benefits of reduced crime

For crime benefits, use the figures in Table 15A.1. Your task is to calculate the expected values for participants and for all of society. You may adjust the dollar value for the cost of each arrest for murder separately, if you wish, based on our analysis of the value of life. (Hints: Watch your signs). The reduction in arrests times the negative benefits associated with each arrest produce a benefit to the rest of society. For property crimes such as burglary, the reduction in arrests lowers the income of JONES members, all else equal, but lowers costs to all of society.

Table 15A.1 Change in arrests per JONES participant[a]

Crime	ΔArrests training period	ΔArrests each year after training	Value per arrest to JONES	Value per arrest to all of society	Expected value (EV) for JONES (training)	EV for JONES (post-training)	EV for all of society (training)	EV society (post-training)
Murder	−0.002	−0.002	$0	−$500,000				
Larceny/ auto theft	−0.06	−0.001	$1,800	−$12,200				
Robbery	−0.002	−0.008	$2,000	−$38,000				
Felonious assault	−0.005	+0.008	$0	−$10,000				
Burglary	−0.052	−0.004	$3,500	−$16,500				
Drug violations	−0.026	0	$0	−$7,000				

[a] These reductions in arrest rates are simplified versions of statistics found in Long *et al.* (1981).

Your job is to do the following
Step 1

Calculate the net benefits for all of society and for Job Corps members over a four-year period made up of one training period and three post-training periods. Start by calculating the net benefits for each year in Table 15A.2.

Step 2

Discount each year's total net benefits for JONES members and for society as a whole. Assume that the training period is year 0 and use a discount rate of 5 percent unless instructed otherwise. Then add the discounted present values as your last mathematical step.

Step 3

Make a recommendation based on the cost–benefit analysis you have performed. Should Basketball JONES be continued or abandoned?

This chart may help organize your information:

The two blank cells in the final column will give you answers for the JONES program's net benefits for participants and for all of society, which are equivalent to the private and social net benefits of the program. If either is negative, the program should be rejected.

Table 15A.2 Net benefit calculations

Net benefit	Training period	Year 1	Year 2	Year 3	Total
Expected income: JONES					X
Expected income: Control					X
ΔExpected income: JONES					X
Expected unemployment: JONES					X
Expected unemployment: Control					X
ΔExpected unemployment: JONES					X
ΔExpected crime value: JONES					X
Total net benefits: JONES					X
Discounted Net Benefits: JONES					
ΔIncome: Rest of society					X
ΔIncome: All of society					X
ΔCrime value: All of society					X
ΔUnemployment benefits: Rest of society					X
ΔUnemployment benefits: All of society					X
ΔTotal: All of society					X
Discounted net benefits: All of society					

Your Turn solutions

Chapter 1

Your Turn 1.1: The benefits of one's university education may extend well beyond added income. It has been argued that higher education improves one's consumption efficiency, appreciation of the arts, health, marital prospects, husband's or wife's income, the health and success of one's children and the operation of democracy, among others.

Your Turn 1.2: In the first two cases, the individuals are not unemployed. In the third, we cannot tell without knowing if the student is actively seeking employment. The student is either unemployed or not part of the labor force.

Your Turn 1.3: Since total U.S. employment in early 2005 was about 135 million, 270,000 jobs equals ⅕ of 1 percent of total employment. These two statements are identical except that one is in terms of a total number and the other is a percentage. However, neither of these numbers is necessarily accurate. There is considerable disagreement about the employment effects of the minimum wage.

Your Turn 1.4: If employment is falling but output is not, the difference could be caused by increases in the average product of labor, or output per worker. New technologies such as improved robotics and computers are major factors in this substantial productivity improvement. Only the percentage of durable goods manufacturing employment to total employment shows a significant decline. Neither the output percentages nor the employment totals support this view.

The distinction between production and employment trends is less stark when viewing data on total manufacturing production than it is for durable goods production only, but there is still a considerable difference. Employment in all U.S. goods-producing industries rose slightly from 20.4 million in 1960 to 25.3 million in 1998. However, as a percentage of total employment it fell from 62 to 25 percent. Measured in 1996 dollars, goods production rose from $777 billion in 1960 to $3,331 billion in 1998, while it fell as a percentage of total gross domestic product from 49 to 37 percent. As a percentage this decline is far less precipitous for production than for employment, and the trend in total production is quite positive. (Source: *Economic Report of the President*, February 2000.)

Chapter 2

Your Turn 2.2: The maxi-min principle would lead to the choice of distribution number one, where the lowest level of income is $15,000. The inequality which exists in the second and third distributions does not improve the income level of person number one, and therefore would violate the difference principle.

Other Your Turn questions in Chapter 2 are discussion questions.

Chapter 3

Your Turn 3.1: Any example with many buyers and sellers and no differences in the product may come close to perfect competition. Markets for individual stocks and bonds are quite competitive, although information issues have led to detailed regulations on financial market behavior.

Your Turn 3.2: (A) D_3; (B) D_2; (C) D_2; (D) D_1 (a change in the price of Coke will not shift its demand curve).

Your Turn 3.3: See the graph.

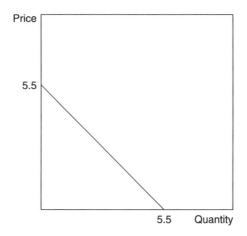

Your Turn 3.4:
(A) S_2
(B) S_2
(C) S_3
(D) S_3
(E) S_1 (a demand shift will move the equilibrium along the supply curve, but will not shift the supply curve in the short run).

Your Turn 3.5: Solution A is as follows: (1) If $P_d = P_s$, then $100 - \frac{1}{2}Q = 20 + \frac{1}{2}Q$. The equality simplifies to $Q = 80$. Substituting 80 for Q in either equation results in an equilibrium price of $60. Example B is the same problem with the demand and supply curves solved for Q. Demand-and-supply equations are acceptable in either form, though by tradition price is always graphed on the vertical axis.

Your Turn 3.6:

(1) $[\Delta Q/\{(Q_a + Q_b)/2\}]/[\Delta P/\{(P_a + P_b)/2\}]$
$[-2/\{(101 + 99)/2\}]/[0.50/\{(4.75 + 5.25)/2\}]$
$[-2/100]/[0.50/5.00]$
$-0.02/0.1$
-0.2
$|-0.2| = 0.2 < 1$ (inelastic)

(2) Elasticity $= -4$ (elastic)

Your Turn 3.7:

(1) Before: $(\$4.75)(101) = \$479.75$ After: $(\$5.25)(99) = \$519.75$
(2) Before: $(\$4.75)(120) = \$570.00$ After: $(\$5.25)(80) = \$420.00$

Your Turn 3.8: The marginal value of fifth mug = $4.00. The total value of all five mugs = $30.00.

Your Turn 3.9: Total value = $175.00.

Your Turn 3.10: Total spending = $100.00.

Your Turn 3.11: Carrie will buy six mugs. Her total spending will equal $18, her total consumer surplus will be $15, and her total value will equal $33. Note that if $3 is the maximum she is willing to pay for the sixth mug, she will buy the sixth mug.

Your Turn 3.12: In Figure 3.6, Consumer surplus = $75.00, Total spending = $100.00, and Total value = $100.00 + $75.00 = $175.00.

Your Turn 3.13: See the adjoining graph.

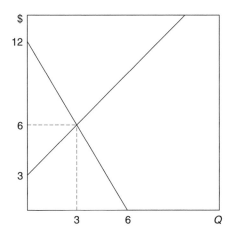

(A) $12 - 2Q = 3 + Q$
$9 = 3Q$
$Q = 3$
$P = 3 + Q$
$P = 6$

(B)   Consumer surplus = ($6.00)($3.00)/2 = $9.00
        Total spending = ($6.00)($3.00) = $18.00
        Total value = $27.00

(C) $12 - 2Q = Q$
        $12 = 3Q$
        $Q = 4$
        $P = Q$
        $P = 4$
        Consumer surplus = ($8.00)($4.00)/2 = $16.00
        Total spending = ($4.00)($4.00) = $16.00
        Total value = $32.00
        Consumer surplus rises by $5.00.

Your Turn 3.14: Six units will be produced. Total revenue is $18. Total producer surplus is $7.50. Opportunity cost is $10.50. Firms will not produce seven units because the marginal cost is greater than the price.

Your Turn 3.15: Producer Surplus = [($4.00)($10.00)]/2 = $20.00. Opportunity cost is the same.

Your Turn 3.16: The water endpoint = $20/$1.25=16 bottles. The soda endpoint = $20/$0.50 = 40 cans. The slope = $-Px/Py$. If water is X, the slope = -2.5. If the person buys 10 sodas, he can afford 12 bottles of water.

   $20.00 - ($0.50/soda)(10 sodas) - ($1.25/bottle of water) $\cdot$ (X bottles of water)
       $= $20.00 - $5.00 - ($1.25)(X) = $15.00 = ($1.25) \cdot X$
   $X = 12$ bottles of water

Your Turn 3.17: The marginal utility of $X = 0$.

Your Turn 3.18: As one moves downward and to the right, the marginal utility of X falls, making the indifference curve slope flatter. Also, the marginal utility of Y rises because one has consumed fewer of them at points lower on an indifference curve. This rising denominator in the slope formula also makes the curve flatter.

Your Turn 3.19: The quantities of each good purchased by the consumer will fall in this graph. Your graph may vary, particularly for X-box games. If both quantities fall, the two goods are complements. If the quantity of X rises while yogurt falls, they are substitutes. In this graph they are complements.

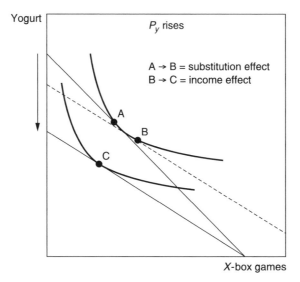

Your Turn 3.20: See the graph

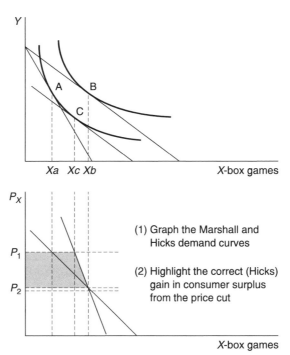

Figure 3.23 Bias in compensating variation, Your Turn 3.20

Chapter 4

Your Turn 4.1:
   (A) Not a Pareto improvement
   (B) No
   (C) No
   (D) Yes

Your Turn 4.2: Rather than being able to sell the first unit for the full $18 and the second for $16, three units can only be sold if the price is lowered to $14 for all three. The total revenue at this price is $42. Had the firm attempted to sell only two units, the price would have been $16 each, so $32 would have been earned. Thus, selling the additional unit yielded only an additional $10, i.e. less than the price of $14.

Your Turn 4.3:
   Private equilibrium is where demand equals supply. $Q_p = 60$, $P_p = 60$
   Social equilibrium: $Q_s = 45$, $P_s = 75$

Your Turn 4.4:
Point b:
$$30 - 4Q = Q$$
$$30 = 5Q$$
$$Q = 6$$
$$P = 6$$

Point c:
$$Q = 6$$
$$P = 30 - 2Q$$
$$P = 30 - 12$$
$$P = 18$$

Your Turn 4.5:
Competitive CS $= (\frac{1}{2}) \cdot (\$20.00) \cdot (10) = \$100.00$
Monopoly CS $= (\frac{1}{2}) \cdot (\$12.00) \cdot (6) = \$24.00$
Competitive PS $= (\frac{1}{2}) \cdot (\$10.00) \cdot (10) = \$50.00$
Monopoly PS $= \$100.00$ (given)

Deadweight loss

	(1) Competitive equilibrium	(2) Monopoly	(1) minus (2)
CS	100	24	76
PS	50	100	−50
Total	150	124	26 (This is the deadweight loss)

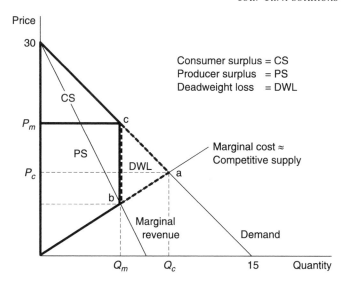

Figure 4.5 Monopoly again

Your Turn 4.6:
Perfect information

$90 - Q = 10 + Q$
$Q = 40$
$P = 50$
Consumer surplus $= (\frac{1}{2})(\$90 - \$50)(40) = \$800$
Producer surplus $= (\frac{1}{2})(\$40)(40) = \$800$
Net gains $= \$1,600$

Consumer is fooled

$110 - Q = 10 + Q$
$Q = 50$
$P = 60$
Consumer surplus $= (\frac{1}{2})(\$90 - \$60)(30) - (\frac{1}{2})(\$60 - \$40)(20) = \$450 - \$200$
$= \$250$
Producer surplus $= (\frac{1}{2})(\$60 - \$10)(50) = \$1,250$
Deadweight loss $= \$1,600 - \$1,500 = \$100$

Chapter 5

Your Turn 5.1: The answers for the consumer tax are as follows. Consumer surplus equals the triangle A + L, tax revenue equals the rectangle B + C + E + F, producer surplus equals area H, and the deadweight loss equals the triangle D + G.

Your Turn 5.2: The transition from the quota system is good for producers, as they gain revenue from increased production and from the subsidy itself. This finding would not be self-evident if the high quota price had been maintained. However, at the lower equilibrium price created by imports, PS is below even its competitive level. Consumers are better off, because increased production leads

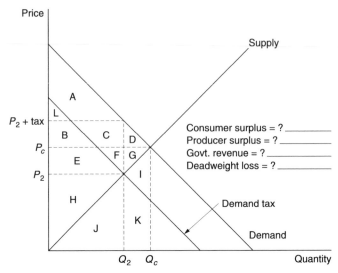

Figure 5.2 Tax on consumers

to lower prices, so in turn the consumer surplus rises. Finally, the government clearly loses, for while the marketable permits could potentially generate some level of profit, the subsidy is simply an outflow of funds.

Your Turn 5.3:

No price ceiling

Price	10	9	8	7	6	5	4
Quantity	2	3	4	5	6	7	8
Total revenue	20	27	32	35	36	35	32
Marginal revenue	xx	7	5	3	1	−1	−3

Price ceiling at $6

Price	6	6	6	6	6	5	4
Quantity	2	3	4	5	6	7	8
Total revenue	12	18	24	30	36	35	32
Marginal revenue	xx	6	6	6	6	−1	−3

Your Turn 5.4: In order to win the election Mrs. Smith must gain votes from over 5,000 voters. Given the voter preferences in the table, favoring any decrease will not gain enough votes to win the election. Candidate Jones is likely to move to the center as well.

Your Turn 5.5: 0.02 times $400 equals $8.

Chapter 6

Your Turn 6.1: If you include operating costs as part of the cost totals, these are the correct answers:

Project 1: Net Benefits = $4m   Benefit/Cost Ratio = 1.36   Rate of Return 36.3%
Project 2: Net Benefits = $2m   Benefit/Cost Ratio = 1.25   Rate of Return 25.0%

Your Turn 6.2: If you now include operating costs as negative operating revenues, these are the correct answers for Project 2. Project 1 will be similar.

Project 2: Net Benefits = $2m   Benefit/Cost Ratio = 1.33   Rate of Return = 33.0%

Your Turn 6.3: A policy analyst would generally recommend building wind farm Project 1, since the benefit/cost ratio is greater than one and the rate of return and net benefits are greater than zero.

Your Turn 6.4:

Table 6.1 Real estate alternatives

	Housing	Industrial park	Outlet mall	Vacant lot
Benefits	$1,000,000	$1,250,000	$1,600,000	$1,000
Costs	$1,100,000	$900,000	$1,200,000	$1,000
Net benefits	−$100,000	+$350,000	+$400,000	$0
B/C ratio	0.909	1.389	1.333	1.000
Rate of return	−9.09%	39%	33%	0%

Rankings:
Net benefits: (1) Outlet Mall; (2) Industrial Park; (3) Vacant Lot; (4) Housing.
B/C ratio or rate of return: (1) Industrial Park; (2) Outlet Mall; (3) Vacant Lot; (4) Housing.

Your Turn 6.5: The optimal budget would be sufficient to fund the industrial park and the outlet mall. The total costs for the two projects equal $2,100,000.

Your Turn 6.6:

Table 6.2 Project choices given a budget

	Housing	Industrial park	Outlet mall	Golf course	Power plant	Vacant lot
Benefits	$1,000,000	$1,250,000	$1,600,000	$1,500,000	$4,200,000	$1,000
Costs	$1,100,000	$900,000	$1,200,000	$900,000	$3,000,000	$1,000
B/C ratio	0.909	1.389	1.333	1.667	1.400	1.000
Net benefits	−$100,000	+$350,000	+$400,000	+$600,000	+$1,200,000	$0

B/C ratio rankings:
(1) Golf Course; (2) Power Plant; (3) Industrial Park; (4) Outlet Mall; (5) Vacant Lot; (6) Housing.

Two alternative strategies could be chosen. First build the golf course (skip the power plant, which you could not afford), and build the industrial park and outlet mall, for a total cost of $3 million and $1,350,000 in net benefits. The second strategy would be to build the power plant, with net benefits of $1,200,000. The first strategy maximizes net benefits, and is the correct choice according to this decision rule.

Your Turn 6.7:

$$MB = MC$$
$$1,800 - \tfrac{1}{3}Q = 300$$
$$\tfrac{1}{3}Q = 1,500$$
$$Q_{total} = 4,500$$

$$MB_R = 1,400 - Q_R = 300$$
$$Q_R = 1,100$$
$$MB_C = 2,000 - \tfrac{1}{2}Q_C = 300$$
$$Q_C = 3,400$$

Your Turn 6.8:

1   Strictly on the basis of benefit–cost analysis, it is not clear that any change in the arsenic standard should be made. Only for the 10 ppb and 20 ppb levels do the benefit and cost estimates overlap. The EPA chose the 10 ppb standard, in part based on other factors.

2   The dollar benefits from lives saved equals $6 million times ½ (the death rate) times the number of cancer cases avoided. Using the high estimates, the dollar values are $414 million for 3 ppb, $300 million for 5 ppb, $168 million for 10 ppb, and $60 million for 20 ppb. If accurate (and they probably are not), these benefits would account for a substantial majority of the total high estimate for health benefits.

Your Turn 6.9:

$4,100,000/100,000 = $41,000 per cop for the training center
$4,100,000/100,000 = $40,200 per cop for the grants

Your Turn 6.10:

Cost of spraying = $1,000
Total effect of spraying = 50
Cost per bug-free apartment = $20
This makes spraying more cost-effective.

Your Turn 6.11:

Table 6.6 A weighted net benefits example

	Weight ($\alpha = 0$)	Weight ($\alpha = \tfrac{1}{2}$)	Weight ($\alpha = 1$)
$10,000 weight	1	2	4
$80,000 weight	1	0.7071	0.5
Weighted benefits to poor youth	$100,000	$200,000	$400,000
Weighted costs to quiche eaters	$120,000	$84,852	$60,000
Net benefits of program	−$20,000	$115,148	$340,000

Chapter 7

Your Turn 7.2:
(A) First year interest = $0.10 \times \$1,000 = \$100$.
   End-of-year total = $\$1,000 \times 1.1 = \$1,100$.
(B) After the second year the total = $\$1,000 \times (1.1)^2 = \$1,000 \times 1.21 = \$1,210$.
(C) After three years her account = $\$1,000 \times (1.1)^3 = \$1,000 \times 1.331 = \$1,331$.
(D) Because of compound interest, the principal on which interest is earned grows faster with higher interest rates, in addition to the higher amount earned on each dollar.

Your Turn 7.3:
$\$1,000 \times (1.05)^{50} = \$1,000 \times 11.467 = \$11,467.40$
$\$1,000 \times (1.10)^{50} = \$1,000 \times 117.39 = \$117,390.85$
$\$1,000 \times (1.05)^{100} = \$1,000 \times 131.50 = \$131,501.26$

Your Turn 7.4:
First year: $\$250,000/1.05 = \$238,095$
Second year: $\$250,000/(1.05)^2 = \$226,757$
Third year: $\$250,000/(1.05)^3 = \$215,959$
20th year: $\$5,000,000/(1.05)^{20} = \$1,884,447$

Your Turn 7.5:

	Now	Year 1	Year 2	Year 3
PV	$= -\$10/1.05^0$ +	$\$(7-3)/1.05^1$ +	$\$(7-3)/(1.05)^2$ +	$\$(7-3)/(1.05)^3$
	$= -\$10/1$ +	$\$4/1.05$ +	$\$4/1.1025$ +	$\$4/1.1576$
	$= -\$10$ +	$\$3.810$ +	$\$3.628$ +	$\$3.456$ $= \$0.894$

Your Turn 7.6: $20 billion/0.05 = $400 billion.

Your Turn 7.7:

	Year 0	Year 1	Year 2
Benefits	$0	$320,000	$320,200
Costs	$200,000	$200,000	$200,000
Net benefits	−$200,000	$120,000	$120,000

At a discount rate of 12 percent, $PV = -\$200,000 + \$107,143 + \$95,663 = \$2,806$.
With a positive net present value, the discount rate is too low. At a discount rate of 13 percent, $PV = -\$200,000 + \$106,195 + \$93,978 = \$173$. So the internal rate of return is roughly 13 percent.

Your Turn 7.8: The discounted B/C ratio equals the discounted benefits divided by the discounted costs. Using the benefit and cost chart from Your Turn 7.7:

$$\frac{\sum_{t=0}^{n} \frac{B_t}{(1+r)^t}}{\sum_{t=0}^{n} \frac{C_t}{(1+r)^t}} = \frac{0 + \$320,000/1.07 + \$320,000/1.1449}{\$200,000 + \$100,000/1.07 + \$100,000/1.1449} = \frac{\$578,565}{\$380,802} = 1.52$$

Your Turn 7.9: The used server's present value for a two-year cycle after subtracting the cost = −$1,000 + $800/1.05 + $800/1.1025 = $487.52. You might verify that the equation in the text produces the same answer for the revenue stream. The two-year annuity value = 1.8594. The used server's EAV then equals $487.52/1.8594 = $262. The new server's present value = $464. Its five-year annuity value = $4.329. Therefore the EAV = $464/4.329 = $107.18. The used servers are the better choice for Brian.

Chapter 8

Your Turn 8.1: If $r_3 = 7$ percent, the social rate of discount is 3 percent, and the project lasts five years, the annualized value of lost consumption equals:

$$X = PV_k \frac{r_3(1+r_3)^n}{(1+r_3)^n - 1} = \$10B \frac{0.07(1.07)^5}{(1.07)^5 - 1} = \$10B \cdot \frac{0.09818}{0.40255} = \$2.439B \text{ per year}$$

The present value of this annual lost consumption for five years can be found using the annuity formula from Chapter 7 or the present value formula. Using a 3 percent social rate of discount, the answer is approximately $11.17 billion.

Your Turn 8.2: The net present value for the first five years is about $11.9 billion.

Your Turn 8.3:
$$Weighted \; r = ar_1 + br_f + (1-a-b)r_3 = 0.2 \cdot 0.03 + 0.2 \cdot 0.03 - 0.6 \cdot 0.07 = 0.012$$
$$+ 0.042 = 0.054$$

Chapter 9

Your Turn 9.1:
$$EV = \$10(18/37) - \$10(19/37) = \$4.865 - 5.135 = -\$0.27.$$

Your Turn 9.2:
$$EV_{Invade} = \tfrac{1}{2} \cdot \$2,000 + \tfrac{1}{2} - \$100 = \$950$$
$$EV_{Not} = \tfrac{1}{2} \cdot \$500 + \$0 = \$250$$
Therefore the model says to invade.
 If there are no WMDs, the EVs are −$100 for invading and $0 for not invading. Not invading becomes the recommended choice.

Your Turn 9.3: The expected value of studying = 3.75, and the expected value of partying and cramming = 2 + whatever value you assign to the parties.

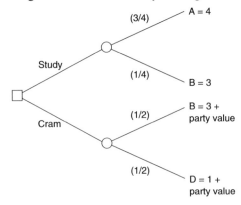

Your Turn 9.4:

(A)   Taking the bet requires risk-preferring behavior. A risk-neutral person would be indifferent.

(B) $EU_{gamble} = \frac{1}{2}\sqrt{\$122} + \frac{1}{2}\sqrt{\$80} = 9.99$ utils

The utility of the initial wealth = 10 utils, so you would refuse the gamble.

(C) $EU_{gamble} = \frac{1}{2}(\$118)^2 + \frac{1}{2}(80)^2 = 10,162$ utils

The utility of the initial wealth = 10,000 utils, so you would accept the gamble.

Your Turn 9.5: Rhonda's expected loss equals $\frac{1}{50} \times \$1,900 = \$38$. Her expected utility without insurance equals 99.8 utils. Her certainty equivalent equals \$9,960. Her maximum willingness to pay for insurance is \$40.

Your Turn 9.6:

(A) $EV_{private} = \frac{1}{4} \cdot \$12,100 + \frac{1}{4} \cdot \$28,900 + \frac{1}{4} \cdot \$34,596 = \$26,124$

(B) $EU_{private} = \frac{1}{4}\sqrt{\$12,100} + \frac{1}{2} \cdot \sqrt{\$28,900} + \frac{1}{4} \cdot \sqrt{\$34,596}$
$= 27.5 + 85 + 46.5 + 159$ utils

$U(\$25,600) = \sqrt{\$25,600} = 160$ utils, a higher value

(C)   The certainty equivalents involve squaring the utility values. For the private account it is \$25,281, less than the dollar value of the fixed payment.

(D)   The new expected utility is

$EU_{private} = \frac{1}{4}\sqrt{\$25,600} + \frac{1}{2} \cdot \sqrt{\$28,900} + \frac{1}{4} \cdot \sqrt{\$34,596} = 171.5$ utils

The certainty equivalent is \$29,412.

Your Turn 9.7: The answer depends on the results of a brief class survey.

Your Turn 9.8:

(A)   If tuition is \$10,000, $EV = \frac{1}{10} \cdot \$5,000$ (half of the tuition) = \$500

(B)   **Without insurance,** $EU = 0.9\sqrt{\$100,000} + 0.1\sqrt{\$90,000} = 284.6 + 30$
$= 314.6$ utils. The certainty equivalent is \$98,973,16.

With insurance, $EU = 0.9\sqrt{\$100,000} + 0.1\sqrt{\$95,000} = 315.422$ utils. The certainty equivalent is \$99,491.04. The option value, or maximum willingness to pay, is $\$99,491.04 - \$98,973.16 = \$517.88$.

Your Turn 9.9:

Asset	Risk-free rate	Market rate of return	Beta	Required rate
Tech	2	8	1.8	**12.8**
Food	2	8	0.8	**6.8**
Gold	4	9	−0.2	**3.0**
Telephone	3	6	0.6	4.8

Your Turn 9.10:
   (A) Required rate $= 3 + 3(7-3) = 15$
   (B) The net present value is about $-\$17.25$ million. Financially the government loses with this arrangement.

Your Turn 9.11:

Discount rates	40 years of benefits	10 years of benefits	Expected value
7%	$14,665	$7,726	**$11,196**
3%	**$25,426**	**$9,383**	**$17,405**

If the cost is $14,000 per employee, the 40-year benefit stream benefits society given either discount rate. The expected value of the two net benefit streams would produce a positive net value for the 3% discount rate only.

Your Turn 9.12:
   A. $EV = \frac{1}{3}(-4.5) + \frac{1}{3}(-2) + \frac{1}{3}(4) = -\frac{5}{6}$ trillion.
   B. $EV = \frac{1}{3}(-2.5) + \frac{1}{3}(0) + \frac{1}{3}(6) = 1\frac{1}{6}$ trillion.
   C. $1\frac{1}{6}-(-\frac{5}{6}) = 2$ trillion.
The quasi-option value is $1 trillion.

Chapter 10

Your Turn 10.1: Most answers will be zero or infinity, depending on the context. Also, no risky action would be rational with an infinite value of life.

Your Turn 10.2: For example, if your required compensation for the extreme skiing position is $10,000, the implicit value of life would be $10,000/0.001, or $10 million.

Your Turn 10.3:
   (A) 45 percent (¾ of 60 percent) of 18.3 milllion would now be riding in car seats because of the law. That's 8.235 million.
   (B) The answer equals the change in lives lost/change in total car seat use. This would equal 161/8,235,000, or 0.00001955. Actually, other interpretations of the denominator might be consistent with the wording of the question.
   (C) $5 million $\times$ 161 = $805 million.
   (D) $30 $\times$ 8.235 million = $247 million.
   (E) Obviously this is an efficient law based on these net benefits. If the value of life was $200,000, costs would outweigh the benefits.

Your Turn 10.4: The low estimate of lives saved is $\frac{1}{10}$ per year. The highest infant flight estimate is $10,000 \times 365$, or 3,650,000. Therefore, the low estimate of the improvement in risk of death is 0.000000027 or 2.7 hundred millionths.

Your Turn 10.5:
   (A) The lowest-cost estimate is $200 \times 5,000 \times 365$, or $365,000,000. The highest would be twice that sum.
   (B) Using the higher value of annual lives saved ($\frac{3}{5}$ per year), the dollar per life saved is $608,333,333, an extremely high value-of-life figure.

Most families are likely to hold their infants rather than buy the extra seat.

(C) More families might choose to drive, a riskier way to travel.

Your Turn 10.6: Some might choose the person with the longest period of foregone life (the infant). Others might choose the most productive.

Your Turn 10.7: The only guideline here is to make sure the lower-quality of life categories are compensated with more total years.

Your Turn 10.8: The weights for each health category are 1 for perfect health, 0.8 for inactive, 0.5 for ill, and 0.2 for bedridden. If the person quits smoking, she will live to 82 (52 more years). If she smokes, she will live to 74 (44 more years).

Step 1:

Table 10.1 Calculating quality-adjusted life years

	Perfect health	*Inactive*	*Ill*	*Bedridden*	*Total*
Smoker (years)	20	16	7	1	44
Smoker (weighted life years)	20	12.8	3.5	0.2	36.5
Smoker (weighted dollar value, undiscounted)	$300,000	$192,000	$52,500	$3,000	$547,500
Former smoker (years)	30	18	3	1	52
Former smoker (weighted life years)	30	14.4	1.5	0.2	46.1
Former smoker (weighted dollar value, undiscounted	$450,000	$216,000	$22,500	$3,000	$631,500

Step 2:

Table 10.2 Benefits of anti-smoking policy using QALY

	Information and incentives				Regulation and enforcement		
Steps in program 1	*Δcost (millions)*	*ΔQALY*	*ΔQALY / Δcost*	*Steps in program 2*	*Δcost (millions)*	*ΔQALY*	*ΔQALY / Δcost*
1	$4	28	7	1	$2	20	10
2	$4	14	3.5	2	$2	8	4
3	$2	4	2	3	$2	6	3
				4	$2	4	2
				5	$2	2	1

Step 3:

(A) Using our decision method from Chapter 6, start with the highest B/C ratio and work down until the next best step doesn't fit in the budget, etc. Therefore you should implement Program 1, Step 1, plus Program 2, Steps 1, 2, and 3. In this case, Program 1, Steps 1 and 2, plus Program 2, Step 1, produce equal benefits.

(B)   Adopt each step where the benefits outweigh the costs. Where the two are equal, there is no Pareto improvement but you might be able to make an ethical case for adoption. At a minimum, Program 1, Steps 1 and 2, and Program 2, Steps 1, 2, and 3, will offer positive net benefits and should be adopted.

Chapter 11

Your Turn 11.1:

	Carlisle	*County*
Spending	1.33	1.59
Employment	1.23	1.38

(A)   Divide the total spending by the direct spending. See above.
(B)   For example, the Carlisle spending multiplier is 1.33. Therefore, $1.33 = 1/(1-MPC_L)$. Using algebra, $MPC_L = \frac{1}{4}$.
(c)   For Carlisle, $88,646,766 \bullet 1.33 \approx \$117,900,199$.
The answers also are available in Table 11.1 in the text.

Your Turn 11.2: $E = 12,000/\frac{1}{2} = 24,000$.

Your Turn 11.3: $20,000/2.5 = 8,000$.

Your Turn 11.4: $0.4/0.05 = 8$.

Your Turn 11.5:

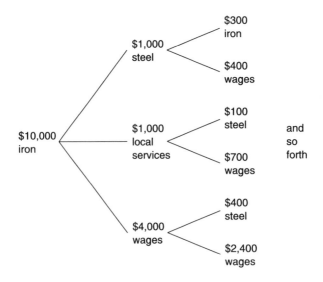

Chapter 12

Your Turn 12.2: The consumer surplus equals areas A + B + C + D. The producer surplus equals areas F + G + H and the external surplus equals areas −(G + H + D + E). The deadweight loss is area E.

Your Turn 12.3: The benefits include the elimination of ambient noise, the creation of open space, and the possible filtering of exhaust fumes before they reach the atmosphere. In addition to the added dollar costs, the operating costs of eliminating water from the system and the possible danger of tunnel collapse and flooding are the major added costs.

Chapter 13

Your Turn 13.1: The primary inputs to consider are energy and materials. Renewable energy sources, including various solar and other natural energy sources such as wind or water, are primary means of achieving sustainable development. Recyclable materials are another. The reduction of pollution is another crucial component of the cycle.

Your Turn 13.2: As proposed in the text, the permits will be bought up by firm 1 and firm 2. This shifts most of the clean-up to the lower-cost firm 3 and reduces the cost of achieving the ¼ reduction.

Table 13.3 Equal abatement vs. permits, 25% reduction

Firm	Pollution	Abatement cost/unit	(1) Pollution after uniform ¼ reduction	(2) Total cost of ¼ reduction	(3) Permits purchased (total = 375)	(4) Abatement cost with permits
Firm 1	100 tons	$20/ton	75	$500	100	$0
Firm 2	300 tons	$16/ton	225	$1200	275	$400
Firm 3	100 tons	$10/ton	75	$250	0	$1,000
Total	500 tons	xxx	375	$1,950		$1,400

Chapter 14

Your Turn 14.2: The 2002 U.S. Gini coefficient (rounded)

The four rectangles are:

$0.2 \times 0.03 = 0.006$
$0.2 \times 0.09 = 0.018$
$0.2 \times 0.15 = 0.030$
$0.2 \times 0.23 = 0.046$

The five triangles are:

$½ \times 0.2 \times 0.03 = 0.003$
$½ \times 0.2 \times 0.09 = 0.009$
$½ \times 0.2 \times 0.15 = 0.015$
$½ \times 0.2 \times 0.23 = 0.023$
$½ \times 0.2 \times 0.50 = 0.050$

The sum of these areas is 0.2, so the Gini coefficient = 0.2/0.5, or 0.4. The actual U.S. Gini coefficient for 2002 was 0.408.

Your Turn 14.3:
  Earnings = wage·hours = 6·10 = $60.
  Public assistance = Base + t·W·H = $75 −1·$60 = $15.
  Total income = earnings + assistance = $75, which is the same as the base payment. She earns nothing extra by working.

Your Turn 14.4: See the graph.

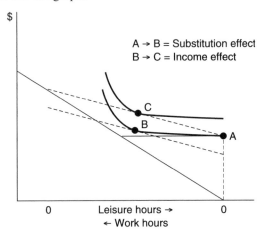

Decrease in implicit tax rate

Your Turn 14.5: Some may feel that in-kind benefits are preferable because government keeps some measure of control over recipients' spending. Those who believe that many of the poor would spend unrestricted cash on intoxicants or extravagant products may favor restrictions of this type. Other reasons may include the self-interest of those supplying the product in question or the positive externalities of some goods. The externalities argument may be particularly true for health expenditures or children's nutrition programs.

Chapter 15

Your Turn 15.1: The generality of your skill set depends on your level and field of study. Skills learned as an undergraduate economics major are likely to be more general than those of a graduate program in public administration or public policy. As for subsidizing general skills, there are many possible positive externalities associated with higher education, any of which would justify some degree of subsidization. For a discussion of a wide range of benefits from higher education, see Robert Haveman and Barbara Wolfe, "Schooling and Economic Well-Being: The Role of Nonmarket Effects," *Journal of Human Resources*, Vol. 19, No. 3 (Summer 1984), pp. 377-407.

Your Turn 15.2: Dimensions of the job search and job choice problem include when to start one's search (early), which information sources to use, how many jobs to apply for, and so forth. The job choice issue also involves Adam Smith's concept of compensating differentials. A job with high pressure, unfavorable location, or other non-monetary disadvantages will be rejected by most people unless the pay is sufficient to compensate for the job's non-monetary costs.

Your Turn 15.3:

Step 1: Organizing the various benefits and costs is a relatively complex step, even for a simple example such as the HIM program. The undiscounted net benefits are compiled in the following table. The government payments are net losses for the rest of society.

Table 15.1 Net benefits for the "HIM" program

	Year 0	*Year 1 to Year 3*
(1) ΔGovernment payments	$110,000	−$10,000
(2) Income for trainees	$50,000	$200,000
(3) Income for control group	$140,000	$140,000
(4) Net benefits for trainees	**−$90,000**	**$60,000**
(5) Net benefits for rest of society	−$110,000	$10,000
(6) Net benefits for all of society	**−$200,000**	**$70,000**

Step 2: The following table includes the undiscounted and discounted totals using both discount rates.

	Year 0	*Year 1*	*Year 2*	*Year 3*	*Total*
Trainee's net benefits	−$90,000	$60,000	$60,000	$60,000	$90,000
2% discount rate	−$90,000	$58,824	$57,670	$56,540	$83,034
10% discount rate	−$90,000	$54,545	$49,587	$45,079	$59,211
Society's net benefits	−$200,000	$70,000	$70,000	$70,000	$10,000
2% discount rate	−$200,000	$68,627	$67,282	$65,963	$1,872
10% discount rate	−$200,000	$63,636	$57,851	$52,592	−$25,921

Step 3: From an efficiency point of view, your recommendation depends on the choice of discount rate. The 7 percent discount rate currently recommended by the Office of Management and Budget would also produce a negative result for all of society. The net benefits to the recipients would justify the program under some ethical criteria, depending on the possible alternative uses of the funds.

Your Turn 15.4: The first portion has a positive implicit tax rate, which acts like a wage increase. Its effect on work hours is theoretically ambiguous. The second portion (not displayed) has a zero implicit tax rate and acts like an increase in unearned income. The income effect will reduce hours worked if leisure is a normal good. Finally, the upper portion has a negative implicit tax rate and acts like a negative income tax. Both the income and substitution effects should encourage fewer hours worked along this segment.

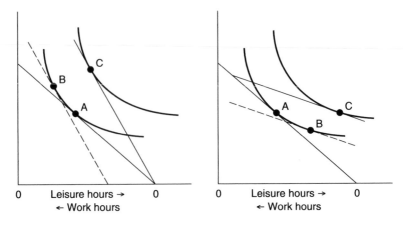

Positive implicit tax rate portion   Negative implicit tax rate portion

Notes

1 The meaning of policy analysis

1 Budda, from the *Kalama Sutra*. Many translations of this passage are somewhat less poetic (http://thinkexist.com/quotation/do not believe in anything simply because you/ 12103.html).
2 From a letter written in London in 1772, reprinted in National Park Service, *Natural Resource Year in Review–2000*, May 2000 (publication D-1459) (http://www2. nature.nps.gov/YearinReview/yir2000/pages/07 new horizons/07 05 haas sub.html).
3 Office of Management and Budget, "Guidelines and Discount Rates for Benefit–Cost Analysis of Federal Programs," Circular No. A-94 Revised, October 29, 1992 (http://www.whitehouse.gov/omb/circulars/a094/a094.html).
4 The progressive era extends from the late nineteenth century to roughly World War I.
5 For example, http://mediamatters.org/ is a liberal website that exposes "conservative bias," while http://www.mediaresearch.org/ is a conservative website exposing "liberal bias." Needless to say, each is likely to be biased in its own right.
6 The Office of Personnel Management's website is a good source of information on civil service protections for federal employees (http://www.opm.gov/Strategic Management of Human Capital/documents/merit/ideal.asp).
7 A good introductory text dealing with the principles of logic and evidence is Phelan and Reynolds (1996).
8 For a user-friendly source for a broad range of U.S. government statistics, see www.fedstats.gov.

2 Ethics for policy analysts

1 Aristotle, *Politics*, Book 4, Part 4 (http://classics.mit.edu/Aristotle/politics.4.four.html).
2 Camus, *Lyrical and Critical Essays*. Available at the Philosophical Society, Bon Mot Archive 10 (http://www.philosophicalsociety.com/bonmot10.htm).
3 George Orwell, *Animal Farm* (Harcourt Brace Jovanovich, 1946), Ch. 10.
4 Rawls realizes this limitation of the difference principle, and proposes a completely different approach to the fair treatment of future versus current generations, known as the just savings principle (Rawls 1971: 285-9).

3 A review of markets and rational behavior

1 Andrew Carnegie, "Wealth," *North American Review*, No. CCCXCI (June 1889).
2 http://creativequotations.com/one/1933.htm.
3 Karl Marx, *Capital: A Critique of Political Economy*, Vol. 1, trans. Ben Fowkes (New York: Penguin, 1990).
4 The marginal utility formula for the slope of an indifference curve can be derived using the mathematical concept of the total differential, along with the fact that moving from one point to another on an indifference curve produces a zero change in total utility.

The proof begins with a general utility function for two goods X and Y and then utilizes the total differential. The partial derivatives of utility with regard to X and Y equal the marginal utilities of X and Y by definition:

$$U = f(X, Y) \tag{1}$$
$$\Delta U = (\partial U/\partial X) \cdot \Delta X + (\partial U/\partial Y) \, \Delta Y = 0 \tag{2}$$
$$-(\partial U/\partial X) \cdot \Delta X = (\partial U/\partial Y) \, \Delta Y \tag{3}$$
$$-(\partial U/\partial X)/(\partial U/\partial Y) = \Delta Y/\Delta X \tag{4}$$
$$-MU_X/MU_Y = \Delta Y/\Delta X \tag{5}$$

In equation (2), the change in total utility (ΔU) equals zero for any movement along a single indifference curve. The right-hand side of equation (5) is the basic rise over run definition of slope. The left is the slope formula in terms of marginal utilities.

4 Efficiency and imperfect markets

1 http://en.thinkexist.com/quotes/jawaharlal_nehru/3.html.
2 http://home.att.net/~jrhsc/wilson.html.
3 http://www.law.mcgill.ca/quid/archive/2003/03110404.html.
4 The Kaldor–Hicks principle as stated above is actually consistent with the work of Kaldor (1939). According to Hicks (1940), a policy should be adopted if the losers could not, in principle, bribe the winners enough to get them to abandon the policy. Technically, the two approaches are not always consistent (see Button 1993: 178-82), though this distinction is rarely noted.
5 Okun (1975: Ch. 4).
6 To prove the relationship between the demand and marginal revenue curves, assume that the **demand curve** is of the form $P = a - bQ$, where a is the Y-intercept and $-b$ is the slope. Since total revenue equals $P \cdot Q$, one can find the total revenue function by multiplying both sides of the demand curve by Q. Therefore, total revenue $(TR) = P \cdot Q = a \cdot Q - b \cdot Q^2$. Marginal revenue equals $\Delta TR/\Delta Q$ by definition, but in basic calculus, marginal revenue also equals the first derivative of the total revenue function, or $\partial TR/\partial Q$. The first derivative of $TR = a \cdot Q - b \cdot Q^2$ is $MR = \partial TR/\partial Q = a - 2 \cdot b \cdot Q$. Comparing the marginal revenue and demand curves, one sees the same endpoint (a) and a slope that is twice as steep for the marginal revenue curve $(-b$ versus $-2b)$.

5 Efficiency and the role of government

1 Adam Smith (1776) *The Wealth of Nations*, Book IV, Chapter IX.
2 If the tax payment by producers was interpreted as an increase in costs, then tax revenue would equal area I + F + C, which is the area between the two supply curves to the left of quantity Q_2. This parallelogram is equal in area to the rectangle described in the text, though it is shaped differently. Producer surplus would then equal area H + E + B, the area above the new supply curve (Supply + tax) and below price P_2. Again, this area is identical to the producer surplus triangle shown in Figure 5.1, but is vertically higher by the amount of the tax.
3 One can also consider the subsidy as a reduction in net private production costs. In this form the subsidy appears as a parallelogram between the two supply curves. If doing so, it is important to remember that the actual opportunity cost of production determines the original supply curve, and that the society's opportunity cost of production hasn't changed. It is being shared by the government.

6 An introduction to benefit–cost analysis

1 William Pollard, *The Soul of the Firm* (Grand Rapids, MI: Zondervan, 2000).
2 *Time*, June 30, 1986.

7 Net benefits over time and present value

1 James Russell Lowell, *The Biglow Papers*, First Series, No. vi (A.L. Burt, 1900).
2 http://www.pbs.org/wgbh/amex/streamliners/peopleevents/p_kettering.html.
3 See Frederick *et al.* (2002) for a detailed review of individual time preference and related factors.
4 The missile defense proposal has been widely debated in the popular press and in specialty magazines. See Brzezinski (2004) and Hall (2003) for overviews of the issue.
5 The derivation of the present value formula for an infinite stream of benefits is presented below. It begins with the assumption that a person will receive $1 each year forever, or until t equals infinity. The present value of this stream is given in equation (1):

$$PV = 1/(1+r)+1/(1+r)^2+1/(1+r)^3+\ldots+1/(1+r)^\infty \qquad (1)$$

Multiply both sides by $1/(1+r)$ and simplify. Notice in (2)′ that the final period can't be raised to a power greater than infinity:

$$1/(1+r)PV = [1/(1+r)\ 1/(1+r)\ ] + [1/(1+r)^2\ 1/(1+r)\ ]+ \ldots + [1/(1+r)^\infty 1/(1+r)] \qquad (2)$$

$$1/(1+r)PV = 1/(1+r)^2 + 1/(1+r)^3 + \ldots + 1/(1+r)^\infty \qquad (2)′$$

Subtract (2)′ from (1). This causes most of the series to cancel. Then solve for *PV* and simplify:

$$PV - 1/(1+r)PV = 1/(1+r) \ \{\text{everything else on the right cancels}\} \qquad (3)$$
$$PV\ [1 - 1/(1+r)] = 1/(1+r) \qquad (4)$$
$$PV\ [(1+r)/(1+r)- 1/(1+r)] = 1/(1+r) \qquad (5)$$
$$PV[(1+r-1)/(1+r)] = 1/(1+r) \qquad (6)$$
$$PV(1-1+r) = 1 \qquad (7)$$
$$PV = 1/(1+r)\cdot(1+r)/r \qquad (8)$$
$$PV = 1/r \qquad (9)$$

In brief, an investment which offers a constant net benefit forever can be discounted using the surprisingly simple formula

$$PV_\infty = \frac{\$\text{net benefit}}{r} \quad \text{where } r \text{ is the discount rate}$$

6 If the inflation rate is "p," each dollar loses value at the rate of $\$1/(1+p)$ each year. Similarly, if the nominal interest rate is "i," each dollar saved will earn interest at the rate $\$1(1+i)$ each year. Therefore, the *real* rate of growth of income will equal:

$$\$1(1+r) = \$1(1+i)/(1+p) \qquad (1)$$

where $1+ i$ equals the number of dollars which will accumulate by the end of the year, and $1/(1+ p)$ equals the change in the purchasing power of each dollar. Now some manipulation of equation (1) will lead to an accurate measure of the real interest rate.

Multiply both sides by $(1+p)$: $(1+r)(1+p) = 1+i$ (2)

Multiply out the left side of (2): $1+p+r+rp = 1+i$

Subtract one from both sides: $p+r+rp = i$

Solve for r, the real interest rate: $r = i-p-rp$

Notice that if r and p are both small fractions (such as 0.05 and 0.02) $r \cdot p$ will be *very* small ($0.05 \cdot 0.02 = 0.001$), and therefore usually can be ignored without causing much inaccuracy. Therefore, it is approximately correct to say that the real interest rate equals the nominal interest rate minus the inflation rate or, in symbols, that $r = i-p$.

7 As in note 6 above, assume that r is the real interest rate, i is the nominal interest rate, and p is the inflation rate. Assume that a policy will offer real net benefits of $\$B$ at the end of one year. If we discount these real benefits using the real interest rate r, their present value will equal

$$B/(1+r) \tag{1}$$

at the end of one year. However, if we have an inflation rate of p, the nominal value of these benefits will rise to $\$B \cdot (1+p)$ by the end of the year. If we discount these nominal benefits using the nominal rate of interest (i), their present value will equal

$$B(1+p)/(1+i) \tag{2}$$

However, from note 5, if $1+r = (1+i)/(1+p)$, then multiplying both sides by $1+p$ implies that $(1+i) = (1+r)\cdot(1+p)$. Substituting the right-hand side of this equation into (2):

$$B(1+p)/(1+r)\cdot(1+p) \tag{3}$$

Since $(1+p)$ now appears in the numerator and denominator, it can be canceled, leaving a present value of $B/(1+r)$, which is the same as equation (1). Therefore, discounting nominal net benefits at the nominal interest rate is equivalent to discounting real net benefits at the real interest rate. Take your pick!

8 This case study is based loosely on the Whitaker Center in Harrisburg, Pennsylvania.

8 Choosing a discount rate

1 William J. Baumol, "On the Social Rate of Discount," *American Economic Review*, Vol. 58, No. 4 (September 1968), p. 788.

2 Raymond Mikesell, The Rate of Discount for Evaluating Public Projects (Washington, DC: American Enterprise Institute, 1977), p. 19.

3 Arnold Harberger is also the primary source of the weighted discount rate approach.

4 Gross private domestic investment averaged 16.2 percent of GDP from 1949 to 2002, and 16.1 percent from 1929 to 2002. It also averaged about 25 percent of personal consumption and about 22 percent of after-tax income.

5 Many or most detailed estimates find the shadow price of capital to be higher than 1.2. Cline (1992: 274) estimates a shadow price of 1.5 to 2, while Zerbe and Dively (1994: 289) suggest a 2.5-3.5 range.

6 For readable reviews of this report on the CPI, see Boskin *et al.* (1998) and Boskin (n.d.).

7 For a readable overview of alternative price indexes and how to use them, see Dalton, *et al.* (1998).

8 For an overview of methods of correcting for quality bias, see Hanoucek and Filer (n.d.).

9 Estimating future interest rates is often accomplished by adopting past average rates or a benchmark such as those of the OMB. However, more sophisticated estimates are also possible. For more information, see Newell and Pizer (2004: 524-7).

10 See Frederick *et al.* (2002: 360-2).

11 Kula (1984) assumed an annual consumption growth rate of 2.25 percent, an elasticity of the marginal utility of consumption equal to 1.56, and the exogenous discount factor as 0.9, an annual mortality rate.

9 Policy analysis involving risk and uncertainity

1 http://www.financial-gurus.com/gurus/3696/Warren-Buffett.

2 Graham and Weiner (1995) provide a readable source for reviewing offsetting risks and their policy implications.

3 The Congressional Budget Office (2004) has issued an informative report on risk adjustment for federal loans and loan guarantees.

4 In reality both the design and analysis of corporate loan guarantees is far more complicated than this discussion suggests. See the Congressional Budget Office (2004).

5 Beta is a commonly reported financial statistic. These values were taken from http://moneycentral.msn.com/.

6 Another version of the Iraq game could be constructed by adding a second piece of new information: the fact that George W. Bush won the 2004 election despite the invasion. If that information is known, invading becomes the best option.

10 The value of life and other non-marketed goods

1 Douglas Adams, *Hitchhiker's Guide to the Galaxy*, Pocket Edition (1979), pp. 179-81.

2 The low end estimate of the reduced risk of death for infants (ignoring indirect effects) equals 0.1/3,650,000, or 0.000000027, or 2.7 hundred-millionths.

3 The primary alternative type of QALY survey question is the "standard gamble" method, which asks subjects about their preferences regarding living a fixed number of years (say, 5) in ill health versus a gamble with some probability h of living the same number of years in perfect health versus the probability $(1-h)$ of dying immediately. At the margin, h will provide the weight for that particular state of ill health. See Adler, (2005: 1).

11 Economic impact analysis: macroeconomics in a micro world

1 This analysis is based partly on Chapter 11 of John McDonald's *Fundamentals of Urban Economics* text (McDonald 1997).

2 The actual derivation of this formula is similar to (11.3):

$$L = E + N \text{ and } N = bL \rightarrow L = E + bL \rightarrow L(1\text{-}b) = E \rightarrow 1/(1\text{-}b) = L/E = \text{multiplier},$$

where $1/(1\text{-}b)$ is the Keynesian spending multiplier, and b is the marginal propensity to consume locally.

3 For example, if the multiplier equals 2, the multiplier formula becomes $1/(1-m) = 2$. Solving for m involves a few basic steps. Cross-multiplying produces $\frac{1}{2} = 1-m$, then adding m and subtracting $\frac{1}{2}$ from both sides gives the final answer, $m = \frac{1}{2}$.

4 These three models can be reviewed on-line. The relevant web addresses are http://www.remi.com/ for the REMI model, http://www.implan.com/ for the IMPLAN model, and http://www.bea.doc.gov/bea/regional/rims/ for the RIMS-II model.

12 Urban transportation policy

1 E.B. White, *One Man's Meat* (New York: Harper & Bros., 1942).

2 For a well-written overview of the economic effects of transportation infrastructure, see Rietveld and Bruinsma (1998: Chs. 2 and 3).

3 Drivers in the eastern U.S. are likely to be familiar with E-Z pass lanes on turnpikes, tunnels, and bridges. E-Z Pass uses electronic sensors to automatically deduct toll charges from a prepaid account balance (see http://www.ezpass.com/). At this time E-Z pass fees do not vary by time of day, so the concept of a congestion fee is not yet built into the system.

4 A proposed monorail project in Seattle provides another interesting transportation study (http://www.elevated.org/project/reports/). The Environmental Impact Statement and the Second Phase Ridership Forecasting Study are recommended reading.

13 Pollution control policy

1 http://www.ontheissues.org/John_Kasich.htm#Environment_1.
2 http://www.presidential-qte.com/reagan.htm.
3 This phrase was originated by René Dubos in a presentation to the United Nations environmental conference, 1972. Source: Eblen and Eblen (1974: 702).
4 A Gaussian equation for stable conditions is as follows (Godish 1997: 230):

$$C_x = \frac{Q}{\pi \sigma_y \sigma_z \varpi} e^{-1/2} \left\{ \frac{H}{\sigma_z} \right\}^2 e^{-1/2} \left\{ \frac{Y}{\sigma_y} \right\}^z$$

where C_x = ground level pollution at distance x downwind, Q = average emission rate, ω = mean wind speed, σ_z and σ_y = the standard deviations of the vertical and horizontal distribution of pollution concentration, H is smokestack height, Y = perpendicular distance from the center of the pollution distribution, and p and e are constants. Adding atmospheric turbulence or other local conditions make the model far more complex.
5 This range of estimates is realistic: "The IPCC (Intergovernmental Panel on Climate Change) projects further global warming of 2.2-10°F (1.4-5.8°C) by the year 2100" (http://yosemite.epa.gov/oar/globalwarming.nsf/content/climateuncertainties. html#known), 2006.

14 Poverty and income support policies

1 http://web.worldbank.org/WBSITE/EXTERNAL/TOPICS/EXTPOVERTY/0,,contentMDK:20153855~menuPK:373757~pagePK:148956~piPK:216618~theSitePK:336992,00.html.
2 *Antelope Valley Libertarian*, August 2001, p. 4.
3 Deb Riechmann, "Wars on Poverty: Battles Exceed Wins," Associated Press, July 9, 1999 (http://www.sullivan-county.com/nf0/dispatch/war_pov.htm).
4 $2.736 per day in 1963, would be worth $14.14 in 1998 dollars if inflated using the food index and $14.57 if inflated using the consumer price index.
5 This total included spending on Temporary Assistance for Needy Families, Supplemental Security Income, the Earned Income Tax Credit, and General Assistance (Schiller 2004: 210).

15 Policies for the working poor: training, worker subsides, and the minimum wage

1 Mark Twain, "As Regards Patriotism," in Charles Neider (ed.), *The Collected Essays of Mark Twain* (New York: Doubleday, 1963).
2 http://money.cnn.com/2005/10/25/news/fortune500/walmart_wage/.
3 Gary Becker, *Human Capital* (1964).
4 Lisa Lynch (1994) provides an informative and readable comparison of the training systems in the United States, Germany, and Japan.
5 For a more critical view of the German apprentice system, see James Heckman (1994).
6 Charles Perry *et al.* (1976) reviewed over 250 early studies, while Friedlander *et al.* (1997) provide a readable and far more recent review.
7 Apologies to Cheech and Chong (1973).

Bibliography

Acs, Gregory and Pamela Loprest, *Leaving Welfare* (Kalamazoo, MI: Upjohn Institute, 2004).

Acton, Jan P., *Evaluating Public Programs to Save Lives: The Case of Heart Attacks*, Report R-950-RC (Santa Monica, CA: The Rand Corporation, 1973).

Adams, Douglas, *Hitchhiker's Guide to the Galaxy* (New York Simon & Schuster, Pocket Edition, 1979).

Addison, John and McKinley Blackburn, "Minimum Wages and Poverty," *Industrial and Labor Relations Review*, Vol. 52, No. 3 (April 1999), pp. 393-409.

Adler, Matthew D., "QALY's and Policy Evaluation: A New Perspective," Washington, DC: AEI Brookings Joint Center for Regulatory Studies, Working Paper No. 05-01, January 2005.

Air Quality Planning and Standards, Environmental Protection Agency, *The Plain English Guide to the Clean Air Act*, EPA-400-K-93-001, April 1993 (http://www.epa.gov/air/oaqps/peg_caa/pegcaain.html).

Alesina, Alberto and Edward Glaeser, *Fighting Poverty in the US and Europe* (Oxford: Oxford University Press, 2004).

Americans for the Arts, "Arts & Economic Prosperity: The Economic Impact of Nonprofit Arts Organizations and their Audiences, National Report," 2003 (http://ww3.artsusa.org/information_resources/economic_impact/).

Anderson, Kathryn and Richard Burkhauser, "The Retirement–Health Nexus: A New Measurement of an Old Puzzle," *Journal of Human Resources*, Vol. 20, No. 3 (Summer 1985), pp. 315–30.

Arrow, Kenneth J., *Social Choice and Individual Values*, 2nd edn. (New Haven, CT: Yale University Press, 1963).

Bailey, Martin J., *Reducing Risks to Life* (Washington, DC: American Enterprise Institute, 1980).

Baranzini, Andrea, Jose Goldemberg, and Stefen Speck, "A Future for Carbon Taxes," *Ecological Economics,* Vol. 32, No. 3 (March 2000) pp. 395-412.

Bardach, Eugene, *A Practical Guide for Policy Analysis*, (New York: Chatham House, 2000).

Barnes, Nora Ganim, Allison Connell, Lisa Hermenegildo, and Lucinda Mattson, "Regional Differences in the Economic Impact of Wal-Mart," *Business Horizons*, (July/August 1996), pp. 21-5.

Baumol, William J., "On the Social Rate of Discount," *American Economic Review*, Vol. 58, No. 4 (September 1968), pp. 788-802.

Bazelon, Coleman and Kent Smetters, "Discounting Inside the Washington D.C. Beltway, J., Ellen R. Dalberger, Robert J. Gordon, Zvi Griliches, and Dale W. Jorgenson, "*Journal of Economic Perspectives*, Vol. 13 (Fall 1999), pp. 213-28.

Becker, Gary, "A Theory of Competition among Pressure Groups for Political Influence," *Quarterly Journal of Economics*, Vol. 98 (August 1983), pp. 371-400.

Becker, Gary, *Human Capital* (New York: National Bureau of Economic Research, 1964).

Bellinger, William, *The Economic Impact of the Carlisle Barracks and U.S. Army War College*, submitted to the Cumberland County BRAC Committee, March 2004.

Big Dig website (http://www.masspike.com/bigdig/index.html).

Blank, Rebecca, "Evaluating Welfare Reform in the United States," *Journal of Economic Literature*, Vol. 40 (December 2002), pp. 1105-66.

Blank, Rebecca, *It Takes a Nation: A New Agenda for Fighting Poverty* (Princeton, NJ: Princeton University Press, 1997).

Blinder, Alan, *Hard Heads and Soft Hearts* (New Year: Addison-Wesley, 1987).

Boskin, Michael, "Prisoners of Faulty Statistics" http://www-hoover.stanford.edu/publications/selections/972/boskin.html.

Boskin, Michael J., Ellen R. Dulberger, Robert J. Gordon, Zvi Griliches, and Dale W. Jorgenson, "Consumer Prices, the Consumer Price Index, and the Cost of Living," *Journal of Economic Perspectives*, Vol. 12, (Winter 1998), pp. 3-26.

Boubel, Richard W., Donald L. Fox, D. Bruce Turner, and Arthur Stern, *Fundamentals of Air Pollution*, 3rd edn. (New York: Academic Press, 1994).

Brajer, Victor and Jane Hall, "Changes in the Distribution of Air Pollution Exposure in the Los Angeles Basin from 1990 to 1999," *Contemporary Economic Policy*, Vol. 23, No. 1 (January 2005), pp. 50-8.

Brown, Charles, "Minimum Wage Laws: Are They Overrated?" *Journal of Economic Perspectives*, Vol. 2, No. 3 (Summer 1988), pp. 133-46.

Brown, Charles, Curtis Gilroy, and Andrew Kohen, "The Effect of the Minimum Wage on Employment and Unemployment," *Journal of Economic Literature*, Vol. 20, No. 2 (June 1982), pp. 487-528.

Brzezinski, Matthew, "How to Make a Missile Miss," *New York Times*, February 8, 2004.

Buchanan, James M. and Gordon Tullock, *The Calculus of Consent: Logical Foundations of Constitutional Democracy* (Ann Arbor, MI: University of Michigan Press, 1962).

Bureau of Labor Statistics, U.S. Department of Labor, "Characteristics of Minimum Wage Workers: 2005," May 19, 2006 (http://www.bls.gov/cps/minwage2005.htm).

Burghardt, John, Peter Z. Schochet, Sheena McConnell, Terry Johnson, R. Mark Gritz, Steven Glazerman, John Homrighausen, and Russell Jackson, *Does Job Corps Work? Summary of the National Job Corps Study,* (Princeton, NJ: Mathematica Policy Research, 2001) (http://wdr.doleta.gov/opr/fulltext/01-jcsummary.pdf).

Burkhauser, Richard, Kenneth Couch, and David Wittenburg, "'Who Gets What' from Minimum Wage Hikes," *Industrial and Labor Relations Review*, Vol. 49, No. 3 (April 1996), pp. 547-52.

Butler, Eamonn, *Hayek* (New York: Universe Books, 1983).

Button, Kenneth J. and Erik Verhoef (eds.), *Road Pricing, Traffic Congestion, and the Environment* (Northampton, MA: Edward Elgar, 1998).

Button, Kenneth, *Transport Economics*, 2nd edn. (Cambridge, UK: Edward Elgar, 1993).

Callan, Scott and Janet Thomas, *Environmental Economics and Management*, 2nd edn. (Fort Worth, TX: Dryden Press, 2000).

Card, David and Alan Krueger, "Minimum Wages and Employment: A Case Study of the Fast-Food Industry in New Jersey and Pennsylvania: Reply," *American Economic Review*, Vol. 90 (September 2000), pp. 1397-420.

Card, David and Alan Krueger, "Minimum Wages and Employment: A Case Study of the Fast-Food Industry in New Jersey and Pennsylvania," *American Economic Review*, Vol. 84 (September 1994), pp. 772-93.

Cheech Marin and Tommy Chong, "Basketball Jones," *Los Cochinos* (Los Angeles: Warner Bros., 1973).

Cline, William, *The Economics of Global Warming* (Washington, DC: Institute for International Economics, 1992).

Coase, Ronald, "The Problem of Social Cost," *Journal of Law and Economics*, Vol. 3, No. 1 (1960), pp. 1-44.

Congressional Budget Office, "Estimating the Value of Subsidies for Federal Loans and Loan Guarantees: A CBO Study" (Washington, DC: Congress of the United States, Congressional Budget Office, August 2004).

Dalton, Pat, Kathy Novak, and Jayne S. Rankin, "Using Price Indexes" (Information Brief, Research Department, Minnesota House of Representatives, February 1998) www.house.leg.state.mn.us/hrd/pubs/indexes.pdf.

Dorman, Peter, *Markets and Mortality: Economics, Dangerous Work, and the Value of Human Life* (New York and Cambridge: Cambridge University Press, 1996).

Downs, Anthony, *Stuck In Traffic* (Washington, DC: Brookings Institution Press, 1992).

Eblen, R.A. and W. Eblen, *The Encyclopedia of the Environment* (Boston, MA: Houghton-Mifflin, 1994).

European Commission: Employment Social Affairs, and Equal Opportunities, "Portfolio of Overarching Indicators and Streamlined Social Inclusion, Pensions, and Health Portfolios" (Brussels, June 7, 2006) (http://ec.europa.eu/employment_social/social_inclusion/ docs/2006/indicators_en.pdf).

Evans, William N. and John D. Graham, "An Estimate of the Lifesaving Benefit of Child Restraint Use Legislation," *Journal of Health Economics*, Vol. 9 (1990), pp. 121–42.

Falwell, Jerry, Ed Dobson, and Ed Hindson, *The Fundamentalist Phenomenon* (New York: Doubleday, 1981).

Federal Reserve Board of Governors, Statistical Release Z-1 (http://www.federalreserve.gov/releases/z1/current/z1.pdf).

Feldstein, Martin, "Distributional Preferences in Public Expenditure Analysis," in H. Hockman and G. Peterson (eds.), *Redistribution through Public Choices* (New York: Columbia University Press, 1974), pp. 136-61.

Fialka, John, "Chief U.S. Regulator Attempts to Find Value of Human Life," *Wall Street Journal*, May 30, 2003.

Fisher, Ann, Lauraine Chestnut, and Daniel Violette, "The Value of Reducing Risks of Death: A Note on New Evidence," *Journal of Policy Analysis and Management*, Vol. 8, No. 1 (1989), pp. 88-100.

Frederick, Shane, George Lowenstein, and Ted O'Donoghue, "Time Discounting and Time Preference: A Critical Review," *Journal of Economic Literature*, Vol. 40, No. 2 (June 2002), pp. 351-401.

Freedman, Richard, "Wal-Mart Collapses U.S. Cities and Towns," *Executive Intelligence Review* (November 21, 2003).

Freeman, Richard (ed.), *Working under Different Rules* (New York: Russell Sage Foundation, 1994).

Friedlander, Daniel, David Greenberg, and Philip Robins, "Evaluating Government Training Programs for the Economically Disadvantaged," *Journal of Economic Literature*, Vol. 35 (December 1997), pp. 1809-55.

Friedman, Milton, *Capitalism and Freedom* (Chicago: University of Chicago Press, 1962).

Galbraith, John Kenneth, *The Anatomy of Power* (New York: Houghton-Mifflin, 1983).

Gangadharan, Lata, "Analysis of Prices in Tradable Emission Markets: An Empirical Study of the Regional Clean Air Incentives Market in Los Angeles," *Applied Economics*, Vol. 36 (2004), pp. 1569-82.

GAO (General Accounting Office), *Observations on EPA's Cost–Benefit Analysis of Its Mercury Control Options*, GAO document GAO-05-252 (Washington, DC: February 2005) (http://www.gao.gov/new.items/d05252.pdf).

GAO (General Accounting Office), "Multiple Employment and Training Programs," Report to the Chairman, House Committee of the Budget, October 2000.

Garms, Walter, "A Benefit–Cost Analysis of the Upward Bound Program," *Journal of Human Resources*, Vol. 6, No. 2 (Spring 1971), pp. 206-20.

Glennerster, Howard, "US Poverty Studies and Poverty Measurement: The Past Twenty Five Years," London School of Economics, Centre for Analysis of Social Exclusion, CASE Paper No. 42, October 2000.

Godish, Thad, *Air Quality*, 3rd edn. (Boca Raton, FL: Lewis, 1997).

Graham, John and Jonathan Weiner (eds.) *Risk versus Risk* (Cambridge, MA: Harvard University Press, 1995).

Griffin, Roger, *Principles of Air Quality Management* (Boca Raton, FL: Lewis, 1994).

Groom, Ben, Cameron Hepburn, Phoebe Koundouri, and David Pearce, "Declining Discount Rates: The Long and the Short of It," *Environmental and Resource Economics*, Vol. 32 (2005), pp. 445-93.

Hall, Mimi, "Shoulder-Fired Missiles: A Concern to U.S. Aviation," *USA Today*, December 3, 2003 (http://www.globalsecurity.org/org/news/2003/031203-manpads.htm).

Hamilton, Bruce and Peter Kahn, "Baltimore's Camden Yards Ballparks," in Roger G. Noll and Andrew Zimbalist (eds.), *Sports, Jobs, and Taxes: The Economics of Sports Teams and Stadiums* (Washington, DC: Brookings Institution Press, 1997), pp. 255-70.

Hanoucek, J. and R. Filer, "Consumers' Opinion of Inflation Bias Due to Quality Improvements" (unpublished) http://home.cerge-ei.cz/hanousek/bias.pdf.

Harberger, Arnold, "On Measuring the Social Opportunity Cost of Public Funds", in Arnold Harberger, *Project Evaluation: Collected Papers* (Chicago: University of Chicago Press, 1976).

Hardin, Garrett, "The Tragedy of the Commons," *Science*, Vol. 162 (December 13, 1968), pp. 1243-8.

Harrison, David, "Turning Theory into Practice for Emissions Trading in the Los Angeles Basin," in Steve Sorrel and Jim Skea (eds.) *Pollution for Sale: Emissions Trading and Joint Implementation* (London: Edward Elgar, 1999), pp. 63-79.

Hartman, Robert W., "One Thousand Points of Light Seeking a Number: A Case Study of CBO's Search for a Discount Rate Policy," *Journal of Environmental Economics and Management*, Vol. 18, No. 2, Part 2 (March 1990), pp. S-3-7.

Hayek, Friedrich von, *The Constitution of Liberty* (Chicago: University of Chicago Press, 1960).

Heckman, James, "Is Job Training Oversold?" *Public Interest*, Issue 115 (Spring 1994), pp. 91-115.

Hicks, J.R., "The Valuation of Social Income," *Economica*, Vol. 7 (1940), pp. 105-24.

Hochman and G. Peterson (eds.), *Redistribution through Public Choices* (New York: Columbia University Pres, 1974), pp. 136-61.

Jarchow, Courtney, Jack Tweedie, and Andrea Wilkins, "Description of State Leaver Studies," National Conference of State Legislatures, May 2002 (http://www.ncsl.org/statefed/welfare/leaverbrief.pdf).

Jencks, Christopher, Joe Swingle, and Scott Winship, "Welfare Redux," *American Prospect*, Vol. 17, No. 3 (March 2006), pp. 36-40.

Jones, W.T., F. Sontag, M.O. Beckner, and R. Fogelin (eds.), *Approaches to Ethics*, 2nd edn. (New York: McGraw-Hill, 1969).

Jones-Lee, Michael, *The Value-of-life: An Economic Analysis* (Chicago: University of Chicago Press, 1976).

Kaldor, N., "Welfare Propositions and Interpersonal Comparisons of Utility," *Economic Journal*, Vol. 49 (1939), pp. 549-52.

Kimenyi, Mwangi, *Economics of Poverty, Discrimination, and Public Policy*, 1st edn. (Cincinnati, OH: South-Western Publishing, 1994).

Klein, Daniel B., Adreian T. Moore and Binyam Reja, *Curb Rights: A Foundation for Free Enterprise in Urban Transit* (Washington, DC: Brookings Institution Press, 1997).

Kula, Erhun, "Derivation of the Social Time Preference Rates for the United States and Canada," *Quarterly Journal of Economics*, Vol. 99, No. 4 (November 1984), pp. 873-82.

Lave, Charles A. (ed.) *Urban Transit: The Private Challenge to Public Transportation* (Cambridge, MA: Ballinger).

Lesser, Jonathan, Daniel Dodds, and Richard Zerbe, *Environmental Economics and Policy* (Reading, MA: Addison-Wesley, 1997).

Locke, John, *Of Civil Government: 2nd Treatise* (Chicago: Regnery Co., 1955).

Long, David, Charles Mallar, and Craig Thornton, "Evaluating the Benefits and Costs of the Job Corps," *Journal of Policy Analysis and Management*, Vol. 1, No. 1 (1981), pp. 55-76.

Luce, R. Duncan and Howard Raiffa, *Games and Decisions: Introduction and Critical Survey* (New York: John Wiley, 1957).

Lukes, Steven, *Marxism and Morality* (Oxford: Clarendon Press, 1985).

Lynch, Lisa, "Payoffs to Alternative Training Strategies at Work," in Richard Freeman (ed.), *Working under Different Rules* (New York: Russell Sage Foundation, 1994), pp. 63-96.

Lyons, David, in Jeffrey Paul (ed.), *Reading Nozick: Essays on Anarchy, State, and Utopia* (Totowa, NJ: Rowman & Littlefield, 1981), pp. 355-79.

MAMRTA (Metropolitan Atlanta Metropolitan Rapid Transit Authority), *Inner Core Feasibility Wrap-Up Report*, submitted by URS Corporation, Atlanta, Georgia, March 2005a (http://www.itsmarta.com/newsroom/innercore_full.pdf).

MAMRTA (Metropolitan Atlanta Metropolitan Rapid Transit Authority), *Inner Core Transit Feasibility Study Executive Summary*, submitted by URS Corporation, Atlanta, Georgia, March 2005b (http://www.itsmarta.com/newsroom/innercore_exec.pdf).

Mathematica Policy Research, *Does the Job Corps Work? Summary of the National Job Corps Study* (Princeton, NJ: Mathematica Policy Research, June 2001).

McDonald, John F., *Fundamentals of Urban Economics* (Englewood Cliffs, NJ: Prentice Hall, 1997), Ch.11.

Mikesell, Raymond, *The Rate of Discount for Evaluating Public Projects* (Washington, DC: American Enterprise Institute, 1977).

Mill, John Stuart, *Utilitarianism* (New York: Bobbs-Merrill, 1957).

Miller, Ted and Jagadish Guria, *The Value of Statistical Life in New Zealand*, Report to the Ministry of Transport, Land Transport Division, 1991.

Miranda, Jose P., *Marx and the Bible: A Critique of the Philosophy of Oppression* (Maryknoll, NY: Orbis, 1974).

Mitchell, Robert Cameron and Richard Carson, *Using Surveys to Value Public Goods: The Contingent Valuation Method* (Washington, DC: Resources for the Future, 1989).

Moffitt, Robert, "Incentive Effects of the U.S. Welfare System," *Journal of Economic Literature*, Vol. 30, No. 1 (March 1992), pp. 1-61.

Mohring, Herbert, John Schroeter, and Paitoon Wiboonchutikula, "The Values of Waiting Time, Travel Time, and a Seat on the Bus," *Rand Journal of Economics*, Vol. 18, No. 1 (1987), pp. 40-56.

Mueller, Dennis C., *Public Choice III* (Cambridge, UK: Cambridge University Press, 2003).

Munger, Michael, "Voting," in William Shugart and Laura Razzolini (eds.), *The Elgar Companion to Public Choice* (Northampton, MA: Edward Elgar, 2001), pp. 197-239.

Murray, Charles, *In Our Hands: A Plan to Replace the Welfare State* (Washington, DC: American Enterprise Institute, 2006).

Murray, Charles, *Losing Ground: American Social Policy, 1950-1980* (New York: Basic Books, 1984).

Nathan, Richard P. and Thomas L. Gais, *Implementing the Personal Responsibility Act of 1996: A First Look* (Albany, NY: Nelson A. Rockefeller Institute of Government, 1999).

National Endowment for the Arts, *Economic Impact of Arts and Cultural Institutions: Case Studies in Columbus, Minneapolis-St. Paul, St. Louis, Salt Lake City, San Antonio, Springfield* (Washington, DC, 1981).

Nelson, Robert, "The Economics Profession and the Making of Public Policy," *Journal of Economic Literature*, Vol. XXV (March 1987), pp. 49-91.

Neumark, David and William Wascher, "Minimum Wages and Employment: A Case Study of the Fast-Food Industry in New Jersey and Pennsylvania: Comment," *American Economic Review*, Vol. 90 (December 2000), pp. 1362-96.

New York City Independent Budget Office, "Estimating the Economic and Fiscal Impacts of the New York Sports and Convention Center" (July 2004) (http://www.ibo.nyc.ny.us/iboreports/stadiumBP.pdf).

New York Times, "Cablevision Wants to Pursue Its Plan to Develop Railyards," June 8, 2005.

Newell, R.G. and W.A. Pizer, "Uncertain Discount Rates in Climate Policy Analysis," *Energy Policy*, Vol. 32 (2004), pp. 518-29.

Nozick, Robert, *Anarchy, State, and Utopia* (New York: Basic Books, 1974).

Nutter Associates and the Economic Development Research Group, "Fort Drum Regional Economic Impact Study" June 1999 (http://www.edrgroup.com/pages/pdf/Ft-Drum-Econ-Impact.pdf).

Office of Management and Budget, "Guidelines and Discount Rates for Benefit–Cost Analysis of Federal Programs", Circular No. A-94, Revised, October 29, 1992 (http://www.whitehouse.gov/omb/circulars/a094/a094.html).

Office of the President, "Executive Order 12866 of September 30, 1993," *Federal Register*, Vol. 58, No. 190 (Washington, DC: October 4, 1993, pp. 51735-44).

Okun, Arthur, *Equality and Efficiency: The Big Tradeoff* (Washington, DC: Brookings Institution Press, 1975).

Olson, Mancur, *The Logic of Collective Action* (Cambridge, MA: Harvard University Press, 1965).

O'Sullivan, Arthur, *Urban Economics*, 5th edn. (New York: McGraw-Hill Irwin, 2003).

Pacific Business News, "Wal-Mart Profits Up 16%," February 17, 2005 (http://www.bizjournals.com/pacific/stories/2005/02/14/daily46.html).

Pastor, Manuel, James Sadd, and Rachel Morello-Frosch, "Waiting to Exhale: The Demographics of Toxic Air Release Facilities in 21st Century California," *Social Science Quarterly*, Vol. 85, No. 2 (June 2004), pp. 420-40.

Peltzman, Samuel, "Toward a More General Theory of Regulation," *Journal of Law and Economics*, Vol. 19 (August 1976), pp. 211-40.

Pennsylvania Economy League, *Higher Education and the Economy 1990: A Survey of the Impacts on Pennsylvania's Economy of its Colleges and Universities, the Statewide Impacts, June 1991*, revised December 1991.

Perry, Charles, R., Bernard E. Anderson, Richard L. Rowan, and Herbert R. Northrup, *The Impact of Government Manpower Programs in General, and on Minorities and Women* (Philadelphia: Industrial Research Unit, Wharton School, University of Pennsylvania, 1976).

Phelan, Peter and Peter Reynolds, *Argument and Evidence* (London: Routledge, 1996).

Radich, Anthony (ed.), *Economic Impact of the Arts: A Sourcebook*, 2nd edn. (Washington, DC: National Conference of State Legislatures, 1987).

Radin, Beryl, *Beyond Machiavelli: Policy Analysis Comes of Age* (Washington, DC: Georgetown University Press, 2000).

Rawls, John, *A Theory of Justice* (Cambridge, MA: Harvard University Press, 1971).

Regional Environmental Center for Central and Eastern Europe, Sophia Initiative on Economic Instruments, Newsletter on Green Budget Reform, a Review of Carbon and Energy Taxes in EU (Issue 6, November 1999) (http://www.rec.org/REC/Programs/SofiaInitiatives/EcoInstruments/GreenBudget/GreenBudget6/carbon.html).

Rietveld, Piet and F. Bruinsma, *Is Transport Infrastructure Effective?* (New York: Springer-Verlag, 1998).

Romich, Hennifer and Thomas Weisner, "How Families View and Use the EITC," *National Tax Journal*, Vol. 53, No. 4 (2000), pp. 1245-66.

Schiller, Bradley, *The Economics of Poverty and Discrimination*, 9th edn. (New York: Pearson Prentice-Hall, 2004).

Schmalensee, Richard, Paul Joskow, A. Denny Ellerman, Juan Pablo Montero, and Elizabeth Bailey, "An Interim Evaluation of Sulfur Dioxide Emissions Trading," *Journal of Economic Perspectives*, Vol. 12, No. 3 (Summer 1998), pp. 53-68.

Schochet, Peter, Sheena McConnell, and John Burghardt, *National Job Corps Study: Findings using Administrative Earnings Records Data*, Final Report (Princeton, NJ: Mathematica Policy Research, 2003).

Schugart, William F. and Laura Razzolini (eds.), *The Elgar Companion to Public Choice* (Northampton, MA: Edward Elgar, 2001).

Schultz, Theodore, "Investment in Human Capital," *American Economic Review*, Vol. 51, No. 1 (March 1961), pp. 1-17.

Sen, Amartya, *Inequality Reexamined* (New York: Harvard University Press, 1992).

Sen, Amartya and Bernard Williams (eds.), *Utilitarianism and Beyond* (Cambridge, UK: Cambridge University Press, 1982).

Shue, Henry, *Basic Rights* (Princeton, NJ: Princeton University Press, 1980).

Sidgwick, Henry, *The Methods of Ethics*, 7th edn. (Chicago: University of Chicago Press, 1962). (Originally published 1907.)

Siek, Foo Tuan, "An Effective Demand Management Instrument in Urban Transport: The Area Licensing Scheme in Singapore," Cities, Vol. 14, No. 3 (1997), pp. 155-64.

Simmons, F. Bruce, III, *The University of Akron and its Economic Impact on its Community, Akron, Ohio* (University of Akron, September 1992).

Singapore Land Transit Authority website: (http://www.lta.gov.sg/motoring_matters/index_motoring_erp.htm).

Small, Kenneth and Jose Gomez-Ibanez, "Road Pricing for Congestion Management," in Kenneth J. Button and Erik Verhoef (eds.), *Road Pricing, Traffic Congestion, and the Environment* (Northampton, MA: Edward Elgar, 1998).

Smart, J.J.C., "Extreme and Restricted Utilitarianism," in W.T. Jones, F. Sontag, M.O. Beckner, and R. Fogelin (eds.), *Approaches to Ethics*, 2nd edn. (New York: McGraw Hill, 1969), pp. 625-33. [Originally in *Philosophical Quarterly*, Vol. 6 (1956), pp. 344-54.]

Smeeding, Timothy, Katherin Ross Phillips, and Michael O'Connor, "The EITC: Expectation, Knowledge, Use, and Economic and Social Mobility," *National Tax Journal*, Vol. 53, No. 4 (2000a), pp. 1187-209.

Smeeding, Timothy, Lee Rainwater, and Gary Burtless, "United States Poverty in an International Context," Luxembourg Income Study, Working Paper No. 244, September 2000b (http://www.lisproject.org/publications/liswps/244.pdf).

Smith, Adam, *An Inquiry into the Nature and Causes of the Wealth of Nations* (Dublin: Printed for Messrs. Whitestone, Chamberlaine, W. Watson, Potts, S. Watson, Hoey, Williams, W. Colles, Wilson, Armitage, Walker, Moncrieffe, Jenkin, Gilbert, Cross, Mills, Hallhead, Faulkner, Hillary, and J. Colle, 1776).

Smith, Daniel, "Political Science," *New York Times*, September 4, 2005.

Stavins, Robert, "What Can We Learn from the Grand Policy Experiment? Lessons from SO_2 Allowance Trading," *Journal of Economic Perspectives*, Vol. 12, No. 3 (Summer 1998), pp. 69-88.

Stigler, George J., "Theory of Economic Regulation," *Bell Journal of Economics and Management Science*, Vol. 2 (Spring 1971), pp. 3-21.

Stigler, George J., "Director's Law of Public Income Redistribution," *Journal of Law and Economics*, Vol. 13, No. 1 (April 1970), pp. 1-10.

Stone, Kenneth "The Effect of Wal-Mart Stores on Businesses in Host Towns and Surrounding Towns in Iowa" (unpublished), November 1988 (http://www.econ.iastate.edu/faculty/stone/Effect%20of%20Walmart%20-%201988%20paper%20scanned.pdf)

Stone, Kenneth, Georgeanne Artz, and Albert Myles, "The Economic Impact of Wal-Mart Supercenters on Existing Businesses in Mississippi" (Mississippi State University Extension Service, 2002) (http://msucares.com/pubs/misc/m1283.pdf

Thaler, Richard and Sherwin Rosen, "The Value of Saving a Life: Evidence from the Labor Market," in Nestor E. Terlecky (ed.), *Household Production and Consumption* (New York: Columbia University Press, 1975), pp. 265–302.

Toh, Rex S. and Sock-Yong Phang, "Curbing Urban Traffic Congestion in Singapore: A Comprehensive Review," *Transportation Journal*, Vol. 37 (1997), pp. 24-33.

Truman, David, *The Governmental Process: Political Interests and Public Opinion* (New York: Knopf, 1951).

Tullock, Gordon, "The Welfare Costs of Tariffs, Monopolies, and Theft," *Western Economic Journal*, Vol. 5 (1967), pp. 224-32.

Urban Institute, The, "A Decade of Welfare Reform: Facts and Figures," 2006 (http://www.urban.org/UploadedPDF/900980_welfarereform.pdf).

U.S. Bureau of Labor Statistics, "Characteristics of Minimum Wage Workers: 2004" (http://www.bls.gov/cps/minwage2004.htm).

U.S. Environmental Protection Agency, "Proposed National Standards for Hazardous Air Pollutants ...", *Federal Register*, January 30, 2004, pp. 4651-752 (http://www.epa.gov/fedrgstr/EPA-AIR/2004/January/Day-30/a1539.pdf).

U.S. Environmental Protection Agency, "National Primary Drinking Water Regulations: Arsenic Clarifications to Compliance and New Source Contaminants Monitoring: Final Rule," *Federal Register*, 50 DFR Parts 9, 141, and 142, Vol. 66 (January 22, 2001),pp. 6975-7066.

U.S. Federal Highway Administration, *A Guide for HOT Lane Development,* March 2003 (http://www.its.dot.gov/JPODOCS/REPTS_TE/13668.html).

U.S. Office of Management and Budget, "Guidelines and Discount Rates for Benefit–Cost Analysis of Federal Programs," Circular No. A-94 Revised, October 29, 1992 (http://www.whitehouse.gov/omb/circulars/a094/a094.html).

Viscusi, W. Kip, "Risk–Risk Analysis," *Journal of Risk and Uncertainty*, Vol. 8, No. 1 (January 1994), pp. 5-17.

Viscusi, W. Kip, "The Value of Risks to Life and Health," *Journal of Economic Literature*, Vol. 31, No. 4 (December 1993), pp. 1912-46.

Viscusi, W. Kip, *Risk by Choice* (Cambridge, MA: Harvard University Press, 1983), Ch 2.

Wallis, Jim, *Agenda for Biblical People* (New York: Harper & Row, 1984).

Walsh, Richard G., Donn Johnson, and John McKean, "Benefit Transfer of Outdoor Recreation Demand Studies, 1968-1988," *Water Resources Research*, Vol. 28, No. 3 (1992) pp. 707-13.

Waters, M. Dane, *The Initiative and Referendum Almanac* (Raleigh, Durham, NC: Carolina Academic Press, 2003).

Webster's New International Dictionary of the English Language (Springfield, MA: G. & C. Merriam Co., 1939).

Weil, David, "Assessing OSHA Performance: New Evidence from the Construction Industry," *Journal of Policy Analysis and Management*, Vol. 20, No. 4 (Fall 2001), pp. 651-74.

Welch, Finis, "Minimum Wage Legislation in the United States," *Economic Inquiry*, Vol. 12, No. 3 (September 1974), pp. 285-318.

Wieman, Clark, "Downsizing Infrastructure," *Technology Review*, No. 4 (1996), pp. 48-55.

Williamson, Samuel, *Fundamentals of Air Pollution* (Reading, MA: Addison-Wesley, 1973).

Willig, Robert, "Consumer's Surplus without Apology," *American Economic Review*, Vol. 66, No. 4 (September 1976), pp. 589-97.

Wilson, Woodrow, "The Study of Administration," *Political Science Quarterly*, Vol. 56 (December 1941), pp. 481-506 (reprinted from 1887 article).

Winkelmann, Ranier, "Co-Payments for Prescription Drugs and the Demand for Doctor Visits – Evidence from a Natural Experiment," *Health Economics*, Vol. 13 (New York: Wiley, 2004), pp. 1081-9.

Zerbe, Richard O. and Dwight Dively, *Benefit Cost Analysis in Theory and Practice* (New York: HarperCollins, 1994).

Index

taxation 8, 118, 119, 201; base payment
353; commuting 300–3; in competitive
markets 119–22; compulsion 35, 89;
consumers 121–2; demand tax 301;
disincentive 94–5; earned income tax
credit 366, 382–4, 385, (effects) 383–4;
emission taxes 327–9; gasoline tax
76–7; implicit tax rate/benefit reduction
rate 353; minimal government and 43;
negative income tax model 353–4;
pollution 129–30, 131–3, 161–2, 165,
337; producers 120–1; property 278–9;
public programs and 92; tax-rebate
problem 76–7; training 369
Temporary Assistance to Needy Families
351, 353, 352, 353, 355, 356, 357, 358,
360, 363, 377, 383, 384; reform 358–9;
unemployed parents 356
Ten Commandments 23
think tanks 4–5
Time 254
time, value of 260
time frame of the project 235
trade, mutually beneficial 59
trade unions 52, 140
traffic *see* transportation
training *see* skills
transfer: disincentive 94–5; just 34–5;
neutral 37, 40, 44, 165–6; non-neutral
38, 40–1, 44, 166; optimal (Rawls) 43;
zero 43–4
transportation: air travel 291; benefit
assessment 307–8; bus travel 291, 292,
303; cost assessment 305–7; cost-
effectiveness 308; data 294–6; demand
291–3; distribution phase 292; lack of
access to 10; line-haul phase 292;
location and development options 308–9;
modal choice 291–3; rail travel 113,
290, 291, 292, 303–4; ships 29;
subsidies 303–4; *see also* highways
travel cost method 261
tree flipping 222
trusts 52
Tullock, Gordon 137, 140
Twain, Mark 366

uncertainty: defined 217; measuring
218–19; policy analysis and 238–41
underproduction 119, 125, 128
unemployment *see* employment
Union of Concerned Scientists 9
unit elasticity 58
United Kingdom: Common Law 6

United Nations: Montreal Protocol 336
United States of America: Base
Realignment and Closure 265, 280, 281;
Bureau of Economic Analysis 209;
Bureau of Labor Statistics 14, 209, 219;
Congress 127, 210, 320; Congressional
Budget Office 210, 211; Constitution 6;
Council of Economic Advisors 343,
344; Department of Agriculture 343;
Department of Defense 4; Department
of Health, Education and Welfare 4;
Department of Labor 367, 369;
Department of Transportation 252;
education 25; Environmental Protection
Agency 160–1, 186, 252, 318, 321, 322,
334, (Envirofacts) 319, (Toxics Release
Agency) 319; Federal Aeronautics
Administration 253–5; Food and Drug
Administration 218; and free trade 16;
GDP 205, 209; General Accounting
Office 322; health and safety 120, 219;
labor force 13; Medicaid 357, 359, 360;
New Deal 126, 369; Office of
Economic Opportunity 4; Office of
Management and Budget 6, 7, 186, 210,
211; Office of Personnel Management
9; output and employment trends 15;
policy analysis 4–5; poverty 343–5,
345–6, 347, 350, 352; public assistance
350–6, 359–61, 370–2; public radio
113; public sector job training 369–72;
Social Security 231, 232, 344, 350–1,
352; Supplemental Security Income
352; unemployment 13; welfare reform
356–61; for legislation and government
programs, see under individual entries
Upward Bound 369, 373
Urban Institute 359
utilitarianism 16–17, 26–30, 59, 93, 166–7,
210, 213; definition (Bentham) 26, 27;
expected utility 225–8; extreme v.
restricted 28–9, 45; risk attitudes 226–8;
social welfare function 39, 212; total
utility 59; utilitarian redistribution 39–43,
44; rule 40; utility function 70–3, 232;
utility maximization 73–4, 92; utility
possibilities frontier 36–9, 44; weaknesses
29–30; *see also* marginal utility
utils 226

value, existence 261
value, expected 219–21, 228; limits 225;
risky decision 219, 220; single outcome
219, 220